T0373053

DUMBARTON OAKS
MEDIEVAL LIBRARY

Daniel Donoghue, General Editor

NIGEL OF CANTERBURY

MIRACLES OF THE VIRGIN

TRACT ON ABUSES

DOML 75

Nigel of Canterbury

Miracles of the Virgin

Edited and Translated by

JAN M. ZIOLKOWSKI

Tract on Abuses

Edited and Translated by

RONALD E. PEPIN

DUMBARTON OAKS
MEDIEVAL LIBRARY

HARVARD UNIVERSITY PRESS
CAMBRIDGE, MASSACHUSETTS
LONDON, ENGLAND
2022

Printed in the United States of America

First Printing

Library of Congress Cataloging-in-Publication Data

Names: Wireker, Nigellus, approximately 1130–approximately 1200, author. | Ziolkowski, Jan M., 1956– editor, translator. | Pepin, Ronald E., editor, translator. | Wireker, Nigellus, approximately 1130–approximately 1200. Miracula sancte dei genitricis Virginis Marie, versifice. | Wireker, Nigellus, approximately 1130–approximately 1200. Miracula sancte dei genitricis Virginis Marie, versifice. English. (Ziolkowski) | Wireker, Nigellus, approximately 1130–approximately 1200. Tractatus contra curiales et officiales clericos. (Pepin) | Wireker, Nigellus, approximately 1130–approximately 1200. Tractatus contra curiales et officiales clericos. English. (Pepin) | Wireker, Nigellus, approximately 1130–approximately 1200. Vita sancti Pauli primi eremitae. (Pepin) | Wireker, Nigellus, approximately 1130–approximately 1200. Vita sancti Pauli primi eremitae. English. (Pepin)

Title: Miracles of the Virgin / Nigel of Canterbury ; edited and translated by Jan M. Ziolkowski ; Tract on abuses / edited and translated by Ronald E. Pepin.

Other titles: Miracles of the Virgin (Compilation) | Tract on abuses | Dumbarton Oaks medieval library ; 75.

Description: Cambridge, Massachusetts : Harvard University Press, 2022. | Series: Dumbarton Oaks medieval library ; DOML 75 | Nigel of Canterbury's Life of St. Paul, the first hermit, edited and translated by Ronald E. Pepin, is included as an appendix. | Includes bibliographical references and index. | Latin and English; introduction and notes in English.

Identifiers: LCCN 2022003952 | ISBN 9780674660267 (cloth)

Subjects: LCSH: Mary, Blessed Virgin, Saint—Poetry—Early works to 1800. | Paul, the Hermit, Saint, –approximately 341—Early works to 1800. | Christian poetry, Latin (Medieval and modern)—Early works to 1800. | Christian saints—Poetry—Early works to 1800. | Great Britain—Church history—1066–1485—Early works to 1800.

Classification: LCC PA8445.W5 M5713 2022 | DDC 871/.03—dc23/eng/20220420

LC record available at https://lccn.loc.gov/2022003952

Contents

Introduction

The writer of the texts edited and translated here is often labeled Nigel of Canterbury. The name, which was first attached to this author in the early eighteenth century, has in its favor that he went by *Nigellus* in Latin and that his surest connection with any place came from being a monk in the Benedictine community of Christ Church in Canterbury.[1] Across the ages he has traveled under a few other aliases. The firmest early evidence supports the Latin *Nigellus de Longo Campo,* which has led to the Anglicized variant Nigel (of) Longchamp and the Gallicized one Nigel de Longchamps.

With the initial element in the genitive *Nigelli* to indicate ownership, authorship, or both, the Latin designation is penned on the first leaf of London, British Library, MS Cotton Vespasian D. xix. This codex comprises four originally independent manuscripts that were bound together in the seventeenth century. The first of the four is fifty-two folios that furnish the unique witness for an assemblage of Nigel's poetry. Cotton Vespasian D. xix presents, in order of appearance, his minor poems (untitled in the manuscript except as *versus* but known by convention as *The Epigrams*), *Miracula sanctae Dei genitricis virginis Mariae, versifice (Miracles of the Virgin, Saint Mary, Mother of God, in Verse), Passio sancti Lau-*

rentii martyris (The Passion of Saint Lawrence, Martyr), and *Vita sancti Pauli primi eremitae (The Life of Saint Paul, the First Hermit)*. The fifty-two folios, in their present form, contain only two items not by him, both of them short verses. A pastedown table of contents suggests that earlier the collection may have embraced nothing but poetry by Nigel. Earlier a portion of the manuscript—*The Passion of Saint Lawrence, Martyr*—could have been the final of eight *libri* ("books," presumably most of them owned rather than composed by Nigel) in the small personal library that he bequeathed to Christ Church.[2] Whenever the first fifty-two folios of the late twelfth- or early thirteenth-century MS Cotton Vespasian D. xix were brought together, all of their components were likely written by scribes under Nigel's direction, possibly including him, and a correcting hand in them may be his own.[3]

Even though neither Nigel's birth nor death can be dated except inferentially, his life probably covered a period from approximately 1135 to 1198. He traveled in Normandy, and he seemingly studied in Paris. By 1170, he took vows and was admitted to Christ Church.[4] Soon before or after withdrawing from the world, he became acquainted with Thomas Becket (ca. 1119–1170), initially chancellor of England and subsequently (as archbishop of Canterbury) primate of all England, whose martyrdom made a major impact on Nigel, but we cannot ascertain whether the latter was already a monk or still a cleric at the time. Nearly a quarter of a century later, Nigel finished what modern editors entitled the *Tractatus contra curiales et officiales clericos* (literally, *Tract against Courtiers and Clerical Officials*). The *Tract on Abuses,* as we will call it, is technically a letter, though protracted and polemic, addressed to William de Longchamp (d. 1197). This man, for a time bishop of Ely and chancellor, ranked among the most influential and controversial figures in England.

Over the centuries, the Latin subscription to Vespasian D. xix has contributed to the poet's being styled first Nigel (de) Longchamp (sometimes with an *s*) and more recently, by way of Nigel Wireker and Weteker, Nigel Whiteacre.[5] Nowadays both Whiteacre and Longchamp are usually interpreted as referring to a manor near Waltham in Kent. Longchamp has been a red herring in efforts to pinpoint the good brother's affiliations and associations. Appearances—or appellations—notwithstanding, Nigel and his politically and ecclesiastically more prominent namesake William apparently did not emerge from the same family or place. In William's case *de Longo Campo* points to a town in Normandy, unrelated to the farmstead in southeastern England.

In the 1170s, many members of Christ Church participated in a communal effort to document the life, martyrdom, and miracles of Saint Thomas. Becket's Canterbury connections ran long and deep. Before becoming archdeacon and eventually archbishop (1162–1170), the future saint served Theobald (archbishop from 1138 until 1161). Brothers William of Canterbury and Alan of Tewkesbury (b. before 1150, d. 1202) composed lives. Alan and a team edited the martyr's letters. Meanwhile, Benedict of Canterbury scouted out miracles. Flanking these colleagues was Gervase of Canterbury (ca. 1145–ca. 1210), who in about 1185 took up service as resident historian.[6] Similarly, Nigel acted in the capacities of what we might call resident poet and occasional political spokesperson.

After finalizing the textual dossier to preserve the memory of Becket, the brethren of Christ Church compiled the correspondence about their frictions with Archbishop Baldwin (1180–†1190) over a planned college of secular canons at Hackington. The black monks were equally opposed when their peers in Coventry were expelled and replaced by a contingent of secular canons there. In both circumstances, the privileging of these clerics threatened to divert funds that would otherwise have flowed to their monastic counterparts. Any elevation of the canons in Canterbury and its environs could also constrict the role and the authority of the Benedictine brothers in determining and directing the archbishop.[7]

Christ Church, as a monastic cathedral, was doomed to be pulled into worldly conflicts. Despite being a monastery, it was located within, had oversight of, and derived revenues from a cathedral (and premier pilgrimage destination). In a highly unusual reporting structure, the abbey's abbot doubled as the cathedral's bishop, who in turn was archbishop of Canterbury and hence primate of all England. Benedict's Rule called for monks to elect their abbot, which in this instance meant that they simultaneously chose the ecclesiastic head of not only their own diocese but in fact the entire realm. For engaging with kings of England and popes of Rome, archbishops required the professional support of lawyers. The arrangement guaranteed collisions between Church and state. It also led to clashes between monks and clerics. The consequences of these frictions entered even into literature.

Nigel brightened the luster of Christ Church through his Latin poetry. His most famous creation is the *Speculum stultorum (The Mirror of Fools)*. This satiric medley in nearly two thousand elegiac distichs was formerly held to have been composed originally by 1179 or 1180 but possibly revised and enlarged from 1185 to 1187. Fifteen years ago a later dating was proposed, placing composition sometime in the 1190s.[8] Whatever its date, the poem recounts the misadventures of a hapless donkey, Burnellus, who seeks a longer tail and greater glory. The Latin survives in dozens of parchment and paper manuscripts, four incunables, and other later printed editions.[9] In the *Nun's Priest's Tale* Chaucer leaves Nigel himself nameless but names "Daun Burnel the Asse." Whereas much medieval Latin literature failed to outlast the leap into the early modern period, *The Mirror of Fools* circulated widely in the Reformation, as Protestants liked its comic criticism of the Church and especially of holy orders.[10]

Beyond this most famous work, Nigel addressed a letter explaining the meaning of *The Mirror of Fools* to a William often understood to be none other than Longchamp.[11] He left further prose in the *Tract on Abuses,* one of the *Epistolae Cantuarienses* (literally, *Canterbury Letters,* but more accurately, *Letters of the Prior and Convent of Christ Church, Canterbury),*[12] and glosses on the *Historia scholastica (Scholastic History)* by Peter Comestor ("the Devourer," so called for voracious reading); scattered among the glosses are marginal poems that Nigel copied or even composed.[13] The verse maker of Christ Church left much more poetry: a metrical prologue to the *Tract on Abuses;* list of archbishops of Canterbury through Richard (d. 1184); epigrams; *The Passion of Saint Lawrence; The Life of Saint Paul, the First Hermit;* and *Miracles of the Virgin.*[14] A verse *Vita sancti Eustachii sociorumque eius (Life of Saint Eustace and His Comrades)* has also been ascribed to him.[15] Even excluding the last, Nigel must be credited with more than six thousand lines of hagiography and counted not just as a preeminent satirist but also as a major producer of Latin lives, passions, and miracles in Angevin England.[16]

Miracles of the Virgin

Thomas Becket's assassination in 1170 may have encouraged writing about other saints: at least thirty works of hagiography were drafted in Angevin England from 1180 to 1220.[17] What guided the choices of the many writers to devote their time and talents to one saint rather than another? Nigel's decision to write *The Life of Saint Paul* was natural, since this holy man embodied one sort of monasticism. Likewise, Lawrence would have resonated at Christ Church as a righteous martyr who stood firm against greedy authorities. The analogy with Becket would have looked strong. An early saint of Rome, Lawrence could have been a good model as the monks embarked upon campaigns to win over popes in contentions with secular canons over benefices, properties that provided income in compensation for the fulfillment of pastoral duties.

Nigel's second-longest poem is the *Miracles of the Virgin*. These seventeen episodes, divided into three books, are the oldest extant collection of versified miracles of the Virgin in Latin. To go a step further, they count among the earliest such assemblages in any language, including the vernaculars. Hundreds of such Marian miracles, possibly even more than two thousand, survive from western Europe in the Middle Ages, when the Latin and vernacular evidence is put together. These accounts often survive in groups, but some are transmitted singly. Many such tales long antedated our monastic poet of Canterbury.

Miracles of the Virgin were attested first in the eastern Mediterranean, in Greek. In the earliest one, possibly from the late fourth century, a dead soldier named Mercurius is reanimated so that he can assassinate the Roman emperor Julian the Apostate. Nigel included this old thriller in his poem. Thereafter came the legend of Mary of Egypt, which he only mentioned in passing. He also incorporated other originally eastern material, in the account of the pact between Theophilus and the devil and in *The Jewish Boy*. The latter narrative had been imported from the East already in the sixth century by Gregory of Tours.[18]

For all the orientalism, the English backdrop to Nigel's *Miracles of the Virgin* should not be underestimated. Marian devotion ran strong in England before the Conquest and intensified afterward.[19] Archbishop Lanfranc of Canterbury (1070–1089) observed that Mary is often invoked in need and is accustomed to offer the benefit of her mercy. Many examples of her assistance are written down, he added, but not all have been committed to memory.[20] The implication is that innumerable miracles of the Virgin circulated orally in England.

The English people supposedly enjoyed a special relationship with the Mother of God. Consequently, the country acquired the title *dos Mariae* (dowry of Mary).[21] A key figure in the rise of Marianism shortly after the Conquest was Anselm of Canterbury (1033/4–1109). Italian by birth, Norman French by his initial monastic affiliation with Bec, but English by becoming archbishop of Canterbury (1093–1109), Anselm focused in his theological work on the doctrines of the Immaculate Conception and Assumption. In literature, medieval English monastic writers elevated the miracle collection as a defining genre.[22] Individual tales of the Virgin had circulated, often first in the East and later in the West, in freestanding literary treatments as well as in short narratives intended for use in sermons. In due course Marian miracles came to be collected, beginning in England.

Pilgrims to Canterbury carried with them their enthusiasm for saints and miracles. Soon the French poet Guernes de Pont-Sainte-Maxence arrived to draft a life of Becket, and the entertainment for the wayfarers would have doubtless encompassed tales about the Virgin's exploits on behalf of her devotees. Marian miracles spread everywhere, and from the late twelfth century on they progressively squeezed out miracles of other saints. Eventually the success of individual tales may have undermined the impulse to gather them. More important, the nature and the function of Latin changed in the face of spoken languages, such as English and French. Nigel's *Miracles of the Virgin* was the last such composition by a Christ Church monk.[23] Collections proliferated in vernaculars, and individual tales are found in narrative poems, theater, and other genres. Miracles also survive in repertories of exempla in Latin for preachers.

The cult of the Virgin Mary expanded along with courtly love and women's devotion. Laity and clergy, women and men, paid ever greater homage to her as a mediator, and the wonders she wrought on earth inspired literature. Her feats, like those of most other saints, were sometimes connected to specific relics, but often to epiphanies that could take place anywhere. The local character of Marianism, with miracles tied to particular religious houses, becomes evident on the Continent in the twelfth century, whereas many English compendia have an international and cosmopolitan sweep.

A case has been made that Marian miracles were composed and compiled especially early in England.[24] Two Latin compositions stand out. Between 1120 and 1130 Dominic (d. ca. 1150), prior of Evesham abbey, assembled the fourteen-miracle "Elements" series (so called because of its themes of earth, wind, fire, and water), among the earliest works to carry the title *Miracles of the Virgin*.[25] By 1137 William of Malmesbury (ca. 1090–ca. 1142) completed his fifty-three *Miracles of the Blessed Virgin Mary*.[26]

Miracles were performed: the last-mentioned William reveals that one episode in his text was a favorite song and another a ballad.[27] These performances would have often been in spoken languages. Compilations of stories about wonders wrought by Mary were also written in the vernaculars. Around 1165 an author conventionally called Adgar, sometimes prefaced by the name William, composed forty-nine *Miracles de la vierge* in octosyllabic Anglo-Norman verse, the first versified *Miracles of the Virgin* extant in a French dialect.[28] He also produced a shorter form, which was given the title *Gracial,* with twenty-two miracles, not all of them overlapping with the ones in the long collection. Adgar allegedly consulted in London, in the library of Saint Paul's Cathedral, a Latin corpus of Marian miracles by *mestre Albri* (Master Albericus).[29]

Sixteen of the seventeen miracles in Nigel's collection are in William of Malmesbury's too, which suggests that the Christ Church poet followed his predecessor's prose or a related version.[30] Nigel's 2,690 verses are in elegiac distichs. Dactylic hexameters, even when enlivened by end rhymes as they are in *The Life of Saint Paul,* better suited the solemnity of conventional hagiography. Elegiacs, associated with love and lighter topics, befit the *Miracles,* with their focus on human failings.

The stories that make up Nigel's *Miracles* show that heinous sins—incest, drunkenness, broken vows—can be washed away through devotion to the Virgin. The selection opens with the tale of Theophilus, a medieval Faust, in which a man, after turning down a promotion to bishop, becomes frustrated and makes a pact with the devil; Mary frees him from the consequences of selling his soul. The poem closes with the tale of an abbess who bears a child, but who is saved from shame by the supreme protector of virginal chastity. Women and men, old and young, laity and clergy count on Mary to intercede with her son Jesus and forgive every sin, no matter how grave, as long as the sinner shows faith in her mercy. Just as she saves souls, so she repairs bodies. Even without Christ's involvement, she nurses the ill back to health with her milk. Merely displaying her clothing routs armies of foes. Her enemies? Obdurate nonbelievers, in this period often Jews. The tales give voice to the anti-Semitism that was widespread in England as in most of then-contemporary Europe and anticipate the Edict of Expulsion, by which King Edward I expelled all Jews from the country in 1290: consider the miracles of Theophilus, the Jewish boy, and the Jewish lender.[31]

Miracle collections dedicated to other saints had a strong local imprint: tales recorded events in shrines with relics that attracted pilgrims and caused wonders. In contrast, Marian miracle books appealed more broadly for not being bound to particular places. The dogma of the Assumption holds that the Mother of God was taken up into heaven at the end of her earthly life. Without bodily remains, medieval Christians focused on contact relics. These remnants included garments that had touched the Virgin and effusions from her body, such as drops of milk. Yet in her great might and mercy, Mary could intervene anywhere on behalf of those who offered up their prayers.

Beyond the sway that Marianism held over many western Europeans even before 1200, Mary occupied the minds of Canterbury monks more than others. Liturgically, the so-called Little Office of the Blessed Virgin Mary offered a cycle of readings to supplement the regular monastic office at Christ Church even before the Conquest, while a commemorative Office of Our Lady came into use there by the twelfth century. Theologically, Archbishop Anselm (ca. 1033–1109) and the precentor Eadmer (ca. 1060–ca. 1126), both Canterbury monks, wrote treatises on the conception and virtues of Mary. Before 1331 the library boasted seven copies of assorted *Miracula,* at least one of which was Nigel's. In 1338 an inventory of missing books mentions miracles of the Virgin in French besides two Marian psalters.[32]

Widely read in Latin poetry, Nigel displays in his own writing a stylistic command that education in the grammar and the rhetoric of the learned tongue granted. He deploys alliteration, internal rhyme and homoeoteleuton, and all manner of wordplay.[33] Had he resorted to a language other than Latin, his *Miracles of the Virgin* might have a place alongside such thirteenth-century vernacular chefs d'oeuvre as Gautier de Coincy's French *Miracles de Nostre Dame,* Gonzalo de Berceo's Castilian *Milagros de Nuestra Señora,* and Alfonso X's Galician-Portuguese *Cantigas de Santa Maria.* This edition and translation of Nigel's *Miracles of the Virgin* offers us a chance to make belated amends, by delving into a Latin poem and poet both deserving of greater appreciation than they have received, while enabling close engagement with the cult of the Virgin that burgeoned in medieval culture from the twelfth century.

Tract on Abuses

By calling England "a paradise of clerks," William Stubbs, the eminent British historian, described the high degree of learning and literature there during the reign of Henry II (1154–1189).[34] He surveyed numerous literary works produced then and saluted many notable scholars and writers from that era, both clerks and monks. Among the latter, Nigel of Canterbury presented a contrasting view of courtiers and secular clerks.

Between 1193 and 1194, Nigel composed the letter whose length, tenor, and tone have elicited the editorial title *Tractatus contra curiales et officiales clericos (Tract against Courtiers and Clerical Officials),* here, more concisely, *Tract on Abuses.* In early catalogs of Christ Church Library and Dover Priory, the treatise was recorded as *Tractatus, Epistola (Epistle),* and *De eruditione praelatorum (On the Learnedness of the Clergy).* The letter resembles a religious pamphlet. It excoriates ecclesiastical abuses, denounces secular activities of prelates and clergy, and summons its episcopal addressee to reform. It expresses sentiments amply supported by scriptural authority, historical sources, contemporary examples, and anecdotes, all graced by classical allusions and an appealing Latin style. Moreover, the *Tract* stands out as its author's most outspoken, forthright, and courageous work.

Nigel had displayed these qualities earlier. He opposed the appointment of Roger Norreys as prior of Christ Church in 1189. That activity resulted in a threat by the archbishop of Canterbury.[35] In the turbulence that roiled Canterbury for forty years after Thomas Becket's assassination on December 29, 1170, the monks of Christ Church clashed with their archbishops over privileges and prerogatives, and this battle inevitably involved kings and clerks.

The *Epistolae Cantuarienses* document the intense strife when Archbishop Baldwin attempted to establish a college of secular canons at Hackington, not far from the cathedral at Canterbury. In the *Tract,* Nigel would express horror over the expulsion of monks from Coventry in 1190 and 1191, events that he witnessed personally *(oculis propriis aspexi).* In the struggle between temporal and ecclesiastical powers, this erudite Benedictine summoned his literary skills to denounce the ambition of courtiers and to uphold monastic ideals of episcopal conduct. This required courage, since his treatise was replete with sharp criticisms addressed to William Longchamp, a man of high station in Church and state.

William retreated from England to the Continent hastily and ignominiously in October of 1191, after a confrontation with barons aligned with King Richard's brother, John, and half brother, Geoffrey. Although Longchamp's enemies had him removed as justiciar, he never stepped down as bishop of Ely, legate of the Papal See, and chancellor of England. Nigel greeted him under these titles in the *Tract.* Nor did Longchamp lose the confidence and support of the king, whom he accompanied when Richard returned to England in 1194.[36] He clearly attempted to balance secular and sacred duties, a duality that Nigel captured in the phrase *in utroque homine* (in each of your offices) early in the treatise.

Certainly, Longchamp's powers, policies, and personality invited reproach and aroused hostility among English noblemen against this Norman courtier. Chronicles and contemporary historians ridiculed his inability to speak English, his short stature and limping gait, his arrogant bearing and intolerable tyranny.[37] His reputation survived, but irreparably damaged, and in *De viris illustribus* (1538), John Leland, "king's antiquary" to Henry VIII, described William Longchamp as "the most hateful *(invidiosissimus)* of all men on whom the sun then shone."[38] He accused Longchamp of "such great tyranny to satisfy his own pomp and glory" that he became "intolerable to nobles, churchmen and the common people alike." Leland credited Nigel with being unafraid to address such a man about "the abuse of ecclesiastical property."

Although Nigel aired complaints and criticisms in the *Tract,* his relations with the addressee, and his ultimate reason for writing the treatise, are not so evident. Indeed, he also dedicated the *Speculum stultorum* to "William," hailing him in Horatian fashion as "greatest part and half of my soul."[39] In the explanatory letter about the poem, he greeted William by name and called him affectionately "beloved, and a brother always to be loved in Christ."[40] The *Tract* similarly addresses him familiarly as "Willelme." Though Nigel both affirms and underscores affection repeatedly, the warm expressions might be more conventional than heartfelt.

The bishop of Ely and the monk of Canterbury may have been students together and friends. The exhortations of the *Tract* might reflect the Christ Church monks' desire to have William as their archbishop.[41] In any case, Nigel's treatise issued a rebuke and called for reform. His intention stands out early in the epistle when he invokes Solomon's proverb: "Better are the wounds of a friend than the kisses of a fawning enemy."[42]

The salutation of the epistle expresses reverence for William in his exalted roles and contrasts his status with that of the author, the "least brother of the brothers of the church at Canterbury," a sinner, a priest, and unworthy.[43] Nigel immediately acknowledges his distress for a friend and anxiety over the insupportable burdens he bears; he hopes that so many cares and vexations might bestow understanding and wisdom on William. He upholds Becket as an example of courage in adversity. Nigel implores the chancellor to forgive his bold criticisms and to pardon the unpolished style, unlike works fashioned for him by others on "golden anvils."[44] He observes that very often rich men brook no criticisms and submit to no correction, but he calls upon his "most beloved" friend to consult his conscience and to embrace instruction.[45]

Just as John of Salisbury had composed an introductory poem to the *Policraticus* that he dispatched to chancellor Thomas Becket in 1159, Nigel also wrote an *envoi* as a verse pendant to the *Tract.* Again, just as Nigel borrowed extensively in his own treatise from John's prose work, so he imitated notably John's *Entheticus in Policraticum.*[46] For example, he employed the elegiac meter, and he copied the device of prosopopoeia, direct address of the book itself. The "little book" is commended to a patron, the bishop of Ely, and sent to him there, just as John's had been directed to Canterbury. Many verses are devoted to the royal court, "a school of vice" *(vitii schola).* Moreover, there are numerous parallels and verbal echoes of John's poem, including his puns on the verb *cancellare* (to cross out), an unmistakable link to the office of royal chancellor held by Becket and Longchamp respectively. Although John's introductory poem is longer at 306 verses, Nigel's 248 lines bear close resemblance to the precedent established by a man whom he clearly admired, and likely had known at Canterbury before John became bishop of Chartres in 1176.

Compared to Nigel of Canterbury's masterpiece, the *Speculum stultorum*—a brilliant satire that has achieved recognition and acclaim from its composition to our own time, and of which two English translations were published in the last century, along with numerous studies of its content and influence[47]—the *Tract* has attracted much less scholarly attention. No English translation has appeared to date, although the Latin has been edited twice. Yet this prose piece certainly merits study. Its themes, use of *exempla,* and sardonic wit resemble *Speculum stultorum,* and these features reflect the author's style as well as abiding interests. Also, the treatise indexes ecclesiastical abuses and offers insights into strife in late twelfth-century England. The *Tract* records useful documentary evidence for the history of its times and stands as a testament to the literary abilities of a major Anglo-Latin writer, one whom Bishop Stubbs called "a monk in a strictish convent, but corresponding with the ministers of a powerful and politic court."[48]

The Life of Saint Paul, the First Hermit

Versified legends of saints are amply represented in the literature of Norman England, especially among Benedictine writers.[49] Nigel of Canterbury's *Miracles of the Virgin Mary, The Passion of Saint Lawrence,* and *The Life of Saint Paul, the First Hermit* all belong to this popular genre, as well as his epigram of twenty lines on Saint Catherine of Alexandria. Elegiac verses on the life of Saint Eustace and his companions have been ascribed to him as well.[50]

The *Vita sancti Pauli primi eremitae (The Life of Saint Paul, the First Hermit)* comprises 747 rhymed dactylic hexameters. The poem is based on Jerome's prose life of Paul.[51] In fact, Nigel followed this account so closely that his verses have been called "a reworking" and "a pretentious adaptation" of Jerome's work.[52] Yet, as a poet and author with his own purpose, Nigel departed from his model's plain, straightforward story by amplifying and embellishing descriptions and details in the prose piece. For example, he occasionally paused to elucidate a doctrine, such as pious love, or to comment on a topic, such as the nature of death or the darkness of superstition.

Nigel's poetic license at times transformed Jerome's blunt statements into florid verses, as when he developed a strained six-line conceit announcing a new day to replace a single six-word sentence in Jerome's text. The result is a purple patch reminiscent of Roman poets' elaborate daybreaks and sunsets. Our poet also introduced images and figures from classical literature, such as Rumor *(Fama)* and the Fates *(Parcae)*. Again, although Nigel sometimes retained Jerome's exact phrasing, as he did with *meretrix speciosa* to describe an enticing harlot, he more explicitly detailed his characterization of her wily seduction of a noble youth. Moreover, Nigel's fondness for alliteration, assonance, and puns is fully evident in his verses. In short, *The Life of Saint Paul* is more ornate, more didactic, than its prose exemplar, and rightly called "a unique composition" by its editor.[53]

In a brief prologue, Saint Jerome clearly states his purpose in composing *The Life of Saint Paul.* After acknowledging a dispute over the identity of the first monk to live in the desert, Jerome records his own conviction that Paul was first, and he expresses his determination to write about him because his story had been passed over. For Nigel's purpose, we must search; he left no such explicit statement of intention.

The hagiographical tradition at Canterbury was strong.[54] Benedictines of Christ Church had contributed to the genre with notable works. At the end of the eleventh century, Osbern had written lives of Dunstan and Alphege; in the twelfth, Eadmer had composed biographies of Saints Dunstan, Oswald, and others, in addition to his celebrated *Vita sancti Anselmi (The Life of Saint Anselm).* Benedict, prior at Christ Church, who later became abbot of Peterborough, wrote of the passion and miracles of Saint Thomas Becket, as did William, monk of Canterbury, at about the same time, 1173–1174. Perhaps Nigel sought to sustain a tradition established by these predecessors in his convent.

Surely, a powerful impetus for Nigel's hagiographic efforts derived from the work of another monk who had flourished at Saint Augustine's earlier in the century. Reginald of Canterbury (d. ca. 1112) had versified the life of Saint Malchus. Coincidentally, the subject of this poem was a desert solitary whose *vita* had been part of the hagiographic trilogy in prose (Paul, Malchus, Hilarion) by Saint Jerome. Thus, the subject, source, and form of Reginald's long account of Saint Malchus's sanctity and struggles would have attracted Nigel and moved him to imitation. Besides affording an opportunity to complement Reginald's life of a desert father and to exercise his own poetic talents too, *The Life of Saint Paul* enabled Nigel to offer instruction and edification to his confreres. As with his *Passion of Saint Lawrence, Martyr,* but for different reasons, it might have provided for the Christ Church community a role model of humility, self-abnegation, and devotion to prayer and monastic practices.

Nigel laces rhymes with didacticism, hortatory passages, and gentle humor. These characteristics did not secure lasting fame for *The Life of Saint Paul,* which survives uniquely in British Library, MS Cotton Vespasian D. xix, folios 45v–51r.

In preparing this volume we have been blessed by the assistance, advice, and encouragement of friends and colleagues, and we take pleasure in acknowledging our debts here.

Everyone on the editorial team has been wonderful. We thank Raquel Begleiter for her welcome guidance of our project in its early stages, and Zachary Fletcher for reviewing and commenting on Ron's translations at that time. Julian Yolles read them with a critical eye and made a host of helpful suggestions, solving some knotty problems in the process. Nicole Eddy has shepherded our book with extraordinary expertise and a genial willingness to assist at every step. We are grateful to Edward Sanger for his invaluable editing and emending of texts, all accomplished with diligence and good humor. Both Danuta Shanzer, the Medieval

Latin Editor, and Michael Roberts, member of her editorial board, gave unstintingly of their latinity, logic, and English style. Father Hugh Feiss, OSB, has been for Ron a kind instructor of Benedictine lore and letters for many years. Our greatest debt of gratitude is owed to each other. During our collaboration we have become friends and colleagues, appreciative of a collaboration that has been marked on both sides by unfailing kindness and wise counsel.

Notes

1 Arthur G. Rigg, "Nigel of Canterbury: What Was his Name?," *Medium Aevum* 56 (1987): 304–7; Arthur G. Rigg, "Canterbury, Nigel of [Nigel Wireker or Whiteacre] (*c.* 1135–1198?)," in *Oxford Dictionary of National Biography* (Oxford, 2004), http://doi.org/10.1093/ref:odnb/20191; Richard Coates, "Nigel of Canterbury's Surname(s) and a Specious Link with Guernsey," *Notes and Queries* 64, no. 1 (2017): 24–27. The designation Nigellus Cantuariensis is recorded first in John Leland, "De Nigello Cantuariensi," in *Commentarii de scriptoribus Britannicis,* ed. Anthony Hall (Oxford, 1709), vol. 1, p. 228.

2 For the listing of these manuscripts in a later inventory of the Christ Church library, see Montague Rhodes James, *The Ancient Libraries of Canterbury and Dover: The Catalogues of the Libraries of Christ Church Priory and St. Augustine's Abbey at Canterbury and of St. Martin's Priory at Dover* (Cambridge, 1903), 101. Alternatively, the poem about the saint could have been Nigel's personal copy of a hagiographic work by another author.

3 Jan M. Ziolkowski, ed. and trans., *The Passion of St. Lawrence, Epigrams, and Marginal Poems,* Mittellateinische Studien und Texte 14 (Leiden, 1994), 49.

4 On Nigel's time in Canterbury, see John D. Cotts, "The Critique of the Secular Clergy in Peter of Blois and Nigellus de Longchamps," *Haskins Society Journal* 13 (1999): 137–50.

5 The supposed surname Wireker, often encountered in older scholarship, is spurious, a corruption from Witeker (corresponding to Whiteacre).

6 On his writings, see Antonia Gransden, *Historical Writing in England, c. 550 to c. 1307* (Ithaca, NY, 1974), 253–60.

7 London, Lambeth Palace, MS 415, containing the 557 *Epistulae Cantuarienses,* documents these and other controversies.

8 Jill Mann, "Does an Author Understand His Own Text? Nigel of Longchamp and the *Speculum stultorum,*" *The Journal of Medieval Latin* 17 (2007): 1–37, especially 32–34.

9 Nigel de Longchamps, *Speculum stultorum,* ed. John H. Mozley and Robert R. Raymo (Berkeley, 1960).

10 In English, see John H. Mozley, trans., *A Mirror for Fools; or, the Book of Burnel the Ass* (Oxford, 1961), and Graydon Wendell Regenos, trans., *The Book of Daun Burnel the Ass: Nigellus Wireker's "Speculum stultorum"* (Austin, TX, 1959).

11 John H. Mozley, "The *Epistola ad Willelmum* of Nigel Longchamps," *Medium Aevum* 39 (1970): 13–20.

12 William Stubbs, ed., *Chronicles and Memorials of the Reign of Richard I,* vol. 2, *Epistolae Cantuarienses: The Letters of the Prior and Convent of Christ Church, Canterbury, from AD 1187 to AD 1199* (Cambridge, 1865), no. 322, pp. 306–7.

13 Ziolkowski, *The Passion of St. Lawrence,* esp. 286–302, and Irene O'Daly, "Reading the Historia Scholastica at the Close of the Twelfth Century: Nigel of Canterbury and Trinity College, Cambridge, MS B. 15.5," *The Journal of Ecclesiastical History* 71, no. 2 (2020): 270–92.

14 *The Passion of Saint Lawrence* is *BHL,* no. 4767, *The Life of Saint Paul* is *BHL,* no. 6597d, and *Miracles of the Virgin* is *BHL,* no. 5365; the last listing is supplemented in *Bibliotheca hagiographica latina antiquae et mediae aetatis: Novum supplementum,* ed. Henryk Fros (Brussels, 1986), 594.

15 Hermann Varnhagen, "Zwei lateinische metrische Versionen der Legende von Placidus-Eustachius," *Zeitschrift für deutsches Altertum und deutsche Literatur* 24, n.s. 12 (1880): 241–54.

16 Robert Bartlett, "The Hagiography of Angevin England," *Thirteenth-Century England* (1995): 37–52.

17 Bartlett, "The Hagiography of Angevin England."

18 John Duffy, "The Jewish Boy Legend and the 'Western Twist,'" in *Byzantine Religious Culture,* ed. Denis Sullivan, Elizabeth A. Fisher, and Stratis Papaioannou (Leiden, 2012), 313–22.

19 For Marian devotion before the Conquest, see Mary Clayton, *The Cult of the Virgin Mary in Anglo-Saxon England,* Cambridge Studies in Anglo-Saxon England 2 (Cambridge, 1990). For the later period, Kati Ihnat, *Mother of Mercy, Bane of the Jews: Devotion to the Virgin Mary in Anglo-Norman England* (Princeton, NJ, 2016), 100–137.

20 *De nobili genere Crispinorum,* in *PL* 150:735.

21 The expression served as the title of a popular book by T. E. Bridgett, *Our Lady's Dowry, or How England Gained and Lost That Title* (London, 1875).

22 Rachel Koopmans, *Wonderful to Relate: Miracle Stories and Miracle Collecting in High Medieval England* (Philadelphia, 2011).

23 Koopmans, *Wonderful to Relate,* 204.

24 Richard W. Southern, "The English Origins of the *Miracles of the Virgin,*" *Medieval and Renaissance Studies* 4 (1958): 176–216, and J. C. Jennings, "The Origins of the 'Elements Series' of the Miracles of the Virgin," *Mediaeval and Renaissance Studies* 6 (1968): 84–93. Southern makes the case that the nephew and namesake of Archbishop Anselm of Canterbury, Abbot Anselm the Younger of Bury Saint Edmunds (d. 1148), was responsible for two key groups of Marian legends.

25 José-María Canal, ed., "El libro *De miraculis sanctae Mariae* de Domingo de Evesham (m. c. 1140)," *Studium legionense* 39 (1998): 247–83.

26 William of Malmesbury, *The Miracles of the Blessed Virgin Mary,* ed. and trans. Rodney M. Thomson and Michael Winterbottom (Woodbridge, UK, 2015).

27 Peter Carter, "The Historical Content of William of Malmesbury's *Miracles of the Virgin Mary,*" in *The Writing of History in the Middle Ages: Essays Presented to Richard William Southern,* ed. R. H. C. Davis and J. M. Wallace-Hadrill (Oxford, 1981), 139.

28 Adgar, *Le Gracial,* ed. Pierre Kunstmann (Ottawa, 1982), and *Le Gracial; Miracles de la Vierge,* trans. Jean-Louis Benoit and Jerry Root (Turnhout, 2021).

29 Within the corpus of Anglo-Norman verse, Adgar anticipated by many decades Evrard of Gateley, a Benedictine of Bury Saint Edmunds who in the second half of the thirteenth century recast his predecessor's miracles into Anglo-Norman French octosyllabic rhymed couplets: see Paul Meyer, "Notice du ms. Rawlinson Poetry 241 (Oxford)," *Romania* 29 (1900): 27–47.

In what little survives of Evrard's text, two narratives overlap with Nigel's: the miracles of Ildephonsus and of the malodorous cleric.

30 The exception is the tenth miracle, on the incestuous matron freed from demonic possession before the senate.

31 Ihnat, *Mother of Mercy,* 138–81.

32 For all the information in this paragraph, see Joan Greatrex, "Marian Studies and Devotion in the Benedictine Cathedral Priories in Later Medieval England," *Studies in Church History* 39 (2004): 157–67, especially 157, 160, 161–63, 164, 165, and Kati Ihnat, "Marian Miracles and Marian Liturgies in the Benedictine Tradition of Post-Conquest England," in *Contextualizing Miracles in the Christian West: New Historical Approaches,* ed. Matthew M. Mesley and Louise E. Wilson, Medium Aevum Monographs n.s. 32 (Oxford, 2014), 63–97.

33 See D. R. Shackleton Bailey, *Homoeoteleuton in Latin Dactylic Verse,* Beiträge zur Altertumskunde 31 (Stuttgart, 1994), 203–6.

34 William Stubbs, *Seventeen Lectures on the Study of Medieval and Modern History and Kindred Subjects* (Oxford, 1887), 150.

35 Stubbs, *Epistolae Cantuarienses,* no. 326, pp. 311–12.

36 Roger of Howden, *Chronica,* ed. William Stubbs (London, 1868–1871), vol. 3, p. 247.

37 Gerald of Wales, *De vita Galfridi* 2.12; William of Newburgh, *Historia rerum anglicarum* 4.2. Based on these and other sources, modern writers continue to paint a dark portrait of William Longchamp; for example, David Boyle, *The Troubadour's Song: The Capture and Ransom of Richard the Lionheart* (New York, 2005), 106–7, 113, 185, 222–24.

38 John Leland, *De viris illustribus,* ed. and trans. James P. Carley (Toronto, 2010), 390–91.

39 "Maxima pars animae dimidiumque meae." Compare Horace, *Odes* 1.3.8, 2.17.5.

40 "Dilecto et in Christo semper diligendo fratri Willelmo." For the letter, see Mozley, "*Epistola ad Willelmum.*"

41 Mann, "Does an Author Understand His Own Text?," 27–28.

42 Proverbs 27:6; see *Tract* 8.

43 *Tract* 1.

44 *Tract* 9.

45 Nigel addresses William as “most beloved” at *Tract* 19, 88, and 106.
46 Twenty-four “clear reminiscences to or borrowings from the *Entheticus Minor*” are detected in Nigel’s distichs by Jan van Laarhoven, ed. and trans., *John of Salisbury’s “Entheticus maior and minor”* (Leiden, 1987), vol. 1, p. 66.
47 The two translations are Mozley, *A Mirror for Fools,* and Regenos, *The Book of Daun Burnel the Ass.*
48 Stubbs, *Seventeen Lectures,* 145.
49 M. Dominica Legge, *Anglo-Norman Literature and Its Background* (Oxford, 1963), 275; Ziolkowski, *The Passion of St. Lawrence,* 59.
50 André Boutemy, ed., *Nigellus de Longchamp dit Wireker: Introduction; “Tractatus contra curiales et officiales clericos”* (Paris, 1959), 69–70, attributed this work to Nigel based on stylistic grounds.
51 Jerome, *Trois vies de moines: Paul, Malchus, Hilarion,* ed. Edgardo M. Morales, trans. Pierre Leclerc, Sources Chrétiennes 508 (Paris, 2007), 144–83.
52 Ziolkowski, *The Passion of St. Lawrence,* 4; Leo M. Kaiser, “A Critical Edition of Nigel Wireker’s *Vita sancti Pauli primi eremitae,*” *Classical Folia* 14 (1960): 63.
53 Kaiser, “A Critical Edition,” 63.
54 Ziolkowski, *The Passion of St. Lawrence,* 59.

MIRACLES OF THE VIRGIN

INCIPIUNT MIRACULA
SANCTAE DEI GENITRICIS
VIRGINIS MARIAE, VERSIFICE.

Virginis et matris celebri memoranda relatu
scribere pauca volo, ductus amore pio.
Paucula de multis placet excerpsisse Mariae
moribus et gestis hac brevitate metri.
Terret opus, sed torret amor; res ardua vires
vincit et ad votum victus amore trahor.
Virginis et matris specialis amor pietatis
spondet opem coeptis quam dabit ipsa suis;
quae velut in caelis superis comitata choreis
dignior est cunctis plusque decoris habet,
sic quoque terrigenis specialis opem pietatis
contulit, innumeris magnificata modis.
Sed quid magnificum si magnificata refulget,
haec ita pro meritis mirificata suis?
Cum Deus in sanctis mirabilis esse probetur,
est mirabilior in genitrice sua;
quique nequit cogi, genitricis amore coactus
quid quod non faciat, qui facit omne quod est?
Sola carens simili, quem virginitate retenta
sola parit mundo, flectere sola potest;
sola Deum flectit, cui soli solus ab aevo
concessit natum flectere posse suum,
non quia flectatur sententia nescia flecti,
sed flectenda tamen flectitur huius ope.

HERE BEGIN THE MIRACLES OF THE BLESSED VIRGIN MARY, MOTHER OF GOD, IN VERSE.

Guided by devout love, I wish to write down a few deeds of the Virgin and Mother that warrant being recalled in oft-repeated retelling. It seems good to have, in the terseness of verse, a selection of a choice few from her many practices and deeds. The task is daunting, but love is ardent; the challenge overcomes my capacities, and yet, overcome by love, I am drawn to my vow.

The Virgin and Mother's special love for devotion promises that she will lend support to what has been undertaken for her. Just as, in the company of celestial troupes, she has greater worth and grace than anyone in heaven, so too, glorified in countless ways, she has bestowed the help of her special kindness upon people on earth.

But what does it glorify her if she shines gloriously, this woman made such a wonder on account of her merits? Though God is proven wonderful in his saints, he is more wondrous in his mother; and he who cannot be compelled, what is there that he would not accomplish, when compelled by love of his mother, he who creates all that exists?

She who alone lacks a peer, she alone can sway him, whom she alone, with her maidenhood intact, brings into the world; she alone sways God, she to whom alone he alone granted from time without end the power to sway his son, not that a verdict incapable of being swayed is swayed, but all the same, one that must be swayed is swayed with her help.

Prima salutis opem dedit haec, pariendo salutem
humano generi, virgo parensque Dei.
Prima salus mundi fuit haec et causa salutis,
quae meruit miseris ferre salutis opem.
Nec miserando pie cessat pia cura Mariae,
excusans miseros, conciliando reos.
Singula si memorem digno memoranda relatu,
deficiet tempus, vita diesque mihi;
sufficiant igitur operi praemissa futuro,
grata sit ut brevitas cum levitate metri.
Sic igitur levitas moderetur opus brevitatis,
quatenus et gravitas sit brevitate levis.

De Theophilo qui Christum negavit

Res levis et fragilis flantique simillima vento
est caro sub carnis condicione sita.
Quae sua sunt quaerit, falsum sub imagine veri
palliat, et casu carpitur ipsa suo.
Labitur ex facili, facilis quia lapsus ad ima,
tum quia mortalis, tum quia firma minus.
Surgere post lapsum decet et timuisse futura
quam sit amara dies quamque timenda malis.
Surgere post lapsum meruisse Theophilus olim
creditur et lacrimis facta piasse suis.
Qualiter excessit, quo sit revocante reversus,
res quia trita, brevis solvere sermo potest.
Res miranda quidem, sed plus miseranda, dolori
laetitiaeque piis mentibus esse solet.

She, Virgin and Mother of God, first gave the help of salvation by bringing forth salvation for humankind. She, who merited bringing the help of salvation to the wretched, was the first salvation of the world and cause of salvation. And Mary's kindly care, excusing the wretched, winning over the sinful, does not cease to take pity with kindliness.

If I should recall everything fit to be recalled in a worthy retelling, time, life, and days would fail me; therefore, let what has been prefaced to the following work suffice, so that the terseness, along with the lightness of the meter, may be pleasing. May lightness then temper the task of terseness, so that even weightiness may by terseness become light.

On Theophilus, Who Denied Christ

The flesh, when subjected to the state of the flesh, is a light and frail thing and most like a gusting wind. It seeks what are its own, it cloaks the untrue beneath the likeness of the true, and it is pulled to pieces by its own downfall. It falls easily, because a fall to the depths is easy, both because the flesh is mortal and because it is unsteady. To rise after a fall is right, and to fear how bitter the day to come is and how fearful because of its torments.

Theophilus is believed, once upon a time, to have deserved to rise after a fall and to have atoned for his deeds with tears. Because the matter is all too familiar, a brief discussion can resolve how he transgressed and at whose summons he was restored. The matter, fit, it is true, to be marveled at but even more to be commiserated, is accustomed to bring grief and joy to devout minds.

Praesulis et cleri populique Theophilus ore
dum fieret celebris, fama fefellit eum.
Gesserat in clero factus vicedomnus et ipse
ecclesiae curas pontificisque vices.
Contulerant in eum cunctorum vota favorem,
principis ac populi pontificisque sui.
Magnus in ecclesiis, in clero maior haberi
coepit et in populo maximus esse suo.
Nil levitatis habens, virtutum culmine famam
emit et exemptam luxuriare dedit.
Non fuit unde queri quisquam potuisset ad horam:
carus et acceptus omnibus unus erat.
Cuncta peregit ita quod eum nec rodere posset
invidus; hinc cunctis invidiosus erat.
Exemplum cleri solum se fecit haberi,
moribus et gestis formula facta gregis,
omnia disponens iustae moderamine legis,
ut nihil in mundo iustius esset eo.
Singula quid memorem? Fuit omnibus omnia factus,
omnibus et solis omnia solus erat.
Praesulis interea de carcere carnis ad astra
spiritus evasit. Sede vacante sua
cumque pari voto clerus populusque rogaret
hunc sibi substitui, substitit hic et ait:
"Absit ut hoc faciam. Satis est sine pontificatu.
Quam vix sustineo, me mea cura gravat.
Absit ut hoc faciam, quia mens et vita remordet.
Absit dulce malum, pontificale decus.
Vix mihi sufficio soli; quid si mihi plures
contingat subici, pastor ovesque luant.

As Theophilus became renowned in the mouths of the bishop, clergy, and people, his fame led him into error. Having been made deputy, he carried out among the clergy the Church's administration and the bishop's functions. The prayers of all—of his prince, people, and bishop—conferred favor upon him. He began to be considered great among the churches, greater among the clergy, and greatest among his people. Having nothing of frivolity, through the eminence of his virtues he acquired fame and allowed it, once acquired, to run riot. There was no reason why, for the time being, anyone could complain: he was the one dear and welcome to all. He carried out every task in such a way that no envious person could gnaw at him; for this reason, he was envied by everyone.

He caused himself to be regarded as the sole paragon for the clergy, having become the standard for his flock in conduct and deeds, managing everything by the exercise of just law, so that nothing in the world was more just than he was. Why should I recall every detail? He became all things to all men, and alone was all things to each individual one.

Meanwhile, the bishop's soul escaped from the flesh's prison to the stars. When, with his see unoccupied, the clergy and people asked with one and the same wish that Theophilus replace him, he stood firm and said: "Heaven forbid that I should do this. I have enough without the bishopric. My care, which I can scarcely shoulder, weighs heavy on me. Heaven forbid that I should do this, since my mind and life bite back. Heaven keep from me this sweet evil, the honor of the episcopate. I am scarcely capable of managing for myself alone; if more people should happen to be put under my control, the shepherd and the sheep would

Quaerite quaerentes sine numine nomen honoris;
quaerite quos agitat ambitionis amor."
Cumque nec assensum plebs extorquere nec illum
vis valet illata flectere, tristis abit.
Alter ad officium sedis de more vocatus
venit et ingressus spernere coepit eum;
utque solet novitas fieri levitatis amatrix,
incipit esse sua sub novitate levis;
utque nihil desit votis, vicedomnus honoris
pulsus ab officio vilis honore caret.
Sustinet ille tamen, portans patienter ad horam,
dissimulando notans praesulis acta novi.
Dissimulare tamen non praevalet ira dolorem.
Altius infligit vulnera raptus honos.
Ira licet simulet modico sub tempore vultum,
non valet illa tamen dissimulare diu.
Cernere se sperni tantum talemque modeste
quis ferat aut quorsum se cohibere queat?
Vivat ut abiectus qui tanto vixit honore,
qua ratione potest quove tulisse modo?
Perdere famosum nomen iactura perennis,
census resque leves perdere cura levis.
Sustinuisse diu celebris dispendia famae
absque dolore gravi vix valet ullus homo.
Rerum damna pati levis est iactura. Favorem
perdere iacturam quis putet esse levem?
Cum sit utrumque grave, famae rerumque ruina,
sunt graviora magis haec duo iuncta simul.
Est gravis haec, gravior tamen illa, gravissima cuius
sub gravitate perit quem gravat haec et ea.

pay. Seek out those who seek a prestigious title without divine will; seek out those whom a desire for advancement motivates."

When the common folk could not elicit his acceptance, nor sway him with the application of pressure, they went off sadly. Another man came, duly summoned, to the episcopal office, and on entering it, started to scorn him; and as a new appointee tends to become fond of fickleness, he began in his new appointment to be fickle; and that nothing might be lacking from his desires, the deputy, driven from the office of honor, worthless, was deprived of honor.

Still, Theophilus endured, suffering patiently for a time, taking note of the deeds of the new bishop but concealing his reactions. Yet anger did not succeed in concealing grief. Deprivation of honor inflicted deeper wounds. Though anger may simulate cheer for a little while, all the same it cannot dissemble for long.

Who could bear with mildness to see himself scorned so much and in such a fashion, or to what end could he restrain himself? In what way or what manner could he bear to live in mean condition, who before lived in such great esteem? To lose a noted name is an everlasting loss; to lose wealth and trivial things a trifling concern. Scarcely any man can endure for a long time without serious grief the diminishment of a renowned reputation.

To suffer material damages is a trivial loss. Who would think losing popular favor to be a trivial loss? Though each of the two is serious, downfall of reputation and of property, these two joined together at one time are more serious. The one is serious, yet the other is more serious; most serious is that under the burden of which a person perishes, burdened

Vivere despectum sub eo quem despiciebat
   se videt et fatis invidet usque suis.
Ingemit ergo gravi graviter stimulante dolore,
   quodque prius placuit displicet omne sibi.
Invidiae stimulos dolor excitat, ira furorem
   gignit et invitat ad scelus omne manus.
Crescit anhela sitis caeco stimulante furore;
   fit sitibunda nimis mens sine mente sua.
Totus ad hoc et in hoc tendit furor ira dolorque.
   Cernere quid deceat mens furibunda vetat.
Cogit ad excessus furor ira tumorque nefandos.
   Nil putat esse nefas quod sua vota iuvet.
Viribus ablatos repetisse iuvaret honores,
   sed desunt vires. Quid iuvet ergo virum?
Non opus est precibus, ne forte superbiat hostis
   fiat et audita surdior ille prece.
Tutius est precibus quam vincere viribus hostem;
   facta negant vires, abnegat ira preces.
Quas modo sprevit opes, modo quos contempsit honores,
   quaerit et affectat esse quod ante fuit.
Hoc amat, hac tendit, hic nocte dieque moratur;
   quaeritur ergo via qua veniatur ad hoc.
Quaeritur ergo magus prudens; inventus aditur.
   Causa retecta patet; spondet Hebraeus opem.
Quaelibet hora dies miseris, lux quaelibet annus
   esse solet cupidis, et mora quaeque gravis.
Terminus ergo rei dudum praefixus adesse
   cernitur. Ad circos urbis uterque ruit.
Conveniunt ad noctis opus sub tempore noctis;
   conveniunt tali noxque locusque rei.

by the one and the other. He sees himself living disdained under one he disdained, and he regards his own fate with constant ill will. Therefore, with grave grief goading him grievously, he groans, and all that pleased him before displeases him now.

Grief rouses the goads of envy; anger gives rise to madness and attracts his hands to all manner of villainy. Panting thirst grows as blind rage goads; the mind, mindless, becomes all too thirsty. Madness, anger, and grief strive wholly toward this and into this. A raging mind prevents him from perceiving what is seemly. Madness, anger, and passion compel him to unspeakable excesses. He thinks nothing to be unspeakable that advances his hopes. It would help his cause to recover the honors taken from him by force, but he has no force. What then may help the man?

There is no call for prayers, for fear that the enemy grow proud and become all the deafer after having heard the prayer. It is safer to defeat an enemy through prayers than through force; the situation excludes force, anger declines prayers. He seeks out the wealth he scorned just now, the honors he despised just now, and aspires to be as he was before. He loves this, he heads in this direction, and he is set on this night and day; the search, then, is for a way by which to come to this. And so a wise magus is sought; he is found and approached. The case, made known, is set forth; the Jew promises help.

To the wretched, any hour tends to seem a day; to the eager, any period from sunrise to sunset, a year; and any delay, burdensome. And so the deadline for the business, fixed long in advance, is perceived to draw near. They both rush to the circuses of the city. They come together for night work at nighttime; the night and place accord with such business.

Affuit interea cum principe daemoniorum
plurima spirituum turba coacta simul.
Accedensque magus regem de more salutat.
Quid velit exponit ipse comesque suus.
Daemon ad haec: "Homini tali Christumque colenti
nescio si potero ferre salutis opem.
Si meus esse cupit, Christum neget atque Mariam,
quatenus optatum perficiatur opus.
Et quia Christicolae me fallunt meque refutant,
confisi Christi de pietate sui,
charta sit inter nos testis, ne forte—quod absit—
ad Christum rediens se neget esse meum.
Suspectos igitur securos cautio curet
reddere, sed propria cautio scripta manu.
Cautio me cautum reddat, ne forte Maria
more suo veniat tollere nostra sibi.
Ustus ab igne timet; laqueos pedicasque tenaces
bestia declinat saepe, retenta semel;
terret aves viscus; pisces exterritat hamus:
me quoque terrere virgo Maria solet.
Haec odiosa mihi, quoniam contraria semper
moribus et votis obviat ista meis."
Talibus auditis miser et miserabilis ille
annuit, effectus immemor ipse sui.
Fallitur infelix, Christum nomenque Mariae
abnegat, et laqueis stringitur ipse suis.
Cautio scripta datur testis, ne forte tepescat
temporis ex tractu pactio firma minus.
Solvitur his gestis, tanto gavisa triumpho,
contio. Pacta placent. In sua quisque redit.

Meanwhile, a most numerous mob of spirits was present, assembled together along with the prince of devils. Approaching, the magus greets the king in customary fashion. He and his companion set forth what he wants. The devil responds to this: "I do not know if I will be able to bring salutary aid to such a person, a worshipper of Christ. If he wishes to be mine, let him deny Christ and Mary, so that the desired task may be accomplished. And because Christians, trusting in the mercy of their Christ, deceive and refuse me, let a charter be as witness between us, that he not return to Christ (may it not be so!) and deny that he is mine. Therefore, let a bond see to rendering the mistrustful free from worry, but a bond written by your own hand. Let a bond render me secure, so that Mary not come in her usual way to take away for herself what is mine. One who has been burned by the fire is afraid; a beast, having been held fast once, often keeps clear of clinging snares and leghold traps; birdlime frightens birds; the hook makes fish fearful: in the same way too, the Virgin Mary is accustomed to make me afraid. She is loathsome to me, since, ever opposed, she goes against my customs and wishes."

After hearing such words, that wretched wretch gives assent, made unmindful of himself. The unfortunate is deceived, denies Christ and the name of Mary, and is bound fast by his own snares. The written bond is given as a witness, so that the compact, made less solid with the passage of time, not weaken. Once these matters have been settled, the assembly breaks up, rejoicing in so great a conquest. The arrangement is agreed. Everyone returns home.

Praesulis interea mens emollita repente
omne quod abstulerat reddit et addit eis.
Rursus ad officium digno revocatur honore
et, velut ante fuit, fit vicedomnus item.
Splendidior cunctis cunctisque beatior unus
effectus, votis cuncta subesse videt.
Quaelibet ad votum succedunt. Cernere caecam
omnia iurares ante retroque deam.
Luxus opum numerum, mensuram copia rerum
vicit et excessit ille, vel illa, modum.
Sola tamen votis sceleris mens conscia facti
obviat et solum sola remordet eum.
Importuna quidem res est et nescia somni
mens sceleris proprii pondere pressa gravi;
tinea corrumpens, vermis numquam requiescens,
mens mala cum propria culpa remordet eam.
Pugna gravis, lis longa nimis, victoria rara
talibus in causis saepe subesse solet.
Nil sapit in mundo nisi mens a crimine munda,
qua nihil in mundo mundius esse potest.
Omnia consumens cum tempore fluxerat aetas,
vix modicum vitae iam superesse videns,
cumque sit haec oneri, mors incipit esse timori:
quae longinqua minus, fit metuenda magis.
Iam quasi pro foribus, "Venies," clamare videtur.
"Ius mihi redde meum; tu tibi tolle tuum!"
Intima deficiunt, teritur mens anxia curis;
terret utrumque virum, morsque scelusque suum.
Aegrescunt vires et amor decrescit habendi;
mens sceleris tanti tristis abhorret opus.

Meanwhile, the bishop's attitude softens all at once; he returns everything that he had taken away, and he adds to it. Theophilus is called back to service again with fitting dignity, and he becomes deputy, just as he was before. He alone, rendered more magnificent than all others and more fortunate than all others, sees all things subject to his wishes. Everything turns out according to his will. You would swear that the blind goddess could see all things both before and behind her. The extravagance of his wealth surpassed reckoning; the abundance of his property, measure. The one and the other exceeded bounds.

Yet his conscience alone, aware of the crime committed, goes against his wishes, and it alone gnaws at him alone. In fact, a conscience oppressed by the heavy weight of its own crime is a relentless thing and incapable of sleep; a bad conscience is a destructive moth, a never-resting worm, when its own guilt gnaws it. In such situations the fight often tends to be harsh, the strife all too long, and victory rare. Nothing in the world has a good taste except a conscience clean from crime; nothing in the world can be cleaner than it.

When age, consuming all things in time, had flowed by, seeing that now scarcely a small portion of life remains, death, since it is a burden, begins to be a cause of fear: less distant, it becomes more frightful. Now it seems to shout as if at his door, "You will come. Render me my due; you take yours for yourself!"

His heart fails, his worried mind is worn down by cares; both his death and his crime frighten the man. His strength grows feeble, and his love of possession dwindles; his sorrowful mind recoils at the commission of so great a crime.

Singula discutiens, in se quandoque reversus,
fluctuat, incertus quid sit et an sit homo;
nam scelus excedit hominem, cum sit tamen ipsum
ipse scelus, sceleris conscius ipse sui.
Vita viam veniae clausit perversa salubri;
se sibi subduxit voce manuque sua.
Paenitet errasse, sed cum via nulla patescat
qua miser errores corrigat ipse suos,
altius inflicto scelerum sibi vulnere, tristis
ingemit, in lacrimas totus abire parans.
Et velut omne scelus scelus hoc superasse videtur
et minus est illo quodlibet orbe nefas,
sic suus iste dolor cunctos superasse dolores
creditur et solum non habuisse parem.
Tristis uterque simul, stimulo stimulante dolorum,
defluit in lacrimas spiritus atque caro.
Nil nisi flere iuvat querulosque refundere questus,
subiungens lacrimis talia verba suis:
"Heu mihi! Quid feci? Quis me furor impius istuc
impulit, ut fierem prodigus ipse mei?
Heu mihi! Quid feci? Quid sum facturus? Et unde
auxilium veniet consiliumque mihi?
Vae mihi! Vae misero! Vae soli! Vae scelerato!
Vae manet aeternum meque scelusque meum.
Quis mihi det quod ego feriam mea guttura cultro,
ultor et exactor in scelus ipse meum?
In scelus ipse meum dixi, seu me scelus ipsum,
cum scelus hoc ipsum sim super omne scelus,
non homo, sed vermis, hominum faex ultima, stercus,
stercore vel si quid vilius esse potest.

Going over every single detail, at times returned to his senses, he wavers, uncertain as to what he is and whether he is human; for the crime outstrips what is human, though he himself still constitutes the crime, conscious in himself of his crime.

A corrupt life shut off the way to soul-saving forgiveness; by his words and deeds he stole himself from himself. He regrets having gone wrong, but since no way lies open by which the wretch himself may right his wrongs, he groans unhappily from the wound the crimes inflicted deeply upon him, making ready to abandon himself entirely to tears.

And just as this crime seems to surpass every crime, and any offense in the world is less than it, so this pain of his is believed to surpass all pains and alone not to have an equal.

With the sting of his pains goading him, the spirit and flesh, both grieving as one, burst into tears. Nothing brings relief to him but weeping and pouring forth plaintive complaints. To his tears he adds the following words: "Alas for me! What have I done? What impious madness drove me to this point, that I should become reckless of myself? Alas for me! What have I done? What am I to do? And from where will aid and advice come to me? Woe is me! Woe to wretched me! Woe to solitary me! Woe to criminal me! Eternal woe awaits me and my crime.

"Who may allow me to slit my throat with a knife, I myself avenger and executioner against my crime? I myself have spoken against my crime, or against myself, myself being the crime, since I am this very crime beyond all crime, not a human being but a worm, the utmost dregs of humankind, dung, or whatever can be more revolting than dung.

Tartara non digne scelus hoc punire nec ulla
  sufficit ad plenum poena piare malum.
Sidera, terra, mare non possunt enumerare
  quaenam sit factis ultio digna meis.
Nonne Petrum legimus, Paulum, David, et Ninivitas
  post lapsum culpas flendo piasse suas?
Plus tamen excessi sceleratior omnibus istis,
  namque meo sceleri subiacet omne scelus.
Quaeque patet cunctis veniae via, clauditur uni
  (non tamen immerito), virgo Maria, mihi.
Forte viam veniae praestaret virgo benigna,
  hanc nisi clausisset lingua manusque mea.
Si quod in hoc mundo miseri meruere levamen,
  hoc venit ex meritis, virgo Maria, tuis.
Quam medicina nequit post mortem ferre medelam,
  hanc solam sola, virgo Maria, potes.
Quam mihi nemo potest meritis apud Omnipotentem,
  tu mihi sola potes ferre salutis opem.
Ergo potens misero miseri miserata medere,
  et, quam non merui, fer pietatis opem.
Fer pietatis opem, miseri miserere, Maria,
  tum quia sola potes, tum quia sola soles.
Omnia sola potes, quoniam super omnia solam
  te statuit solus, quem paris, ipse Deus.
Et quia te sprevi, te liqui teque negavi,
  si mihi subvenias, plus pietatis habes.
Hostibus exhibita cum sit pietas specialis,
  hoc speciale decus convenit esse tuum.
Humani generis tu spes, tu causa salutis,
  tu via duxque viae qua reparatur homo,

The underworld is not enough to punish this crime fittingly, nor any penalty to expiate the misdeed fully. The heavens, earth, and sea cannot recount what kind of retribution is fitting for my deeds.

"Do we not read that Peter, Paul, David, and the Ninevites atoned for their faults by weeping after falling? Yet I, more wicked, have transgressed more than all these, for all wickedness is inferior to my wickedness. Whatever way of forgiveness lies open to all others is closed to me alone (yet not undeservedly), Virgin Mary. Perhaps the kindly Virgin would furnish a way of forgiveness, if my tongue and hand had not shut it off.

"If in this world the wretched have merited any comfort, it comes from your merits, Virgin Mary. The cure that medicine cannot bring after death, this alone you alone, Virgin Mary, can. The aid of salvation that no one else can achieve for me through merits before the Almighty, you alone can bring me. Therefore, powerful one, heal the pitiful, taking pity on the piteous, and bring the aid of compassion that I have not deserved. Bring the aid of compassion, take pity on the piteous, Mary, both because you alone can do so and because you alone are accustomed to do so. You alone are capable of everything, seeing that God himself alone, to whom you give birth, established you alone above everything.

"And because I spurned you, abandoned you, and denied you, you show still greater compassion if you bring help to me. Since compassion displayed to enemies is extraordinary, this extraordinary honor is fittingly yours. You are the hope of humankind, you are the source of salvation, you are the way and leader of the way by which a human being is

humani generis tu gloria, tu reparatrix,
tu decus atque decor, tu speciale decus,
tu via qua Christus veniens invisere mundum
venit et effecit te sibi vita viam,
tu sine nocte dies, radius sine pulvere, lumen
quod mundi tenebras irradiare solet,
luna carens umbris, quam sol Deitatis obumbrat.
Per te fulget humo qui deus est et homo.
Hinc, pia, redde pium miserando, benigna, benignum.
Effice ne pereat, te miserante, miser."
Talia clamanti miserorum mite levamen
affuit et modicum turbida dixit ei:
"Quid lacrimas fundis? Quid palmis pectora tundis?
Mene putas lacrimis flectere posse tuis?
Quid gemis incassum? Quid me cupis aut petis? Adsum,
cum tibi non valeam ferre salutis opem.
Nonne meum natum blasphemus et ipse negasti?
Quid petis hoc a me, quod negat ipse tibi?
Me pariter cum prole mea tua lingua negavit.
Testis adest facti cautio scripta tui.
Sim licet humani generis pia semper amatrix,
non possum nati probra tulisse mei.
Nemo tibi nisi tu quicquam nocuisse probatur;
nemo tibi nisi tu vimque necemque tulit.
Te tibi surripuit tua lingua manusque profana;
non alius nisi tu te tibi surripuit.
Derogat ergo mihi quisquis contempserit illum,
contemptorque mei derogat omnis ei.
Sed ne dira nimis tibi sit dum dura videtur,
hac vice victa, volo mitior esse tibi.

restored, you are the glory of humankind, you are its restorer, you are its honor and ornament, its extraordinary honor, you are the way by which Christ came into the world to visit it with his coming, and life made you the way for itself; you are day without night, a sunbeam without dust, the light that is accustomed to enlighten the darkness of the world, a moon without shadows that the sun of divinity shades. Through you, he who is God and man shines forth on earth. Therefore, righteous one, make a wretch righteous by showing mercy; kindly one, make him kindly. By showing your mercy, ensure that he not perish."

As he shouted such words, she who is the gentle solace of the wretched was by his side and with some agitation said to him: "Why do you pour forth tears? Why do you beat your breast with the palms of your hands? Do you think you can sway me with your tears? Why do you groan to no effect? What do you desire or seek from me? I am here, though I do not have the ability to bring you the resource of salvation. Didn't you in your blasphemy yourself deny my son? Why do you seek from me what he denies you? Your tongue denied me together with my offspring. The written bond here bears witness to your action.

"Though I am always a devoted lover of humanity, I cannot bear the abuse of my son. No one but you is proven to have done you any harm; no one but you inflicted violent death on you. Your sacrilegious tongue and hand have wrested you from yourself; no one but you wrested you from yourself. So whoever has held him in scorn detracts from me, and everyone who scorns me detracts from him. But, swayed by these circumstances, so they might not be too extreme for you though they seem harsh, I wish to be rather

Me lacrimae gemitusque tui meruisse videntur,
non quia tu iustus, sed quia mitis ego.
Ergo fidem cordis confessio nuntiet oris,
ut testis fidei sit tua lingua mihi.
Cor nimis immundum mundet confessio munda,
ne si munda minus polluat ipsa nimis."
Dixit. At ille, quasi mortis de funere surgens,
surgit et exponit facta fidemque suam.
Dicta placent; placido vultu placata recessit,
talia post triduum verba reversa ferens:
"Cessent singultus, lacrimae, suspiria, planctus;
dimissum facinus noveris esse tuum.
Iam satis est cecidisse semel; semel ergo resurgens,
ne moriaris item, nocte dieque cave!"
Talia suadenti iamiamque redire volenti
obviat et maesto pectore tristis ait:
"O pia stella maris, decor orbis, honor specialis,
virgo carens simili, sponsa parensque Dei,
restat adhuc scriptum quod me movet amplius, illud
quod male daemonibus contulit ista manus.
Et nisi tu dederis, nisi tu revocaveris illud,
nunquam tutus ero, liber ab hoste meo."
Tertia lux aderat cum iam lux nescia noctis
affuit, egregia virgo parensque pia.
Hostibus invitis scriptum quod ab hoste negatum
viribus extorsit, reddit, at inde redit.
Charta retenta manet, sed abit cum virgine somnus.
Somnus abit: verbis facta dedere fidem.

indulgent to you. Your tears and groans seem to have won me over, not because you are justified, but because I am indulgent. Therefore let confession from your mouth proclaim the faith of your heart, so your tongue may be witness of your faith to me. Let a cleansing confession cleanse an all-too-unclean heart, for fear that if unclean, it may be too defiling."

She spoke. Then that man, as if rising from the grave, rises and declares his past deeds and his faith. His words find favor; appeased, she withdrew with a kindly countenance and returned after three days, saying the following words: "Let sobs, tears, sighs, and lamentations cease; know that your villainy has been pardoned. To have fallen once is already enough; so now you have risen once again, take care by night and day not to die in the same way!"

As she gives this advice when wishing at this very moment to retire, he meets her and unhappily addresses her with sad heart: "Oh kindly star of the sea, ornament of the world, special honor, peerless Virgin, Betrothed and Mother of God, there remains still to upset me further the contract that this hand ill-advisedly consigned to demons. If you do not grant it, if you do not recover it, I will never be safe, free from my enemy."

The light of the third day was at hand, when now the light that knows no night, the noble Virgin and kindly Mother, made her appearance. Against the will of the enemy she returns the contract that she wrested away by force from her foe when he withheld it, and then she retires. The charter remains in his possession, but sleep departs with the Virgin. Sleep departs: the actions confirm the truth of the words.

Et quia festa dies populos collegit in unum,
currit et ecclesiae limina laetus adit.
Singula pontifici referens ex ordine, cunctos
terret et a simili se cohibere monet.
Qualiter errasset causamque modumque revelat,
auctor et interpres criminis ipse sui.
Spem veniae lapsis dedit hinc, sed et inde timorem
stantibus incussit res manifesta satis.
Charta datur flammis; populo pia forma salutis
redditur, ecclesiae portio digna sui;
cumque sacrum Domini corpus gustasset, honorem
contulit ecce novum virgo Maria viro:
provocat aspectus quos luce reverberat ipsa
clara viri facies, sole micante novo.
Sol novus in facie radiis scintillat acutis—
angelus ex vultu, corpore cum sit homo.
Vix igitur triduo vivens, moriendo recessit,
de mundo mundus, ad loca sacra sacer.
Terra subit terram, subeunt caelestia caelum.
Spiritus astra petit, terrea castra caro.
Virginis in populo timor et devotio crevit,
ex tunc usque modo non habitura modum.

De sancto Dunstano

Optima terrarum, fecunda Britannia, muris
clauditur aequoreis, insula grata satis,
alter in hoc mundo paradisus deliciarum,
deliciis plenus creditur esse locus.

Because a feast day brought together as one the people, he runs and happily approaches the threshold of the church. Recounting in order each and every detail to the bishop, he frightens one and all and cautions them to restrain themselves from anything similar. Himself the agent and interpreter of his own misdeed, he discloses how he went astray and the reason and manner. On the one hand the all-too-evident facts of the matter gave hope of forgiveness to the fallen, but on the other they struck fear into those still standing.

The charter is consigned to the flames; a pious model of salvation is restored to the people, a worthy share of its own to the Church. When he had tasted the sacred body of the Lord, behold, the Virgin Mary conferred a new honor upon the man: she calls forth visible forms that Theophilus's bright face reflects with identical light, as a new sun gleams. A new sun glitters with piercing rays in his face—an angel in his countenance, though he may be human in body. Living thereafter barely three days, he passed away in death, in purity from the world, sanctified to sacred places. Earth enters earth; heavenly things enter heaven. The spirit seeks the stars; the flesh, the earthly stronghold. Awe and devotion for the Virgin grew among the people, from then to now not observing any bounds.

On Saint Dunstan

The best of lands, fertile Britain, is closed within watery walls, a quite charming island, a second paradise of delights in this world, a place believed to be full of delights.

Mellea terra favi mellis, gens lactea lactis,
fertilitate fluens, dulcia quaeque parit.
Deliciis variis opibusque fluens pretiosis
pullulat, innumeris terra referta bonis.
Hoc speciale tamen habet insula quod speciali
quadam prae reliquis gens pietate nitet.
Accidit unde piae specialius esse Mariae
gentem devotam, quae pietate viget.
Hinc Dorobernensis Dunstanus adest mihi testis,
Dunstanus patriae flosque decusque suae.
Testis adest genti pariterque Dei genitrici,
gloria pontificum, forma decusque pium.
Monstrat utramque piam, gentem simul atque Mariam,
Dunstanus, patriae flosque decusque piae.
Coeperat a puero Dunstanus habere Mariam
exemplum vitae praesidiumque suae.
Huius in obsequium totum se devovet; huius
certat amore frui corpore, mente, manu.
Hanc amat, hanc sequitur; amor incipit esse timori;
dumque timet quod amat, crescit amore timor.
Crevit amor pueri puero crescente. Iuventus
excoluit pariter facta fidemque senis.
Cuius ad exemplum dum se componit amando,
viribus et vitae vim facit ipse suae.
Vicit amor vires; puerum devicit amantem
verus amor pueri, non puerilis amor.
Moribus aetatem transcendit, viribus annos.
Mirares iuvenem corpore, mente senem.
Annorum numeris amor innumerabilis annis
obviat. Exactor fit gravis ipse sibi.

A honeyed land of honeycomb, a milky nation of milk, flowing with fertility, it gives birth to every sort of sweetness. It teems with a flood of various delights and precious riches, a land packed with countless good things. Yet the island has this special quality, that its nation shines before all others with a special piety. Therefore it happens that this nation, which is distinguished by its holiness, is specially devoted to holy Mary.

From this place Dunstan of Canterbury comes forward for me as witness, Dunstan, flower and honor of his homeland. The glory of bishops, their model and pious ornament, he comes forward as witness to his nation as well as to the Mother of God. Dunstan, flower and honor of his pious homeland, shows that both are pious, at once his nation and Mary.

From boyhood Dunstan began to hold Mary as the example and protection of his life. He dedicates himself wholly to her service; he strives with body, mind, and hand to win enjoyment of her love. He loves her, he follows her; love begins to be a cause of fear; and as he fears what he loves, fear grows with love. The boy's love grew as the boy grew. Youth practiced equally the actions and faith of an old man. As he shapes himself on that one's model in loving, he uses force on his own vim and vigor. Love conquered vim; a boy's true love, not boyish love, thoroughly conquered a boy who is a lover.

In moral conduct he surpasses his age, in vigor his years. You would marvel at a youth in body, an old man in mind. A love that is numberless in years contradicts the actual numbers of his years. He becomes a hard taskmaster over

Spiritus ad nutum carnem servire coegit,
ancillam dominae restituendo suae.
Sic subiecit Agar Sarae, ne forte rebellis
vinceret et dominam sperneret ipsa suam.
Nec mora, Glastoniae claustrum subeundo Mariae
colla iugo studuit subdere seque Deo.
In novitate viae, donatus amore Mariae,
incipit esse novus miles ad arma nova.
Induit exterius monachum quem gesserat intus,
dum sub veste nova vota vetusta tegit.
Velle vetus sub veste nova conservat; amorem
auget et augmentis proficit ipse suis.
Munda fit a mundo pueri mens munda. Mariae,
quam colit, esse comes virginitate studet.
Haec via duxque viae: vitam meditando Mariae,
hanc habet ad patriam qua cupit ire viam.
Se sibi subducens, carnem castigat ad unguem,
quam premit ipse prius quam premat ipsa virum.
Ne rediviva caro carnis consurgat in hostem,
subtrahit huic somnum, subtrahit atque cibum.
In cinerem redigens cinerem quandoque futuram,
monstrat et attendit quid sit et unde caro.
Sic igitur vivus mortis sub imagine vixit,
viveret ut Christo mortificata caro.
Quicquid honestatis, quicquid pietatis amorem
excitat, instituit protinus esse suum.
Saepius unde suus meruit, mediante Maria,
spiritibus superis spiritus esse comes.
Cernere psallentes et cum psallentibus ipse
psallere spiritibus, raptus ad astra, solet.

himself. The spirit compelled the flesh to serve at its beck, restoring it as maidservant to its mistress. In this way he subjected Hagar to Sarah, so that she might not in mutiny overcome and scorn her mistress.

Without delay, by entering the cloister of Glastonbury he desired to subject his neck to Mary's yoke and himself to God. Favored with the love of Mary, he begins to be a new soldier on a new path to new arms. He dons outwardly the appearance of a monk that he had worn inwardly, as he cloaks old-established vows beneath new clothing. Beneath new clothing he preserves his old desire; he increases his love, and he profits by his increases. The clean mind of the boy becomes cleansed of the world. He strives to be a companion in virginity to Mary, whom he venerates. She is the way and the leader of the way: by contemplating Mary's life, he has her as the way by which he wishes to go to the homeland. Rescuing himself from himself, he subdues completely the flesh, which he overpowers before it overpowers him as a man. So that the flesh not return to life and arise against the foe of the flesh, he deprives it of sleep and deprives it of food. Reducing to ash what will someday be ash, he shows and heeds what flesh is and from where it comes. So then, he, while alive, lived in the likeness of death, so that the flesh mortified would live in Christ. Whatever enhances the love of integrity, whatever enhances that of piety, he established immediately as his own.

For this reason his spirit deserved very often, through the intercession of Mary, to be a companion to the spirits above. Carried off to the stars, he is accustomed to see the spirits chanting and himself to chant with them as they chant.

Nec semel hoc in eo, sed saepius est repetitum,
virgine matre tamen hoc tribuente sibi.
Iam totiens fuerat Dunstanus ad astra vocatus,
quod sibi vita foret et via nota poli;
et nisi condicio carnis mortalis obesset,
angelus esse magis quam videretur homo.
Neumata spirituum retinendo melosque supernos,
saepe suos docuit redditus ipse sibi.
Praesulis ipsa sui celebris Dorobernia testis
eius adhuc hodie neuma melosque canit.
Quid quod et hic Satanam per nasum forcipe sumptum
fortiter ignita fecit inire fugam,
huncque revertentem multatum verbere multo
ipsa flagellantis fracta flagella probant.
Quo magis ad superos meruit transire videndos,
daemonis insidias pertulit inde magis.
Plura futura suis quasi facta referre solebat,
multa quidem referens, multa silendo tegens.
O novitatis opus, o res memoranda modernis,
o veneranda viris vita venusta viri!
Cum semel in caelum solito de more redisset,
venit in occursum virgo Maria viri.
Obvia virgineis venit comitata choreis,
applaudens miro mater honore viro.
Dextra datur dextrae, sociatur amicus amicis,
virginibus virgo, civibus hospes amans;
dumque corona datur quasi merces virginitatis,
his modulando melis ora resolvit era:

This did not happen just once in him, but rather was repeated very often; the Virgin Mother bestowed this upon him. Now Dunstan had been called to the stars so many times that the life and way of heaven were known to him; and if the circumstance of mortal flesh were not an obstacle, he would seem to be an angel rather than a human being. Retaining the musical notes and heavenly melodies of the spirits, he often, once restored to himself, taught them to his followers. Canterbury itself, as witness of its renowned bishop, sings still today his music and melodies.

What is more, this man also caused Satan to take flight after grabbing him by the nose with intensely red-hot pincers, and the very whips that were broken as he whipped him confirm that upon returning, Satan was punished with many a lash. The more Dunstan merited making the passage to see heavenly beings, the more thereby he endured the demon's schemes.

He was accustomed to relate to his followers numerous things to come as if they had already happened, relating many things indeed, while covering many in silence. Oh how novel an experience, oh how worthy an event of being commemorated by people today, oh how pleasing this man's life, worthy of men's reverence! When once he had returned to heaven in his accustomed manner, the Virgin Mary came to encounter the man. She came to meet him, accompanied by virginal troupes, a mother acclaiming this man with wondrous honor. Right hand is clasped with right hand, friend is joined with friends, virgin with virgins, loving visitor with citizens. As a garland is given, by way of reward for virginity, Our Lady gives voice, chanting these melodies:

"Cantemus Domino, sociae, cantemus honorem:
dulcis amor Christi personet ore pio."
Alternando chori versus moderamine dulci
excipiunt, reliquos continuando melos.
Obstupuit tanta praesul dulcedine captus;
iussus et ipse melos intonat orsus ita:
"O rex Christe, piae meritis largire Mariae
humano generi te sine fine frui.
Ne peregrinetur a te tua plebs, revocetur
ad vitae patriam, te tribuente viam."
Plura quidem cecinit quorum brevitatis amator
sub brevitate stili non valet esse memor.
Singula quis numeret? Quod opus, quae lingua retexat
gaudia Dunstani tanta videntis ibi?
Matris amor propriae trahit hinc, trahit inde Maria.
Gaudet utroque pio tractus amore trahi.
Sic igitur dum distrahitur, vir tractus ad astra,
rursus ad ima soli carne trahente redit.
Visa refert rediens. Specialius esse colendam,
quam colit ipse monet, huius amore coli.
Praesulis ergo fides non est fraudata fidelis,
quem suus ex nulla parte fefellit amor.
Cuius enim studuit fieri dum vixit imago,
corpore deposito fit sine fine comes.

De Iuliano apostata interfecto

Pessima faex hominum, Iulianus apostata, regum
pessimus, ecclesiae subdolus hostis erat.
Dogmata Catholicae fidei quandoque secutus,
vestierat falsa simplicitate dolum.

"Let us sing in honor to the Lord, let us sing, my companions: may the sweet love of Christ resound from pious mouths." Choirs take up the versicles antiphonally in a sweet strain, carrying on the rest of the tunes. The bishop, enthralled by such great sweetness, was astounded, and as bidden, himself intones melodies, beginning thus: "Oh Christ the King, through the merits of kindly Mary grant to humankind to enjoy you endlessly. That your folk not wander from you, let them be called back to the homeland of life, by offering them the way yourself."

He sang of many more things, in fact, which a lover of conciseness cannot recollect in a concise style. Who could enumerate every single one? What work, what tongue could recount such great joys as Dunstan saw there?

On one side love of his own mother draws him, on the other Mary. Drawn by pious love, he rejoices to be drawn by both. And so, as he is torn in this way, the man is carried off to the stars, but returns, as flesh draws him down again to the lowlands of the earth. On his return he reports his visions. For love of this destiny, he advises that she, whom he himself venerates, ought to be venerated more particularly. So the faith of the faithful bishop was not misplaced, for his love in no way failed him. By laying down his body, he becomes, to be sure, the unending companion of her whose likeness he strove to become while he lived.

On the Killing of Julian the Apostate

The worst of the dregs of humanity, Julian the Apostate, the worst of kings, was a sly foe of the Church. Having followed for a time the doctrines of the Catholic faith, he cloaked

Dissimulando diu, celans sub melle venena,
pelle sub agnina coeperat esse lupus;
quamque puer didicit, postquam pervenit ad annos,
Catholicae fidei certior hostis erat.
Omnibus exosus nullique benevolus unquam,
acrior ecclesiae depopulator erat.
Unde triumphales sub eo meruere coronas
multi, sanctorum martyriique decus.
Contigit ergo semel quod, cum properaret in hostes,
magnus Basilius obvius esset ei.
Vir bonus et iustus nullique secundus in urbe,
praesul Caesareae Capadocensis erat.
Sed Iulianus eum graviter commotus in iram
spreverat et spreto multa minatus erat.
Praesulis excidium si forte rediret et urbis
sternere iurarat moenia more suo.
Nectere bella moras prohibent; vocat hostis in arma.
Accelerare studet quem sua damna trahunt.
Praesulis interea geminam cautela medelam
prospicit oppressis civibus atque sibi.
Civibus accitis, dum tempus et hora supersunt,
congregat hinc aurum, congregat inde preces.
His placare Deum cupit, hoc prosternere regem.
Haec via tuta satis, tutior illa tamen.
Auri sacra fames fulvo satianda metallo,
sed superanda magis vis violenta prece.
Nusquam tuta fides: timor et tremor occupat omnes,
principis adventum sexus uterque timet.
Rara quies populis; spes pacis nulla remansit.
Vindicat omne sibi ius timor atque dolor.

treachery in false simplicity. By long pretense, concealing poisons under honey, he undertook to be a wolf beneath a lambskin; and after reaching adulthood, he was a committed enemy of the Catholic faith which he learned as a boy. Hateful to all and never kindly to anyone, he was a keen despoiler of the Church. As a result, many earned under him garlands of victory, the distinction of saints and martyrdom.

It happened then once that, as he hastened against enemies, Basil the Great encountered him. A good and just man, second to none in the city, he was bishop of Caesarea in Cappadocia. But Julian, stirred to vehement anger, spurned him and after so doing uttered many threats against him. He swore, if he should happen to return, to destroy the bishop and to lay flat the city walls as was his practice. War forbids contriving delays; the enemy calls him to arms. He is keen to make haste; he is drawn to his detriment.

In the meantime the providence of the bishop foresees a twofold remedy for the overwhelmed citizens and himself. Summoning the citizens, while a period of time is left, he amasses gold on this side and prayers on that. By the second he desires to mollify God, by the first to lay low the king. The one way is safe enough, but the other still safer. The execrable hunger for gold is satisfied by tawny metal, but destructive force is better overcome by prayer.

Faith is nowhere safe: fear and trembling take hold of everyone; each sex fears the coming of the emperor. For the people tranquility becomes rare; no hope of peace remained. Fear and grief monopolize everything for themselves. No

Nulla salus miseris restat, regnante tyranno.
Res odiosa nimis, rex pietate carens!
Sola tamen superest fessis quam spondet adesse
praesul opem: precibus sollicitare Deum.
Praesulis ad nutum, tanto concussa timore,
offert dives opes, paupera turba preces.
Vim sibi quisque facit: quoniam sic cogit, oportet.
Otia non patitur luxuriare dolor.
Auro dives, egens precibus se multat; et hostem
vincat ut alteruter, certat utroque modo.
Postulat auxilium gens tristis adesse supernum;
pulsat et apertas invenit ipsa fores.
Affuit et miseris miserorum mite levamen:
contulit auxilium virgo Maria pium.
Neve diu doleant, celeri virtute medelam
moribus et morbis contulit ipsa suis.
Virginis et matris fuerat prope moenia templum
montis in excelso vertice grande situm.
Hic offerre preces, hic solvere vota Mariae
coepit ab antiquo tempore cura patrum.
Huc petiturus opem populus cum praesule sancto
confluit et querulis questibus ora replet.
Defluit in lacrimas quas aut timor aut dolor urget
tota cohors; lacrimis sexus uterque madet.
Terra madet lacrimis, resonant clamoribus aethra.
Unica plangentum publica causa fuit;
cumque tot et tantis amicta doloribus esset,
hostibus ut fieret plebs miseranda suis,
affuit afflictis hominum speciale levamen,
virgo Maria, citam dans pietatis opem.

security is left for the wretched, under a despot's rule. An all-too-hateful thing, a king lacking in mercy! Yet one resource alone remains, which the bishop promises is available to the weary: to entreat God with prayers.

At a nod from the bishop, the crowd of rich people, stricken by great fear, offers wealth; the crowd of poor, prayers. Everyone is compelled to force himself: because circumstances so oblige, it is necessary. Grief does not permit indulging in idleness. The rich pay the price in gold; the needy in prayers; and each, to overcome the enemy, strives in one of these two ways. The distressed people ask for heavenly aid to come to their side; they knock and find the doors open. The gentle solace of the wretched came to them in their wretchedness: the Virgin Mary bestowed her kindly aid. So that they might not grieve for long, she bestowed upon her followers a remedy with swift effect for their dispositions and diseases.

A large church of the Virgin and Mother was near the walls, located on the lofty summit of a mountain. Here from olden times the fathers, in their solicitude, offered prayers; here they fulfilled vows to Mary. To this place the people, with their saintly bishop, stream together to seek aid, and they give full voice to bitter laments.

The entire troop bursts into tears that either fear or grief prompts; each sex is awash with tears. The earth is drenched with tears; the sky resounds with cries. There was a single cause for the public lamentation; and when the populace had been encompassed by so many great griefs that it became pitiable to its own enemies, she made herself present as a particular solace to the distressed of humankind—she, the Virgin Mary, granting swiftly the aid of her compassion.

Cumque soporiferae praesul lassata quieti
membra daret, somno lumina fessa levans,
undique virgineis circumvallata choreis
venerat in templum virgo Maria suum;
cumque resedisset, vultu veneranda, vocari
Mercurium iussit. Nec mora, iussus adest.
Astat et armatus, iussis parere paratus
virginis et matris. Cui pia mater ait,
"Ibis et accelerans interficies Iulianum.
Ne mora tardet opus, acceleretur iter.
Occidat exosus, te percutiente, tyrannus.
Perge redique celer, caelica iussa sequens."
Miles ad arma ruit, adiens in Perside regem
inflictoque gravi vulnere victor abit.
Talibus inspectis, praesul descendit in urbem
ut probet auditis quae sit habenda fides.
Nomine Mercurius miles celeberrimus olim
martyrium celebre concelebrarat ibi.
Clarus et insignis et in urbe sepultus eadem
morte triumphata carne iacebat ibi.
Cuius ob insigne meritum celebremque triumphum
militiae signum lancea mansit adhuc.
Hanc modo sublatam cum praesul abesse videret,
coepit maiorem rebus habere fidem;
dissimulansque tamen rem censuit esse tegendam,
rebus in incertis certior esse volens.
Crastina lux aderat cum lancea forte reperta
corporis humani tincta cruore madet.
Quod cum tota simul urbs admirata fuisset,
affuit antistes, visa referre studens.

When the bishop gave over his wearied limbs to sleep-inducing repose, relieving his tired eyes with sleep, the Virgin Mary, on all sides surrounded by virginal troupes, came into her church; and when, venerable in countenance, she had taken a seat, she ordered Mercurius to be called. Without delay, he is present as ordered. He stands by, armed, prepared to obey the orders of the Virgin and Mother. To him the kindly Mother says, "You will go and, making haste, kill Julian. Don't let delay slow the task; be quickly on your way. Let the hated despot drop dead from your blow. Go off and come back again swiftly, following heavenly orders." The soldier rushes to arms; he approaches the king in Persia and, having dealt a serious wound, departs as victor.

When he had seen all this, the bishop goes down into the city to verify what stock should be placed in what he has heard. Long ago a most famous soldier, Mercurius by name, made famous there his celebrated martyrdom. Renowned and distinguished, he lay buried in the flesh there in the same city, after having triumphed over death. On account of his distinguished merit and celebrated triumph, the lance still remained as a token of his soldiery. When the bishop saw that it had now been removed and was gone, he began to put greater stock in the story. Yet, maintaining a pretense, he resolved that the matter should be concealed, out of a desire to have certainty in uncertain matters. Daylight on the following day had come when the lance happened to be found, moist and tinged with gore from a human body. When the whole city all wondered at this, the prelate came before them, keen to report what he had seen.

Nuntiat extinctum transacta nocte tyrannum
virginis ex iussu Mercuriique manu.
Exhilarata diem, tempus, designat et horam
urbs, ex post facto facta probare volens.
Exitus acta probat: rex nocte peremptus eadem
militis ignoti dicitur esse manu.
Principis impietas sic est pietate perempta:
illa necis causam praebuit, ista manum.
Grata quies populo, pax urbi, civibus aurum,
redditur ecclesiae pontificique salus.

De sancto Ildefonso

Nobilis antistes fuit Ildefonsus in urbe,
nomine Tholeto, nobilitatis honos,
vir sacer et celebris ac summae religionis,
sedis honor, populi gloria, forma gregis.
Hic in amore piae devotior esse Mariae
coepit et inceptis institit usque suis.
Unde fide plenum, verbis insigne volumen
virginis in laudem scripsit amica manus,
quo satis egregie falsos reprehendit aperto
dogmate Iudaeos Elvidiique nefas.
Praemia digna labor, devotio sancta favorem
virginis et matris promeruere sibi;
sicque sui memoris studuit memor esse Maria,
quatenus effectu res manifesta foret.
Quid labor exspectet vel quid devotio speret,
pontifici monstrant munera, monstrat amor.

He announces that during the past night the despot was killed by the Virgin's order and by Mercurius's hand. Exultant, the city records the day, time, and hour, wishing through subsequent actions to confirm earlier ones. The outcome confirms the deeds done: the king is stated to have been slain on the same night by the hand of an unknown soldier. In this way the impiety of the emperor was slain by piety: the former supplied the motivation for the violent death; the latter, the hand. Welcome repose is restored to the people, peace to the city, gold to the citizens, safety to the Church and bishop.

On Saint Ildephonsus

Ildephonsus was a noble prelate in the city named Toledo, the high esteem of nobility, a holy man, renowned, of highest saintliness, the esteem of his see, glory of his people, model for his flock. This man undertook to show special devotion in love to kindly Mary and dedicated himself to her in all his undertakings. For this reason, with loving hand he wrote a book, full of faith and remarkable in its language, in praise of the Virgin. In it, in a most excellent way he takes to task with lucid doctrine the deceitful Jews and the sacrilege of Helvidius.

His toil earned for him worthy rewards from the Virgin and Mother; his holy devotion, her favor. In this way Mary strove to be mindful of one mindful of her, so that the reality would be evident from the result. The rewards and love show to the bishop what toil could expect or devotion hope

Nam cum more suo psallendo silentia noctis
solveret antistes, astitit alma parens.
Dulcibus alloquiis grates referendo, volumen
monstrat et acceptum praedicat esse sibi.
Collaudatur opus operis preciosus et auctor;
Virgine teste, placent auctor opusque suum.
Neve minus dignas digno retulisset honori
grates, grata refert munera virgo viro.
Quem postquam dulci visu verboque refecit,
cum cathedra vestem contulit huic et ait,
"Haec allata tibi duo munera de paradiso,
vestem cum cathedra suscipe, care meus.
Haec duo dona, tibi soli concessa, teneto;
haec duo dona mei pignus amoris habe."
Dixit et, ex oculis subito collapsa, reliquit
pignus amicitiae munus utrumque sibi.
Nemo satis cathedram tibi sufficienter ad horam
describat, qualis quaeve vel unde fuit.
Vestis candorem, speciem, decus atque decorem
cum careat simili quis notet arte styli?
Talia pontificem decuerunt, talia matrem
munera pontifici distribuisse suo.
Munera pontificem commendant, munera matrem,
quae meritis dignis munera digna dedit.
Quid sibi vult cathedra, nisi spem requiemque laboris?
Veste nitet nivea virginitatis amor.
Ne terrena tamen reputet sua dona fuisse,
quae dedit ipsa docet caelica quaeque fore.

for. For when the prelate according to his custom broke the silence of the night with singing, the fostering Mother stood nearby. Rendering thanks in sweet words, she shows the book and makes known that it is pleasing to her. The work and the valued author of the work are commended; with the Virgin as witness, the author and his work win approval. In order not to render unworthy thanks for a worthy honor, the Virgin renders welcome rewards to the man.

After she brought him refreshment with her sweet sight and speech, she bestowed upon him the vestment along with the throne of a bishop and said, "Receive, my dear one, these two rewards brought to you from paradise, the bishop's vestment and throne. Hold fast to these two gifts, granted to you alone; keep these two gifts as a token of my love."

She spoke and, abruptly slipping from sight, she left behind for him the two rewards as pledges of friendship. No one could describe the throne to you at all satisfactorily in a short time—what it was, of what kind, or from where. Who could express by the art of the stylus the brightness, splendor, beauty, and attraction of the vestment, since it has no like? Such rewards befitted the bishop; such rewards it befitted the Mother to have bestowed on her bishop. The rewards reflect credit on the bishop; the rewards reflect credit on the Mother, who gave deserved rewards for deserving merits. What does the throne convey, if not hope and repose for toil? Love of virginity shines in the snow-white garment.

Yet so that he not consider her gifts to have been earthly, she shows him that everything that she gave is heavenly.

His iubet hunc uti solum solique licere
vestis et exhibitae sedis honore frui.
Neve minus prudens quisquam sibi sumat honorem
quem dedit huic soli, virgo venusta vetat.
Hoc quotiens voluit dum vixit honore potitus,
corpore deposito, liber ad astra redit.
Cuius successor vetito semel usus honore
ne resecundaret, mors cita causa fuit.
Vix erat indutus vestem, vix sede locatus,
cum rueret subita morte peremptus homo.
Quod male praesumpsit praesul, ne forte revertens
hoc iteraret item, mors cita clausit iter.
Terminus erroris terror fuit omnibus horis,
re faciente fidem ne repetatur idem.
Presulis errorem vetitum rapientis honorem

INCIPIT LIBER SECUNDUS.

De liberatione Carnotensium

Presserat obsessis Carnoti civibus urbem
dux Normannorum, Rollo, dolore gravi.
Arma necem, furor excidium, numerosa triumphum
turba minabantur civibus atque loco.
Arridens Fortuna duci ventura timere
praedicat a simili condicione sui.
Sumptibus absumptis, virtutibus attenuatis,
urbs emarcuerat obsidione gravi.

She orders him alone to use them and permits him alone to enjoy the honor of the vestment and throne she had presented to him. The comely Virgin forbids anyone less wise to take up for himself the honor that she gave to this one alone. While alive, he availed himself of this honor as often as he wished; after laying down his body, he returns in freedom to the stars.

His successor took advantage of this forbidden honor one time. A swift death was the reason that he did not try a second time. The man had hardly donned the vestment, hardly taken a place on the throne, than he collapsed, destroyed by a sudden death. Swift death barred the way for the bishop to return and repeat this course of action that he had wrongly presumed to take. Unceasing dread put an end to sin, as the incident guaranteed that the same thing would not be done again. The bishop's sin in seizing a forbidden honor . . .

HERE BEGINS THE SECOND BOOK.

On the Liberation of the Chartrians

The citizens of Chartres were besieged. The duke of the Normans, Rollo, had afflicted the city with heavy grief. Arms threatened the citizens and locality with murder; rage with destruction; the numberless throng with conquest. Fortune, smiling upon the duke, proclaims from her constant state that the future is to be feared.

The city, its resources consumed and powers diminished, had wasted away from the harsh siege. Fear cast out hope;

Spem timor exclusit. Auxit ducis ira timorem.
  Fit suspecta magis gens feritate sua.
Causa viam paci clausit, Fortuna saluti,
  quam negat inclusis ira furorque ducis.
Carnotum iam carcer erat; quasi carcere clausos
  undique vallarat vis violenta ducis;
cumque resistendi miseris spes omnis abesset
  et prohiberet iter hostis et arma fugam,
ad Deitatis opem tandem sibi confugiendum
  consensu parili tutius esse putant.
Iam prope limen erat furibundus et hostis et ignis—
  viribus iste viam praeparat, ille dolo—
cum iam tota simul novitatis ad arma recurrit
  urbs et inaudito vincere Marte parat:
virginis et matris quae servabatur ibidem
  interulam rapiens, ad nova bella ruit
hancque, super turrim vexilli more locatam,
  hostibus opponit ignibus atque neci.
O novitatis opus, o res memoranda modernis,
  o nova bellandi forma modusque novus!
Quisquis in hanc oculos vestem convertit iniquos,
  frustratus proprio lumine caecus abit.
Lumine cassatas divina potentia turmas
  terruit et subitam fecit inire fugam.
Dux confusus abit, fugit hostis et ignis ab urbe,
  ordine confuso turba reversa redit.
Victor abit victus; premitur qui presserat ante.
  Incidit in laqueos gens furibunda suos.
Turba, superba prius, humilis ruit; inque ruendo
  reddit quam tulerat hostis ab hoste vicem.

the duke's anger increased the fear; his nation became even more distrusted for its fierceness. That cause blocked the road to peace, Fortune the one to safety, which the anger and madness of the duke denies to those besieged.

Chartres was now a prison; the violent might of the duke had blockaded the people on all sides, as if shut up in prison. When all hope of offering resistance was gone for the wretches, and the armed enemy precluded a way out and flight, they thought at last, with common consent, that it would be safer for them to flee for refuge to the assistance of the Deity. The enemy and fire, both raging, were already at their doorstep—the second makes its way by might, the first by stratagem—when now the whole city resorts at once to weapons of a novel sort, and prepares to win victory by an original form of combat: seizing the tunic of the Virgin and Mother that was kept there, it sallies forth to new warfare and sets the tunic, placed above a tower in the style of a banner, against the enemy, fire, and slaughter. Oh what a novel turn of events, oh what a story worthy to be recalled by people today, oh what a new form and new manner of warring!

Whoever sets hostile eyes upon this garment goes off blind, deprived of his own sight. The power of God struck fear into troops stripped of sight and caused them to take sudden flight. The bewildered duke goes off, the enemy and fire flee from the city, the multitude turns and retraces its steps in disorder. The victor goes off vanquished; he who had previously oppressed is now oppressed himself. The raging nation falls into its own snares. The multitude, earlier haughty, collapses in humiliation; and in collapsing, the enemy paid back in turn what it had inflicted on its enemy.

Pro vice quisque vicem dignam tulit hostis ab hoste.
  Sic variat varias virgo Maria vices.
Hostibus extinctis, pax est data civibus, urbi
  grata quies, Domino gloria, laus et honor.

<De sancto Fulberto Carnotensi>

Multa licet calamum revocent alias, tamen istud
  gestum Carnotho chartula nostra notet.
Sedis honor, non sedis onus, Fulbertus in urbe
  sedit Carnotho, gemma decusque loci.
Extulit officium meritis, cumulavit honorem
  moribus, auxit opes vita pudica viri.
Invigilans studiis vigilanter, honestus honestis,
  instituit fieri forma sequenda gregi.
Nobilis ingenio, scripturae dogmata sacrae
  hauserat a puero, corpore mente sacer.
Pervigil in studiis, studiosius ipse Mariae
  coepit in affectum mente manuque trahi,
utpote qui fuerat sedis ratione vocatus,
  eius in obsequium prosequeretur idem.
Unde fidem factis tanto faciebat amori,
  virginis in laudem plura notante stylo.
Hic prior instituit celebrari virginis ortum,
  extulit et celebrem laudibus ipse diem.
Primus in urbe sua Fulbertus honore perenni
  hunc statuit celebrem laudibus esse diem;
utque dies festus festivior esset, eidem
  consona composuit cantica clara melis.
Hoc opus, iste labor, haec est sententia mentis,
  non sibi, sed soli velle placere Deo.

In turn each enemy took from its enemy a fitting recompense: thus the Virgin Mary rings the changes on changing circumstances. After the enemies have been killed, peace was granted to the citizens; welcome repose to the city; glory, praise, and honor to the Lord.

On Saint Fulbert of Chartres

Though many events call for the pen in other places, all the same let our little document record this incident at Chartres. The honor of the see, not the burden of the see, Fulbert was enthroned in the city Chartres, the gem and glory of the place. The man's modest life elevated the post through meritorious actions, amassed honor through his character, and increased resources. Keeping watch watchfully in his studies, honorable to the honorable, he undertook to become a model to be followed by his flock. Remarkable in intellect, holy in body and mind, he absorbed the teachings of holy scripture from boyhood.

Ever watchful in his studies, he was drawn in mental and manual labor more eagerly to devotion to Mary—as it is natural, that one who had been called up because of the bishop's throne would persevere in the same service to her as before. As a result, he gave proof of his great love by his deeds, recording with his pen many things in praise of the Virgin. He first established that the birth of the Virgin be honored, and he himself celebrated the famed day with praise. Fulbert first, with enduring honor, ordained in his city that this day be famed with praise. And so that the feast day would be more festive, he composed for it in harmony famous songs with tunes. This is the work, this the toil, this the cast of his mind, to wish to please not himself but God alone.

Contigit interea subito languore gravatum
pontificem lecto decubuisse diu;
cumque mori potius quam vivere praesul ad horam
crederet et vitae spes sibi nulla foret,
astitit et, morbi causamque modumque requirens,
virgo, parens veri luminis, inquit ei:
"Mi Fulberte, quid est? Quis te timor aut dolor urget?
Ne metuas mortem! Non morieris adhuc.
Surge, nihil timeas. Tibi me mediante salutem
corporis et mentis noveris esse datam."
Dixit et ecce sinu producta virgo mamilla
lactis rore sacri morbida membra rigat;
quoque Deum pavit in terris, hoc relevavit
ubere pontificem, pro vice dando vicem.
Lactis ad attactus, morbus fugit omnis abactus.
Membra vigent subito, tacta liquore sacro.
Lac quoque virgineum, condigno vase receptum,
certa dedit fidei signa subesse rei.
Re faciente fidem verbis, lactis liquor idem
virginis et matris mirificavit opus.
Mira rei novitas prospexit posteritati,
perpetuam verbis re faciente fidem.

Fessa quies reparet; calamus respiret ad horam.
Det requiem calamo pagina, cera stylo.
Sensus hebes requiem, requiem manus arida poscit:
convenit haec calamo, convenit ista stylo.
Fessa petant requiem; repetant lassata quietem,
qua sine nulla queunt posse vel esse diu.
Exspirare magis quam respirare videtur,
quem labor assiduus obsidione premit.

In the meantime it happened that the bishop, oppressed by a sudden sickness, languished in bed for a long time; and since the bishop believed that he was now dying rather than living and that there was no hope of life for him, the Virgin, Mother of the true light, stood nearby and, seeking the cause and nature of his illness, said to him: "My Fulbert, what is it? What fear or grief besets you? Don't dread death! You will not die yet. Rise, fear nothing. Know that, through my mediation, health of body and mind has been given to you."

She spoke and behold, the Virgin, bringing forth her nipple from her bosom, moistens his sickly limbs with the dew of holy milk. With the breast with which she fed God on earth, she relieved the bishop, furnishing one service for another. At the touch of the milk, all illness flees in banishment. The limbs, touched by the holy liquid, suddenly revive. The virginal milk also, collected in a vessel worthy of it, gave sure signs of the faith that underlay the event. With the event giving credence to her words, the same liquid milk made miraculous the action of the Virgin and Mother. The miraculous novelty of the event looked ahead to future generations, with the event giving unending credence to her words.

Let rest restore what is tired; let the pen recover its breath for a time. The page should let the pen rest; the wax, the stylus. A blunted wit demands rest, a desiccated hand demands rest: the second rest befits the pen, the first befits the stylus. Let what is tired seek rest; let what is wearied seek again repose, without which nothing can avail or exist for long. The person who is beleaguered by constant toil seems to breathe his last rather than to recover his breath.

Absque quiete, labor non est durabilis ullus.
 Omnia consumit absque quiete labor.
Deficit in nihilum labor absque quiete. Quietem
 si cupis, ecce quies absque quiete: labor.
Absque labore gravi requies tibi nulla paratur.
 Det labor ergo tibi posse quiete frui.
Viribus et votis mediante quiete resumptis,
 Musa regat calamum mente manuque stylum.
Accelerare precor. Ne sit mora longa periclo,
 curre vias longas per brevitatis iter.
Restat iter longum, labor arduus, area lata;
 sed mediante stylo sit via longa brevis.
Semper, in hac vita dum vivimus, unde queramur
 pluribus ex causis causa subesse solet;
quam sit enim fragile, quam futile quamque caducum
 vas hoc quod gerimus, plurima gesta probant.

De monacho resuscitato

Fugerat in claustrum, mundum fugiendo sequentem,
 clericus, ut monachus nomine reque foret.
Nominis officio mutata veste recepto,
 re tamen abiecta, dimidiarat opus.
Vestibus induerat monachi sine numine nomen,
 ostendens sine re significata rei.
Nomen habens sine re monachi, sub nomine mundo
 conservabat adhuc mente manuque fidem.
In duo divisus, homo duplicitatis iniquum
 dissimulabat iter vestis honore sacrae;
sicque tegens vitium, crimen discriminat omne
 vestis honestate mens inhonesta viri.

Without rest, no toil is lasting. Toil without rest devours all capacities. Toil without rest fades to nothing. If you desire rest, here is rest without rest: toil. Without hard toil no repose is provided for you. Let toil then grant you the ability to enjoy rest. Once your powers and wishes have been regained through the intervention of rest, let the Muse guide the pen with mind and the stylus with hand.

I pray to speed up. For a long stretch of time not to pose danger, run long distances by a short route. A long route remains, difficult toil, a broad open space; but by means of the stylus let a long distance be short. Always, while we live in this life, there tends to be one reason for complaint out of many; for numerous events attest how frail, how brittle, and how perishable this vessel is that we carry.

On a Monk Raised from the Dead

A cleric had fled into a cloister, fleeing the world that pursued him, to be a monk in name and reality. In taking on the obligations of the name, he changed his clothing, yet disregarded the real work; he performed only half the duty. With the clothing, he donned the name of monk but not the inclination, making a show of what was signified by the substance without the substance itself. Having the name without the substance of a monk, he still maintained beneath that name allegiance in mind and body to the world. Split in two, the duplicitous man disguised his wicked ways with the dignity of holy clothing; and so cloaking his vice, the man's indecent mind excuses all his crime with the decency of his

Palliat arte dolum, sub religione reatum,
ne pateat mundo res manifesta Deo.
Iustus in aspectu populi fratrumque suorum,
ementitus erat simplicitatis ovem.
Pellis ovina lupum texit quoadusque venirent
viribus et votis tempora grata suis;
cumque loci custos factusque sacrista fuisset,
coepit iure sui liberiore frui.
Si qua fuit levitas in eo quam iure notares,
excusabat eam crimine fama vacans.
Fama sed et tacite tacita quid in aure sonasset,
adnihilata fuit viribus ipsa suis.
Si qua sacris solito minor est reverentia rebus,
hanc labor excusat officiumque grave;
cumque liceret ei vetitis pro velle potiri,
fasque nefasque sibi cuncta licere putat.
Arserat interea miseram miser in mulierem
ignibus illicitis luxuriosus homo.
Hanc precis, hanc pretii nimis importunus eidem
munere multiplici sollicitare studet.
Flectitur illa prece pretio mediante precantis.
Non prece, sed pretio flectitur omnis homo.
Quaeritur ergo rei tempus, locus aptus et hora;
quaeritur illicito tempus et hora stupro;
cumque reperta forent locus aptus et hora vicissim,
conveniunt celeres accelerando nefas.
Nec monachi mulier sed nec monachus mulieris
horruit amplexus ille vel illa suos.
Turpis utrique sua placuit commixtio carnis,
quam repetisse iuvat saepe superque satis.

clothing. He cloaks deceit with craft, sin beneath religion, so that a reality evident to God is not obvious to the world.

Righteous in the view of the people and his fellow brothers, he pretended to be a guileless sheep. Sheep's clothing clothed a wolf until the occasion favorable to his power and prayers came. When he had been made custodian and sacristan of the place, he began to enjoy a freer rein over himself. If there was any inconstancy in him that you would rightly stigmatize, a reputation devoid of blame pardoned him. But what rumor sounded silently in a silent ear was brought to nothing through his influence. If there is any reverence less than customary in holy matters, toil and burdensome duty pardon it; and since he is permitted to avail himself as he wishes of things forbidden, he thinks that all things right and wrong are permitted him.

In the meantime, the wretch, a licentious man, was ablaze with the fires of unlawful lust for a wretched woman. Far too persistent toward her, he strives to seduce her with all sorts of gifts of pleading and payment. With the payment as go-between, she is swayed by his plea as he pleads. Everyone is swayed, not by pleading but by payment. So a time, place, and hour suited to the affair are sought; a time and hour are sought for illicit sex. When in turn a suitable place and hour are found, they come together speedily to speed up the sin. Neither the woman shuddered at the embraces of the monk, nor the monk at those of the woman. Their foul commingling of flesh pleased each of the two; they took great pleasure in repeating it often and then some.

Plurima fluxerunt annorum tempora postquam
ista frequentarant nocte dieque mala.
Nec tamen illicitas exstinguunt ut satientur,
sed magis accendunt tempora longa faces;
cumque libido frequens totiens repetita placeret,
usus et ars veneris lege ligavit eos:
quodque prius libitum fuerat, facit esse necesse
usus; et illicita cogitur ire via.
Allicit affectus; consentit iniqua voluptas
inveterata; ligat usus, ut ipse solet.
Damna tamen famae multa gravitate redemit,
ne damnaret eum fama nefasque grave.
Huius erat moris, quotiens transire per aram
contigit, ut supplex solveret illud "Ave."
Sicque salutata submissa voce Maria,
ibat quo voluit quoque necesse fuit.
Hoc quotiens repetebat iter, repetebat et illud
dulce salutantis hanc Gabrielis "Ave."
Sed neque cura gravis neque transitus acceleratus
hoc dum transiret surripiebat "Ave."
Cumque suis vitiis miser insenuisset et annis,
nec resipiscentem cerneret ulla dies,
sed neque mors praesens neque mortis imago futurae
posset ab illicitis hunc revocare viis,
quadam nocte tamen, solito de more Maria
ante salutata, exit abitque celer.
Claustra monasterii furtim, prout ante solebat,
egressus solitum carpere coepit iter.
Forte monasterii muros ingentis obibat
fluminis unda rapax, unda profunda nimis.

After a long period of years flowed by, they had repeated these evils night and day. Yet they do not quench the unlawful flames until they are sated, but the long passage of time kindles them more; and since frequent lust so often repeated was pleasing, practice and skill bound them by the law of sexual passion. What earlier had been pleasure, practice causes to be a necessity; and they are bound to continue down an unlawful path. Desire entices them; sinful pleasure, become chronic, concurs; practice constrains, as it is accustomed to do.

Yet he compensated for the damages of hearsay by much austerity, so that hearsay and grievous sin would not damage him. He had this custom, however often he happened to pass by the altar, as a suppliant to offer that well-known "Hail, Mary." Having thus greeted Mary in a humble voice, he would go where he wished and where it was necessary. However often he repeated the route, he would repeat also that sweet "Hail, Mary" of Gabriel greeting her. What's more, neither weighty care nor his haste in passing would steal from him this "Hail, Mary" as he passed.

When the wretch had grown old in his vices and years, and no day saw him regain his senses, but neither the immediacy of death nor the specter of death to come could summon him back from his unlawful ways, on a certain night, having greeted Mary beforehand in his usual way, he goes out all the same and departs swiftly. Having stealthily left the confines of the monastery, as he had been accustomed to do previously, he began to take his customary route.

As it happened, a river's ravenous and exceedingly deep waters surrounded the walls of the vast monastery. The

Fluminis ergo vadum subito transire volentem
devorat absorptum fluminis unda vorax.
Obrutus ergo miser, sed non ablutus in undis,
indignus digna morte peremptus obit.
Obruit unda scelus quod non tamen abluit unda;
sicque diu tectum detegit unda scelus.
Terminat excessus carnisque refrigerat aestus
fluminis unda fluens frigiditate sua.
Nox abit, hora fluit, conventus abesse sacristam
percipit, officio deficiente suo.
Ordinis et noctis fregere silentia passim
murmure cum signis pastor ovesque gregis.
Quaeritur absentis praesentia; crimina noctis
multiplici redimit lumine flamma facis.
Invenit exanimem fluviali margine mersum
multa ministrorum cura, vagata diu.
Concurrunt fratres, ruit altus ad aethera planctus:
unica plangendi causa sacrista fuit.
Triste sed et tristes fratres psallendo frequentant
funeris officium, munera dando precum.
Exsequiis igitur multa pro parte peractis,
mortis ab officio surgere coepit homo.
Mira rei novitas primo dubitare coegit,
ne phantasma novum falleret arte nova.
Sed res vera fidem dubiam confirmat et ille
omnibus exponens omnia fatur ita:
"Cum miser a rapida moriens submergerer unda,
protinus accessit plurima turba nigra.
Venit et econtra niveo candore corusca
turba, sed haec modica maestaque visa mihi.

river's devouring waters gulp him down and consume him as he wished hastily to cross by a ford. Then the wretch, overwhelmed but not absolved in the waters, undeserving of a deserving death, passed away, slain by a deserved one. The waters overwhelm the crime, but even so the waters do not wash it clean; and thus the waters uncovered a crime long covered. The river's flowing waters ended his transgressions and cool the heat of the flesh with their coldness.

Night departs, the hours flow by, the religious house notices that the sacristan is absent, as his functions are left unfulfilled. Everywhere the shepherd and sheep of the flock broke the nighttime silence of the monastic order with murmuring as well as with gestures. The presence of the one absent is sought out. The blaze of a torch, with its abundant light, atones for the misdeeds of nighttime. An extensive search by the servants, lengthy and wide-ranging, discovers him lifeless and drowned at the river's edge.

The brethren run together, loud lamentation surges to the heavens: their sole reason for lamenting was the sacristan. Still the saddened brethren, making an offering of their prayers, in great numbers perform with their singing the sad funeral ritual. But then, when the burial rites were in large part complete, the man begins to arise from the office of the dead. The miraculous novelty of the event at first compels them to hesitate, in case a strange illusion was deceiving them through strange powers. But the true reality strengthens their doubtful faith, and he explains all of it to them all, speaking as follows:

"When, a dying wretch, I was drowned by the swift waters, a very great, dark crowd immediately approached. From the opposite direction there came a crowd, gleaming with snow-white brightness, but it seemed to me modest

Omnibus ergo malis ex una parte locatis,
coeperunt alia parte locare bonum.
Sed trutinando bonis mala praevaluere, malorum
maxima namque fuit copia, parva boni.
Pauca quidem mecum, sed contra me faciebant
omnia quae feci crimina multa nimis.
Spiritibus taetris miser et miserabilis illis
traditus, ad poenas iam rapiendus eram.
Solus ab aspectu solo terrebar; et ultra
quam credi poterat exanimatus eram.
Vallarant miserum timor et tremor undique. Nulla
spes fuit auxilii consiliive mihi.
Cumque miser traherer, decus orbis honorque, Maria,
affuit et torvo lumine dixit eis:
'Quis furor, o miseri, quae vos, o mente maligni,
causa trahit? Quonam contio vestra ruit?
Sistite! Quem rapitis meus est. Quo iure nefandas
mittere temptastis in mea iura manus?'
Daemon ad haec: 'Tuus est, tibi qui contraria semper
egit et in nullo destitit esse meus?
Si tuus, unde tuus, cui tecum, de ratione,
nil commune fuit tempore sive loco?
Qui meus usque modo mihi se servire probavit
corpore, mente, manu, quis neget esse meum?
Ad mea iura frequens mea iussa secutus ubique,
qua poterit fieri de ratione tuus?
Moribus et vita mihi se sociavit. In illo
nil proprium poteris iure dicare tibi.
Quae mea sunt iuste noli, iustissima, noli
tollere, iusta minus ne videare mihi!

sized and mournful. Then when all the bad deeds had been placed on one side, they began to place the good on the other side. But in weighing them, the bad deeds outdid the good, because the supply of bad ones was exceedingly great, that of good small. Few things counted on my side, but against me were all the very many misdeeds that I committed. Pitiful and pitiable, I was handed over to those hideous spirits, and was now to be snatched away for punishment. All alone, I was frightened by their mere appearance, and disheartened beyond what could be believed. Terror and trembling ringed me round on all sides, wretch that I was. I had no hope of help or guidance.

"When in my wretchedness I was being dragged off, the glory and honor of the world, Mary, came beside me and spoke to them with a fierce glare: 'What madness, oh wretches, what motive, oh evil-minded ones, attracts you? Where is your company rushing off? Hold up! The man you are snatching away is mine. By what right have you tried to lay your wicked hands upon what is rightly mine?'

"The evil spirit responded to these words: 'Is he yours, who has always acted in opposition to you and has ceased in no act to be mine? If he is yours, on what basis is he reasonably yours, with whom you have had nothing in common in time or place? Who could deny him to be mine, who as mine has demonstrated he serves me even now in body, mind, and hand? He, following my commands regularly everywhere in keeping with my laws, by what reason could he become yours? In manners and life, he allied himself with me. In him you will be able to claim rightly nothing proper to yourself. Don't, most just of women, don't take away things that are justly mine, for fear that you seem unjust to me!

Non nisi iusta peto. Si iusta negaveris, ipsam
quis neget iniustam, quae mihi iusta negas?
Semper oboedivit mihi meque secutus ubique.
Fecit multa mihi consona, pauca tibi.
Quid nam luxuriae cum virginitatis honore?
Num Belial Christo consociandus erit?
Vita placet tibi? Non. Via? Non. Spurcissima mors? Non.
Mors, via, vita mihi consona tota placet.
Quae mea sunt vel me contingunt de ratione,
his mihi contingat de ratione frui.
In propriam messem falcem, sed non alienam
mittere iure licet. Quid mea rura metis?'
Talia causanti, respondit talibus orsa
splendida stella poli, virgo parensque Dei:
'O male mentitos, o singula falsa locutos,
o furor, o subitus in mea damna dolus!
Quamvis vita mihi sua displicuisset, honore
gratuito placuit gratior ipse mihi.
Crimen displicuit; placuit veneratio digna
et decus exhibitum nocte dieque mihi.
Damna quidem vitae reverentia digna redemit
voxque mihi totiens multiplicantis "Ave."
Corpore, mente, manu, quicquid deliquit inique,
omnia dulce meum crimina lavit "Ave."
Absit ut illud "Ave" tam sanctum tamque suave
depretiet prave spem memorantis "Ave."
Absit ut illud "Ave" necis hunc non eruat a vae,
hunc in conclave ne premat omne grave.
Omne nefas operis lavit devotio mentis,
abstulit et virus mellea lingua viri.

I seek nothing but justice. If you deny justice, who would deny that you are unjust yourself, you who deny justice to me? He has always obeyed me and followed me everywhere. He did many things in conformity with me, few with you.

"'For what does sexual misconduct have to do with the honor of virginity? Belial will surely not be associated with Christ, will he? Does his life please you? No. His conduct? No. His foulest of deaths? No. His death, conduct, and life all are pleasing for being in conformity with me. Whatever is mine or reasonably falls to my lot, let it reasonably fall to my lot to enjoy. It is properly permitted to lay a sickle on one's own harvest but not on another's. Why do you reap my land?'

"To him as he made such protests, the shining star of heaven, the Virgin and Mother of God, began to speak in reply with these words: 'Oh wicked liars, oh you who have spoken nothing but falsehoods, oh madness, oh deceit endured to my detriment! Though his life has displeased me, he himself pleased me and became more welcome to me by his freely given honor. His wickedness brought displeasure; the fitting reverence and honor shown me night and day were pleasing. His fitting veneration and voice, repeating "Hail, Mary" so many times to me, compensated for the failings of his life. Whatever sins he committed wickedly with body, mind, and hand, all those crimes his "Hail, Mary," my delight, washed away. Let it not be the case that that "Hail, Mary," so holy and so sweet, should perversely diminish the hope of one who remembers his "Hail, Mary." Let it not be the case that that "Hail, Mary" should fail to wrest him from the wailing of death, so that every grievous sin not weigh upon him in the conclave. Dutifulness of mind has washed away every sacrilege of deed, and the man's honeyed tongue

Si miser erravit, precibus errata redemit.
Criminis ipsa sui conscia nonne fui?
Nonne salutavit me supplex quando recessit
meque salutata mortuus est in aqua?
Quaeque meam laudem mors est festina secuta,
nonne meae laudi continuata fuit?
Exitus ergo probat quoniam meus esse probatur,
quem mihi commendat tempus et hora necis.
Ne tamen iniusta videar nimiumve proterva,
iudicium nati terminet ista mei.'
Dixerat et subito, cum nec sententia caelo
lata foret nec adhuc pulsus ad ima forem,
restituor, subito subita de morte reductus
viribus et vitae, virgine matre duce."
Talia desierat postquam narrare, reversus
nota monasterii claustra relicta subit;
neve per anfractus rursus descendat iniquos,
obiecto vitiis obice claudit iter.
Obice multiplici vitio via clauditur omni.
Fit novus ex veteri, redditus ipse sibi.
Carnis ad excessus pateat ne forte recessus,
castigat vetera tempora lege nova.
Temporis indulti spatium rapiendo, salubri
consilio redimit perdita quaeque prius.
Alter, non alius, veteres novus alterat actus.
Virtutum studio fit novus alter homo.

has banished his poisons. If the wretch erred, he compensated for the errors with prayers.

"'Was I not myself aware of his misdeed? Did he not as a suppliant hail me when he went away, and did he not die in the water after hailing me? And the death that promptly followed his praise of me, did it not come directly after praise of me? So the outcome confirms that he is confirmed as mine, whom the time and hour of death entrust to me. Yet so that I not seem unfair or too obstinate, let the judgment of my son bring these matters to a close.'

"She spoke and in an instant, since no judgment was passed by heaven and I was not yet banished to the nether regions, I was restored, suddenly brought back from instant death to vim and vigor, with the Virgin Mother leading the way."

After he had stopped this narrative, he returns and enters the well-known confines of the monastery he had forsaken; and so as not to fall again through wicked diversions, he closes the route to vices by interposing a barrier. The way to every vice is closed by many a barrier. Restored to himself, he becomes a new man from the old. So that a return to the transgressions of the flesh not chance to lie open, he corrects his conduct in old times by a new law. Taking advantage of the period of time now granted him, he compensates for all his past depravities through a salutary way of thinking. An altered but not another person, new, he reforms his old actions. Through eagerness for virtue, he becomes a new and altered man.

De monacho ebrioso

Alter amore piae monachus coenobita Mariae
fervebat studio nocte dieque pio.
Moribus implevit fuerat quam voce professus
vitam, ne vesti dissona vita foret.
Mens, devota prius, devotior esse Mariae
coepit et obsequiis invigilare suis.
Omnia postponens, solum praeponit amorem,
virginis et matris dignus amore frui.
Amplius affligit spes, dum differtur, amantem;
afflictum recreat spes properata magis.
Sed quia praecipue virtutibus invidet hostis,
amplius instigat ad mala quaeque bonos.
His magis infestus quos cernit ad ardua gressu
tendere praecipiti, praecipitare studet.
Totus in insidiis non cessat ubique malignus
sollicitare bonos fraudibus atque dolis.
Circumit insidiis, quaerens quem devoret, hostis
implens officii debita iura sui.
Contigit ergo semel oblitum sobrietatis
indulsisse nimis potibus atque cibis.
Vis violenta meri subito surrepsit et, ultra
quam decuisset ei, dedecoravit eum.
Pondere pressa meri, solita gravitate relicta,
aestuat absque modo mens sine mente modo.
Frons rubet, igniti sine lege vagantur ocelli.
Luxuriat multo lingua manusque mero.
Solvitur in risum sine causa vultus ineptum.
Castigat calices ventris anhela sitis.

On a Drunken Monk

Another monk, a cenobite, out of love for kindly Mary was fired with devout zeal by night and day. He fulfilled in conduct the life he had professed in speech, so that his life would not be in discord with his clothing. His mind, already previously devout, began to be even more devoted to Mary and to keep vigil in service to her. Treating all else as secondary, he, worthy of enjoying the love of the Virgin and Mother, gives priority to love alone. Hope, when it is put off, causes a lover greater distress; hope, when hastened even more, refreshes one who is distressed.

But because the Adversary is especially hostile to virtues, he incites good people even more to all manner of wickedness. Particularly antagonistic to those whom he perceives hastening with headlong progress on high, he strives to cast them headlong down. Engrossed entirely in his schemes, the Evil One does not cease to afflict the good everywhere with treachery and deceits. The Enemy, fulfilling the due prerogatives of his office, besets with schemes, seeking someone to devour.

So it happened once that, forgetful of temperance, the monk indulged excessively in food and drink. The powerful potency of the wine suddenly crept up on him and disgraced him, beyond what befitted him. Overwhelmed by the weight of the wine, his mind, now mindless, with its accustomed seriousness abandoned, is inordinately agitated. His face reddens, his inflamed eyes wander uncontrolled. His tongue and hand run riot with much wine. His countenance dissolves, for no reason, into unbecoming laughter. His belly's panting thirst chastises the chalices. His words lack

Pondere verba carent; cervix, hirsuta capillis,
deturpata riget; mens rationis eget.
Immoderatus amor dulcisque libido bibendi
privant officio singula membra suo.
Lingua fit elinguis, nutat sine vertice vertex,
pes suus absque pede vix sinit ire pedem.
Viribus ergo viri victis virtute Falerni,
claustrum noctivagus intrat et errat ibi.
Taliter erranti taurum simulando ferocem
cornibus, erroris obvius auctor adest;
cumque ferire fero vellet fera pessima cornu,
cornibus obiecit virgo Maria manum.
Cuius ad aspectum subito tremefactus ad horam
se simulat subitam taurus inire fugam.
Sed variando dolum, canis ementita figuram
rursus adest, rabido bestia dente furens.
Obvia fit rursum pia virgo reversa reverso,
se canis opponens morsibus atque minis.
Territus aufugit rursum; rursumque leonis
affuit in specie qui fuit ante canis.
Quae, quid, et unde sit haec tribus his variata <figu>ris
bestia, designant causa modusque rei.
Sub specie triplici tauri, canis atque leonis
monstrant multimodos daemonis esse dolos.
Daemonis insidias totiens redeuntis inultas
non tulit ulterius virgo parensque Dei.
Verbere castigat quem castigare perennis
poena nequit, tandem talibus usa minis:
"Effuge, damnate! Procul hinc, maledicte, recede,
ne tibi contingat his graviora pati.

weight; his neck, shaggy haired, dirtied, grows stiff; his mind lacks reason. Intemperate love and sweet passion for drinking strip of their function every one of his limbs. His tongue becomes tongueless; his head nods, lacking its head; his foot, without footing, hardly allows him to go a foot.

When the man's capacities have been overcome by the power of wine, he enters the cloister in his nighttime rambling and wanders there. As he wanders in this way, the author of sin, taking the form of a fierce bull with horns, comes to encounter him. Though the most wicked beast wished to strike him with a savage horn, the Virgin Mary blocked its horns with her hand. Immediately terrified at the sight of her, for a moment the bull pretends to embark upon sudden flight. But varying the deceit, he appears again, taking on the guise of a dog, a beast raging with maddened jaws. The kindly Virgin, returning, confronts him again on his return, opposing herself to the barks and bites of the dog. Frightened, he again takes flight; and he who had before been a dog appears again in the guise of a lion. The reason for this event and the form it took indicate who this beast is, differentiated by these three forms, and why and from where he comes. In the threefold appearance of a bull, dog, and lion, they show that the demon's wiles are manifold.

The Virgin and Mother of God no longer permitted the schemes of the demon, with his many manifestations, to go unpunished. She chastises with a blow one whom everlasting punishment cannot chastise, resorting at last to the following threats: "Take flight, damned one! Withdraw far from here, accursed one, in order that you not chance to suffer more grievous things than these. How or why, wicked

Unde meum monachum vel qua ratione, nefande,
ausus es insidiis sollicitare tuis?
Quis tibi concessit, cum sis pollutus ab aevo,
mittere pollutas in mea iura manus?
Nonne reformidas quicquid mihi iure dicatum
noveris aut titulo quolibet esse meum?"
Talibus auditis, tenues elapsa per auras
consuluit celerem pestis iniqua fugam.
Praevia virgo virum manibus sustentat euntem
perque gradus templi dirigit illa gradum.
Quem postquam proprio manus officiosa cubili
reddidit aptatis vestibus, inquit ei,
"Quam citius poteris, cum crastina fulserit hora,
surge celer, scelus hoc purificare studens,
mundet ut immundum scelus hoc confessio munda.
Ille meus monachus cras adeundus erit;
criminis admissi maculas meus ille minister
abluet: ille tibi consiliator erit."
Talibus auditis, miser et miserabilis ille
quaeve vel unde sit haec quaerit, et illa refert,
"Virgo Dei genitrix ego sum, vitae reparatrix,
sponsa parensque Dei, vita salusque rei.
Sola, carens simili, sine semine virgo virili
caelestis merui prolis honore frui.
Noveris ergo piam quam conspicis esse Mariam,
quae pariendo Deum traxit ad astra reum.
Fons ego signatus per quem sine semine natus
est in carne Deus, filius ipse meus."
Dixit et hoc dicto monacho mundoque relicto
linquens ima soli scandit ad alta poli.

one, have you dared to plague my monk with your schemes? Who allowed you, even though you have been defiled from time immemorial, to set your defiled hands upon what is rightly mine? You shrink, do you not, from whatever you know has been duly consecrated to me or is mine by any right of claim?"

After hearing such words, the evil pest, vanishing into thin air, decided upon swift flight. The Virgin, leading the way, supports with her hands the man as he goes, and she guides his step on the steps of the church. After her dutiful hand restored him to his own bed and tucked the bedclothes, she said to him, "As fast as you can, when tomorrow's first hour has shone, rise swiftly, zealous to purify this crime, so that cleansing confession may cleanse this unclean crime. Tomorrow you must go up to that monk of mine; that servant of mine will wash away the stains of the misdeed you have acknowledged: he will be a conciliator for you."

After hearing these words, he asks, pitiful and pitiable, who this woman is and where she is from, and she replies, "I am the Virgin, begetter of God, restorer of life, betrothed and Mother of God, life and salvation of the sinner. Alone, with no peer, a virgin, I deserved without male seed to enjoy the honor of heavenly offspring. Know then that the one you see is holy Mary, who by giving birth to God bore a sinner to the stars. I am the fountain sealed up, through whom God, my very son, was born in the flesh without seed."

She finished speaking, and with these words, leaving the monk and this world, abandoning the lowlands of the earth, she ascends to the heights of heaven. The lees of drunken-

Iam digesta satis fuerat fex ebrietatis
visque soporiferi depopulata meri,
cum celer a lecto surgens, torpore reiecto,
quo dea mandarat protinus ire parat.
Pervigili cura redimit confessio pura
excessus pravi damna dolore gravi.
Abstergunt crimen lacrimae, suspiria, vimen.
Fit novus ex veteri, non hodie quod heri.
Lapsus, virtutis casus, fit causa salutis,
ne ruat ulterius mens male lapsa prius.

De monacho resuscitato

Viribus atque viris bene culta Colonia dignum
ex re nomen habet, urbs populosa satis,
urbs opulens, iucunda situ, fecunda virorum,
vernans perpetua religione patrum.
Contigit hic celebre sacri sub nomine Petri
esse monasterium religione sacrum.
Inviolatus ibi sacer ordo monasticus olim
floruerat, sacri ductus amore Petri.
Sed quia multotiens facilis discordia morum
in coenobitarum moribus esse solet,
inter eos parilem quos contigit esse professos
vitam, disparilis moribus unus erat.
Veste quidem monachus, sed moribus a monachatu
longe fuit, factus faexque luesque gregis.
Vestis honestate monachum mentitus honestum,
hunc inhonestabat corpore, mente, manu.
Vitam quam fuerat monachi sub veste professus
demonachabatur moribus ipse malis.

ness had already been digested sufficiently, and the potency of the sleep-inducing wine had been neutralized when, rising swiftly from bed and casting away sloth, he gets ready to proceed immediately where the goddess had bidden.

With ever-watchful care, innocent confession redeems through intense sorrow the damage of his perverse transgression. Tears, sighs, and the rod wash away the offense. He becomes new from old, not today what he was yesterday. A moral failing, a fall of virtue, becomes the cause of salvation, that a mind, which earlier failed wickedly, not fall further into ruin.

On a Monk Brought Back to Life

Cologne, well endowed with might and men, possesses a worthy name from that reality, a very populous city, a sumptuous city, pleasing in its situation, prolific in men, flourishing in the enduring piety of its forefathers. There chanced to be here under the name of holy Peter a renowned monastery, holy for its religious devotion. A holy monastic order had long flourished there unblemished, guided by love of holy Peter.

But because many times moral discord is accustomed to exist readily in the conduct of cenobites, there was one dissimilar in conduct among those who chanced to have professed the same course of life. If nothing else, he was a monk in clothing but far from monastic in his morals, becoming the scum and contagion of the flock. Simulating in the propriety of his clothing a proper monk, he defiled that status in body, mind, and hand. Through wicked conduct he rendered unmonastic the life that he had professed under the cover of a monk's clothing.

Vicerat hunc subito propriae petulantia carnis,
ingluvies ventris et muliebris amor.
Castra quidem Veneris plus quam sua claustra colebat;
rarius in cella vir sceleratus erat.
Iam meretricalis potius quam vir monachalis
promeruit dici de ratione rei.
Cur tamen ex monacho fuerit cito factus adulter,
causa subest quoniam deliciosus erat.
Debilitant animi vires venus, otia, vinum;
quem non debilitent otia, vina, venus?
Luxuriosa quidem res est et religioni
non bene conveniens cum meretrice merum.
Nascitur interea miserabilis ex muliere
testis adulterii, filius unus ei.
Fama sinistra rei crevit crescente reatu;
quaeque prius fuerat tecta, retecta volat.
Criminis occulti scelus occultare nequibat,
filius incesta de muliere satus.
Coeperat ergo suo tanto de crimine fidus
testis et interpres filius esse patri.
Sed puer aetatem pueri praevenit et annos,
moribus ante diem facta sequendo senum.
Cernitur in facie similis puer esse parenti,
cum sit dissimilis moribus atque fide.
Quem licet induerit facie natura parentis,
hunc tamen a vitiis exuit illa patris.
Virtutum pretio pueri pretiosa redemit
fama sui generis degenerando notam.
Nobilitas hominis proprii de stipite cordis
plus quam de carnis nobilitate fluit.

The wantonness of his own flesh, the gluttony of his gut, and the love of women had suddenly overcome him. Truth be told, he frequented the camps of Venus more than his cloisters; the scoundrel of a man was quite seldom in his cell. Now he earned the right, as the reality confirms, to be called as a man a debauchee rather than a devotee. For all that, the underlying reason why he quickly became an adulterer from being a monk is that he was self-indulgent. Lovemaking, leisure, and wine wear down his mental capacities; whom would leisure, wine, and lovemaking not wear down? Strong wine along with a wanton woman is indeed a licentious thing and does not comport well with religious devotion.

In the meantime a son is born to him by a woman, pitiable evidence of his adultery. As his sinfulness grew, malicious rumor about the affair grew; and what had been covered previously, takes wing uncovered. The outrage of his hidden misdeed could not remain hidden, a son fathered from an unchaste woman. So the son became for his father the convincing evidence and token of his great sin.

But the boy outstripped the age and years of a boy, in his character imitating the actions of the old before that age. The boy is observed to be like his parent in appearance, though unlike in morals and faith. Though birth clad him in his parent's appearance, even so it stripped him of his father's vices. The boy's renown, valued for the value of his virtues, compensated for the stigma of his parentage by falling away from it.

The nobility of a person emanates more from the stock of his own heart than from the nobility of his flesh.

Nobilitant homines virtus, sapientia, mores,
non genus aut proavi nomina clara sui.
Sola virum virtus animi reddit generosum;
quemlibet a vitiis degenerare licet.
Ut luat ergo patris redimatque piacula natus,
fit monachus iuvenis, tractus amore patris.
Invidet interea laetis sors invida rebus,
tollit et e medio mors inopina patrem.
Post obitum carnis, mortali carne relicta,
spiritus ad poenas non obiturus abit;
cumque fuisse suum monachum Petrus hunc meminisset
deque monasterii fratribus esse sui,
Iudicis ante pedes veniens veniam petit, orans
ut fiat misero mitior ira Dei.
Nil tamen obtinuit quia stat sententia flecti
nescia, veridico commemorante David:
"Rex, in monte tuo sancto quisnam requiescet
aut habitator erit arcis in aede sacrae?
Qui mala non fecit, qui iustitias operatus
ingreditur maculae nescius atque notae."
Hinc, patiente Petro iusta ratione repulsam,
affuit acta Petri virgo Maria prece.
Cum prece cumque Petro venit veniamque petivit
ante thronum nati virgo benigna sui.
Obvia fit matri venienti gloria nati;
auditaque prece virginitatis ait,
"Cum nequeant pacto quovis mea verba refelli
ore prophetarum vaticinata prius,
nec decet aut debet mea sustinuisse repulsam
mater et a voto cassa redire suo.

Virtue, wisdom, and morals ennoble people, not their ancestry or the famous names of their forefathers. The virtue of character alone renders a man noble; anyone at all can be debased by vices. So that the son, then, may expiate and compensate for the wrongdoing of his father, the young man, impelled by love of his father, becomes a monk.

But then envious chance envies his happy circumstances, and an unexpected death takes away from their midst the father. After the death of the flesh, when mortal flesh was left behind, the spirit, not subject to death, goes off to its punishments; and when Peter remembered that this man had been his monk and was one of the brethren of his monastery, he comes to the feet of the Judge and seeks forgiveness, praying that the wrath of God might become gentler to the wretch. Yet he obtained nothing because the verdict that cannot be swayed stood firm, as truthful David declares: "King, who will rest on your holy mountain or will be a dweller in the sanctuary of the sacred citadel? He who has committed no wrongs, who, having performed acts of justice, enters without blemish and stigma."

Then, as Peter was with good reason suffering rejection, the Virgin Mary joined him, impelled by Peter's prayer. She came with a prayer and in the company of Peter, and the kindly Virgin sought pardon before her son's throne. The glory of the son goes to meet his mother as she approaches, and after hearing the prayer of virginity, says, "Though my words, foretold previously by the mouth of prophets, cannot be refuted in any manner whatsoever, neither is it right or proper for my mother to endure rejection and return having achieved nothing from her entreaty.

Spiritus ad corpus redeat vivensque resurgat,
pro quo decrevit fundere virgo preces.
Corrigat excessus mortali carne resumpta,
mortem perpetuam ne patiatur item."
Dixit et, in corpus anima redeunte, revixit,
dandus iam tumulo iamque tegendus humo.
Suscipiunt alacres tristi de morte reversum
fratres, gavisi de novitate rei.
Funere frustratum supplevit terra sepulchrum.
Mortem pressa prius vita reversa premit.
Laeta dies rediit post maesta silentia noctis;
gaudia tristitiae surripuere locum.
Grex congaudet ovi de fauce lupi redeunti;
gaudet ovis proprio consociata gregi.
Crevit amor populi, laus et devotio cleri,
spes et amor fidei de novitate rei.
Laeta rei novitas cunctis sublata reformat
gaudia, luctus abit, causa doloris abest.
Ipse suos casus cunctis manifestat, ut illis
quilibet auditis cautior esse queat.
Alter ab alterius trahit argumenta salute.
Unica multiplicis causa salutis erat.
Conscia quaeque sui mens, tacta dolore salubri,
plangere festinat quod superesse videt.

De matrona a daemone coram senatu liberata

Militis uxorem Romanis civibus ortam
contigit optata prole carere diu.

May the soul, on behalf of which the Virgin resolved to pour forth prayers, return to the body and, coming to life, rise again. When the mortal flesh has been taken up again, let him amend his transgressions, that he not suffer death again, this time everlasting."

He spoke and, as the soul returned to the body, the monk lived again, though already on the point of being consigned to the tomb and covered by soil. The brethren, rejoicing in the novel turn of events, receive him eagerly upon his return from gloomy death. Earth filled up the tomb that had been deprived of the corpse. Life, previously oppressed, returns and oppresses death. Glad daylight returned after the sad silence of night; joys usurped the place of sadness. The flock rejoices together for the sheep returning from the wolf's jaws; the sheep rejoices, reunited with its own flock. The people's love, the clergy's praise and devotion, and hope and love placed in faith grew from the novel turn of events.

The novel turn of events happily restores to everyone the joys that had been taken from them, mourning departs, all reason for sorrow is absent. The monk himself makes his misadventures known to all, so that after hearing them, everyone may be able to be more on guard. One person derives instruction from another's salvation. A single instance of salvation brought salvation to many. Each mind, in its self-awareness, was touched by healthy grief, and makes haste to lament what it sees remaining.

On a Matron Freed from a Demon before the Senate

It chanced that a knight's wife, born of Roman citizens, for a long time lacked hoped-for offspring. Everything else

Prospera cuncta satis dederat Fortuna, sed unum
defuit unde forent cetera grata magis.
Anxietas animi cupientis habere quod optat
aestuat et votis carpitur usque suis.
Res et opes, fundos, generosi stemmatis ortum,
cum careat subole, computat esse nihil.
Uxorem sterilem causatur habere maritus;
se sterilem queritur uxor habere virum.
Imputat illa viro quod vir suus imputat illi;
sicque diu steriles tempora longa terunt.
Prospera cuncta forent nisi sola prole carerent,
qua sine quicquid habent vile nihilque putant.
Tristis uterque nimis animo languescit amaro
quodque magis cupiunt, amplius urit eos.
Quaeque solent animis fieri solacia maestis
sunt magis his oneri: gloria, census, honos.
Consulitur super his medicorum cura, sed illud
quod natura nequit, reddere nemo potest.
Si qua tamen miseris superest medicina salutis,
pendet in arbitrio Iudicis illa Dei.
Fluxerat interea cum tempore prolis habendae
temporis ex tractu spesque fidesque simul.
Sed Domini pietas, tandem commota precantum
vocibus et votis, prole beavit eos.
Nascitur ergo patri sterili de coniuge natus
qui patris et matris frons et imago foret;
quique seni tribuit sterili de matre Iohannem,
contulit his subolem gratia sola Dei.
Transierat metas pueri iam fortior aetas;
iam iuvenum iuvenis flosque decusque fuit,

Fortune had granted was utterly positive, but one thing was lacking that would make everything else more pleasant. The soul seethes in agitation, wishing to have what it desires, and is continually tortured by its wishes. It sets no store by property and wealth, estates, and origin from a noble lineage, so long as it lacks progeny. The husband protests at having a barren wife; the wife complains that she has an infertile husband. She ascribes to the husband what her husband ascribes to her, and, long childless, they waste extended periods of time in this way. All things would be positive except only that they lacked offspring, without which they regard as contemptible and of no value whatever they possess.

Each of them, in grief, sickens in extreme bitterness of soul, and the more they crave something, the more it torments them. Everything that is accustomed to give solace to sad spirits—glory, wealth, esteem—is instead a burden to them. Treatment from doctors is sought out for these symptoms, but no one can deliver what nature cannot. Instead, if any healing medicine is available for wretches, it depends on the determination of God the Judge.

Meanwhile, in the course of time, hope and faith together slipped away along with the time for having progeny. But the goodness of the Lord, at last moved by the voices and vows of them praying, blessed them with offspring. A son is born then to an infertile father by a barren wife, to be the spitting image of the father and mother; and the grace alone of God, who granted John to a sterile old man by a barren mother, bestowed upon them a scion.

Now a sturdier age had passed the bounds of boyhood; now the youth was the flower and glory of youth when, after

cum, patre defuncto, spes una relicta superstes
matris erat natus, unica cura, suae.
Unica spes matri luctum de morte mariti
temperat et matris mite levamen erat,
quodque carere patre quod et unicus esse parenti
cernitur, hoc puerum cogit amare magis.
Artior innatus amor est in pectore matris.
Creditur omnis amor matris amore minor.
Iam puer in iuvenem forma facieque venustum
creverat et cunctis carus in urbe fuit.
Iam satis attigerat tempus virtutibus aptum;
sed vitiosa parens hac vetat ire via.
Castus in incestum, moderatus in immoderatum
est conversus amor. Fas parit omne nefas
atque, quod horrendum dictu nimis esse videtur,
tangitur illicito prolis amore parens.
Alloquium, tactus, visus, locus aptus amori
illicito licitas supposuere faces.
Passio mentis, amor, qua nil subtilius umquam,
intrat et ingressa depopulatur eam.
Nascitur ex nihilo; nullum tamen orta periclum
ferre timet. Timidis imperat atque feris.
Luxuriosa parens, castae sub imagine matris,
in thalamum puerum suscipit inque thorum.
Res levis ad lapsum nimis est levitas iuvenilis
et venus ex facili cor iuvenile movet.
Nox, thorus et mulier nimio correpta calore
prima fuit tanti causa caputque mali.
Consensu parili pariter iunguntur; uterque
pronior in venerem quam Venus esse monet.

his father's death, the surviving son was the one remaining hope and the only care of his mother. His mother's only hope, he tempers her mourning about her husband's death and is his mother's gentle solace. Because he is perceived to lack a father and to be the only one left for his parent, this compels her to love the boy the more. A more intense love arises in the mother's heart. All love is believed to be less than a mother's love.

The boy had grown now into a young man, attractive in figure and face, and he was dear to everyone in the city. He had arrived now at a stage well attuned to virtue, but his corrupt parent forbids him from taking this route. Chaste love turned into unchaste, moderate into immoderate. Right gives birth to every wrong and, what seems to be all too disgusting to say, the parent is touched by unlawful love for her offspring. Conversation, touching, seeing, and a convenient location set lawful torches to unlawful love. A passion of the mind, love, than which nothing ever is more insidious, enters her and, having done so, wreaks havoc on her. It is born out of nothing; yet, once arisen, it fears to endure no danger. It gives orders to the bashful and brash alike.

The licentious parent, in the guise of a chaste mother, receives the boy into her bedchamber and bed. A youth's folly makes him a thing all too ready to fall, and sex easily stirs a youthful heart. Night, the bed, and a woman seized by extreme passion were the first cause and beginning of such great wickedness. They are joined together with shared consent; each of them gives sign of being more inclined to lovemaking than Venus is. No witness is present, apart

Conscius omnis abest nisi qui videt omnia solus.
  Dissimulando scelus celat uterque suum.
Quis tamen inter eos castum nisi credat amorem
  vel cui suspectus ille vel illa foret?
Unicus est matri defuncti forma mariti;
  artius hinc illum diligit atque fovet.
Complacet ambobus scelus hoc novitatis et ambo
  occultare student quod placet atque iuvat.
Concipit interea proprio de germine germen
  mater, et a nato fit gravis ipsa suo.
Crescit amara seges dulci de semine; ventrem
  torquet et excruciat dulcis in ore cibus.
Pestiferos fructus furtivi seminis edit
  tempore decurso femina foeda nimis.
Ne tamen hoc pateat, sceleri scelus accumulare
  quaerit et abiecta matre noverca subit.
Protinus ex utero proles miseranda sepulchro
  redditur et facti fama sepulta iacet.
O quam saeva parens, propriae quam prodiga prolis,
  o manus immitis, o mulieris opus!
Perdere progeniem mavult quam perdere famam;
  infamis fieri non homicida timet.
Dulcis odor famae sibi quam servire coegit
  munere virtutum magnificarat eam.
Iudicium populi nec non et praesulis urbis
  dulcis odor famae conciliarat ei.
Sola sui sexus speculum virtutis in urbe
  iudicio iuvenum creditur atque senum.
Quicquid honestatis, quicquid virtutis in ulla
  cernitur, huic soli creditur esse datum.

from the one who alone sees everything. They both conceal their crime by dissembling. Yet who would believe the love between them to be anything but chaste, or to whom would either he or she be an object of suspicion? For his mother, he alone has the outward appearance of her dead husband; for this reason she loves and cherishes him the more intensely. This novel crime meets the approval of both, and both strive to hide what pleases and delights.

Meanwhile, the mother conceives a seed from her own seed, and she becomes pregnant by her own son. A bitter crop grows from a sweet seed; food that is sweet in the mouth tortures and torments the belly. When her term has elapsed, the all-too-foul woman brings forth the pernicious fruits of her stealthy insemination. Yet, that this circumstance not be evident, she seeks to heap villainy upon villainy and, casting aside the role of mother, assumes that of stepmother. At once the miserable offspring is handed over from the womb to the tomb, and the report of the deed lies buried. Oh how savage the parent, how reckless with her own offspring, oh merciless hand, oh woman's work!

She prefers to destroy her progeny rather than to destroy her reputation; she fears to become an object of infamy, not a murderer. The sweet aroma of a reputation that she compelled to serve her interests had glorified her with an endowment of virtues. The sweet aroma of her reputation had won over for her the judgment of the people and of the bishop of the city. Alone of her sex, she is believed to be a mirror of virtue in the city, in the estimation of young and old. Whatever decency, whatever virtue is perceived in any woman is believed to have been conceded to her alone.

Crimine fama carens, populi favorabilis aura
huius in obsequium prona dedere manum.
Fama favorque sui populum compellit ut illam
praedicet, extollat, laudet, honoret, amet.
Praedicat hanc populus, hanc princeps, hancque senatus;
praedicat hanc etiam quisquis in urbe manet.
Casta, modesta, pia, sapiens, verecunda, benigna
et quodcumque potest ulla fuisse, fuit.
Mira Dei pietas, cuius patientia mira
sustinet atque diu dissimulare solet,
parcit et exspectat. Nec se miserator in ira
continet, immo malis dat bona quaeque bonus.
Nec punire reos statim nec praemia iustis
reddere consuevit iustus ubique Deus.
Non tamen ulterius sceleris discrimina tanti
daemonis invidia sustinuisse potest.
Consulit ergo suos quos possidet ille nocendi
mille modos; super his, quae sit habenda via—
quae via, quisve modus, quae convenientior hora,
quis locus aut tempus aptius esse queat.
Induit humanos ficta sub imagine vultus,
confisus propriis artibus atque dolis.
Et senis indutus formam faciemque vetustam,
singula prosequitur quae senis esse solent.
Fit gravis incessu, fit et in sermone modestus,
omnibus in gestis aptus et absque nota.
Omnibus imbutum studiis se fingit ad unguem;
omnia scit. Nihil est quod latet orbe virum;
quodque magis mirum multis solet esse, futura
praedicat et pandit abdita quaeque prius.

Sinless reputation and the breeze of popular favor readily surrendered to her service. Her reputation and popularity constrain the people to proclaim, extol, praise, honor, and love her. The people, prince, and senate proclaim her; all dwelling in the city proclaim her too. She was chaste, modest, dutiful, wise, discreet, kindly, and all any woman could be.

God's mercy is wondrous; his wondrous forbearance endures and usually turns a blind eye for a long time, shows restraint, and waits. Taking pity, he does not remain in a state of anger; on the contrary, in his goodness he gives all manner of goods to the wicked. God, universally just, is not accustomed immediately either to punish the guilty or to render rewards to the just.

Yet the devil's ill will can endure no further the trials of such great wickedness. Therefore he considers the thousand means of causing injury that he possesses; in addition to these, he considers what approach should be taken—which approach, which means, or which hour can be more suitable, what place or time more fitting.

He dons human features beneath a feigned likeness, trusting in his own crafts and tricks. Having donned the aged figure and face of an old man, he adopts the individual traits that are typical of an old man. He becomes plodding in gait, and he becomes restrained in speech, appropriate in all his gestures and without blemish. He makes himself out to be perfectly informed in all studies; he knows everything. There is nothing in the world that escapes the man; and, what is accustomed to be still more wonderful to many, he proclaims things to come and reveals all that were previously hidden.

Facta fidem verbis faciunt; quodcumque futurum
dicit, in instanti res manifesta probat.
Moribus atque fide Petrus alter adesse putatur;
aut Petrus aut similis creditur esse Petro.
Vestibus et victu contentus paupere, pauper
spernit opes mundi, nil nisi munda sequens.
Lumina, lingua, manus quasi quodam carcere clausa
moribus et famae consuluere suae.
Angelus exterius (cum sit tamen angelus intus,
sed malus) a populo creditur esse bonus;
cumque satis regi toti placuisset et urbi,
metas propositi sperat adesse sui.
Regis in aspectu veniens, spectante senatu,
substitit et, solito tristior, inquit ei:
"Caesar, in hac urbe scelus est, pro crimine cuius
digna foret subito tota ruisse solo;
horrendum facinus, scelus exsecrabile, solo
aera quod dictu commaculare potest;
crimen inauditum, crimen quod totus abhorret
mundus et illicitum iudicat esse nefas.
Gentibus et populis res est incognita talis;
tale nefas veterum pagina nulla refert.
Hoc genus incestus refugit genus omne ferarum;
hoc genus, hanc speciem despicit omne pecus.
Quod fera, quodque pecus refugit, quod bestia campi,
solus non refugit bestia factus homo.
Illa quidem mulier, mulier venerabilis illa
errat et est nato succuba facta suo.
Nec semel aut iterum rediit satiata retrorsum,
sed iacet in vitiis inveterata suis.

His deeds make for belief in his words; whatever he says will come to be, in a moment an event clearly bears it out. In morals and faith another Peter is thought to be at hand; he is believed to be either Peter or like Peter. A poor man, satisfied with poor clothing and diet, he holds the world's wealth in contempt, pursuing nothing but the pure. His eyes, tongue, and hand, as if constrained in some prison, paid heed to his morals and reputation.

An angel outwardly (though he is an angel inwardly too—but an evil one), he is believed by the people to be good; and since he had well pleased the king and the whole city, he hopes that the goals of his plan are nearby. Coming into the presence of the king, as the senate watches, he stands firm and, sadder than usual, says to him:

"Emperor, in this city is a wickedness, for the sinfulness of which the whole city would deserve to crash suddenly to the ground; a hideous act of wrongdoing, an execrable crime, the mere mention of which can defile the air; an unheard-of crime, a crime from which the whole world recoils and which it holds to be an unlawful abomination. Such a deed is unknown to nations and peoples; no page of the ancients recounts such an unspeakable thing. Every genus of wild beasts shuns this kind of unchasteness; every domestic animal disdains this genus and this species. Only a human being, made bestial, does not shun what a wild or domestic animal, what a creature of the field shuns.

"That woman, in fact, that respectable woman, commits a sin and has become a mistress to her son. She did not return satisfied just once or twice, but wallows habitually in

Nuper enim proprium proprii de semine nati
quem peperit puerum, saeva peremit eum.
Huius ob incestus causam ne tota per orbem
gens tua depereat, urbs quoque Roma, cave,
et nisi quam citius res haec manifesta patescat,
noveris excidium gentis adesse prope.
Principis et populi res est suspecta saluti.
Sollicitus studeat quisque cavere sibi.
Haec nisi vera fore certa ratione probarim,
quo meruit plecti crimine plectar ego.
Nec dubium quin vera loquar; manifesta probabit
res ex post facto singula vera fore."
Dixerat. At cuncti communi voce resistunt,
haec sua dicentes verba carere fide.
Hac vice deceptum super hac muliere fatentur.
Talia de tali credere nemo potest.
Ille sed econtra penitus contrarius illis
quam dicunt sanctam praedicat esse ream,
accendique rogum media rogat ipse platea.
Assistat populus, adsit et ipsa rea,
et nisi convicta fuerit vel confiteatur
sponte sua, legem quam tulit ipse ferat.
Interea populum tandem dubitare coegit
quod prius in cunctis vera locutus erat.
Hoc movet et regem, quod nil nisi vera locutum
noverat et verbis facta dedisse fidem.
Ergo diem statuunt certum, quo certiorari
partibus accitis contio tota queat.

her vices. Indeed, she recently did away savagely with her own child, whom she bore from the seed of her own son. You too, city of Rome, take heed that your entire people not suffer utter ruin throughout the world because of this incest, and unless this affair is revealed and becomes open knowledge as fast as possible, know that the downfall of the people is near at hand. The affair is dangerous for the welfare of the ruler and people. Let everyone anxiously strive to watch out for himself. If I do not establish these things to be true in an indisputable manner, may I be punished for the crime for which she has deserved to be punished. There is no doubt that I speak truths; the affair, when revealed after the fact, will establish the details to be true."

He spoke. But all balk with shared voice, saying that these words of his lack credibility. They declare that on this occasion he has been misled about this woman. No one can believe such things about such a person. But in rejoinder, flatly opposed to them, he declares that the woman whom they call a saint is a sinner, and he requests that a pyre be kindled in the middle of the town square. Let the people attend, let the woman who sinned also be present, and if she is not convicted or does not confess of her own free will, may he endure the legal consequence that he has brought forward.

Meanwhile, he forced the people at last to have doubts, because in the past he had spoken the truth on all scores. This influences the king too, because he knew that the man had spoken nothing but the truth and that the facts had lent credence to the words. Accordingly, they establish a set date on which the entire assembly can be apprised, once the parties have been summoned.

Comperit haec postquam mulier male conscia, toto
corpore diriguit; dissimulatque tamen.
Quid tunc mentis ei, penitus ubi mente careret,
quisnam sufficiet mente vel ore loqui?
Quam scelus et sceleris sibi mens male conscia tanti
damnat et accusat, quid sibi mentis erat?
Quid sibi mentis erat, quae iam quasi proxima morti
flens sedet et scelerum facta revolvit ita?
"O nimis infelix, o femina, faex mulierum,
o nimis infelix, femina foeda nimis!
Femina, sed foetor, sed faex foetore repleta;
femina foetoris, femina faecis ego.
Femina, faex foeda, sed faex foedissima foedi
foetoris, fetu femina feta suo.
Intus ficta, foris fera pessima faxque furoris:
fax, furor, et flamma, femina facta fera."
Talia commemorans, tristi terebrata dolore,
urbis pontificem tristis adire parat.
Vir sacer et celebris praesul, Lucianus, in urbe
praesulis officium tempore gessit eo.
Praesulis ante pedes terrae prostrata, salubre
postulat auxilium consiliumque sibi.
Singultus, lacrimae, gemitus, suspiria, planctus
contritae mentis signa fuere satis.
Talibus aspectis, praesul ratione modesta
quae sit causa rei quaerit et illa refert,
"O pater, o patriae pastor praesulque beate,
fer, precor, auxilium. Fer pietatis opem.
En trahor ad mortem. Miserere, precor, morientis;
ne moriar misere, tu miserere mei.

After the woman, conscious of her guilt, learns of these things, she stiffened throughout her whole body; and yet she continues to dissemble. Who will have enough capacity in mind or speech to describe what her frame of mind was then, when she was completely out of her mind? What was her frame of mind, when the sin and her mind, in its guilt conscious of so great a sin, condemn and accuse her? What is her frame of mind, she who now sits wailing as if very close to death and reflects in the following way on her sinful deeds? "Oh all too unfortunate, oh woman, dregs of womankind, oh all too unfortunate, all too foul a woman! Not a woman but a stench, dregs filled full of a stench; I am a woman of stench, a woman of dregs. A woman, foul dregs, foulest dregs of a foul stench, a woman pregnant by her own offspring. Inside false, outside the worst of wild beasts and a firebrand of fury: firebrand, fury, and flame, a woman become a wild beast."

With such a speech, pierced by sadness and grief, she prepares sadly to approach the prelate of the city. A holy man and renowned bishop, Lucian, filled the office of bishop at that time in the city. Prostrate on the ground at the bishop's feet, she asks for healing aid and advice for herself. Sobs, tears, moans, sighs, and lamentations were signs of a very contrite mind.

Seeing this, the bishop asks in moderate manner what the cause is of her situation, and she replies, "Oh father, oh pastor of the country and blessed bishop, bring aid, I entreat. Bring the comfort of pity. See, I am being carried off to death. Have mercy, I entreat, on one who is dying; have

Me iuvenum, me turba senum, me tota senatus
curia condemnat. Tu miserere mei!
Vatis ab ore novi iam praedamnata repente,
carnis ad interitum maesta gemensque trahor.
Sola mihi miserae superest sententia mortis.
Ergo quid ulterius iam moritura querar?"
Questibus et lacrimis praesul commotus amaris
"Non es digna mori, nec morieris," ait.
"Fama, quod est famae, sine causa saepe laborat.
Rodere summa solet. Nescia stare loco,
quae numquam stabilis vacuas vaga circinat auras.
Litus arans sterile, plurima vana serens,
currit in incertum, dum spe frustratur inani,
falsa sed in nihilum tota redire solet.
Principis et populi si te sententia damnat,
errat et errasse iure probabis eos.
Quin etiam pro te mihi si iurare liceret,
iurarem super his. Tune vel inde times?
Criminis obiecti cum non sis conscia, vatis
errat et augurio fallitur ipse suo."
Tunc ea: "Nequaquam, pater alme, sed est ita totum
sicut praedixit ore propheta suo.
Femina, faex urbis, fera pessima, faex mulierum,
his ego sum vitiis commaculata meis.
Vas ego pollutum, vitiis subiecta nefandis,
sordibus innumeris sordeo, sumque rea.
Femina, foeda lues, proprio quasi nupta marito
succubui nato luxuriosa meo.

mercy, you, on me, that I not die miserably. Crowds of young men, crowds of old, and the whole council of the senate condemns me. You, at least, have mercy on me! Already hastily damned in advance from the mouth of a new prophet, I am dragged off, sorrowful and moaning, to the demise of my flesh. Only the sentence of death remains for wretched me. So then why, as I am now about to die, should I complain further?"

The bishop, stirred by the bitter complaints and tears, said, "You do not deserve to die, and you will not die. Rumor, as is characteristic of rumor, often operates without basis. It is accustomed to malign the most prominent. Incapable of staying in place, never stable, it circles aimlessly through the empty air. Plowing a barren shore, sowing many groundless reports, it scurries after the dubious, as it is disappointed of its idle hope, but, false that it is, is regularly reduced entirely to nothing.

"If the verdict of the ruler and of the people condemns you, it is wrong, and you will duly establish that they have gone wrong. What is more, if I should be permitted to take an oath on your behalf, I would take one on these charges. Do you fear even then? Since you are not complicit in the crime charged, the prophet is wrong and is himself deceived by his prognostication."

Then she says: "That's not at all the case, kindly father, but it is all just as the prophet foretold from his mouth. I am a woman who is the dregs of the city, the worst wild beast, the dregs of womanhood, defiled by these vices of mine. A defiled vessel, in thrall to unspeakable vices, I am soiled with countless forms of filth, and I am a sinner. A woman, foul contagion, I lay down wantonly under my son, like a

Quin etiam puerum proprii de semine nati
concepi; peperi crimen onusque mihi.
Nec satis id fuerat, sed adhuc scelerata nefandis
ausibus adieci multiplicare nefas.
Addo scelus sceleri, veteri nova damna furori;
in mea crudeles viscera mitto manus.
Quem male concepi, peius pariendo peremi,
saeva parens partum nil miserata suum.
Vix fuit in lucem materna fusus ab alvo,
cum necis in tenebras mater abegit eum.
Prima dies misero fuit ultima; membra sepulchro
foeda iacent, foedo contumulata solo.
Haec ego, serve Dei, mulier miseranda peregi;
his ego multimodis sum maculata modis.
Nulla piare meos poterunt tormenta reatus.
Quaelibet est tanto crimine poena minor."
Talia clamanti miseramque reamque fatenti,
compatiens miserae, vir miserator ait,
"Noli, cara mihi, noli, mea filia, flere,
sperans multimoda de pietate Dei.
Ter dominum Petrus una sub nocte negavit;
septem daemonibus plena Maria fuit:
flevit et in fletu sua damna redemit uterque.
Accipit hic claves, abluit illa pedes.
Conversi veniam meruere viri Ninivitae;
gratia conversis summa pepercit eis.
Coniugis ob causam David interfecit Uriam,
sed lavit lectum flendo propheta suum.
En Aegy<ptiacae> pia virgo Maria Mariae
spem tribuit veniae, duxque comesque viae.

bride under her own husband. Yes, and I conceived a child from the seed of my own son; I bore a crime and burden for myself. Nor was that enough, but, still sinful, I continued to multiply my criminality through criminal outrages. I add sin to sin, new disgraces to former madness; I lay cruel hands upon my womb. A savage parent showing no mercy to her offspring, I did a worse thing by killing at birth the child I was wrong to conceive. Scarcely was he brought forth into daylight from his mother's womb, when his mother banished him to the darkness of death. His first day was the last for the wretch; his foul limbs lie in a tomb, interred in foul soil. Servant of God, I, a pitiable woman, carried out all these things; I am stained in these many ways. No torments will be able to expiate my sins. Any punishment at all is less than so great a crime."

Taking pity, the man, feeling compassion for the wretch as she loudly proclaims these words and confesses herself a wretch and a sinner, takes pity and says, "Don't, my dear, don't, my daughter, weep, but hope for the manifold goodness of God. Peter denied the Lord three times in one night; Mary was filled with seven demons: they both wept and in weeping redeemed their failings. The one receives the keys, the other washes feet. The men of Nineveh, changed in heart, merited pardon; the highest grace spared them after their change of heart. David killed Uriah because of the latter's wife, but the prophet washed clean his bed by weeping.

"See too, the merciful Virgin Mary, as leader and companion for the route, granted hope for forgiveness to Mary of

Porta patet veniae, miseratio sola Mariae;
haec et non alia restat habenda via.
Si scelerum veniam cupis obtinuisse, Mariam
vocibus et votis sollicitare stude.
Spem fonti veniae totam committe Mariae,
ut precibus noxas abluat illa tuas.
Haec tibi sola potest morbi conferre medelam;
haec tibi sola potest ferre salutis opem;
nilque reformides quia mundo mitior illa
res a principio nulla creata manet.
Sola salus miseris, miserorum mite levamen
est, erit atque fuit, fons pietate fluens."
Dixit et, iniuncta digna pro tempore poena,
crimina confessam iussit abire domum.
Praesulis ad nutum, mulier conversa retrorsum
corpore, mente domum iussa redire redit.
Inveterata diu veteris contagia vitae
tergit et abstergit temporis hora brevis.
Fletibus irriguis lavat et rigat omnia cordis
intima, castigans artius acta prius.
Tempora flens redimit; gemitu sua damna relaxat,
luctibus et lacrimis nocte dieque vacans.
Sic tamen assidue nomen memorale Mariae
invocat, ut causae consulat ipsa suae:
"Virgo carens simili, spes invictissima mundi,
sola tui sexus flos, decus atque decor,
gloria terrarum, paradisus deliciarum,
pneumatis hospitium, numen et ipsa pium,
virgo, parens Christi, sine semine quae peperisti,
splendida stella poli, gloria summa soli,

Egypt. The door of forgiveness lies open, the compassion alone of Mary: she and no other remains the route to which to hold fast. If you wish to procure forgiveness of sins, strive to entreat Mary with your words and vows. Entrust all hope to Mary, the wellspring of forgiveness, that she wash away your offenses in response to your prayers. She alone can grant you a cure for sickness; she alone can bring you the gift of salvation; and fear nothing, for not a thing created in the world from the beginning is gentler than she. She alone is, was, and will be salvation for the wretched, gentle relief of the wretched, a wellspring flowing with goodness." He spoke and, imposing a suitable punishment for the time being, ordered the woman who had acknowledged her crimes to go off home.

When ordered to return home at the bishop's command, the woman, changed back again in body and heart, returns. A brief hour's time wipes away and wipes clean the long-standing pollutions of her old life. With tearful weeping she washes and waters all the inmost parts of her heart, chastising severely her past deeds. With tears, she compensates for past times; with groans, she relieves the losses she has suffered, devoting herself to weeping and wailing night and day. In this way she constantly calls on the name of Mary, worthy of remembrance, that she take up her case:

"Peerless Virgin, the world's most invincible hope, sole flower, honor, and ornament of your sex, glory of the world, paradise of delights, lodging of the Holy Spirit, Virgin, Mother of Christ, who yourself also without seed gave birth to the merciful Godhead, shining star of heaven, highest

virgo, favus mellis, cunctis praelata puellis,
fons veniaeque via, digna, benigna, pia,
vas Domino gratum, vas mundum sanctificatum,
undique signatum, vas in honore datum:
tu thalamus regis, tu consummatio legis,
tu caeli facies, tu sine nocte dies,
lumen sensificum, summae Deitatis amicum,
Christum magnificans, lux sine fine micans,
mater, in hac hora pro me misera, precor, ora.
Crimina terge prece, crimina digna nece.
Me tibi, virgo pia, tibi me committo, Maria.
Sum tua, teque sequor teque sequendo precor:
Splendida stella maris, fer opem quam ferre rogaris.
Tu mea spes hodie, duxque comesque viae.
Virgo, decus morum, decor orbis, flosque polorum,
flos, decus atque decor, suscipe vota, precor.
Humano generi per te statuit misereri
gratia summa Dei; sis memor ergo mei."
Iamque dies aderat parti praefixus utrique,
facturusque fidem clericus actor adest.
Affuit et Caesar, sacro comitante senatu;
affuit et praesul, tristior ipse tamen.
Contio multa nimis populi convenit in unum,
rebus in incertis certior esse volens.
Illa sui generis multa comitante caterva
intrat et, aspecto rege, salutat eum.
Contio tota silet. Rex, maesta silentia solvens,
vaticinatorem iussit adesse virum.
Astat et astanti rex, "En," ait, "en mulierem
quam praedixisti criminis esse ream."

glory of earth, Virgin, honeycomb, preferred to all young women, wellspring and way of forgiveness, deserving, kind, and good, a vessel pleasing to the Lord, a pure and hallowed vessel, sealed on every side, a vessel granted as an honor: you are the king's bridal chamber, you are the law's fulfillment, you are heaven's face, you are day without night, light that illuminates the senses, dear to the highest Deity, extolling Christ, light that shines without end, mother, I entreat, pray in this hour for me, wretch that I am. Wipe away my crimes with prayer, crimes deserving of death. I entrust myself to you, kindly Virgin, to you, Mary, I entrust myself. I am yours, and I follow you, and in following you I pray: Shining star of the sea, bring the assistance you are requested to bring. You are my hope today, and leader and companion of my journey. Virgin, glory of morals, ornament of the world, and flower of the heavens, flower, glory, and ornament, receive my prayers, I entreat. Through you, the highest grace of God resolved to take pity upon humankind; may you then be mindful of me."

Now the day appointed by the two parties was at hand, and the cleric who was going to testify was present as plaintiff. The emperor also attended, in the company of the holy senate; the bishop also attended, yet he was rather downcast. A very great assembly of people came together as one, wishing to have greater certainty in uncertain matters. The woman enters, accompanied by a great throng of her family, and, on seeing the king, greets him. The whole assembly falls silent. The king, breaking the gloomy silence, ordered the man and prophesier to present himself. He stands near and as he does so, the king says to him, "See, see, the woman whom you foretold to be guilty of crime."

Obstupuit subito vates confusus et illam
  esse negat de qua vaticinatus erat.
"Absit," ait. "Non est, o rex, haec femina. Non est!
  Absit ut illa sit haec. Sit procul ista, precor.
Ista nihil turpe, nihil haec commisit iniquum;
  sed magis est mulier sancta placensque Deo.
Absit ut haec mulier quicquam commiserit horum.
  Urbe vel orbe parem non habet ista sibi.
Corpore, mente, manu mulier mundissima, totum
  illustrat populum sanctificatque suum.
Civibus angelicis haec circumsaepta, Mariae
  virginis et matris itque reditque comes.
Virgo parensque Dei celebri comitante caterva
  huic comes assistit, huic favet, hancque fovet.
Sit procul ergo, precor, virtus vultusque Mariae,
  quae magis est odio quam fuit ante mihi."
Dixerat et subito tenues collapsus in auras
  spiritus abscessit, non rediturus item.
Principis ante pedes vestigia foeda relinquens,
  consuluit subitam pestis iniqua fugam;
quique putabatur verus prius esse propheta,
  omnibus immundus spiritus esse patet.
Daemonis insidiae nil praevaluere Mariae;
  artibus atque dolis fallitur ipse suis.
Fraus patet, hostis abit, mulier salvata recedit;
  mirantur populi magnificantque Deum.
Plebs devota piam devotius inde Mariam
  laudat et ad veniam praedicat esse viam.

Immediately the bewildered prophet was shocked and denies that she is the woman about whom he prophesied. "Perish the thought," he said. "Oh king, this is not the woman. It is not she! Perish the thought that this is she. Send this woman far away, I pray. This woman has committed nothing offensive, nothing wrongful; rather, she is a holy woman and pleasing to God. Perish the thought that this woman has committed any of these acts. She has no equal in Rome or the world. The purest of women in body, mind, and hand, she gives luster to her entire people and hallows them. Surrounded by angelic citizens, this woman comes and goes as companion of the Virgin and Mother, Mary. The Virgin and Mother of God, in the company of a glorious host, is attending her as companion, showing favor to her, and cherishing her. Send the virtue and visage of Mary far away, I pray, for she is more detestable to me than she was before."

He had finished speaking and the spirit abruptly departed, vanishing into thin air, not to return again. Leaving his foul calling card before the feet of the emperor, the evil pest decided upon sudden flight; and he who was thought previously to be a true prophet is revealed to all as an unclean spirit. The demon's schemes held no power over Mary; he is outwitted by his own crafts and tricks. The deceit is revealed, the enemy retreats, the woman, saved, withdraws; the people marvel and extol God. The devout common folk praise merciful Mary for this more devoutly and pronounce her to be the way to forgiveness.

De puero Iudaeo cum Christianis communicante

Forte dies aderat quo sacrae carnis ad esum
agni paschalis turba venire solet.
Fonte renata sacro, plebs circumquaque fidelis
Christicolis celebrem gaudet adesse diem.
Omnis ad ecclesiam concurrit sexus et aetas,
angelico cupiens participare cibo.
Laetus ad ecclesiam properat cum paupere dives.
Sexus uterque ruit; hinc puer, inde senex.
Quod puer Hebraeus cernens accurrit et ipse
intrans cum pueris participansque sacris.
Ignorans igitur quisnam puer esset et unde,
presbyter angelico pane cibavit eum.
Contigit ergo domum puerum de more reversum
utque solent pueri visa referre domi,
simplicitas pueri mentiri nescia verum
simplicitatis opus in sua damna refert.
Quo pater audito, graviter succensus in iram,
irruit in puerum, mente manuque furens.
Nulla patrem pietas potuit revocare furentem,
quo labem nato parceret ipse suo.
Ardentis clibani puerum proiecit in ignem
dextera saeva patris, dextra nefanda nimis.
Maesta parens pueri, misero compassa dolori,
clamat et infestis unguibus ora secat.
"Me miseram, quid agis, quid agis, scelerate virorum?
Ignibus innocua viscera nostra cremas!
Vae, quid agis, quid agis? Quae tanti causa furoris?
Quid miser admisit, curve vel unde furis?

On a Jewish Boy Taking Communion with Christians

The day had chanced to arrive when crowds customarily come to eat the holy flesh of the Easter lamb. Reborn in the holy font, the faithful common folk all round rejoice that the day, renowned among Christians, has arrived. Each sex and every age hurry together to church, desiring to share in the angelic food. The rich man hastens happily to church with the poor. Each sex rushes to join in; here is a boy, there an old man. A Hebrew boy, perceiving this, hurries up himself too, entering with other boys and sharing in the holy rites. The priest fed him with angelic bread, not knowing then who the boy was and where he was from.

It happened then that the boy returned home in his usual way and, as boys are accustomed to report at home on what they have seen, the guileless boy, incapable of misrepresenting the truth, reports to his detriment his guileless act. When the father heard it, he was inflamed to violent anger and, frenzied mentally and physically, attacked the boy. No kindheartedness could restrain the frenzied father, for him to spare his son catastrophe. The father's savage hand, his all too wicked hand, flung the boy into the fire of a blazing oven. The boy's distraught mother, taking pity on his grievous pain, shouts out and tears her face with violent fingernails.

"Wretched me, what are you doing, what are you doing, you scoundrel among men? You are consuming with fire our own innocent flesh and blood! Woe, what are you doing, what are you doing? What is the reason for such great rage? What offense did the wretch commit, or why or from what

Parce, pater, puero; miserae reminiscere matris!
   Criminis impietas dedecet ista patrem."
Civibus excitis miserae clamore parentis,
   ocius accurrunt aspiciuntque nefas,
cumque putaretur corpus puerile resolvi—
   nam rogus in cineres iam resolutus erat—
accidit astante populo res digna relatu,
   res memoranda satis de novitate sua:
cum puer illaesus exiret ab igne camini,
   Catholicae fidei dogmata sacra probans,
flamma nihil puerum sed nec tetigisse capillum
   cernitur aut vestem contaminasse suam!
Stat puer illaesus quem sic transisse per ignem
   contigit, ut nec odor ignis inesset ei.
Mira rei novitas magis ac magis esse stupori
   coepit et astantes sollicitare magis;
sed puer, accedens causamque modumque revelans,
   simplicitate sua talibus orsus ait:
"Cum pater ecce meus me proiecisset in ignem
   spesque mihi misero nulla relicta foret,
quae super altare templi residere videtur
   astitit illa mihi, femina pulchra nimis.
Femina, quae puerum gremio fovet atque Maria
   dicitur a populo, venit opemque tulit.
Cuius heri populo puer est partitus in escam,
   ignibus in mediis affuit illa mihi.
Illa parens pueri, cuius de carne cibavit
   hesterno populus atque cruore bibit,
illa quidem miserum me conservavit ab igne;
   contulit haec misero se mihi meque sibi.

cause do you rage? Spare the boy, father; have a thought for his wretched mother! The pitilessness of this crime dishonors you as a father."

The citizens were aroused by the shouting of the wretched mother; they run up swiftly and see the unspeakable act. When the boy's body was thought to have been reduced to ashes—for the pyre had already been so reduced—a thing worth reporting happened as the people stood by, a thing extremely memorable for its novelty: when the boy came forth unharmed from the fire of the furnace, professing the holy doctrines of the Catholic faith, the flame is perceived to have touched the boy not at all, not even a hair, or to have marred his clothing! The boy stands unharmed who had the fortune to pass through the fire in such a way that not even the scent of fire was upon him. The miraculous novelty of the event began to be the cause of more and more astonishment and to rouse the bystanders even more; but the boy, approaching and revealing the cause and manner of what had happened, in his guilelessness began with the following words:

"When my father (mark my words!) flung me into the fire, and no hope remained to me in my wretchedness, that woman stood near me, extremely beautiful, who is to be seen seated upon the altar of the church. The woman, who coddles a boy in her lap and is called Mary by the people, came and brought aid. She, whose boy was shared among the people yesterday as food, stood near me in the middle of the flames. That mother of the boy, on whose flesh the people fed and from whose blood they drank yesterday, it was she who saved wretched me from the fire; this woman devoted herself to wretched me, and me to her. That mother

Illa parens pueri quam plebs devota frequenter
invocat, illa fuit, illa Maria bona.
Huius in accessu candentis tota camini
friguit ut glacies flamma, calore carens.
Flammam fornacis tepidi quasi flamina roris
fecit; et ardentes nil nocuere faces."
Talibus auditis, matrem pietatis honorat
plebs pia dulcisonis laudibus atque melis.
Catholicae fidei Iudaea lege relicta,
talibus aspectis, credit uterque parens.
Laetus uterque parens puero comitante tenello
gaudet Catholico subdere colla iugo.
Narrat adhuc hodie gens haec Pisana, Mariae
pronior obsequiis officiisque piis.

De puero cum alio ludente

Solvere vota volens, puero praeeunte tenello,
virginis in templum venit honesta parens.
Oblatisque prius precibus, procedit ad aram
oblatura piae munera grata deae.
Vota precesque piae mulier devota Mariae
solvit et a voto solvitur ipsa suo,
dumque parens precibus pro se puerique salute
instat et optatam virginis optat opem,
stat puer, intendens puero quem matris imago
cernitur in gremio laeta fovere suo,
cumque puer puerum vivum verumque putaret,
venit et oblato quem gerit ipse cibo
"Papap," ait, "mecum!" Quo dissimulante, rogare
institit ille magis, ingeminando preces.

of the boy whom the pious common folk often invokes, was that woman there, that good Mary.

"At the approach of this woman, the whole flame of the white-hot furnace, losing its heat, grew cold as ice. She made the flame of the still warm bake-oven like gusts that bring dew; and the blazing firebrands harmed not at all."

After hearing these words, the devout common folk honors the mother of goodness with sweet-sounding praise and melodies. Both parents, after seeing such things, believe in the Catholic faith, abandoning the Jewish law. Both parents, in the company of their boy of tender years, rejoice happily to submit their necks to the Catholic yoke. The people of Pisa still tell of these things today, even more devoted to pious service and the liturgical hours in honor of Mary.

On a Boy Playing with Another

Wishing to fulfill vows, a respectable mother, with her boy of tender age preceding her, came into the Virgin's church. After first offering prayers, she proceeds to the altar to offer gifts pleasing to the benevolent goddess. The pious woman fulfills her vows and prayers to benevolent Mary, and she is released from her vow.

As the mother perseveres with prayers for herself and the boy's well-being, and requests the Virgin's hoped-for aid, the boy stands, looking at a boy whom a mother's likeness is perceived to cherish happily on her lap; and since the boy thinks that that boy is living and real, he comes and, offering the food that he is carrying, says, "Eat with me!" As the other disregards him, he perseveres even more in asking,

Semper idem repetens, porrecti panis ad esum
nunc prece, nunc lacrimis sollicitare studet;
extentaque manu panem protendit in altum,
vim faciens puero quo valet ille modo.
Simplicitas pueri puerum de more rogantis
digna favore fuit simplicitate sua.
Compatiens igitur puero, respondit imago
viventis pueri more modoque pari:
"Hac vice non comedam tecum. Tu vero cibabis
mecum post triduum, me tibi dante cibum."
Forte loci custos, audita voce loquentis,
astitit inquirens quis loqueretur ei,
cui puer, "Iste meus socius," digitoque sacristae
eminus ostendens insinuavit eum.
Mente quidem tacita puerorum verba sacrista
pensat et hoc triduum quid velit esse notat.
Cognatos igitur pueri vocat atque parentes,
rem satis exponens mysteriumque rei.
Nec mora, post triduum puero moriente fidelem
fecerunt verbis facta secuta fidem.

INCIPIT LIBER TERTIUS.

Stupendum miraculum de clerico

Exstitit Europae iuvenis de partibus ortus.
Clericus officio, iuris amator, homo

redoubling his prayers. Always reiterating the same thing, he strives now with entreaty and now with tears to persuade him to eat the bread he held out. With hand outstretched, he raises the bread up high, exerting pressure on the boy in whatever way he can.

The guilelessness of the one boy, in asking the other in a typical way, was in its very guilelessness deserving of a favorable response. Accordingly, the likeness, sympathizing with the boy, replied in a manner and way comparable to a living boy's: "This time I will not eat with you. But you will share food with me after three days, and I will be the one giving you food."

By chance the custodian of the place, having heard the voice of a person speaking, came to his side and asked who was speaking to him. The boy replied to him, "This playmate of mine," and, pointing with a finger from a distance, he indicated him to the sexton. In the silence of his heart the sexton ponders the words of the boys and recognizes what this three-day period means. So then, he calls the relatives and parents of the boy, giving a thorough explanation of the event and its hidden meaning. Without delay, after three days, when the boy dies, the events that followed confirmed belief in his words.

HERE BEGINS THE THIRD BOOK.

An Amazing Miracle about a Cleric

There lived a young man who hailed from the continent of Europe. He was a cleric by profession, a lover of the law, a

moribus et vita cunctis venerandus honesta,
virginis et matris vir venerator erat.
Cuius in obsequium solitas qui psalleret horas,
clericus hic toto primus in orbe fuit.
Virginis et matris meritum, celebremque triumphum
horarum titulis extulit iste prior.
Hoc speciale decus primus dedit iste Mariae,
cuius adhuc hodie clerus ad instar agit.
Praesulis et cleri sibi conciliarat amorem
et morum probitas et Deitatis amor.
Principis et procerum populique favore solemnis
promeruit fieri vita pudica viri.
Crimine fama vacans nec quavis parte laborans
ex operum fructu fragrat odore bono.
Quicquid agant alii, super omnia religioni
corpore, mente, manu nocte dieque vacat.
Hoc opus, hoc studium: nihil huic praeponit amori,
hunc opibus cunctis praeposuisse studet.
Sed quia felices gravior fortuna frequenter
tangit et immemores non sinit esse sui,
sors adversa virum—sors toti flebilis urbi!—
tangit et attactu fit gravis ipsa suo.
Mira Dei pietas et dispensatio mira
(cuius iudicia solvere nemo potest),
quid, quo consilio, quare vel qua ratione
ista vel illa facit, omnia corda latet.
Vulnerat et sanat, prosternit et erigit idem,
ista vel illa tamen de ratione facit.
Hunc igitur pietas quae percutit et miseretur
percutiens tetigit, sed miserando tamen.

person revered by all for his character and respectable life, and a man who venerated the Virgin and Mother. This cleric, who would chant the customary hours in her service, was foremost in the whole world. He was first to extol the merit of the Virgin and Mother and her renowned triumph under the headings of the hours. He first gave this special honor to Mary, and today the clergy still acts according to his model. Both the propriety of his moral character and his love of the Deity won for him the love of bishop and clergy. Through the goodwill of the ruler, nobles, and people, the man's modesty of life acquired a claim to become highly regarded.

His reputation, free of crime and not suffering in any particular, is fragrant with a good aroma from the fruit of his deeds. Whatever others do, he devotes himself by night and day, with mind, body, and hand, to religious devotion above all things. This is his work, this his pursuit: he prefers nothing to this love, he strives to give this preference over all material concerns. But because fortune frequently affects the blessed more oppressively and does not allow them to be forgetful of it, misfortune—a misfortune lamentable for the whole city!—touches this man and with its touch it weighs heavily on him.

It lies hidden from all hearts why, with what plan, with what cause, or with what reason the marvelous goodness and marvelous dispensation of God (whose judgments no one can fathom) does one thing or another. He both wounds and heals, he lays low and raises high, yet he does one thing or another with good reason. Accordingly, the goodness that smites and shows pity touched this man, smiting and yet pitying him.

Frons tumet et, labiis serpentis vulnere cancri
turpiter exesis, foetet odore gravi.
Defluit in saniem tandem corruptio carnis,
ulcere pestifero depopulata prius.
Subtrahit accessus hominum faciemque suorum
foetor et aspectu fit gravis ipse suis.
Vix superest misero de tot modo milibus unus
qui velit aut possit illius ire comes.
Omnibus est oneri quibus antea vixit honori.
Vilis et abiectus, solus in urbe manet.
Vir quondam celebris nunc est abiectio plebis,
ultimus in populo qui modo primus erat.
Qui modo tantus erat, modo tot numerabat amicos,
nunc extra numerum se dolet esse suum.
Fortunae socios et prosperitatis amicos
abstulerant penitus poena pudorque suus.
Divitiis, opibus, sociis, mundo vel amicis
expertus didicit quae sit habenda fides.
Creverat interea longo cum tempore morbus;
inque dies gravior coeperat esse dolor.
Arcet ab accessu solo foetore clientes
vulnus et exesi vulneris atra lues.
Rebus in humanis nil iam superesse videtur
quod queat, excepta morte, iuvare virum.
Hanc miser exspectat, quia vita vivere tali
quid nisi saepe fuit et sine fine mori?
Taliter afflicto solita pietate salubrem
virginis affectus acceleravit opem.
Hunc igitur, somno dum se de nocte dedisset,
angelus assumptum ducit ad alta poli.

His face is swollen and, because his lips have been foully eaten away by the lesion of a spreading cancer, it stinks with an oppressive stench. In the end the infection of the flesh, first ravaged by the noxious ulcer, drains off as discharge. The stench deprives him of human company and the sight of his kin; because of his appearance, he becomes burdensome to his kinsfolk.

To the wretch there is left now scarcely one out of so many thousands who wants to be or can be his companion. He is a burden to all to whom previously he was an honor. Repulsive and cast out, he remains in the city, but alone. A man formerly renowned is now an outcast among the common folk, he who just recently was first is last among the people. He, who just recently was so great and just recently counted so many friends, now grieves that he is outside their number. His suffering and shame had deprived him altogether of the comrades of his good fortune and the friends of his success. He learned by experience what credence is to be put in riches, prosperity, comrades, the world, or friends.

Meanwhile the illness had increased with the long passage of time, and the pain began to be more severe from day to day. The lesion, by its stench alone, and the black canker of the lesion that has been eaten away kept his retainers from approaching.

In the human realm nothing seems left now that can help the man except death. The wretch awaits this, because to live such a life, what else was it but to die often and endlessly? To him afflicted in this way, the compassion of the Virgin with her accustomed goodness hastened healing aid. For when he had surrendered himself to sleep in the night, an angel takes him up and guides him to the heights of heaven.

Grata loci facies, odor optimus, aura salubris
    aspectus fragiles detinuere diu.
Herbarum species bis denas tresque venustas
    ridenti facie florida gignit humus.
Quarum prima quidem, septeno flore referta,
    omnibus excessit sola decore suo.
Cetera tota cohors herbarum floribus octo
    vestit odorifero germine laeta solum.
Vernat humus, vario florum depicta colore.
    Quaelibet in flores pullulat herba virens.
Fragrat odor florum, spirans quasi nectar odorum;
    balsama dulcifluo vincit odore locus.
Herbarum numerus sed et haec distinctio florum
    quid notet, exponit angelus orsus ita:
"Herbarum species psalmos designat et horas
    virginis et matris quos in honore canis.
Herba bis undena centeni terque quaterni
    et sexti psalmi signa sacrata gerit.
Distinctas species signat distinctio psalmi;
    unde vides flores versibus esse pares.
Celsior illa tamen species psalmum notat illum,
    qui quinquagenus tertius esse solet.
Pulchrior haec aliis, septeno flore referta,
    septem dona sacri pneumatis esse docet.
Psalmorum numerus varius varias notat herbas,
    quae duo si numeres, invenis esse pares.
Sic etiam psalmis quot versus cernis inesse,
    tot flores etiam quaelibet herba parit.
Hic locus, ista quies, decus hoc, floresque venusti
    debita sunt meritis singula quaeque tuis.

The pleasant appearance of the place, the most excellent scent, and the healthy air long detained his feeble gaze. The flowering earth, with smiling face, brings forth twenty-three charming types of vegetation. The first of them in fact, replete with sevenfold flower, alone surpasses all others with its beauty. The entire remaining troop of plants, abounding in fragrant growth, clothes the earth in eight flowers. The ground blooms, decorated with diverse colors of flowers. Every verdant plant sprouts into flowers. The scent of flowers spreads its aroma, breathing as it were a fragrant nectar of scents; the place outdoes balsam with its sweet-flowing scent.

The angel, beginning with these words, explains what the number of the plants and this division of the flowers signify: "The kinds of plants stand for the psalms for the hours that you sing in honor of the Virgin and Mother. The twenty-two types of plant serve as sacred symbols of Psalm 118. The division of the psalm corresponds to the different types; from this you perceive that the flowers are equivalent to verses. But that taller type designates that psalm that is conventionally the fifty-third. More beautiful than the others, laden with a sevenfold flower, it teaches that the gifts of the Holy Spirit are seven. The differing numeration of psalms designates different plants; if you number the two of them, you find they correspond. So too, you perceive that there are as many verses in the psalms as also flowers that each herb produces. This place, this tranquility, this beauty, and these lovely flowers are every one due to you for your merits.

Haec tibi pro meritis digne reddenda reservat
omnia post obitum virgo parensque Dei."
Dixerat et subito caelestis limina portae
ingreditur laetus ipse comesque suus.
Quae sit forma loci, quae gloria, quisve paratus
materiae species quaeve vel unde foret,
omnia non solum cum sint bona, sed bona valde,
nec sua cernentis dicere lingua potest.
Currit in occursum caelestis curia, tanti
hospitis adventu laetificata pio.
Ipsa parens Christi venientem mitis in ulnas
excipit et gremio confovet ipsa suo.
Ubera quin etiam matris suggenda ministrans
inter complexus obtulit haec et ait:
"Quae mihi dilectus in terris filius olim
ubera suxit homo, tu quoque suge modo.
Ubera quae suxit in terris conditor orbis,
haec mea suge meus ubera, care mihi.
Ubera suge, precor, caelesti lacte referta;
ubera sunt labiis haec mea digna tuis.
Lacte meo satiare meus; lac dulce parentis
dignus amore meo, dulcis amice, bibe.
Os, mihi quod totiens tot dulcia munera laudum
obtulit, ulterius nolo dolore premi.
Absit ab his labiis foetor, furor et dolor omnis,
quae mihi tot laudes totque dedere preces.
Non decet ut pereat, putri consumpta dolore,
laudibus et titulis lingua dicata meis."
Talibus auditis, subito sopor et dolor omnis
cedit et abscedunt tristia quaeque prius.

The Virgin and Mother of God is keeping all these things for you as a fitting return for your merits after your death."

The angel spoke, and immediately he and his companion joyfully cross the threshold of the heavenly gate. Not even the tongue of an eyewitness can say what the beauty of the place is, what the splendor, what the adornment, what the type of material used, or what its origin, since everything is not only good but supremely good. The heavenly council, rejoicing at the blessed arrival of so great a guest, runs to meet him. On his arrival the mother of Christ herself gently receives him in her arms and cherishes him in her bosom. Moreover, while attending to him, she offered amid her embraces a mother's breasts to suckle and said:

"You too now suck the breasts that my beloved son once sucked while a man on earth. Suck these breasts of mine that the creator of the world sucked on earth, you who are mine and dear to me. Suck these breasts, I pray, engorged with heavenly milk; these breasts of mine are appropriate for your lips. Sate yourself, you who are mine, with my milk; worthy of my love, sweet friend, drink a mother's sweet milk. I do not want the mouth that has so often offered me so many sweet gifts of praise to be oppressed any further by pain. Begone all stench, madness, and pain from these lips, which have given me so many praises and so many prayers. It is not fitting that a tongue, consecrated to my praises and titles, perish, worn down by festering pain."

After he heard these words, all sleep and sorrow suddenly leave him, and all previous sadness departs. The house, filled

Fragrat odore domus, caelesti nectare plena;
balsama fusa putes et thymiama loco.
Morbus abit subito, vestigia nulla relinquens
vulneris in toto corpore sive cute.
Caelitus indulta tanto medicamina morbo
sentit et attactu comprobat ipse suo.
Visio vera fuit; res est manifesta secuta;
verbis virgineis facta dedere fidem.
Foetor in eximium subito conversus odorem
defecit, causa deficiente sua.
Nusquam foeda lues, nusquam corruptio carnis:
ubere virgineo fit rediviva caro.
Pristina forma redit. Facies renovata colorem
contrahit antiquum, contrahit atque statum.
Nulla quidem desunt, quia singula quaeque reformat
in melius medica virgo Maria manu.
Fit novus ex veteri, cum nec vestigia tanti
vulneris in tota carne relicta manent.
Non est qui fuerat, subito mutatus in illum
qui fuit ante virum, virginitatis ope.
Vulnera melliflua matris medicante mamilla,
gutture mellito stillat in ore favus.
Inveterata diu sanat medicina novella,
virginis et matris lacte mamilla sacra;
utque prius fuerat nimio foetore repulsus,
nunc revocando gradum certat odore frui.
Quos prius atra lues, quos ulceris abstulit horror,
hos medicina nova reddit odorque novus,
quique sepultus erat longa sub nocte, suorum
fit redivivus amor, fit rediviva fides.

with heavenly nectar, has a fragrant scent. You might think that balms and aromatic gums had been spread upon the place. Suddenly the sickness goes away, leaving no traces of the lesion on his whole body or skin. He feels the effects of heaven-granted medicines on so severe an illness and confirms it by his touch. The vision was true; the event that followed clearly showed it; the facts lent credence to the Virgin's words. The stench disappears, suddenly changed into an exceptional fragrance, as its cause disappeared. The foul contagion is nowhere, the corruption of the flesh nowhere; the flesh is restored to life by the Virgin's breast. His former appearance returns. His face, renewed, takes on its previous complexion and takes on its previous condition. Nothing at all is lacking, because the Virgin Mary, with healing hand, refashions every single thing for the better.

The new comes into being from the old, since no trace of so great a lesion remains left in the whole of his flesh. He is not who he had been, suddenly changed into the man he was before, with the help of virginity. While the mother's breast, flowing with honey, cures the lesions, a honeycomb drips in his mouth as his throat is honey coated. The new medicine, the breast of the Virgin and Mother with its sanctified milk, heals long-standing wounds. And he who previously had been driven off by the overpowering stench now retraces his steps and vies to enjoy the fragrance. The new medicine and new fragrance bring back those whom the black canker and revulsion at his sore earlier took away. He who had been buried in long night became a renewed object of love for his family and friends, a renewed proof of faith. He who just

Qui modo solus erat, nullo comitante suorum,
   redditus ipse sibi fit comes ecce suis.
Fama rei subito totam vulgata per urbem
   laeta ruit, populo nuntia facta suo.
Ipse quid acciderit causamque modumque retexens
   insinuat populo pontificique suo.
Res manifesta patet, celebri res digna relatu;
   confirmat dubiam res manifesta fidem.
Matris mellifluae miseratio magna Mariae
   magna manet, magnis magnificata modis.
Quam pia, quamque potens, quam sit studiosa suorum
   virgo, memor memorum, dicere nemo potest.
O quam dulce decus, quam sanctum, quamque suave
   virginis obsequiis invigilare piis,
cuius amor tantus, cuius miseratio tanta
   non cessat famulis semper adesse suis.

De presbytero qui nescivit aliam missam nisi de sancta Maria

Moribus ornatus plus quam sermone Latino
   presbyter exstiterat, simplicitatis homo,
qui minus artis habens, multum virtutis habebat,
   culmine virtutum dives et artis egens.
Sed pia vita dabat quod et ars et lingua negabat;
   his minus instructus, aptior inde fuit.
Damna suae linguae multa virtute redemit
   simplicitatis homo simplicitate sua.
Vir vitae celebris et religionis honestae
   moribus implebat quod minus artis erat.

now had been alone, with no one of his intimates keeping him company, becomes, when restored to himself, take note, a companion of those very people.

The report of the episode, broadcast at once throughout the whole city, rushes forth gladly as messenger to his people. He himself conveys to his people and bishop what happened, recounting its cause and extent. The plain truth of the episode is obvious, an episode worthy of frequent reporting; the plain truth of the episode strengthens wavering faith.

The great compassion of Mary, the mother sweet as honey, proves great, her greatness extolled in great ways. No one can say how kindly, how powerful, how devoted to her followers the Virgin is, attentive to those attentive to her. Oh how sweet, how saintly, and how agreeable the honor, to keep vigil in dutiful service to the Virgin, whose great love and great mercy never cease to be at hand for her servants.

On the Priest Who Knew No Other Mass but of the Virgin Mary

There lived a priest, a simple person, distinguished by morals rather than by the Latin language, who despite having little skill had great virtue, rich in the eminence of virtues and impoverished in skill. But a devout life gave what both skill and language refused him; less educated in the two last mentioned, he was better qualified in the first.

A simple person, in his simplicity he compensated with much virtue for the failings of his tongue. A man of renowned life and of respected piety, he made up through morals for what he lacked in skill. He was an upright man,

Rectus homo, non rhetor erat, nec multus in arte
grammatica, gratus non minus inde Deo.
Cordis et oris egens, vir hebes, vir simplicitatis,
vir qui grammaticae nescius artis erat,
vir sacer et simplex, qui nullas noverat artes,
hac placet arte Deo, simplicitate sacra.
Quid sit grammatica, quid vox, quid littera, quidve
syllaba sive sonus, haec sibi cura minor.
Non quae verborum, sed quae sit regula vitae
sedulus inquirit, sollicitusque tenet.
Quid genus a specie, quid res a nomine differt,
mentibus astutis scire reliquit hebes.
Non est grammaticus, neque rhetor quaerit haberi;
Quintilianus eum denegat esse suum.
Usus et auditus modicum quod habere videtur
(si tamen est aliquid) contulit illud ei.
Cumque deceret eum missam celebrare frequenter
ordinis atque loci de ratione sui,
semper idem repetens, missam celebravit eandem,
nil varians aliquo tempore sive loco.
Virginis et matris illud venerabile "Salve,
sancta parens" semper et sine fine canit.
Hoc et non aliud anno volvente revolvit;
hoc iteravit heri, cras iterabit idem.
Omnibus hoc annis, hoc tempore quolibet anni,
hoc est cotidie quod canit atque legit.
Hoc est officium quod sancto convenit omni;
omnibus et solis convenit illud idem.
Hoc Patris, hoc Nati, sed et hoc est Flaminis almi;
convenit hoc uni, convenit atque tribus.

not a rhetorician, and unskilled in the art of grammar, but no less pleasing to God on that account. Lacking good sense and eloquence, a dull-witted man, a simple man, a man who was ignorant of the art of grammar, a saintly and simple man, who knew no arts, by this art—saintly simplicity—he pleases God.

What grammar is, what utterance, letter, syllable, or sound, these are a lesser concern to him. He investigates diligently and observes conscientiously not what are the rules for language but what are the rules for life. A dullard, he leaves to sharper minds to know how genus differs from species and the real from a name. He is not a grammarian, and he does not seek to be considered a rhetorician; Quintilian denies that he is his follower. Practice and hearing conferred upon him that modest portion which he seems to possess (if it is anything at all).

Since by virtue of his rank and position it was proper for him to say the Mass often, he said the same Mass, always reiterating the same thing, changing nothing at any time or in any place. He sings always and endlessly that revered refrain of the Virgin and Mother, "Hail, holy Mother." As the year rolls by, he falls back on this one refrain and no other; he repeated this yesterday, he will repeat it the same tomorrow. Through all the years, at whatever time of year, this is what he sings and reads daily. This is the office that suits every saint; this same one suits each and every one. This is the office for the Father, the Son, and also the Holy Spirit; this suits each one and suits all three. This has the power to

Solvere defunctos habet hoc, veniamque precari;
hoc habet et vivos conciliare Deo.
Hoc est officium quod ad omnia convenit unum;
omnibus hoc solum sufficit estque satis.
Praesulis hoc igitur postquam pervenit ad aures,
rem iubet inquiri, quae sit et an sit ita.
Archilevita celer, qui terram circuit omnem
ut scelus acceleret, accelerare studet.
Nec mora, more sacro, super his conventus ab ipso,
vir sacer et simplex esse fatetur ita.
Praesulis in vetitum cupidos traxere ministros
lucri spes et odor, non Deitatis amor.
Ipsa, licet tenuis, rerum substantia clerum
pontificemque suum traxit, amore sui;
dumque sacerdotis quae sit substantia pensant,
hunc magis insimulant criminis esse reum.
Non quod sit facinus, sed quae vel quanta facultas
adsit avaritiae pensat anhela sitis.
Non homo sed census hominis peccasse putatur;
protinus ergo luat quem liquet esse reum.
Corporis et mentis oculos dum vana voluptas
vincit et excaecat, fallitur omnis homo.
Luxus opum leviter solet enervare potentes,
inque suos pietas absque rigore cadens.
Indiscretus amor, pietas et cura suorum
plus viget in clero plusque rigoris habet.
Unde sacerdotem gravius peccasse fatentur
et gravioris eum criminis esse reum.
Causa sacerdotis gravis est: coniurat in illum
praesulis et cleri contio tota sui.

perform last rites and to pray for pardon; this has the power also to reconcile the living with God. This is the office that by itself befits all; this alone suffices and is enough for all.

Well then, after this reached the bishop's ears, he orders the matter to be investigated, what it actually is and whether it is as reported. The archdeacon, who goes around the whole earth to hasten crime, in haste applies himself to hastening it. Without delay, the saintly and simple man, when approached by him about these matters, admits in his saintly manner that it is so.

Hope for and the whiff of gain, not love of the Deity, attracted the bishop's greedy attendants to what is forbidden. Though meager, the substance of his property enticed the clergy and their bishop, out of love for themselves. As they weigh what the priest's assets are, they accuse him all the more of being guilty of a crime. The covetous thirst of greed does not ponder what the misdeed is but what or how great the resources are. Not the man but the man's wealth is deemed to have sinned; accordingly, let him pay immediately, since he is clearly guilty. As empty pleasure overcomes and blinds the eyes of his body and mind, every man is deceived. Extravagant wealth is accustomed easily to weaken the powerful, and so too is devotion to family that degenerates for want of severity. Undiscriminating love, loyalty, and concern for family have greater force and greater severity among the clergy.

For this reason they declare that the priest sinned even more seriously and that he is guilty of a more serious crime. The priest's case is serious. The whole assembly of the bishop and his clergy conspire against him. He is said to

Subversor populi, derisor mysteriorum
dicitur et fidei nescius esse sacrae.
"Vir sine doctrina legis nec in arte peritus,
qua ratione gregem pascet et unde suum?
Sic abit in nihilum vigor ecclesiasticus omnis
inque sacerdotum deperit ipse manu.
Excessus igitur tantos et tam manifestos
absit ut ecclesia dissimulare queat.
Scandala tollantur, gravior ne forte ruina
accidat exempli de ratione sui.
Sic vigor ecclesiae, sic est servanda potestas,
ne status illius decidat atque decus.
Presbyter ergo gradu careat, succedat et alter
dignus ut officium suppleat atque locum.
Rebus et officio debet de iure carere,
debet et a propriis finibus esse procul.
Cur dispensandum vel mitius esset agendum?
Sufficiens causa nulla subesse potest.
Si genus attendas vel quae sit origo parentum,
omnia servilis condicionis erunt.
Sed neque magnorum quisquam sibi propitiatur,
nec gravis est super his ira timenda ducis.
Sed neque res quicquam regem contingit, ut ipsa
debeat aut possit displicuisse sibi.
Forte tamen populi sibi conciliavit amorem.
Cur? Quia favit ei virque remissus erat.
Unde velut populus, sic cernitur esse sacerdos;
immo magis populo desipit ipse suo.
Cesset ab officio. Cedat sua portio clero
aut cui clerus eam praesul et ipse dabit."

be an underminer of the people, a mocker of sacraments, and ignorant of the holy faith.

"A man without instruction in the law and with no expertise in the liberal arts, how and on what will he feed his flock? In this way all the Church's authority dissolves into nothing, and it perishes utterly in the hands of its priests.

"So then, perish the thought that the Church could overlook transgressions so great and evident. Let the bad influence be removed, for fear that a more serious disaster perhaps come about by reason of his example. The Church's strength and power must be preserved in this way, that its status and glory not decay. Let the priest then be deprived of his rank, and another worthy of fulfilling his office and position succeed him. By law he must be deprived of property and office, and must be removed far from his own parish. Why should any exemption be accorded or the action be mitigated? No sufficient reason can support doing so.

"If you examine his family or what the background is of his parents, they will be entirely of servile status. What is more, no one from among the grandees is favorably disposed to him, nor is the earl's severe anger to be feared in these matters. What is more, this matter is not one to concern the king in the least, that it should or could displease him. Still, perhaps he has won over for himself the people's love. Why? Because he showed favor to them and was an easygoing man. As a result, the priest is perceived to be just like the people; in fact, he is even more foolish than his people.

"Let him resign from his office. Let his benefice pass on to the clergy or to whomever the clergy and bishop himself grant it."

Talibus auditis, commotus amore suorum
contulit assensum praesul et ipse suum.
Dissimulando tamen se finxit longius ire,
hoc velut invitus vique coactus agens.
Sic voluit cogi, qui sic est forte coactus.
Verba negantis habet, facta volentis habens.
Nec desunt lacrimae laeto de pectore tristes,
quas praelatorum constat habere chorum.
Nacta locum, lacrimas tristes mens laeta propinat,
anxia vindictae, mente manuque furens.
Hae non sunt lacrimae quas Petri sive Mariae
fudit amor, veniae ductus amore piae.
O dulces lacrimas, o luctus deliciosos,
quos furor et vindex iudicis ira parit!
Talibus in lacrimis solet ebullire venenum,
corde quod absconsum contigit esse diu.
Quoddam laetitiae genus est species lacrimarum
talis, et hac specie praesulis ora madent.
Rebus et officio quoniam spoliatus inique,
presbyter abscessit, praesule flente tamen.
Humana viduatus ope, Deitatis in aure
clamat et assiduis fletibus orat opem.
Nec mora, clamantem solita pietate benigna
audit et exaudit virgo parensque Dei.
Praesulis ante thorum media de nocte corusca
astitit et torvo lumine dixit ei:
"Pessime pontificum, nec re nec nomine dignus
pontificis, quid agis? Cognita sumne tibi?
Summi regis ego genitrix, ego virgo Maria,
quam male laesisti, quam male laedis adhuc.

After hearing this, the bishop, motivated by his love for his family and friends, gave his personal assent. Yet, dissembling, he pretended that he was proceeding reluctantly, as if doing this unwillingly and coerced by force. He, who as chance would have it was coerced in one way, desired to be coerced in the other. He offers words of a person refusing, deeds of one assenting. Sorrowful tears, which it is well known that the troupe of prelates possesses, are not missing from his happy heart. Having secured the post, his mind, though happy, worried about retribution and, frenzied mentally and physically, serves up a draft of sorrowful tears. These are not the tears that Peter's or Mary's love shed, induced by the longing for merciful forgiveness. Oh sweet tears, oh delightful lamentations, to which the judge's avenging madness and wrath give rise! Venom that has happened to be long hidden in the heart is accustomed to bubble up in such tears. Such a semblance of tears is a type of happiness, and with this semblance the bishop's face is wet.

Seeing that he has been stripped unjustly of property and office, the priest went away, while the bishop still wept. Deprived of human aid, the priest raises his cry to the Deity's ear and beseeches his aid with insistent weeping. Without delay, the kindly Virgin and Mother of God hears his cries and hearkens to him with her accustomed goodness. In the middle of the night she stood, radiant, before the bishop's bed and said to him with menacing gaze:

"Basest of bishops, worthy of neither the reality nor the name of bishop, what are you doing? Am I familiar to you? I am the mother of the highest king, I am the Virgin Mary, whom you have wickedly injured, and whom you are still

Ille meus famulus et cancellarius idem
ille meus nocuit quidve vel unde tibi?
Presbyter ille meus a te spoliatus inique
rebus et officiis qua ratione fuit?
Iuris forma tui fuit haec, tua sola voluntas,
non aliud, cleri voce favente tibi.
Te carnalis amor, te sollicitudo tuorum
traxit et illicitas fecit inire vias.
Te tibi surripuit amor indiscretus eorum
quos de stirpe tua contigit esse satos.
Quam male pontificem decet et raptoris habere
nomen et hoc factis promeruisse suis!
Ex re nomen habes; raptorem res manifesta
te probat et populi contio tota tui.
De pastore lupus, factus de praesule praedo,
hoc quod debueras parcere, praedo voras.
Talia pontificum non sunt bene convena gestis;
talia pontificem dedecuere pium.
Parcere simplicibus et debellare superbos
debet pontificis dextra sacrata pii.
Vita pudica viri, morum gravitate venusta
simplicitasque sua digna favore fuit.
Ergo virum iustum, nullo prohibente tuorum,
rebus et officiis illico redde suis.
Quod si distuleris, pro certo te moriturum
infra ter denum noveris esse diem."
Dixit et, angelicis digne comitata choreis,
unde prius venit virgo reversa redit.
Virginis ad vocem praesul turbatus et ultra
quam credi poterat contremefactus ait,

wickedly injuring. That servant of mine and chancellor of mine, what harm has he done to you, or for what reason? On what basis has that priest of mine been stripped unjustly by you of his property and offices? This has been the provision of your legal system, your will alone, not anything else, with the vocal support of the clergy. Fleshly love and the interests of your family and friends have impelled you and made you travel down unlawful ways. Your indiscriminate love of those who happened to be born from your family stock got the better of you.

"How ill it befits a bishop both to have the reputation of a robber and to have earned that reputation through his deeds! The reputation you have is based on fact; the clear facts and the entire assembly of your people prove you to be a robber. Having become a wolf instead of a shepherd, a brigand instead of a bishop, you devour as a brigand what you were obliged to spare.

"Such things do not conform well with the behavior of bishops; such things have dishonored a good bishop. The sanctified hand of a good bishop ought to spare the simple and to crush the proud. This man's modest life and his simplicity, along with the pleasing sobriety of his conduct, have been worthy of favor. So then, return this just man instantly to his property and offices, and let none of your people prevent him. If you put this off, be assured that you will certainly die before the thirtieth day."

The Virgin spoke and, duly accompanied by angelic troupes, turned round and went back from where she had come earlier. The prelate, distressed by the Virgin's utterance and quite terrified to an unbelievable degree, said,

"Erravi, fateor." (Miserum sua facta remordent.)
"Sanguinis et carnis me superavit amor.
Errorem fateor: amor indiscretus ad ima
traxit et excessi carnis amore meae.
Me miserum, fateor. Miseri miserere, benigna!
Omnia restituam, sed miserere mei!
Mos praelatorum et consuetudo cavenda
me plus quam reliquos fecit amare meos."
Accelerans igitur, mortis terrore coactus,
praesul praedictum iussit adesse virum.
Iussus adest. Cunctis visum de nocte revelat
praesul et ablata cuncta reformat ei.
Res, gradus, officium, locus, et substantia tota
redditur et solito gaudet honore frui.
Praesul enim supplex errasse fatetur in illo;
supplicis et cleri lingua fatetur idem.
Virgo, sui memorum memor, indefessa per aevum
hoc meruit titulo clarior esse suo.
Praesulis et cleri fastum fraudemque refellit
conservans servum virgo benigna suum.
Nos quoque servare dignetur et associare
his quibus ad patriam dat Deus ire viam.
Postquam divitiae virtuti praevaluere,
virtutes pretium dedidicere suum.

De imagine Iudaeum convincente

Civis in urbe fuit Constantinopolitana
nobilis et nimiae simplicitatis homo.
Vir mercator erat, nomenque Theodorus illi;
exstitit et census non mediocris ei.

"I made a mistake, I confess." (His deeds inspire remorse in the wretch.) "Love of flesh and blood overcame me. I confess my mistake: undiscriminating love induced me to base actions, and I transgressed for love of my flesh. Woe is me, I confess. Kindly one, take pity upon a wretch! I will restore everything, but take pity upon me! The common custom of bishops and conduct to be avoided have made me love my own kin more than others."

So then, making haste, compelled by fear of death, the bishop ordered the aforesaid man to appear. As ordered, he appears. The bishop discloses to all his nighttime vision and restores to the priest all that had been taken away. Property, rank, office, position, and entire substance are returned to him, and he rejoices to enjoy his accustomed status. Indeed, the bishop, as a suppliant, confesses to have sinned against that man, and the tongue of the clergy in supplication confesses the same.

The Virgin, mindful of those mindful of her, untiringly merited, time without end, to enjoy special fame for this quality of hers. The kindly Virgin, by keeping her servant safe, gave the lie to the arrogance and deceit of the bishop and clergy. May she deign also to keep us safe and to unite us with those to whom God grants to make their way to their homeland.

After riches prevailed over virtue, virtues lost their value.

On an Image Convincing a Jew

In the city of Constantinople there was a noble townsman, a person of exceeding simplicity. The man was a merchant, his name was Theodore, and he possessed no small fortune. But

Sed quia luxus opum levis est citiusque recedit,
cesserunt leviter luxus opesque leves;
utque solet subito pauper de divite factus,
mercibus absumptis coepit egere nimis;
quique prius fuerat cunctis venerandus in urbe,
omnibus est factus vilis in urbe sua.
Omnia deficiunt, Fortuna deficiente.
Cum parat haec reditum, cuncta redire parant.
Cogitur extremo mendicus ad ostia victum
quaerere, quo saltem vivere possit inops.
Cum sit egestatis onus importabile semper,
inter concives plus gravitatis habet.
Duplex poena mali gravat: hinc rubor, inde ruboris
nescia paupertas degenerare facit.
Omnibus est odio quibus esse putabat amori.
Absumptis pretiis, nil valuere preces.
Dum bene successit, nomen sapientis habebat;
nunc quia res periit, desipientis habet.
Pluribus expertis sed prosperitatis amicis,
Iudaei tandem poscit egenus opem.
Respondens Abraham (quia sic erat ille vocatus):
"Compatior fatis, tristis amice, tuis.
Si vadium vel pignus habes, miserebor egenti,
quae cupis et quanti ponderis aera dabo.
Vade, vadesque para, quia nudis credere verbis
Nolo, nec id tutum creditur esse mihi."
"Accipe," pauper ait, "fidei venerabile pignus,
qua nihil in mundo carius esse potest,
quaeque meae fidei spes est, caput et mediatrix,
virgo, Dei genitrix: hanc tibi pono vadem.

because the luxury of riches is unstable and very quickly departs, his unstable luxury and riches went unstably on their way. As is prone to happen when a poor man is suddenly created out of a rich one, he began to suffer great want after his property was taken away. He who previously had been held in reverence by everyone in the city became worthless to all in his city. Everything departs when Fortune departs. When she makes ready a return, everything makes ready to return. Finally he is compelled to seek sustenance at doors as a beggar, so that in his destitution he can at least stay alive. Though the burden of need is always unbearable, it has more severity among fellow townspeople. The penalty for the hardship oppresses doubly: first shame, then poverty that knows no shame, makes for degradation.

All hate him who he used to think loved him. When payouts ceased, prayers counted for nothing. So long as business prospered, he had the reputation for being wise; now, because his wares vanished, he has one for folly. After sounding out many friends—but fair-weather ones—he at last in his need calls for the help of a Jew.

In reply, Abraham (for so he was called) said: "I feel sympathy, sad friend, for your bad luck. If you have a surety or pledge, I will take pity on you in your need, and I will give money of as much weight as you desire. Go and prepare a surety, because I am not willing to trust mere words, nor is that believed by me to be safe."

"Receive," the poor man said, "a revered pledge of my faith, than whom nothing in the world can be dearer, and who is the hope, source, and intercessor of my faith, the Virgin, Mother of God: I offer her as surety for you. The

Nomine sub cuius nulla ratione licebit
fallere, testis erit virgo Maria mihi.
Ista vades vadiumque mihi; pretiosius isto
pignere nil habeo, nil habiturus ero.
Ista meae fidei caput est et conscia voti;
haec etiam pacti testis et obses erit.
Quam violare mihi nulla ratione licebit,
sit, precor, ista loco pigneris atque vadis."
Cogitur assensum precibus praestare petentis
creditor, antiquo ductus amore viri.
Stabat in ecclesia cui nomen Summa Sophia
matris imago <Dei> more dicata loci,
quae tamen in tabula vario vestita colore
artificum manibus picta decenter erat.
Hac igitur statuunt ut fiat imagine coram
virginis hoc pactum, ne violetur idem.
Conveniunt igitur pariter Iudaeus et alter
quo statuere die, quo statuere loco.
Virginis et matris iurat sub nomine pauper
reddere depositum remque carere dolo.
Ille bonae fidei committens cuncta Mariae
mox exponit opes quas sitiebat inops.
Nec mora, perceptis opibus discedit ab urbe
ascensaque rate longius ire parat.
Artis et officii veteris memor, instat emendis
mercibus ut lapsas sic revocaret opes.
Aspirat Fortuna viro; substantia rerum
crescit et excrescit multiplicata nimis,
inque brevi spatio factus de paupere dives
res et opes varias vix numerare potest.

Virgin Mary will be a witness for me, in whose name it will be permitted in no way to deceive. She will be my surety and pledge; I have, and I am going to have, nothing more valuable than this pledge. This woman is the source of my faith and aware of my vow; she will also be the witness and guarantor of the agreement. Let her, whom I may in no way disrespect, take the place, I pray, of a pledge and surety."

The creditor, led by his long-standing love of that man, is compelled to acquiesce in the petitioner's prayers. In the church named Highest Wisdom there stood a likeness of the Mother of God, consecrated to her according to the custom of the place, which had been finely painted by artists' hands on a panel clad in various colors. So then, they specify that this agreement, so that it not be breached, be made before this image of the Virgin.

Well then, the Jew and the other man come together on the day and in the place they appointed. The poor man swears in the name of the Virgin and Mother that he will return the deposit and that the deal is without fraud. That Jew, entrusting everything to the good faith of Mary, immediately makes available the resources that the poor man was craving. Without delay, once he had received the resources he took his leave from the city; boarding a boat, he prepares to go far away. Mindful of his old skill and profession, he devotes himself to buying goods in order to recoup in this way the wealth that had slipped away.

Fortune favors the man; the substance of his property grows and grows, multiplied many times over. And in a short period of time, becoming a rich man from a poor one, he can hardly count his sundry property and riches. Everything

Prospera cuncta viro succedunt, nilque sinistrum
accidit; ad votum cuncta fuere suum.
Ergo redire domum festinat ut omnia solvat
debita Iudaeo faenoris ante diem.
Multa tamen votis obstant contraria iustis,
quodque magis cupimus, tardius omne venit.
Obstat hiems votis. Obstat mare, sidera, venti.
Ventus et unda furens aequoris obdit iter.
Attemptare fretum prohibet sub turbine tanto
ventorum rabies atque procella gravis.
Instat hiems gravior, ventus crebrescit et aurae
spiritus aequoreum saevit in omne solum.
Anxius ille nimis ne fama fidesque laboret,
quam natura negat, invenit arte viam.
Ergo thecam modicam subtili vimine textam
praeparat, imponens credita quaeque sibi.
Hanc etiam proprio studuit signare sigillo,
scripsit et exterius hoc breve carmen, habens:
"Accipe, care meus Abraham, mihi credita quondam,
quae genitrice Dei teste remitto tibi."
Taliter inscriptam ventis committit et undis.
Ne tamen erret, ita virginis orat opem:
"Quae mihi, virgo parens, te sunt vade credita, serva.
Cuncta tuae fidei sunt data, nulla meae.
Quo mihi non licuit nec adhuc licet ire volenti,
transfer opes meritis per freta longa tuis.
Terminus ecce prope solvendi faenoris instat,
quod mihi commissum te quoque teste fuit.

turns out positively for the man, and nothing negative happens; everything was in keeping with his wishes.

Accordingly, he hastens to go back home to pay off all his debts to the Jew before the date for interest payment. Yet many obstacles oppose his righteous wishes; the more we want anything, the slower it comes. Winter weather opposes his wishes. The sea, stars, and winds are opposed. The wind and raging wave of the ocean block his route. The fury of the winds and a severe storm rule out attempting the strait during such a great gale. The rough winter weather presses more violently, the wind intensifies, and blasts of air vent upon the entire ocean surface.

The man, much concerned that his reputation and good credit not suffer, finds by craft a way that nature refuses. Accordingly, he readies a small chest woven of flexible withies, putting into it all that was lent to him. He also took care to mark it with his own seal, and he wrote on the outside this brief poem, reading: "Receive, my dear Abraham, what was formerly loaned to me, which I remit to you, with the Mother of God as my witness."

He entrusts the chest, bearing this inscription, to the winds and waves. Yet so that it would not go astray, he prays as follows for the Virgin's assistance: "Virgin Mother, protect what has been lent to me with you as surety. Everything has been entrusted to your good credit, nothing to mine. Through your merits convey these resources over the long reaches of the sea, where, despite wishing to go, I have not been and still am not allowed to do so. Now see here, the deadline looms near to pay off the debt which was entrusted to me with you indeed as witness.

Sint, precor, ergo tuae fidei commissa soluta,
solvere quo teneor te quoque teste die.
Terra tibi servit, tibi servit et ignis et aer;
et maris unda, precor, serviat ista tibi.
Sidera, terra, mare tibi sunt commissa regenda:
haec quoque committo, virgo Maria, tibi.
Tu rege, tu serva. Sint omnia te duce salva.
Accelerare, precor! Terminus ecce prope!
Te duce serventur, te propitiante per undas
litora certa petant quaque iubentur eant.
Te duce regna petant Constantinopolitana;
te duce percipiat creditor ista meus.
Si bene perveniant illuc, tibi cedet honori.
Si pereant, culpam quis neget esse tuam?
Virgo parensque Dei, quorum tu testis et obses
esque relicta vades, sis, precor, ipsa comes.
Quod potui super his feci nec sufficit illud.
Fac quoque posse tuum sufficietque satis."
Anxius interea nimium Iudaeus ab urbe
litora multotiens incomitatus adit.
Litora lata maris languentia lumina frustra
detinuere diu, spe pereunte sua.
Ventus et unda patent sed puppis in aequore toto
nulla; nec ad votum cernitur ire suum.
Maestus adesse diem queritur quo credita solvi
debuerant nec adest qui sibi solvat ea.
Virginis et matris nomen maledicit et illam
criminis istius asserit esse ream;

Accordingly, I pray, let what has been entrusted to your good credit be discharged on the day, with you indeed as witness, on which I am bound to discharge it.

"The earth serves you, both fire and air serve you; may this sea wave, I pray, serve you too. The heavens, earth, and sea have been entrusted to you for governance; I entrust these items too to you, Virgin Mary. Govern and protect them. May they all be safe with your guidance. Make haste, I pray! Now see here, the deadline is near. May they be protected with your guidance; with your propitious aid may they seek out sure landfall through the waves and go where they are bidden. May they seek out the realm of Constantinople with your guidance; may my creditor receive these with your guidance.

"If they were to arrive there safely, it will redound to your glory. If they were to perish, who would deny that the blame is yours? Virgin and Mother of God, may you yourself, I pray, accompany these things, for which you are witness and guarantor and have been left as surety. I have done what I could regarding them, but it is not enough. You too exert your power and it will be more than enough."

In the meanwhile the Jew, greatly distressed, goes unaccompanied many times from the city to the coast. The broad coastline of the sea occupied his wearying eyes for a long time in vain, as his hope waned. The wind and waves are evident, but on the whole ocean no ship; nor is one perceived moving according to his wish. He laments sadly that the day is near on which the loan should be paid, and no one is at hand to pay it to him.

He curses the name of the Virgin and Mother and declares that she is guilty of this crime; but when he gets ready

cumque redire parat, cernit spumantibus undis
nescio quid modicum quod maris unda trahit.
Leniter appulsum flatu famulante secundo
arripit. Arreptum quid sit et unde videt.
Littera scripta docet cui quis transmiserit illud;
quo duce, quave via venerit unda notat.
Taliter inventa clam tollit clamque reponit,
artius observans ne manifesta forent.
His igitur gestis, tandem cessante procella
grata quies pelago redditur atque solo.
Anxius ad patrias remeare Theodorus oras
rebus dispositis acceleravit iter.
Ventus et unda vocant; ventis dat vela secundis,
limite fluctivago litora nota petens.
Uxor in occursum turba comitante parentum
proruit et populi contio multa sui.
Nec mora, Iudaeus commissa talenta reposcit,
acrius insistens ut cito solvat ea.
Temporis et fidei metas violasse Mariam
arguit, hunc pretio depretiasse suo.
Iste sed econtra se persolvisse talenta
virgine teste sibi dicit; at ille negat.
Lis gravis et longa super his protracta quietem
obtinuit tandem, condicione tamen:
in commune placet veniant ut imaginis ante
vultum quo pactum constituere prius,
quique reposcit opes iuret Iudaeus ab ipso
reddita nulla sibi, reddat et alter ea.
Conveniunt igitur multis comitantibus illuc
quo fuerat finem lis habitura suum.

to return, he perceives on the foaming waves a small unidentified object that the sea swell is carrying along. He seizes it, as it is gently driven ashore by a favoring wind. He sees what he has seized and where it has come from. The written text indicates who sent it to whom; the wave manifests with whose guidance and by what course it came. He stealthily takes up what he discovered in this way and stealthily stores it away, keeping very close watch that it not be revealed.

Then, after he had done these things, as the storm at last dies down, a welcome peace is restored to sea and land. Once his affairs had been put in order, Theodore, anxious to return to his native shores, speeded his passage. The wind and wave summon him; he lets out his sails to favoring winds, seeking a familiar coast on a wave-borne course. His wife, with a throng of relatives accompanying, and a large assembly of his fellow people rushed forth to meet him.

Without delay, the Jew demands back the talents that had been loaned, insisting rather harshly that Theodore quickly pay them back. The Jew accuses Mary of having broken the deadline for the credit—of having defrauded him of his recompense. In rejoinder, Theodore says that he paid the talents off in full, with the Virgin as his witness; but the other denies this. A serious and long-drawn-out dispute about these issues achieved at last a peaceful outcome, but with a proviso: it is resolved jointly that they should come before the face of the image where they earlier established their agreement, and that the Jew who is demanding money back swear that nothing had been returned to him by Theodore and that the other should return it.

Then they come together, with many accompanying them, there where the dispute was about to reach its

Virginis et matris Iudaeus imagine tacta
iurat et abiurat quas habet intus opes.
Talia iuranti subito respondit imago
virginis et matris. Talibus orsa modis,
"Cur mentiris?" ait. "Numquid non plena talentis
me mediante tamen arca reperta fuit?
Quam tibi restitui, per me tibi restituendam
fluctibus in mediis tradidit iste mihi.
Haec tibi nota satis scripto fuit atque sigillo,
quo, cui, quid veheret, quaeve vel unde foret.
Quae solvenda petis, tibi sunt me teste soluta,
haec licet absconsa sint et in aede tua.
Nonne fui praesens in litore quando talenta
quae petis ante tuos attulit unda pedes?
Me sunt teste data, sunt me quoque teste relata
quae dedit unda tibi me tribuente sibi."
Protinus erubuit animo confusus et ore
Iudaeus facti conscius ipse sibi.
Cor stupet, ossa tremunt, rubor et confusio vultus
criminis interpres ore tacente fuit.
Abdita quae celat Iudaeus, imago revelat
et convincit eum criminis esse reum.
Quae detestari, quae non valet infitiari,
omnia Iudaeus detegit, immo Deus.
Protinus ergo sacri baptismi fonte renatus
credidit et sectae plurima turba suae.
Mira rei novitas, subito vulgata per urbis
compita, finitimis fit manifesta locis.

conclusion. The Jew, touching the image of the Virgin and Mother, takes an oath and swears not to have the riches which he has in his possession. As he swore this, the likeness of the Virgin and Mother suddenly replied to him. Beginning in this manner, she said, "Why do you lie? Surely, despite what you say, the coffer filled with talents has been found through my mediation, has it not? The coffer that I have now restored to you, this man handed over to me, to be restored to you with the waves as intermediaries. This was made amply known to you by the text and seal—where it was conveying what for whom, and what it was and from where. The debts that you seek to have discharged have been discharged to you with me as witness, though they are concealed, and in your house.

"Was I not present on the shore when the wave brought before your feet the talents that you seek? They were given with me as witness, they have been returned also with me as witness; the wave gave to you what I consigned to it."

Straightaway the Jew blushed for shame, embarrassed in mind and countenance, aware of what he had done. His heart is stunned, his bones shudder, the blushing and embarrassment of his face were a spokesperson for his misdeed, though his mouth kept silent. The image discloses the secret that the Jew is hiding, and it convicts him as guilty of the misdeed. The Jew, or rather God, uncovers everything that he cannot repudiate, that he cannot deny. Straightaway, accordingly, reborn in the font of sacred baptism, he and a very great throng of his sect became believers.

The miraculous novelty of the matter, immediately broadcast throughout the city's meeting points, becomes well known in neighboring localities. The miraculous nov-

Mira rei novitas populum trahit et patriarcham;
ad novitatis opus sexus uterque ruit.
Res nova, res celebris, celebri res digna relatu
laude nova celebrem contulit esse diem.
Ex hoc ergo die populus Iudaeus ibidem
vilior est habitus huius amore rei,
sicque fide populi crescente, refriguit aestus
gentis barbaricae detumuitque tumor.

De clerico pro puella Deum negante

Arserat illicito correptus amore puellae
clericus a cleri condicione procul.
Otia longa faces primo tribuere furori;
tela secunda dedit desidiosa quies.
Virginis in risu Venus illaqueavit amantis
lumina. Feminea forma fefellit eum.
Nemo quid expediat sed quid iuvet optat amantum;
acrius in vetitum nititur omnis amans.
Omne quod optat amans licitum putat, immo necesse;
nec quodcumque libet non licuisse putat.
Quod cupit et sperat mens obtinuisse laborat
anxia, nunc pretio, nunc prece, nuncque dolo.
Virgo tamen prudens, precibus pretiisque remissis,
depretiat pretio dona precesque suo.
Dona, preces, iuvenem spernit, fugit atque repellit,
indignum reputans huius amore frui.
Dona remissa domum, dolor et despectus amantis
acrius accensas exacuere faces.

elty of the matter attracts the people and the patriarch; people of both sexes rush to see the novel exploit. A novel event, a renowned event, and an event worthy of a renowned narration, with its new praise made the day one to be renowned. Accordingly, from this day forward, out of attachment to this event, the Jewish people there was held in lower esteem, and so, as the people's faith grew, the seething agitation of the barbarous nation cooled and its inflated arrogance deflated.

On a Cleric Denying God for the Sake of a Girl

A cleric, who was far removed from the state of being clerical, had caught fire and burned with unlawful love for a girl. Long periods of inactivity supplied the flames for the first madness; lazy repose provided the second armory. In the virgin's smile, Venus ensnared the lover's eyes. Female beauty led him astray.

Among lovers, no one wishes for what is right but for what brings delight; every lover strives more keenly for what is forbidden. A lover thinks that everything he longs for is allowed—no, even necessary—and does not think that whatever brings pleasure is not allowed. The mind toils anxiously to obtain, now by payment, now by plea, and now by trickery, what it desires and hopes for.

Nevertheless, sending back his pleas and payments, the wise virgin through her own worth treats gifts and pleas as worthless. She spurns gifts, flees pleas, and rebuffs the young man, thinking it unworthy to enjoy his love. The gifts sent back to his home, and the grief and contempt felt by her lover, intensified more keenly the flames that had been

Saucius igne novo novitatis ad arma recurrit,
ignibus illicitis arte parando viam.
Carminibus magicis satagit revocare repulsam
quam nimis indigne sustinuisse dolet.
Quam prece nec pretio valet emollire, nefandis
carminibus studuit sollicitare suis.
Praestigiis igitur et daemonis arte dolosa
instat et instanti fallere fraude parat.
Ars tamen effectu caruit; solitumque vigorem
miratur magicis augur abesse suis;
impatiensque morae, stimulo stimulante furoris,
artibus elisis daemonis orat opem.
Nec mora, daemon adest spondetque cupita libenter,
hac interposita condicione tamen:
"Si cupis," inquit, "amans tibi me praestare quod optas,
te facies servum tempus in omne meum.
Insuper accepta fidei documenta negare
expedit et Christum cum genitrice sua.
Haec sunt quae nostros decet observare ministros;
haec observabis si meus esse cupis."
Clericus "Absit," ait, "Christum sine fine negare
cum genitrice sua; cetera quaeque placent.
Absit enim Christum sanctamque negare Mariam,
omnia si mundi tu mihi regna dares.
Cuncta libens faciam, salvo Deitatis honore
et pariter salva virgine matre Dei."
Qui modo liber erat nullo dominante, maligno
in servum datus est seque subegit ei.
Nox abit et noctis princeps cum nocte recedit,
inflammans animos virginis igne novo.

kindled. Wounded by a new fire, he resorts to arms of a new sort, readying by craft a way for unlawful fires. Through magic spells he busies himself to reverse the rebuff that he grieves to have endured, all too undeservedly. He endeavors to win over with his evil spells the woman whom he can soften by neither plea nor payment. So then, he importunes her with the demon's illusions and treacherous craft, and prepares to lead her astray with importunate deceit. Yet the craft lacks efficacy, and the wizard marvels that his sorcery lacks its accustomed force. Intolerant of delay, prodded by the goad of mad desire, he begs a demon's aid once his own crafts have been crushed.

Without delay, the demon appears and gladly pledges what is desired, but adding this proviso: "If you desire," he says, "for me to furnish you what you as a lover want, you will make yourself my servant for all time. On top of that, it is expedient to deny the received doctrines of faith and Christ along with his mother. These are things that it is proper for our servants to uphold; you will uphold them, if you desire to be mine."

The cleric says, "Perish the thought of denying Christ with his mother unendingly; all the other provisos are acceptable. Perish the thought indeed of denying Christ and holy Mary, even if you should give me all the realms of the world. Everything else I will gladly do, while leaving intact the glory of the Deity and likewise the Virgin Mother of God."

He, who only recently was a free man with no overlord, was given as a serf to the Evil One and subjected himself to him. Night departs and the Prince of Night withdraws along with night, inflaming the virgin's heart with a new fire. The

Clericus in mentem rediit; placuitque repente
qui modo displicuit, qui modo nullus erat.
Forma, decor, probitas, fervens in amore iuventus,
omnia iudicio grata fuere suo.
Paenitet errasse, piget et sprevisse rogantem.
Decertant pariter hinc amor, inde pudor.
Frangit amor vires, torpor gravis occupat artus,
intima consumit ignis amoris edax.
Nox abit insomnis. Suspiria pectus anhelum
crebra trahit, lacrimas fundit ocellus amans.
Lumina, lingua, manus solito viduata vigore
deficiunt. Tristis pallor in ore sedet.
Dissimulando tamen multumque diuque reluctans,
quid patiatur amans dissimulare studet.
Sed color et facies, mentiri nescia morbum
quem fovet, invita dissimulare n<equit>.
Vulnera tecta diu facies macilenta revelat.
Quae sit causa mali pallida membra notant.
Praevaluit tandem penitusque pudore reiecto
vicit et evicit imperiosus amor.
Nec superare valens nec dissimulare furorem,
omnibus exponens quid patiatur, ait,
"En ego iam morior, nisi se mihi clericus ille
iunxerit et voto perfruar ipsa meo.
Huic et non alio me desponsate marito;
omnibus invitis, hunc ego sola sequar.
Hunc et non alium citius date, quaeso, maritum,
ne manus in iugulum saeviat ista meum.
Hic placet, hunc cupio, nihil est mihi dulcius isto:
hunc mihi ne moriar accelerate, precor."

cleric comes back into her mind, and he who just now was displeasing and just now was a nobody suddenly is pleasing to her. His figure, beauty, integrity, and youth, ardent in love, all were pleasing in her judgment. She regrets having made a mistake and is irked at having spurned her suitor. On the one side love and on the other shame struggle together. Love breaks down her self-control, heavy sloth lays hold of her limbs, and the voracious fire of love destroys her inner being.

Sleepless night departs. Her panting breast draws frequent sighs, her loving eye pours forth tears. Eyes, tongue, and hand fail, bereft of their customary vitality. A sad pallor settles on her countenance. Yet by dissembling, and resisting long and hard, the lover strives to disguise why she is suffering. But the color of her face, incapable of concealing the sickness that she harbors, is unwilling and unable to dissemble. Her emaciated face discloses her long-hidden wounds. Her pale limbs make known what the cause is of her illness.

At last, domineering love gained the upper hand and, with shame completely cast aside, defeated and overcame her. Having the strength neither to overmaster nor to dissemble the mad desire, explaining to everyone what she suffers, she says, “See, now I die, unless that cleric unites himself with me and I fully enjoy my desire. Betroth me to this and no other husband; if all are opposed, I will follow this man by myself. Grant me quite swiftly, I beg, this and no other husband, in order that this hand of mine not commit violence against my throat. This man pleases me, this man I desire, nothing is sweeter to me than he: I pray, speedily bring him to me so I not die.”

Talia clamantem tristes rapuere parentes,
artius instantes cesset ut ista loqui.
Vincula, flagra, minas manibus perpessa suorum,
fortius inceptis perstitit illa suis.
Viribus in vacuum consumptis, cura parentum
cedit et assentit victus uterque parens.
Praesulis assensus et dispensatio cleri
quaeritur ut liceat lege coire thori.
Praesul adesse iubet iuvenem ductumque seorsum
convenit et super his quid velit ipse rogat.
Ille licet timide retegit tamen omnia, solis
daemonis exceptis artibus atque dolis.
Cuius in arbitrio mors est et vita rogantis,
pectore, voce, manu praesulis orat opem.
Praesulis assensum meruit qui cuncta meretur
sanguinis et carnis immoderatus amor.
Dispensare quidem pro tempore proque nepote,
praesulis ad tempus quis negat esse pium?
Temperat austerae legis patriarcha rigorem,
proque bono pacis proque nepote suo.
Quicquid praesumit levitas aut impetus irae
praesulis, hoc sanctum dicitur atque pium.
Non est difficilis interprete causa benigno:
praesulis ad nutum pagina quaeque canit.
Praesulis et cleri placet haec sententia cunctis
et toleranda satis ista statuta probant.
Clericus ista probat cupidus, probat ista puella;
subscribit votis laetus uterque suis.
Clericus et clerus bene dispensasse fatentur
pontificem, facti sit nova forma licet.

Her sad parents seized her as she cried out in this way, pressing her severely to desist from saying such things. After enduring shackles, whips, and threats at the hands of her kin, she persevered more strongly in what she had begun. Her concerned parents, their strength exhausted to no avail, gave up and, defeated, both gave assent. The bishop's assent and the clergy's dispensation are sought to allow them to come together by the law of the marriage bed. The bishop orders the young man to appear before him, takes him aside to confer, and asks what he intends in these matters. The youth, though timidly, nevertheless uncovers everything, excepting only the demon's crafts and wiles. He prays with heart, voice, and hand for the help of the bishop, upon whose judgment the life and death of the petitioner depend.

Unrestrained love for flesh and blood, which wins out in everything, won the bishop's assent. Who really can deny that it is rightful during a bishop's period of office, to make a special dispensation for a nephew as the occasion demands? The patriarch moderates the strictness of the stern law, for the good of peace and for his nephew. Whatever the bishop's inconstancy or fit of passion presumes, this is declared holy and dutiful. With a well-disposed advocate, the case is not challenging: every page sings at the bishop's beck and call.

This verdict of the bishop and clergy is agreeable to everyone, and they approve these ordinances as perfectly admissible. The cleric, filled with desire, approves them, the girl approves them; the two each happily confirm their vows. The cleric and clergy declare that the bishop made a proper dispensation, though the type of action is new. On

Nubere virginibus post votum virginitatis
ordinibusque sacris hac ratione licet.
Venerat ergo dies quo nubere nympha marito
debuit atque viri virgo subire thorum;
mysteriisque sacris solemni more peractis
indulgent variis potibus atque cibis.
Hinc hymenaea vocant, vario sonat aula tumultu,
exhilarat facies organa, vina, dapes.
Turba ministrorum iucunda ministrat abunde
omnibus ad votum singula quaeque satis.
Pronus ad occasum iam sol vergebat et umbras
crescere declinans fecerat orbe suo.
Sed fugiente die iuvenis meminisse Mariae
coepit et horarum virginis esse memor.
Restat adhuc nona soliti solvenda tributi
quae solito nondum more soluta fuit.
Hanc sibi subripuit, reliquas cum psalleret horas,
missa sacerdotis accelerata nimis.
Tardior hora monet ne plus tardando moretur,
si placet, et solita solvere vota velit.
Oblitum solitam solitus monet usus ad horam,
quem tamen ex facili dedidicisse nequit.
Usus et hora vocant solitum persolvere pensum:
serior hora rogat, imperat usus ei.
Haec vocat, ille monet; rogat haec, iubet ille. Coactus
tum prece, tum monitis, quo vocat usus abit
dumque vetus iuveni praeiudicat usus amori
cogitur hic sperni, cogitur ille coli.

this basis it is allowable for virgins and those in holy orders to wed after a vow of virginity.

Accordingly, the day came on which the bride was due to wed her groom and the virgin to enter her husband's marriage bed. After the holy sacraments had been completed with customary solemnity, they indulge in various foods and drinks. Next they give voice to wedding songs, the hall resounds with a variety of revelry, and musical instruments, wines, and fine fare gladden countenances. An agreeable throng of servants serves absolutely everything in abundance, to satisfy everyone's wish.

Now the sun was sloping downward to its setting, and as it grew lower in the sky, in its course it caused the shadows to increase. But as the day took flight, the young man began to recall Mary and to be mindful of the Hours of the Virgin. Of the customary tribute, the hour of Nones, which he has not yet performed in the accustomed manner, remains still to be performed. Though he chanted the rest of the hours, the priest's Mass, sped up too much, stole this one away from him.

The belated hour suggests, if it is acceptable, that he not waste time by delaying further and that he be ready to perform his accustomed prayers. At the customary hour his accustomed practice, which despite everything he cannot readily unlearn, prompts him, though neglectful. His practice and the hour call him to perform his accustomed duty: the belated hour asks, his practice commands him. The hour calls, the practice prompts; the hour asks, the practice orders. Compelled by both prayer and promptings, he goes off where practice calls. As long-established practice outweighs young love, the latter is compelled to be spurned, the former to be performed.

Nox cita, virgo recens, venerisque coaeva iuventus
causantur subitas has in amore moras;
dumque novum subito vincit vetus usus amorem,
cedit amor quoniam vim facit usus ei.
Hinc vulgi strepitum fugiens populique tumultum,
clericus ecclesiae limina solus adit
inceptaque diu dilata virginis hora,
altaris supplex sternitur ante gradum.
Verba soporifero clauserunt lumina somno:
vox et verba silent, lumina somnus habet.
Nec mora, virgo parens, aspectu torva minaci,
astitit, inquirens an sibi nota foret.
Quo respondente quia non cognosceret illam,
illa refert, "Ego sum virgo parensque Dei.
Virgo Dei genitrix ego sum, de qua modo nonam
cantabas, quam tu despicis atque fugis.
Virgo Maria potens ego sum regina polorum,
cuius amore frui spernis amore novo.
Me quasi nulla forem novitatis amore repellis;
sed patior, novitas dum placet ista tibi.
Maesta tamen doleo quod me pro paelice spernis.
Spernor, et in thalamum ducitur illa meum;
quodque magis doleo, specie seductus inani
spernis coniugium pro meretrice meum.
Numquid me melior, numquid me pulchrior illa?
Pulchrior et melior haec est visa tibi?
Cur tibi vilis ego, vel cur despecta videri
debeo? Sumne minus casta minusve decens?
A puero tibi sum casto sociata tenore
et specialis amor te dedit esse meum.

The swift passing of night, the newly won maiden, and youth, the age suited for lovemaking, protest against these unexpected delays in love. As a long-established practice suddenly overcomes a new love, love yields, because practice overpowers it. And so, fleeing the hubbub of the common folk and the uproar of the people, the cleric approaches the threshold of the church by himself, and after beginning the long-deferred hour of the Virgin, as a suppliant he prostrates himself before the steps of the altar. The words closed his eyes in drowsy slumber: his voice and words fall silent, sleep takes possession of his eyes.

Without delay, the Virgin Mother, stern with a menacing demeanor, stood near, inquiring whether she was familiar to him. When he replies that he does not recognize her, she answers, "I am the Virgin and Mother of God. I am the Virgin Mother of God, concerning whom you were just now chanting Nones, but whom you despise and flee. I am the Virgin Mary, powerful queen of the heavens, whose love you scorn to enjoy, because of a new love. For love of novelty you reject me, as if I were nothing; but I tolerate it, so long as that novelty pleases you. All the same, I am saddened and grieve because you scorn me for a mistress. I am scorned, and she is led into my marriage chamber. What grieves me more, led astray by hollow beauty, you scorn marriage with me for a prostitute.

"Can it be said that she is better than I, more beautiful than I? Did this woman appear more beautiful and better to you? Why should I appear cheap to you, or why despised? Am I less chaste or less becoming? From your boyhood, I have been united in chaste observance with you, and a special bond of love made you mine. But now I am despised and

Sed modo despicior et pro meretrice repellor,
spernor et intuitu turpis amoris ego.
Vincula coniugii novitatis amore resolvis.
Desipis et sponsus desinis esse meus.
Displicet illa mihi quia me tibi displicuisse
fecit et antiquum vicit amore novo.
Noster amor castus nec daemonis arte petitus.
Hic perit, at noster non periturus erat.
Quem mihi delegi, raptum tenet altera sponsum.
Sum vetus, illa nova. Me magis illa placet.
Sed si virgo parens ego sum quam praedicat orbis,
ultio non deerit, si volo, crede mihi.
Numquid non potero citius punire reatum,
quae Christum peperi, si mihi poena placet?
Si matrem Christi mundo me constat haberi,
numquid non potero quatenus ista luas?"
Talibus auditis, timor et tremor occupat artus;
vix quoque pro multis pauca locutus ait:
"O Deitatis amor, o mundi gloria sola,
quae paris absque pari, virgo parensque Dei,
mater ubique potens, mitissima virgo Maria,
etsi non merui, mitis adesto mihi!
Non ego te fugio, nec te fugiendo relinquo;
sed sequor atque sequar tempus in omne meum;
sumque fuique tuus et ero per saecula. Solam,
si placet, hanc noxam, virgo, remitte mihi,
quodque magis vereor, quia me mea crimina terrent,
daemonis insidias destrue, tolle, preme.
Eripe, ne peream, me daemonis a dominatu,
cedat et illius vis violenta tibi.

rejected for a prostitute, and I am scorned out of consideration for a vile love. For a newfangled love you undo the bonds of marriage. You are losing your wits and cease to be my betrothed. That woman displeases me, because she caused me to displease you and outdid an old love with a new one. Our love is chaste and not courted by a demon's craft. That love is perishable, but ours was not going to perish. Another has seized and possesses the betrothed I chose for myself. I am an old love, she is a new one. She is more pleasing than I. But if I am the Virgin Mother whom the world proclaims, believe me, my retribution will not fail, if I so desire. Will I, who bore Christ, not be able swiftly to punish the offense, if punishment is to my liking? If it is established that I am acknowledged Christ's mother by the world, will I not have in my power to have you atone for these things?"

As he heard such words, fear and trembling lay hold of his limbs. Likewise, with difficulty he spoke a few words rather than many: "Oh God's love, oh the world's sole glory, you who without equal give birth, Virgin and Mother of God, universally powerful mother, gentlest Virgin Mary, even if I have not deserved it, stand gently by me! I do not flee you, nor in flight abandon you; but I follow and will follow for all my days; I am and have been and will be yours throughout all ages. If it please you, pardon me, Virgin, this single offense; and, what I dread more, because my misdeeds terrify me, demolish, remove, and suppress the demon's schemes. For fear that I die, snatch me away from the demon's dominion, and let his fierce violence yield to you.

Me mihi subripuit propriae violentia carnis
multiplicesque doli daemonis arte sua.
Me mihi subripuit fera pessima faxque furoris,
femina: sed, fateor, causa cupido fuit.
Traxit amor cupidum, species seduxit amantem;
materiam morbo dura repulsa dedit.
Aetatis levitas confusa, repulsa pudore,
dum voluit vires vincere, victa subit.
Actus abest; voluisse piget, quia sola voluntas
sufficit et poenam promeruisse potest.
Corde quidem volui, sed non pervenit ad actum
velle meum; satis est me voluisse tamen.
Peste venenifera totum corrumpere corpus
fermenti modicum contaminando solet.
Paenitet, excessi: miserere, piissima Christi
intemerata parens virgo Maria, mihi."
Plura loqui prohibent gemitus, suspiria, planctus,
quaeque fluunt lacrimae fontis ad instar aquae.
Virgo sed a lacrimis cessare piissima iussit
visaque post modicum mitior inquit ei,
"Pone metum, lacrimas, gemitum, suspiria, planctum.
Sunt satis ad praesens ista; futura time.
Prima quidem gravis est graviorque ruina secunda
esse solet. Satis est te cecidisse semel.
Neve per illicitos rursus rapiaris amores,
amplius illicitis abstinuisse stude.
Quae tibi causa mei, quid amor, quid pignus amoris,
ex operum fructu res cito scire dabit.
Facta fidem verbis facient, si forte sequantur;
pendet in arbitrio res tamen ista tuo.

The violence of my own flesh and the manifold wiles of the demon by his craft stole me from myself. Woman, worst of wild beasts and the inflamer of frenzy, stole me from myself: but, I admit, the motivation was desire. Love attracted my desire, beauty seduced me as lover; a hard rebuff provided the fuel for my illness.

"The inconstancy of age was confused and recoiled in shame; it suffers defeat even as it wished to defeat the strength of its feelings. Action is absent, but it is painful just to have wanted, because wanting alone is enough and capable of deserving punishment. To be sure, I wished in my heart, but my wish did not arrive at the action; still, to have wanted is enough.

"A little leaven is accustomed to defile a whole body by polluting it with its venomous virus. I regret, I transgressed: take pity on me, most pious Mother of Christ, unblemished Virgin Mary."

Groaning, sighs, lamentations, and tears that flow like water from a fountain prevent him from speaking more. But the most pious Virgin ordered him to desist from tears and, seeming gentler after a little while, said to him, "Lay aside your fear, tears, groaning, sighs, and lamentation. For the present these are enough; fear events to come. A first downfall is certainly serious, but a second is accustomed to be more so. It suffices for you to have fallen once. So that you are not swept away again into unlawful loves, strive to refrain any more from the unlawful ones. From the outcome of my actions, events will swiftly allow you to know what my purpose is with respect to you, what my love is, and what the token of that love is. My deeds will lend credence to my words, if they chance to follow; yet this outcome depends

Ne tamen hoc facias quasi nolens atque coactus,
liber es atque tui iuris, ut esse soles.
Omnis enim leviter, vel quem simulatio fingit
vel timor extorquet, adnihilatur amor.
Hoc tamen, hoc unum certo tibi certius esse
noveris et super his ne dubitare velis,
quod nisi paeniteas et ab his citius resipiscas,
puniet excessus ultio digna tuos."
Transiit his dictis tristemque reliquit amantem,
splendida stellifero stella recepta polo.
Territus expavit iuvenis vultumque repente
et color et sanguis deseruere suum;
utque solent fragiles quas vellit ab arbore frondes
vis violenta Noti, sic sua membra tremunt.
Corporis ebibitum testantur membra cruorem,
frigidiora gelu, pallidiora croco.
Ardor abit veneris carnisque refriguit omnis
aestus et illicitae condicionis amor.
Conscius omnis abest, nisi mens quae conscia sola
criminis imprimis prima remordet eum;
dumque sui secum causamque modumque reatus
discutit, ulterius displicet ipse sibi.
Accelerans igitur, vicinas praesulis aedes
intrat et illius se iacit ante pedes.
Visa refert seriemque rei totius ad unguem
explicat, interpres criminis ipse sui.
Intima deficiunt, vires dolor ebibit omnes.
Nil nisi flere iuvat: hoc licet hocque libet.
Quam sit amarus amor et quam sit amoris amarus
exitus illiciti, res manifesta probat.

on your judgment. Yet so that you do not do this as if unwilling and coerced, you are free and independent, as you are accustomed to be. For every love that either pretense feigns or fear extorts is readily reduced to nothing. Yet be aware that this thing, this one thing, for certain, is quite certain for you, and on this matter have no doubt: that unless you repent and from this behavior return swiftly to your senses, a worthy retribution will punish your transgressions."

After saying these things, she passed on to be welcomed as a shining star in starry heaven, and left behind the sad lover. The panic-stricken young man turned pale, and at once both color and blood left his countenance; and his limbs quiver just as frail fronds are accustomed to do that the brutal force of the south wind tears from a tree. His limbs, colder than ice, paler than saffron, give evidence that the blood has been drained from his body. The heat of sexual impulse departs, and all passion of the flesh and love of a forbidden nature grew cold.

Everyone aware of his sin is absent, apart from the mind which, alone aware of it, first and foremost gnaws at him. As he examines within himself the motivation and manner of his sin, he finds fault with himself even more. So making haste, he enters the bishop's church nearby and throws himself before his feet. He relates the vision and, informing on his own misdeed, unfolds the sequence of the whole affair completely. His inner being grows faint, grief drains all his strength.

Nothing but weeping helps: this is permitted, and this brings pleasure. The affair, once revealed, demonstrates how bitter love is and how bitter the outcome of unlawful

Tristis et exsanguis, commissa piacula plorans,
plangit et in lacrimas totus abire parat.
Sic igitur saevos compescuit ignibus ignes,
incestos castis continuosque novis.
Flebilis astantem cunctum cum praesule clerum
ad lacrimas lacrimis compulit ipse suis.
Protinus illiciti placet in commune resolvi
foedera coniugii factaque nulla fore.
Irrita quaeque fore decernit et absque vigore
praesulis et cleri contio tota simul.
Pactio turpis erat, et fraus sub imagine veri
nec de post facto convaluisse potest.
Solvitur illicitus iuvenum consensus utrique;
alter ab alterutro dissociatus abit.
Nexibus illicitis iusta ratione solutis
clericus ecclesiae redditur, illa patri.
Virtutum studio vitae commissa prioris
mox statuit redimi redditus ipse sibi.
Actibus illicitis animi virtute repressis,
se premit et licita vix licuisse licet.
Ne caro consurgat viresque recolligat ignis,
asperitate gravi membra domare studet.
Vimine, veste, cibo carnem macerando rebellem,
singula defraudat membra vigore suo.
Erudit ad lacrimas oculos risumque refrenat.
Debilitat vires somnus et esca brevis.
Spiritus in tenui vix corpore solus anhelans
palpitat et vitam mortis imago premit.
Iam sine carne caro, corpus sine corpore; mundum,
sit licet in mundo, deseruisse putes.

love. Sad and utterly devoid of vitality, mourning the sins he has committed, he laments and prepares to give himself over entirely to tears. So then, he checked fierce fires with fires, unchaste with chaste ones, and long-running with new ones. Weeping, by his tears he drove to tears all the clergy standing close with the bishop.

Straightaway, it meets general approval that the bonds of unlawful matrimony be dissolved and annulled. The whole assembly of the bishop and clergy together determines them all to be entirely null and void. The compact was disgraceful, and deceit in the guise of truth cannot become valid even after the fact. The unlawful agreement is dissolved for both the two young people; each goes off divorced from the other. When the unlawful bonds were justly dissolved, the cleric is restored to the Church, the young woman to her father.

Restored to himself, the young man soon resolves that the misdeeds of his former life be redeemed through the zealous pursuit of virtues. After his unlawful deeds were quashed by spiritual virtue, he brings himself under control, and even what is lawful is hardly allowed to be allowable. So that the flesh not experience a resurgence and the fire regain strength, he strives to subdue his body parts through severe austerity. Mortifying the insubordinate flesh with rods, clothing, and food, he deprives every body part of its strength. He trains his eyes to tears and reins in laughter. Scant sleep and food weaken his strength. His breathing, all that is left in his gaunt body, hardly a body at all, falters in labored panting, and the appearance of death overwhelms life. Now there is flesh without flesh, body without body; you would think that, though still in the world, he had forsaken it.

Talibus intentus, extremi temporis horam
sedulus exspectat sollicitusque timet.
Qua veniente tamen, cum iam de corpore mortis
spiritus ad vitam progrederetur ovans,
visa palam nivea morientis ab ore columba
exit, inoffenso tramite summa petens.
Sicque solutus abit carnis de carcere liber
spiritus, angelicis raptus ad astra choris.
Sic abit eductus de valle necis tenebrosa
clericus ad vitam, virgine matre duce.

<*De abbatissa praegnante*>

Plurima cum revocent tendentis ad ardua gressum,
fortius obsistunt spiritus atque caro.
Lis gravis et longa nimis est redivivaque semper
quae solet in carnis condicione geri.
Bella timenda magis quaecumque domesticus hostis
sub specie pacis continuare solet.
Saepe quidem vincit, sed raro vincitur. Unde
fortius exsurgens rursus ad arma ruit.
Moribus et gestis fuit abbatissa venustis,
virginei custos formaque facta gregis.
De sibi commissis ovibus studiosa regendis,
artius instituit se prius ipsa regi,
quoque magis timidam reddenda de ratione
hinc et sollicitam contigit esse magis.
Saepius ad mentem revocans quid culmen honoris
exigat, officii fit memor ipsa sui.
Non quis honos, set quod sit onus dum pensat honoris,
hunc fugit, illius pondera saeva timet.

Concentrating upon such matters, he waits attentively and fears anxiously the final hour of death. Yet when it comes, when the spirit was now setting forth rejoicing to life from the mortal body, a snowy-white dove is clearly seen going out from the mouth of the dying man, seeking the heights on an unobstructed path. The spirit, released in this way, free, departs from the prison of the flesh, carried off to the stars by angelic choirs. In this way the cleric departs, led forth to life from the dark valley of death, with the Virgin Mother as guide.

On the Pregnant Abbess

Though very many factors hold back the progress of someone aiming for the heights, the spirit and flesh resist most strongly. The dispute that is customarily waged in the condition of the flesh is very long and serious, and constantly renewed. Especially to be feared are all wars that the familiar foe is accustomed to prolong under the guise of peace. He often conquers, but he is seldom conquered. Rising up more strongly from such a reverse, he rushes again to arms.

An abbess possessed a graceful character and actions, and she had become the guardian and model for a virgin flock. Zealous about governing the sheep entrusted to her, she laid it down that she first should be governed more stringently; but it happened that the more fearful she became about the reckoning to be rendered, the more anxious because of this she became too.

Time and again calling to mind what the summit of glory demands, she becomes mindful of her own office. As she ponders not what the honor is but what the onus of the honor is, she flees the first and fears the harsh weight of the

Hinc praelatorum quae pro mercede laborum
praemia dantur avet; inde pericla timet.
Cogitat assidue quia quo gradus altior omnis,
quaelibet hinc gravior esse ruina solet,
dumque nimis rigida studet ordinis esse magistra,
seque gregemque gravat, prima rigore suo.
Invidiae stimulos rigor immoderatus et iram
excitat inque brevi plurima corda replet.
Ira, parens odii subitique ministra furoris,
semina discidii germinat atque fovet.
Hinc maledicta minas parit et dissentio rixas;
vixque suo capiti membra subesse sinit.
Foedera dirumpit zelus indiscretus amoris
et nimium rigida regula damna parit,
dumque sub austera regitur caro religione,
corporis et mentis paxque quiesque perit.
Nec tamen illa minus coeptis desistit, at illud
quod semel incepit fortius usque tenet;
nilque remittendum concepti dura rigoris
aestimat; immo magis addere plura studet.
Viderat haec postquam totum qui circuit orbem,
protinus invidit spiritus ille malus,
quaque putat fieri citius leviusque quod optat,
hac magis insistit viribus atque dolis.
Et quia mortalis naturam condicionis
infirmam didicit, fortius arma capit
quosque quibus vitiis cognovit saepe vacare,
amplius hos aliis sollicitare studet.

second. On the one hand, she craves the rewards that are given as compensation for the labors of prelates; on the other, she fears the dangers. She thinks constantly that the higher each step is, the more severe any downfall from it is accustomed to be. As she strives to be an overstrict mistress of the order, she weighs heavily on herself and her flock, leading in her severity. Untempered severity sets in motion the goads of hostility and anger, and in a short time fills very many hearts.

Anger, the parent of hate and the attendant of sudden madness, germinates and nurtures the seeds of dissent. From this situation, cursed disagreement gives birth to threats and quarrels, and it scarcely permits the limbs to be subject to their head.

Indiscriminate zeal bursts apart the pacts of love, and an overstrict rule gives birth to harmful consequences. As the flesh is ruled over by severe religious practice, the peace and tranquility of the body and mind die. Yet she desists not at all from her undertakings, but holds even more strongly to what she once undertook. In her strictness, she reckons that nothing should be slackened in the severity she has adopted; on the contrary, she is keen to increase it even more.

After he who traverses the entire globe had seen these things, straightaway that evil spirit grew hostile, and wherever he thinks that what he desires can be achieved more swiftly and easily, there he presses on more with force and wiles. Because he has learned that the nature of the mortal state is weak, he takes up arms more vigorously. He is eager to harass more than others those who, he has recognized, give themselves over to these vices. And because he sees

Et quia femineum sexum corpusque tenellum
quemlibet ad lapsum pronius esse videt,
luxuriae stimulos caecosque libidinis ignes
virginis in mente suscitat arte sua.
Incipit ergo rudis rudibus subiecta ligari
legibus et cursum dedidicisse suum.
Lumina, lingua, manus solita gravitate relicta
mirantur studia deseruisse sua.
Uritur igne novo, subito succensa calore,
cum tamen ignoret quidve vel unde sit hoc.
Mitior est solito multoque remissius instat
ordinis officio, mitis amore novo.
Quod prius austera nulla ratione volebat
sustinuisse, modo sustinet atque probat.
Quod damnare prius quod et exhorrere solebat,
nunc minus est odio quam fuit ante sibi.
Ergo quod affectat, stimulo stimulante furoris,
nocte dieque studet conciliare sibi.
Incidit in iuvenem tandem—miseranda iuventus!—
concipiens utero crimen onusque suo.
Criminis admissi mentem dum culpa remordet,
mitior atque minus imperiosa manet.
Dissimulando diu, multa gravitate reatum
texerat et facti conscia rara fuit.
Tecta diu latuit, astutia sed mulieris
quid non percipiat calliditate sua?
Quid patiatur amans vel quo patiatur amore
percipit a simili condicione sui.
Haec vultus varios, varias notat illa diaetas.
Haec somno gravidam percipit, illa gradu.

that the female sex and a delicate body are more susceptible to falling of any kind, by his craft he arouses the impulses of lechery and the hidden fires of lust in the maiden's mind.

Accordingly, she in an unfamiliar role begins to be bound in subjection to unfamiliar laws and to unlearn her routine. Her eyes, tongue, and hand, their customary dignity forsaken, marvel at having abandoned their usual pursuits. Inflamed with sudden heat, she is burned by a new fire, though even so she does not know what or from where it is.

She is gentler than usual and, gentle because of her new love, insists much more laxly on the duties of the order. She tolerates and approves now what previously in her sternness she wished on no account to countenance. What previously she would condemn and shudder at, now is less a cause of loathing for her than it was before. So, as the goad of madness pricks her, day and night she is eager to win over to herself what she aspires to have. At length she throws herself upon a young man—oh pitiable youth!—in the process conceiving in her womb a sin and burden. As the guilt of the sin she has committed gnaws at her mind, she becomes gentler and less demanding.

Dissembling for a long time, she had concealed her offense with much austerity and rarely was any sister aware of her crime. For a long time she escaped notice in her concealment, but what can a woman's cunning in its subtlety not detect? From its similar nature it detects what she suffers as a lover, or even from what love she suffers. One sister observes her changing appearance, another her changing choices of food. One detects that she is pregnant by

Singula signa notant; quae postquam consona cernunt,
quod prius audierant, verius esse putant.
Et color et facies et quae male cetera produnt
viscera praegnantis signa fuere satis.
Laeta quod ulcisci se contio tota sororum
posset et optatum tempus adesse videns,
quatenus accedant et certius experiantur
an ita sit, clerum pontificemque rogat.
Obstupefactus ad haec, clerus cum praesule certum
quo veniant statuunt ista probare diem.
Quod postquam miserae miseras pervenit ad aures,
ingemuit graviter, tacta dolore gravi.
Anxia quid faciat, cui se committat, et unde
postulet auxilium, nescit amara nimis,
quodque sui sexus proprium primo solet esse,
solvitur in lacrimas, sola relicta sibi.
Cum sit utrumque grave, graviter formidat utrumque:
hinc gregis insidias, praesulis inde minas.
Omnibus exosa, cunctorum sola favorem
maesta (nec immerito) demeruisse videt.
Ante diem partus sic parturiendo dolores
fit velut in partu deperitura parens.
Singula dum memorat et secum sola retractat,
unica spes superest de genitrice Dei.
Hanc et non aliam solam superesse Mariam
quam cupit ad veniam conspicit esse viam.
Ergo recepta loco quo multiplicare Mariae
illud dulcisonum saepe solebat "Ave,"

her sleeping, another by her gait. They observe all the individual symptoms; after they see those are in agreement, they think what they had heard earlier to be even truer. Coloring, complexion, and the other things that tellingly betray the womb of a pregnant woman were sufficient evidence.

The whole assembly of sisters, happy that it could avenge itself and seeing that the longed-for opportunity was drawing near, asks the clergy and bishop to come and to find out by experience for certain whether it is so. Shocked by these matters, the clergy along with the prelate set a definite date on which to come to examine them.

After this reached the wretched ears of the wretched woman, she groaned deeply, touched by intense sorrow. Deeply distressed, in her anxiety she does not know what to do, to whom to entrust herself, and from where to entreat aid. When left alone to herself, she dissolves into tears, as is a first recourse customarily characteristic of her sex. Since both are grave, she fears each of them grievously, the schemes of her flock on the one hand, the threats of the prelate on the other. Detestable to all, alone, and mournful, she sees that (not undeservedly) she has forfeited the favor of all. In this way, by giving birth to pains before the day of childbirth, she becomes like a mother who will die in childbirth.

As she recalls and reflects within herself on everything, the only remaining hope is in the Mother of God. She realizes that this woman and no other, Mary alone, remains as a route to the forgiveness she desires. Accordingly, after being admitted to the place where she was accustomed often to repeat for Mary that sweet-sounding "Hail, Mary,"

materiam verbis causa praestante doloris,
  taliter optatam virginis optat opem:
"O sine sola pari, quae virgo parensque vocari
  sola potes, solam respice, virgo parens.
Hanc peccatricem, peccati nescia sola,
  respice respectu quo potes atque soles.
Sordidior cunctis, sceleratior omnibus una,
  en ego sum quam tu solvere sola potes.
O pia, postque Deum miseris spes prima salutis,
  da, precor, auxilium consiliumque mihi.
Quam mihi nemo potest nisi tu, largire salutem,
  quam sim sola videns quamque relicta tibi.
O sine qua nullus et per quam quisque fidelis
  sperat opem veniae, virgo parensque, veni!
Virginitatis honos, decus et decor o mulierum,
  offensum placidum redde, benigna, Deum.
Te moveant gemitus, lacrimae, suspiria, planctus;
  nec memor admissi criminis esse velis.
O sine fine pia, mitissima virgo Maria,
  virgo parensque Dei digna, memento mei.
Sim licet horribili polluta libidinis aestu
  sed quasi sus foedo contaminata luto,
tu tamen una potes meritis precibusque benignis
  me miseram nato conciliare tuo.
Mater ab instanti poteris tu sola pudore
  si placet eruere meque iuvare modo.
Virgo parens, hodie si me salvaveris, ipsam
  me tibi devoveo tempus in omne meum."
Talia deplorans, modicum soporata quievit,
  fletibus irriguis lumina fessa rigans.

the occasion of her grief supplies the subject for her words, and she prays in the following fashion for the aid of the Virgin she longed for:

"Oh you, alone without peer, who alone can be called Virgin and Mother, have regard for me in my loneliness, Virgin Mother. You, who alone are unknowing of sin, have regard for this sinner with attention as you are able and accustomed to do. Behold, fouler than everyone else, a single person more wicked than all others, I am one whom you alone can release. Oh benevolent one, after God the first hope of salvation for the wretched, grant aid and counsel to me, I pray. Bestow on me the salvation that no one but you can, seeing how alone and how abandoned to you I am. Come, oh Virgin and Mother, without whom no one hopes for the blessing of forgiveness, and through whom every one of the faithful has such hope! Oh glory of virginity, honor and ornament of women, kindly one, render God indulgent, whom I have offended. Let groans, tears, sighs, and lamentations move you, and do not be mindful of the offense committed. Oh endlessly benevolent, gentlest Virgin Mary, Virgin and worthy Mother of God, remember me.

"Though I have been defiled by the dreadful fire of lust, and what is more, polluted like a sow by foul mud, yet through your merits and kindly prayers you alone can reconcile wretched me with your son. Mother, you alone, if it pleases you, can rescue me from the looming shame and can help me now. Virgin Mother, if you save me today, I dedicate myself to you for all my time."

Lamenting in these words, she rested for a while in sleep, watering her tired eyes with the water of weeping. Without

Nec mora, spiritibus mater comitata duobus
astitit angelicis, talibus orsa modis:
"En ego virgo parens, quam tu miseranda vocasti;
en adsum, precibus sollicitata tuis;
en ego, quam fueras multumque diuque secuta,
grata comes, grata dum tua vita foret.
Nonne sacrata Deo vitam cum veste professa
virginitatis eras meque pudica sequi?
Foedera rupisti quibus agno iuncta fuisti,
ut sequereris eum munda sequendo Deum.
Irrita fecisti quaecumque Deo pepigisti,
dum sine lege ruis, legibus usa tuis.
Irrita sunt facta tua vota priora, subacta
carne tua vitiis luxuriaeque viis.
Sed quia sum memorum memor indefessa meorum,
non possum meriti non memor esse tui.
Hac vice subveniam nec dura nimis tibi fiam,
<detur> ut ad veniam me duce nosse viam.
Noveris ergo Deum tibi dimisisse reatum
quodque petis tibi me subveniente datum."
Dixit et exceptum puerum de ventre parentis
angelicis manibus misit ab urbe procul,
hoc in mandatis vicino dans eremitae
ut puerum foveat instituatque bene
donec septennis factus maioribus aptus
esse queat studiis tunc adhibendus eis,
sicque levans gravidam furtiva prole parentem,
virgo parensque Dei talia rursus ait:
"Praesulis ecce timor, populi pudor, ira sororum
morbi materia depereunte perit.

delay, the mother, accompanied by two angelic spirits, stood near and began to speak in the following manner: "See me, the Virgin Mother, whom you in your wretchedness summoned; see, I am here, petitioned by your prayers; see me, whom you followed long and greatly, an agreeable companion, so long as your life was agreeable. Consecrated to God, did you not make vow of a life of virginity, along with the nun's habit, and of following me chastely? You broke the covenants by which you were joined to the lamb, to follow him in your purity while following God. You rendered void whatever you pledged to God, as you rushed lawlessly to ruin, following your own laws. Your previous vows have become void, as your flesh has been made subject to vices and to the paths of lechery. But because I am untiringly mindful of those mindful of me, I cannot be unmindful of your merit. On this occasion I will support you and not become overharsh to you, so that you may be permitted to know with my guidance the way to forgiveness. Accordingly, know that God has pardoned your crime and that what you seek with my support has been granted you."

She spoke and, taking the child from his mother's belly, sent him by angelic hands far from the city, giving to a nearby hermit this as a command, that he should watch over the child and raise him well until, after turning seven years old and becoming suited for more advanced studies, he could then be given over to them. So unburdening the pregnant mother of her illegitimate son, the Virgin and Mother of God again speaks with the following words:

"Behold, once the substance of the sickness perishes, the prelate's fear, people's shame, and sisters' anger will perish

Quicquid in instanti timuisti ferre pericli,
en ego deposui compatiendo tibi;
iamque nihil superest, nisi quod redimendo reatum
de reliquo studeas vivere casta Deo.
Criminis admissi semper memorando, studeto
virtutes vitiis opposuisse tuis.
Nec nimium rigidam, sed nec nimis esse remissam
expedit, at mediam tuta teneto viam.
Sit moderata tui discreti norma rigoris.
Non tibi sed reliquis mitior esse velis.
Qualiter alterius et quam cito te misereri
conveniat, docui prima miserta tui."
Dixit et abscedens tristem laetamque relinquens
scandit ad aetherei lumina clara poli.
Surgit at illa celer, veteri gravitate relicta
qua graviter gravidam contigit esse diu;
cumque novi partus vestigia nulla manerent,
miratur partus de novitate sui.
Absque dolore quidem nec visceribus patefactis,
contra naturam se peperisse videt.
Qualiter intacta puer est exceptus ab alvo,
nec sensisse potest nec ratione capit.
Venerat ergo dies causae praefixus eidem,
venerat et populus urbis ad illud idem.
Sederat hinc praesul iudex, stetit inde sororum
turba procax, dictis exhibitura fidem.
Affuit et timida nimis abbatissa, Mariam
patronam causae constituendo suae.
Quam procul aspectam statim secedere iussit
praesul ab aspectu. Cesserat illa cito

too. Whatever danger you feared to suffer at that moment, see, I have removed in taking pity on you; and now nothing is left, except that in the remaining time you should strive in redeeming the sin to live chastely for God. Always remembering the offense you have committed, strive to pit virtues against your vices. It is beneficial to be neither too strict nor too lax, but to hold safely to the middle way. Let the rule of your discerning strictness be restrained. Be gentler not to yourself but to others. By first pitying you, I have demonstrated how it is appropriate that you pity another and how quickly."

So she spoke and, in her departure leaving the woman both sad and happy, she ascends to the bright lights of the celestial heavens. And then the abbess swiftly rises, the former heaviness abandoned with which she happened for a long time to be heavily pregnant. Since no traces remain of the new form of childbirth, she marvels at the novelty of her birthing. Without pain and without her uterus being laid open, she sees that she gave birth contrary to nature. How the child was taken from her untouched womb, she neither can perceive by her senses nor grasp by reason.

Then the day set in advance for the lawsuit under discussion had come, and the people of the city had come too for that same event. On this side sat the prelate as judge, on that stood the assertive throng of nuns, to give credence to the words. Also present in great fear was the abbess, appointing Mary as advocate for her suit. When the bishop sighted her a long way off, he ordered her to withdraw immediately from his sight. She quickly retired. Sending two

transmittensque duos ad eam de more ministros,
   certius inquiri singula quaeque iubet.
Explorant igitur primo quae venter at inde
   ubera quae super his signa referre solent.
Quid color aut pulsus, quid cetera membra loquantur,
   quaerere districte sollicitenque student.
Sed nihil est in ea signo quocumque repertum
   quod vel praegnantem vel peperisse notet.
Nam macilenta nimis facie gracilisque per alvum,
   nil quod dedeceat subtus inesse docet.
Ubera dura nimis et prorsus sicca sorores
   obiecti faciunt criminis esse reas.
Et color et facies et cetera quaeque notata
   mendacem faciunt criminis esse notam.
Nec mora, transmissi redeunt, iurare parati
   quod nihil est quicquid publica fama sonet.
Deceptum graviter dicunt cum praesule clerum
   et populum falsa suspicione fore.
Talibus auditis, alii mittuntur, at illi
   hoc referunt primi quod retulere prius.
Obstupefactus ad hoc, praesul festinat et ipse
   corruptos metuens munere sive dolo;
cumque nihil vitii penitus reperisset in illa,
   protinus illius sternitur ante pedes,
confessusque palam quoniam peccasset in illam,
   postulat ignosci civibus atque sibi.
Vidit ut haec populus numerosaque turba sororum,
   talia mirari non potuere satis.
Talibus aspectis, confusa rubore recessit
   Fama loquax, telis vulnera passa suis.

attendants to her according to custom, he orders that every detail be examined more exactly.

So then, they scrutinize first the indications that the belly and then the breasts customarily display concerning these matters. They are eager to investigate attentively and carefully what her coloring and heart rate as well as what the other body parts tell. But nothing is discovered in her as any indication whatsoever to signal either that she is pregnant or that she has given birth. For quite lean in her face and slender in her belly, she shows that nothing unbecoming lies hidden within below. Her breasts, extremely firm and utterly dry, make the nuns guilty for leveling the charge. Her coloring, face, and everything else observed give the lie to the slur of the charge.

Without delay, those dispatched return, ready to swear that whatever common gossip proclaims is of no account. They say that, along with the bishop, the clergy and people have been grievously deceived by false suspicion. After hearing this, others are sent, but they report what the first ones reported previously. Astonished at this, the bishop hurries there himself too, fearing that they have been suborned by bribery or trickery. When he discovered absolutely no vice in her, he throws himself immediately at her feet and, after acknowledging publicly that he had sinned against her, he asks for pardon for his countrymen and himself.

When the people and vast throng of sisters saw these things, they could not marvel enough at such developments. After seeing such things, talkative Rumor, blushing in embarrassment, withdrew, having suffered wounds from her

Praesul et a cella nec non et ab urbe sorores
utpote mendaces iussit abesse procul.
Quod tamen illa videns subito compuncta, seorsum
praesule deducto tecta retexit ei.
Qualiter acciderit proprium retegendo reatum,
singula pontifici prona referre studet.
Qualiter in somnis peperisset et absque dolore
narrat et in partu viscera clausa fore,
qualiter ex utero puer est eductus et ad quem
missus alendus erat, quo duce, quave via;
quin etiam puero quotus est praefixus alendo
annorum numerus enumeravit ei.
Talibus auditis, eremitam iussit adiri
praesul, ut inquirat de novitate rei.
Nuntius ergo celer eremo redit atque reversus
inventum puerum nuntiat atque senem.
Quo celer audito puerumque senemque videre
currit et antistes certior esse volens.
Hinc infans vagiens, hodie genitricis ab aluo
editus; annosus cernitur inde senex;
poscentique senex quisnam puer esset et unde
pontifici tandem talibus orsus ait:
"Hunc ex parte sua puerum transmisit alendum
angelicis manibus virgo Maria mihi,
omnimodam puero mandans impendere curam
donec adimpletus septimus annus eat.
Angelicis manibus huc est allatus ab ipsa,
quae super angelicos considet alma thronos."
Talibus auditis, puero compassus et ipse
praesul sollicitum postulat esse senem;

own weapons. The bishop ordered the nuns, because they were liars, to stay far from both their cells and the city.

Yet she, upon seeing this, struck by sudden compunction, took the bishop aside separately and uncovered to him what had been covered up. In revealing her own sin, and how it happened, she strives, prostrate, to report to the prelate every detail. She recounts how she gave birth in her sleep and without pain, and how her uterus remained shut in childbirth, how a boy was delivered from her womb and to whom, with whose guidance, and in what way he was sent away to be reared. In addition, she reckoned for him what number of years was set in advance for the boy's rearing.

After hearing these words, the bishop ordered the hermit to be approached, to question him about the unprecedented event. Accordingly, a messenger swiftly goes back to the hermitage and on his return announces that the boy and old man have been found. After hearing this, the bishop too runs swiftly to see the boy and old man, wishing to verify the story. On one side is to be seen the wailing newborn, brought forth today from his mother's belly; on the other, the long-lived old man. In reply to the bishop asking who the boy was and where he was from, the old man at last began his speech with the following words: "By way of angelic hands, the Virgin Mary conveyed to me on her own authority this boy to be reared, enjoining me to devote all manner of care to the boy until the seventh year has been completed. By way of angelic hands, he has been brought here from her, who graciously takes her seat above angelic thrones."

After hearing these words, the very bishop himself takes pity upon the boy and entreats the old man to be attentive.

magnificansque Deum super his, conversus in urbem
virginis obsequiis artius inde vacat;
utque puer primos septem compleverat annos
iuxta quod statuit virgo parensque Dei,
praesulis ex eremo cura mediante reversus
maiorum studiis erudiendus abit.
Moribus et gestis qui postquam crevit honestis,
praesule defuncto fungitur ipse throno;
moxque gradum nactus, implevit praesulis actus,
invigilans studiis nocte dieque piis.
Damna sui generis morum probitate redemit.
Omnibus et solis omnia solus homo,
in domino servus, ovis in pastore, minister
in primate fuit, in dominante cliens.
Cuncta resarcivit quae vel nota condicionis
fortunaeve status destituere prius.
Moribus egregiis materni probra pudoris
abstulit, excusans ille quod illa fuit.
Damna pudicitiae suboles genitricis ademit;
abstulit et naevum nobilitate sua;
sicque, quoad vixit, magis officiosa Mariae
vota (nec immerito) solvit amore pio.

Glorifying God for these events, he turns back to the city and from then on applies himself more rigorously to the service of the Virgin. When the boy had completed his first seven years in keeping with what the Virgin and Mother of God prescribed, he returns from the hermitage through the intercession of the bishop and goes off to be educated in study of more advanced subjects.

After advancing through respectable character and actions, he accedes to the episcopal throne himself when the bishop passes away. Immediately, having obtained the rank, he carried out the activities of a bishop, devoting himself to pious studies by day and night. He compensated for the detriments of his lineage by the integrity of his conduct. Alone, he was all things to each individual person, a servant as a master, a sheep as a shepherd, a minister as a magnate, a vassal as a lord.

He mended everything that either the stigma of his state or the circumstances of his lot left damaged previously. By his outstanding conduct he took away the disgrace of his mother's ignominy, himself atoning for what she had been. As his mother's offspring he removed her affronts to modesty; he took away too, through his distinction, her defect. And so, as long as he lived, he discharged to Mary (and not without good reason) the most dutiful prayers with devout love.

TRACT ON ABUSES

TRACTATUS CONTRA CURIALES ET OFFICIALES CLERICOS

Postquam tristis hiems zephyro spirante recessit,
grando, nives, pluviae consuluere fugae;
Terra parens florum, vires rediviva resumpsit,
exseruitque caput exhilarata suum.
Ver, caput atque comes aestatis, in otia curas
laxat et ablato frigore flore nitet.
Vernat fronde nemus, vestitur gramine tellus,
veris odoriferi spirat ubique vapor.
Quicquid hiems hiemisque graves rapuere ministri,
reddidit aestatis gratia vere novo.
Veris ad imperium surgens statione soluta,
clausa sub aestivo carcere cedit hiems.
Flante levi zephyro dum ver lascivit in herbas,
aestas multiplici flore maritat humum.
Temporis atque loci facie redeunte serena,
saltibus et silvis redditur exul avis.
Quaeque diu siluit philomena silentia solvit,
voce sua redimens verba negata sibi.
Cuius ad exemplum, sterili torpore remoto,
morem temporibus qui gerit, ipse sapit.
Ergo quid hic latitas? Quid, parve libelle, moraris?
Ne mecum pereas, i cito, rumpe moram.
Pergere securus poteris quocumque placebit,
nil sibi quod cupiat praedo cruentus habes.

TRACT AGAINST COURTIERS AND CLERICAL OFFICIALS

After grim winter has departed, while the west wind blows, hail, snow and rain have taken to flight. Alive again, Earth, the mother of flowers, has renewed her strength, and, now refreshed, has lifted up her head. Spring, the source and companion of summer, now eases our cares in leisure, and flourishes with flowers after cold is swept away. Groves grow green with foliage, the ground is covered with grass, the perfume of fragrant spring is everywhere alive. Whatever winter and winter's harsh helpers have ravaged, the kindness of summer has restored with the new spring. Rising up and abandoning its post at spring's command, winter gives way, shut up in summer's prison. While spring frolics in the grass with gentle breezes blowing, summer sows the soil with various flowers. When the cloudless face of time and place returns, the banished bird is restored to glades and woods. The nightingale which was long silent breaks the silence, setting free with her song sounds that were suppressed. At her example, free from sterile sluggishness, he is wise who suits his ways to the seasons.

And so, why do you hide here, little book? Why do you tarry? Break off delay! Go quickly, lest you perish with me. You can go carefree wherever you please; you have nothing that a bloodthirsty bandit wants for himself.

Neve reformides propterque pericula cesses:
est via tuta tibi, liber; abire potes.
Cur? Quia secure coram latrone viator
cantabis vacuus cum nisi verba feras.
Nec tamen unde venis, vel quo mittente, vel ad quem
dixeris, aut subitae quae tibi causa viae.
Omnia sint suspecta tibi, semperque timere
sollicitus studeas quicquid obesse potest,
non quia laesisti quemquam, nec feceris unde
debeat infestus quilibet esse tibi;
sed quia multotiens multi quo non meruerunt
ex odio domini deperiere sui.
Crimen ob alterius multi cecidere, fiuntque
plus aliena mali quam sua causa sibi.
Ne nihil ergo tibi valeat nocuisse vianti,
haec duo verba tene: dic bona facque bene.
Neve tuos timeas hostes, in rebus agendis
non sis securus sollicitusve nimis.
Nec nimium facilem nec difficilem nimis esse
te volo, sed medium velle tenere locum.
Non usurpabis quicquam quod vendicet alter,
sed sis contentus conditione tua.
Non opibus studeas, ne sit suspecta potestas
quae leviter tollit parta labore gravi.
Paupertas tutum, sed non facit esse disertum;
si sapias, omni tempore dives eris.
Novit abundare sapiens, et novit egere,
insipiens omni tempore pauper erit.
Multa scias cum nil habeas, sic dives haberi
et liber poteris teque tuoque frui.

Nor should you fear and hold back because of dangers: your way is safe, my book; you can depart. Why? Because as an empty-handed wayfarer you'll sing safely in a robber's face, since you carry nothing but words. However, don't say where you're from, or who sends you, or to whom, or the reason for your sudden journey. Be suspicious of everything and always anxiously strive to fear whatever can be a hindrance, not because you've injured anyone or done anything for which anybody is rightly hostile toward you, but because often many have perished on account of their lord's hatred, which they have not deserved. Many have fallen for another's offense, and the cause of their calamity is more another's than their own. Thus, so that nothing can harm you as you travel, keep these two precepts: say good things and be beneficial. And don't fear your enemies, nor in conducting affairs should you be too confident or excessively anxious. I want you to be neither too easy nor too difficult, but willing to hold the middle ground. You will not take possession of anything that another claims, but be content with your own circumstances. Do not strive for riches, so that the power that easily appropriates what has been acquired by hard toil will not be mistrusted in you. Poverty makes one safe, but not skilled in speaking; if you're wise, you'll be rich all the time. A wise man knows how to have plenty and how to be needy; a foolish man will be poor all the time. Know many things, although you possess nothing; in this way you can be considered rich and free to enjoy yourself and your property.

Nec preciosa putes studeas vel parta tueri
quae possunt adimi iure dolove tibi;
non tibi res propria sed res aliena videtur
quam fortuna potest tollere sive dare.
Ut tibi sit proprium quod habes, et non alienum,
tu quod habent alii deforis intus habe.
Sint tibi divitiae, sed quae comitentur ubique
nec possint dominum deseruisse suum.
His comitatus erat, licet incomitatus abiret
exul ad ignotos Naso poeta Getas.
Ecce viae comites dedimus, ne devius erres,
hi comitentur iter nocte dieque tuum.
Ut quid adhuc dubitas, nectisque moras in eundo,
et cupis invito me residere domi?
Plurima causaris, et te nescire fateris
quis status atque modus debeat esse tuus,
quis cultus, quae lingua tibi, quis gestus habendus,
quove loqui liceat quove tacere loco,
qui mores hominum, quae consuetudo locorum,
curia cur reprobet ista vel illa probet,
quid cui conveniat, quo tempore quid sit agendum,
rebus in incertis quae sit habenda fides.
Quod petis, expediam, paucis breviterque docebo
te quibus addictum legibus esse velim.
Nolo rudem nimium, sed nec nimis esse facetum,
ne videare sequi summa vel ima nimis.
Tempore sive loco sis circumspectus ab omni,
ne levis in gestu, nec nimis esto gravis.
Damna pudicitiae redimas sectator honesti;
sobrius esse stude, pectore, voce, manu.

Don't count as precious or strive to protect possessions that can be snatched away from you by law or by guile; property that fortune can take away or give is clearly not your own but another's. So that what you have may be your own and not another's, keep within what other men keep outside. By all means have riches, but the kind that accompany you everywhere and that cannot desert their master. The poet Ovid kept company with these, although he went unaccompanied as an exile to the unknown Getae.

See, we've given you companions for the way, so that you not wander astray; they will attend your journey night and day. How is it that you still hesitate and invent delays in departing, and want to stay at home against my will? You give many reasons and confess that you don't know what your attitude and manner ought to be, what style, what speech, what bearing you should have, where you are allowed to speak or where to be silent, what are the manners of men, what the customs of places, why the court disapproves of these things or approves of those, what suits whom, what should be done at what time, what trust one should have in doubtful matters. What you seek, I'll explain, and in a few words briefly teach the rules to which I want you to be bound.

I don't want you to be too clumsy, but not altogether elegant either, so that you won't seem to strive too much for the heights or the depths. In every time or place, you should be circumspect: do not be fickle in attitude, nor too severe. As a follower of virtue, shun damage to your modesty; strive to be sober in heart, word, and hand.

Iustitiae cultor maneas, dissuasor iniqui,
consona sint verbis singula facta tuis.
Sordida ne maculent mundam tibi munera dextram,
suspectos Danaos et sua dona time.
Omnia sint odio quae non commendat honestas;
quicquid honestati convenit, illud ama.
Hic status, iste modus est, hic tibi cultus habendus,
qui placeat sola simplicitate sua.
Lumina, lingua, manus, nulla ratione vagentur,
sed sint perpetuo carcere clausa tibi.
Haec tria conservant vitam, mortemque ministrant;
haec tria custodias tempus in omne tuum.
Haec tria sunt quae se semper servantia servant,
spretaque dant sperni conditione pari.
Ista precor serves, ut tu serveris ab istis,
haec tua vota regant si meus esse velis.
Haec tria sunt hominis speculum quo cernitur extra
quicquid in arcano pectoris intus habet.
Haec tria sic homine sese comitantur in omni,
exponant dominum semper ut ipsa suum.
Haec tria non possunt morum non esse fidelis
interpres, tribus his se probat omnis homo.
Haec tria sub tanta semper gravitate gubernes,
ut numquam levitas frena relaxet eis.
Haec tria si serves, aliorum discere mores
et levius poteris composuisse tuos.
Haec tria te facient virtutis amore placere,
et quibus ista placent displicuisse nequis.
Forsan adhuc quaeris quae sunt quae curia curet,
cur leviter reprobet ista vel illa probet.

Be a supporter of justice, an opposer of the unjust; let all your deeds accord with your words. Let sordid gifts not stain your clean right hand; suspect and fear Greeks and their gifts. Hate all things that virtue does not commend; whatever accords with virtue, love that. You must have this attitude, this manner, this style, to be pleasing for solely simplicity itself.

Do not let your eyes, tongue, or hands stray for any reason, but keep them shut up in a perpetual prison. These three preserve life, and they serve death; keep watch on these three at all times. These are three that always guard the things that guard them, and likewise, if spurned, cause them to be spurned. Guard them, I pray, that you may be guarded by them; let them guide your desires, if you want to be mine. These three are the mirror of a man, in which is seen on the outside whatever he has inside, in the secret recesses of his heart. These three so join together in every man that they always reveal their master. These three cannot but be a faithful indication of character; through these three every man shows himself. Govern these three always with such great dignity that levity never slackens the reins on them. If you preserve these three, you'll be able to learn the character of others and easily to regulate your own. These three will make you pleasing for your love of virtue, and you cannot displease those whom they please.

Perhaps you still ask what things the court cares about, why it lightly disapproves of some things or approves of

Curia curat opes, inopum fastidit amores,
nausea divitibus pauper amicus adest.
Curia suspendit tales in poste salutes,
quae vacuis manibus nil nisi verba ferunt.
Curia sollicitas parit omni tempore curas,
et facit ut placeant aspera, dura iuvent,
gratia cuius, amor cuius, constantia cuius
in pretio pretium constituere suum.
Curia cura gravis, labor improbus, error inanis,
otia multa serit, seria nulla sequens.
Ridet, adulatur et fingit amare quod odit,
sicque quod est album praedicat esse nigrum.
Plurima si dederis, modicum tibi forte refundet,
colligat ut rursum fertiliore manu.
Curia quos hodie summissa voce salutat,
cras subsannabit, sorte cadente sua.
Curia, crede mihi, sine munere nescit amicum,
munera si dederis hostis amicus eris.
Suscipit ad pondus trutinatque negotia quaevis,
reddit et ad pondus omnia lance pari.
Nec tamen ad pondus ratione reponderat aequa,
sed redimit gravia pondere saepe levi.
Munera parva probat, promissaque grandia spernit,
et vacuas surda suscipit aure preces.
Curia non curat quemquam sine munere cuius
pendet ab obsequio gratia, vita, salus.
Curia causa mali, vitii schola, fabrica falsi,
fomes luxuriae, fons et origo gulae.
Sed de fallaci fieret si forte fidelis,
disceret et cursum dedidicisse suum,

others. The court cares for wealth; it disdains love of the needy; a poor friend is an object of loathing to the rich. The sorts of greeting the court hangs on its door for empty hands bring nothing but words. The court constantly gives rise to anxious cares, and makes harsh times agreeable, hard ones pleasing, whose favor, whose love, whose constancy assess their value in financial terms. At court, anxious care, restless toil, misspent time-wasting beget much idleness, while pursuing nothing serious. The court laughs, flatters, and pretends to love what it hates, and thus what is white, it declares to be black. If you've given very much, perhaps the court will restore a little to you, so that it can collect again with a more profitable hand. Those whom the court hails today with a humble voice, tomorrow, when their fortune is sinking, it will sneer at.

Believe me, the court knows no friend without a bribe; if you've given bribes as a foe, you'll become a friend. The court undertakes and evaluates all business by weight, and by weight it assigns all equally. Yet it does not repay by weight with a fair reckoning, but often buys back heavy weights with a light weight. The court approves of small bribes and spurns grand promises, and it receives empty entreaties with a deaf ear.

The court does not care about anyone whose favor, life, and welfare depend on allegiance to the court without a bribe. The court is a cause of evil, a school of vice, a workshop of fraud, the tinder of lust, the source and origin of gluttony. But if by chance the court were to become faithful instead of false, and would learn to unlearn its present

posset adhuc merito nomen famamque mereri,
    quam constat meritis demeruisse suis.
Non tamen haec dicas cum tu perveneris illuc,
    et prodas dominum nuntius ipse tuum,
sed magis accelerans memori mandata reconde
    pectore, festinus ique redique cito.
Dum peregrinaris vultum sapias peregrinum,
    vox quoque cum veste sit peregrina tibi.
Postquam transieris pontes, vada, stagna, paludes,
    est quibus Elysii gloria saepta loci,
virginis Eldredae venies devotus ad aram,
    dignaque pro meritis dona precesque dabis.
Praesulis inde domum tacito pede solus adibis,
    qua tibi dant patulam claustra gradusque viam.
Si tibi porta patet, mox ingrediaris ut hospes,
    mixtus ut hospitibus interiora petas.
Non tamen accedas donec plebs tota recedat,
    et vacet hora, locus, praesul et ipse tibi.
Tunc habitu posito vultuque simul peregrino,
    ante salutatum pronus adibis erum.
Lingua tamen caveas ne sit materna, sed illa
    quam dedit et docuit lingua paterna tibi.
Excipiet vultu te quo solet omnia laeto,
    quaque nequit larga non habuisse manu,
indutusque suam quam nec gravis abstulit umquam
    ira viri faciem vina petita dabit,
vimque tibi faciet Cererem redimente Lyaeo,
    servato patriae more modoque loci.
Tu tamen esto memor cui, quis sis missus, et a quo,
    ne tibi fecundus obstruat ora calix.

course, it could yet deservedly earn the reputation and renown which it has clearly forfeited by its faults. However, do not say these things when you've arrived there, nor as a messenger make known your master, but rather, going swiftly, store your instructions in your heart's memory; go in haste and return quickly. While you are a stranger, have a stranger's appearance, and also along with your attire, let yours be a stranger's speech.

After you've crossed over bridges, streams, ponds and marshes, with which the glory of Ely is surrounded, you'll come devoutly to the altar of Etheldreda the virgin, and offer due gifts and prayers according to her merits. From there you'll go alone with silent step to the bishop's house where the cloister and your rank will grant you ample access. If the gate is open, quickly enter as a guest, so that, mingling with the guests, you may seek out the inner rooms. Yet do not approach until all the common folk depart, and the hour, the place, and the bishop himself have time for you. Then, after your habit and stranger's appearance have been put aside, bowing down, approach your lord to greet him in his presence. However, take care not to use your mother tongue, but that which your father's tongue gave and taught you. He will receive you with the same happy countenance he does all things, and with the generous hand that he cannot fail to maintain, and, adopting the expression that serious anger has never taken away, he will produce wines he has called for. He will assail you, making up for food with drink, following the custom of his homeland and the practice of the place.

Yet you should keep in mind who you are, and to whom, and by whom you are sent, so that the copious cups don't

Praesulis ergo manu facieque potitus amica,
sollicitus caveas ne videare rudis.
Sed si te fuerit oculis dignatus et ore,
offer quicquid habes officiosus ei.
Nec leve vel modicum quicquam suppresseris, immo
omnia fac pateant interiora tui.
Crimina pontifici studeas tua quaeque fateri,
possis ut solvi praesulis ore tui.
Forte rubore gravi facies suffusa tacebit
plurima nec poterit omnia verba loqui.
Nulla tamen taceas, sed singula quaeque reveles,
nec palpes vitium conscius ipse tuum.
Nec medicum timeas, nec ei tua vulnera celes,
nam magis absconsa vulnera peius olent,
quamque prius potuit facilis medicina salutem,
postea vix valuit reddere cura gravis.
Et quia non tantum medici sed manus amici,
tractabit levius vulnus amica manus.
Auribus hinc tutis nec ab ulla parte timendis
securus poteris dicere quicquid habes.
Ergo nihil dubites, nec te pavor aut pudor urat,
quin pateant medico vulnera cuncta tuo.
Ipse quod hinc sanum, quod viderit inde secandum
dicat, et arbitrio cuncta relinque suo.
Esto tamen patiens, quoniam diuturna secari
vulnera non possunt absque dolore gravi.
Et resecare semel praestat quam saepe dolores,
et breve tormentum quam tolerare diu.
Utile cauterium quod ad omnia vulnera praestat,
quod simul atque semel omnia sana facit.

impede your speech. And having gained the bishop's friendly hand and expression, be careful, be wary, so that you not seem uncouth. But if he's deemed you worthy of his sight and speech, dutifully offer him whatever you have. Do not conceal anything, however trivial or small, but, on the contrary, see to it that all your inner secrets are exposed. Be eager to confess all your sins to the bishop, so that you can be absolved by the words of your bishop. Perhaps your face, blushing with great shame, will pass over many sins in silence and will not be able to express all your words. Yet be silent about nothing, but disclose every detail, and do not knowingly cosset your faults. Don't fear the physician and don't hide your wounds from him, for the more wounds are concealed the worse they stink, and what deliverance an easy remedy could bestow before, a painful cure can hardly render afterward. And since it is not only the hand of a physician, but of a friend, that friendly hand will treat the wound more gently. Hence, into ears that are safe and in no way to be feared you can say securely whatever you must.

And so, don't hesitate at all, and don't let fear or shame vex you, but rather let all your wounds be exposed to your physician. Let him say what he's seen that's healthy, and what must be cut out; leave all to his judgment. However, be patient, because long-lasting wounds cannot be operated on without severe pain. It is better to cut out painful parts once rather than often, and to endure a brief torment rather than a long one. A cautery is useful, which is efficacious for all wounds, which makes all well at one and the same time.

Omnibus expositis quicquid tibi dixerit ipse,
hoc fac et vives tempus in omne meum.
Si stes, stabis ei, si forte cadis, cadis illi;
seu stes, sive cadas, non minus eius eris.
Si non cancellat te cancellarius, immo
approbat, ulterius irreprobatus eris.
Pontificum flori si complaceas Elyensi
non potes aut poteris displicuisse mihi.
Quicquid enim de te dictaverit ipse sequendum,
hoc sequor hocque sequar, tuque sequeris idem.
Ipse tibi nomen dabit et tibi nominis omen,
vivat ut illius nomen in ore tuo.
Sicque relativo praesul gaudebit honore,
cui tribuit vitam vivat ut eius ope.
Hoc decedenti debet praestare superstes
alter ut alterius sit sine fine memor.
Postquam pontificis fueris satis ore sereno
usus et alloquio pocula dante mero,
si licet atque vacat monachorum claustra subibis,
portans multiplicis verba salutis eis.
Protinus occurret meus ille tibi Nicholaus,
dicere nec Petro vix patietur, "Ave."
Totus in amplexus et in oscula tantus abibit,
cedat ut anguillae filia febris ei.
Organa nec deerunt, licet ordinis hora reclamet;
virginis Eldredae festa redisse putes.
Ergo, liber, propera, tibi nec baculus neque pera
deficit, aera tibi sunt satis atque cibi.
Perge, nihil dubites, fuge iurgia, subtrahe lites,
ne sit terrori vivere sive mori.

After you have set forth everything, do whatever he says to you, and you'll live for all time as my own. If you stand, you'll stand as his; if perchance you fall, you fall as his. Whether you stand or whether you fall, you'll be his no less. If the chancellor doesn't cancel you, but rather approves of you, thereafter you'll be beyond reproach. If you're pleasing to Ely, the flower of bishops, you cannot, now or in the future, displease me. For whatever course he says you should follow, this I follow and this I shall follow, and you will follow the same. He will give you a name and fame from that name, so that his name will live on your lips. Thus the bishop will rejoice in the reflected glory of the one he granted life, namely to live by his aid. When this one departs, a second should succeed it and guarantee that it preserves the memory of the other forever.

After you've sufficiently enjoyed the bishop's cheerful countenance and conversation, while he's offering goblets of pure wine, if he permits and there's time, you'll enter the monks' cloister, bringing words of multiple greeting to them. My friend Nicholas will present himself to you immediately, nor will he hesitate to permit you to greet Peter with "Hail." He'll so wholly abandon himself to embraces and kisses that an eel's offspring, a fever, would be bested by him. There'll be no lack of music, though the canonical hour should sound out; you'd think that the feast of Etheldreda the virgin had returned.

And so, my book, make haste; you lack neither staff nor satchel; you have enough money and food. Go on, don't

Perge, nec expensis parcas dum sol Elyensis
exstat et exstabit seque videre dabit.
Perge nec exspecta, patet exitus et via recta;
fata sed et prona sunt tibi, suntque bona.
Perge libens, perge, lacrimas preme, lumina terge,
quodque facis nolens fac videare volens.
Si mihi credideris nulla ratione moreris,
perficies leviter hoc brevitatis iter.
Nec timeas enses, quia, seu statuant Elyenses
proelia, sive ioci sint ibi more loci,
praesule tutus eris, vita votoque frueris,
legatusque tibi non erit hostis ibi.
Nec cancellatus, sed ab ipso canonizatus,
iure reverteris, sicque perennis eris.

hesitate, flee from quarrels, stay away from strife, so that you won't dread to live or die. Go on, don't spare expenses, while the sun of Ely exists and will go on existing and grant sight of himself. Go on, don't wait, the way out is open and the path is straight, but also the fates are favorable to you and they are prosperous. Go on willingly, go on, check your tears, wipe your eyes, and what you do unwillingly, may you seem to do willingly. If you trust me, you'll not delay for any reason; you'll complete this brief journey with ease. Don't fear swords, because either the men of Ely will stage battles or there might be sport there in accordance with the local custom. With the bishop you'll be safe, you'll enjoy life and what you desire, and the legate will not be your enemy there. By him you'll not be canceled, but canonized; you'll return rightfully, and thus live without end.

1. Reverendo patri et domino Willelmo, Dei gratia Eliensi episcopo, apostolicae sedis legato, regis Angliae cancellario, Canturiensis ecclesiae fratrum minimus frater Nigellus veste monachus, vita peccator, gradu presbyter, sed indignus sentire de Domino in bonitate et in simplicitate cordis quaerere illum.

2. Sincere et sine simulatione diligentis est saepe esse sollicitum et raro securum, citius timore concuti quam spe consolari, amici fortunam non solum suam dicere, sed esse operum effectu comprobare, si quid est quod non deceat vel correctione indigeat humiliter suggerere, non publice aut impudenter improperare.

3. Haec mihi consideranti et mecum saepius postquam claustro meo, immo mihi redditus sum, diligentius retractanti, non potui de te non esse sollicitus, quem in caritate non ficta diligo, cuius profectum in utroque homine toto corde desidero, cui comes individuus amando adhaereo, pro quo etiam preces Domino licet indignas, devotas tamen, effundo. Dum enim considero quid honoris, quid oneris, immo quae onera et quam importabilia imposita sunt umeris tuis, in tantum ut pondere sub tanto sudaret maximus Athlas, timeo *ne titubes mandataque frangas,* cum scriptum sit: *Si vis vitam, serva mandatum.*

1. To my reverend father and lord, William, by the grace of God bishop of Ely, legate of the Apostolic See, chancellor of the king of England, Nigel, least brother of the brothers of the church at Canterbury, a monk in vesture, a sinner in life, a priest in office, but unworthy in goodness to know the Lord and to seek him in simplicity of heart.

2. It is the nature of a man who loves sincerely and without simulation to be often anxious and rarely secure, more quickly shaken by fear than comforted by hope, not only to call his friend's fortune his own, but to prove it to be so by the performance of deeds; to suggest humbly if there is anything that is not seemly or needs correction; not to reproach publicly or impudently.

3. While considering these matters after I returned to my cloister—indeed to myself—and often thinking them over very attentively, I could not but be anxious about you whom I love with true charity, whose advancement in each of your offices I desire with my whole heart, to whom I cling as a companion inseparable in loving, for whom also I pour forth prayers, devout though unworthy, to the Lord. For when I consider what honor, what a burden, in fact, what the burdens are and how unsupportable they are that have been placed on your shoulders, to the degree that mighty Atlas would sweat under such a great weight, I fear *lest you stumble and break the commandments,* since it is written: *If you want life, keep my commandment.*

4. Et dum his intuendis diutius immoror et moras quas cogitatio inexplicabilis extendere avidius amplector, artius obligor, amplius affligor, navisque mea spatioso cogitationum pelago exposita, a portu longius abducitur, et tempestati addicitur graviori, et *terit in rapido tempora longa freto.* Unde consumptis in huiusmodi nonnumquam diebus et noctibus in hoc labyrintho, quaerens exitum et non inveniens, obambulo et oberro. Et non invento prae diluvio aquarum multarum ubi requiescat pes meus, cum beato Iob compellor clamare et dicere: *Dies mei transierunt; cogitationes meae dissipatae sunt, torquentes cor meum.*

5. Video enim quam multae curae et inextricabiles te premant, quot et quantae occupationes te opprimant, quae et quanta incommoda tibi cotidie accidant, quibus laboribus afficeris, quibus necessitatibus occuparis, qua sollicitudine distraheris, qua mentis quiete fere semper defrauderis, qui tota die et tota nocte cum Martha circa plurima intentus sollicitaris, ita ut vix aliquando liceat vel ad modicum Mariam imitari, sed ita frequens sit vexatio tua quod continua, ita vehemens quod vicissitudinis nescia, ita valida quod vix convalescas. Sed utinam vexatio ista tam continua, tam vehemens, tam valida, tibi valeat dare intellectum ut sapias et intelligas, ac novissima praevideas ne ex improviso in praecipitium descendas.

6. Vitae enim praesentis, immo praetereuntis, in stadio positus, non tantum forsitan restat currendum quantum cucurristi; feliciter autem currit qui sic currit ut comprehendat, sic agonizat in stadio dum tendit ad bravium, ut cum

4. And while I linger longer in contemplating these matters and eagerly embrace delays which unavailing reasoning extends, I am more firmly bound, I am more fully distressed, and my ship is exposed to an immense ocean of thoughts; it is led farther away from port, it is surrendered to a more severe storm, and *endures for a long time in a raging sea.* And so often spending such days and nights in this labyrinth, seeking and not finding a way out, I aimlessly walk about and wander. Finding no place for my foot to rest because of the vast watery flood, I am compelled to cry out with blessed Job and say: *My days have passed away; my thoughts are scattered, tormenting my heart.*

5. For I see how many inescapable cares press upon you, how many and how great the affairs are that oppress you, what and how great the troubles that daily befall you, by what hardships you are afflicted, with what obligations you are occupied, by what anxiety you are distracted, and what peace of mind you are almost always denied, who all day and all night are anxious about many things, like Martha, so that you are hardly ever permitted to imitate Mary even a little. But so frequent is your vexation that it is constant, so vehement that it knows no vicissitude, so vigorous that you hardly recover. But would that this so constant, so vehement, and so vigorous vexation could grant you the understanding to know, to perceive, and to foresee the end, lest you unexpectedly fall headlong.

6. For positioned on the racecourse of this present life, nay rather, this passing life, perhaps not so much remains to be run as you have already run; moreover, he runs successfully who runs in such a way as to attain the prize; he competes in the race as he strives for the prize, to win the reward

laboris praemio honoris percipiat et triumphum. Sicut autem gloriosum est currere, gloriosius vero cursum consummare, ita ignominiosum est medio in cursu deficere, et multo ignominiosius, cum iam e vicino meta respicitur, et currentis animus spe apprehendendi accenditur, qualibet occasione subsistere, cum in perpaucis passibus pendeat gloria vel confusio, haereditas vel exhaeredatio, exilium vel patria, carcer vel corona. Melius fuisset non currere quam citra metam cursum terminare.

7. Quia sicut victoria unius pugilis multi animantur ad virtutem, concipiuntque animos et audaciam ardua aggrediendi, ita unius occasus et inertia multis timorem incutit ad ruinam, et tepidos adhuc et timentes durioris pugnae congressum adducit consequendae victoriae in desperationem. Quamvis et nostro tempore in quo fines saeculorum devenerunt, viderimus virum illum desideriorum (beatum dico martyrem Thomam), quem vidimus oculis nostris, et manus nostrae contrectaverunt, cum quo manducavimus et bibimus, qui senescentis saeculi et inveterati dierum malorum malitiae virtute mascula resistens, et solus ad exemplum multorum ex adverso ascendens et murum pro domo Domini se opponens, vestigia imitanda reliquerit universis, et viam virtutis et veritatis ad oculum ostenderit omnibus episcopis sui temporis. Qui utinam opera eius, ut ea imitarentur, tam crebro satagerent ad memoriam reducere, quam non solum facere sed etiam fastidiunt audire. Sed quorsum ista? Absit ut *ponam os meum in caelum,* et *tangam christos domini.* Ad te mihi sermo, Willelme, sed non quem animi impetus aut spiritus exacerbatus excitet, sed quem intimae dilectionis devotio propinet.

for his toil and an honorable triumph. Furthermore, just as it is glorious to run, but more glorious to complete the course, so it is shameful to cease in midcourse, and much more shameful, when the goal is already seen nearby and the runner's spirit is inflamed with the hope of attaining it, to stop for any reason at all, since on a very few paces depends glory or shame, inheritance or disinheritance, exile or homeland, prison or crown. It would have been better not to run than to end the race short of the goal.

7. For just as many men are inspired to valor by the victory of one boxer, and they are fired with the courage and audacity to attempt arduous tasks, so do the downfall and inaction of one man strike fear in many to their ruin, and lead the lukewarm and those fearing the contest of a longer fight to despair of obtaining victory. Yet even in our time, in which the end of the world has arrived, we have seen that man of our desires (I speak of the blessed martyr, Thomas), whom we have seen with our own eyes and whom our hands touched, with whom we have eaten and drunk. He resisted with manly courage the malice of evil days in a world growing old and hardened, and, rising up alone against it as an example to many, and placing himself in opposition as a wall before the house of the Lord, he left a path for all to follow, and he showed the way of virtue and truth as a display for all the bishops of his time. Would that they would trouble themselves to recall his works to mind, in order to imitate them as often as they are loath not only to do them, but even to hear them. But to what end these words? God forbid that *I set my mouth against heaven,* and that *I touch the Lord's anointed.* To you, William, is my discourse directed, but it is not one that a passionate impulse of mind or a heated spirit arouses, but one that the devotion of deepest love offers up.

8. In primis igitur, iuxta Salomonis sententiam, qui ait, "*Meliora sunt amici vulnera quam inimici blandientis oscula,*" obsecro ut detur temeritati meae venia, et si quid dixero quod aliquem urat, illud amor et intentio dicentis temperet, immo totum exstinguat; non enim ex amaritudine cordis os loquitur, sed ex abundantia dilectionis. Unde peto ut eo spiritu quo dicta sunt intelligantur, et quo exterius stylo exarata sunt interius scribantur, sitque procul malignus interpres, quia nihil adeo sobrie dictum quod sinistro interprete non sit insipidum et superciliosum. Accipe itaque rudi stylo nuper exarata, placeatque limam correctionis verbis adhibere incompositis, quodque cancellarii spectat ad officium, cancelletur quod aut male cadit aut cantat, verumtamen sermonis inculti asperitatem ne abhorreas, quod aridum est et exsangue; ne spernas quod forte taediosum est; ad tempus potius portes quam proicias.

9. Memini me quandoque vidisse quod, inter delicias quibus aliquando prae aliis affluebas, olera herbarum sumebas, vinoque seposito pocula minus pretiosa persaepe admisisse. Opus igitur rude, immo penitus rusticum, inter alia quae tibi cotidie aureis incudibus ore rotundo et lingua elimata fabricantur admitte, sed illud nequaquam cum eis repone nisi forte ut quae splendida sunt ex vicina tenebrarum caligine magis resplendeant, et ex vasis fictilibus vasa aurea

8. First, therefore, in keeping with the proverb of Solomon, who says, "*Better are the wounds of a friend than the kisses of a fawning enemy,*" I pray that pardon be granted to my boldness, and if I have said anything which riles anyone, may love and the speaker's purpose temper it, nay rather, totally negate it; for my mouth speaks not from bitterness of heart, but from abundance of love. Hence, I ask that my words be understood in this spirit in which they were said, and that they be written in the inner heart in the style in which they were outwardly composed. And may a malicious interpreter be kept far away, because nothing is said so modestly that it is not tasteless and haughty when the interpreter is treacherous. And so, accept what has been recently composed in an unpolished manner, and may it please you to apply a file for the correction of my disordered words. And since it pertains to the office of chancellor, let that which either has a faulty ending or sounds so be canceled out, but yet do not shudder at the roughness of my uncultivated speech, or what is dry and lifeless; do not scorn what perhaps is tedious; bear with them for a while rather than throw them out.

9. I remember that sometimes I observed that among the delicacies which you once had in abundance, you used to prefer green vegetables, and setting the wine aside, you very often introduced less costly cups. Therefore, accept an unpolished work, or rather, an utterly coarse one, among others which are fashioned on golden anvils for you daily with eloquent voice and refined tongue. But by no means set this work with those, unless, perhaps, so that their brilliance may shine more brightly in juxtaposition with the murky darkness nearby, and by comparison with vessels of clay, the

et argentea admirationem ampliorem consequantur et gratiam. Quae enim esset diei iocunditas nisi noctis molestia interveniret? Aut quis rogaret ea quae ad pacem sunt, si nulla belli formidine tangeretur?

10. Sane unum est quod timeo, sed nec immerito, scilicet ne insolentiae aut temeritatis me arguas, quod tibi aliquatenus scribere attemptaverim, qui tot scripturarum scientiam penes te non tantum in codicibus sed etiam in corde tuo habes reconditam, ita tamen quod omni loco et tempore quantumvis et quomodovis *proferas de thesauro tuo nova et vetera* non praemunitus aut praemeditatus, et talia quidem quae et aedificent audientes, et ex operis venustate commendent artificem. Unde nihil aliud est tibi scribere quam ligna in silvam et in mare magnum et spatiosum aquam mittere.

11. Rem igitur tam mirandam, immo tam miraculosam, tibi insitam primo in tantum mirabar, quod nec credidi sed neque adhuc credidissem, nisi ex commoratione familiari crebra experientia vulnus incredulitatis amputasset. Venient igitur stillicidia fontis exigui in mare magnum, non ut illud augeant, vel aliquid, quasi quod desit, adiciant, sed ut ad originem suam revertentia refluant unde prius fluxerunt, quia omnia flumina intrant in mare, et mare non redundat. Rursumque *omnia habenti dabitur.*

12. Sed et temeritati meae non minimum praestat audaciae, quod audivi, quod et expertus sum, *quia mitis* es *et humilis corde.* Tantumque habens Mosaicae mansuetudinis, quod

vessels of gold and silver might attain more admiration and esteem. For what would be the delight of day if the oppression of night did not intervene? Or who would seek the blessings of peace if he felt no fear of war?

10. However, there is one thing that I fear, but not without cause, namely, that you accuse me of insolence and rashness because I have attempted to write in some measure for you who have in your possession the knowledge of so many writings, stored not only in books, but even in your heart, yet in such a way that in every place and time *you may bring forth from your treasure things new and old* to whatever extent you wish and in whatever way you wish, without forewarning or forethought, and that they are such as to edify those hearing them, and to commend the author for the elegance of the work. Thus, to write to you is nothing but to furnish wood for a forest and water for a great and spacious sea.

11. Therefore, at first I marveled so much that a circumstance so marvelous, nay rather, so miraculous, was implanted in you, that I did not believe it, nor would have believed it yet, if repeated observation borne out of intimate familiarity had not extirpated the wound of disbelief. And so, little drops from a small spring will come into the great sea, not to increase it or to add anything, as if it were lacking, but that, returning to their source, they might flow back to the place from which they first flowed, since all streams go into the sea, and the sea does not overflow. And again, *to the one who has all will it be given.*

12. But also, audacity is not the least responsible for my rashness, for I have heard and I have experienced *that* you are *meek and humble of heart.* And you have so much of the

aut facile remittas aut iniuriarum raro reminiscaris, licet aemuli tui aliter sentiant, et hi maxime quorum aciem hebetavit invidia, eo usque gradiens et progrediens ut non revereantur nec confundantur dicere malum bonum et bonum malum, ponentes tenebras lucem et lucem tenebras. Quos tamen ego non iudico, sed eius iudicio derelinquo cui a Patre datum est omne iudicium, qui cum venerit non solum manifesta sed etiam occulta cordium iudicabit. Nolo enim falcem meam in messem alienam mittere, nec *servum alienum iudicare, suo enim domino stat aut cadit.*

13. Habeat igitur sanctitas tua me excusatum, nec mihi succenseat, si quid ab ore meo elapsum fuerit quod aut non placeat aut penitus displiceat, attendens quod *os fatuorum ebullit stultitiam,* et lingua labitur ex facili, quoniam versatur in habendo. Duobus autem malis subiacet persaepe conditio et consuetudo divitum. Unum est quod non est, quicquid enormitatis vel inhonestatis attemptent, qui eos impediat vel saltem reprehendat, sed etiam cum male fecerint et abominationes pessimas perpetraverint laudantur et magnificantur a suis, et quasi obsequium Deo praestiterint publice commendantur. Aliud est quod quamvis remordeat eos conscientia interius, non admittunt correptionem exterius, sed subsannatur correptio ne subsequatur correctio. Si quis vero deprehensus fuerit qui quod vitiosum est aegre ferat, nec voce et vultu hilari triumphaliter applaudat, statim suspectus habetur, accepti beneficii ingratitudinis arguitur,

mildness of Moses that either you readily forgive or rarely remember injuries, although your enemies think otherwise, and especially those whose vision envy has dimmed, which reaches and progresses to such a point that they are not afraid or ashamed to say bad is good and good is bad, making darkness light and light darkness. Yet I do not judge them, but I leave them to his judgment, to whom all judgment was given by the Father, who will judge, when he comes, not only what is evident to view, but even things hidden in our hearts. For I do not want to send my scythe into another's harvest, nor *to judge another's servant, for he stands or falls by his own lord.*

13. And so, may your holiness hold me excused and not be angry at me if anything has escaped my lips which either does not please you or utterly displeases you, considering that *the mouth of fools spouts foolishness* and the tongue errs easily, since it is occupied in making speech. Moreover, the condition and conduct of rich men is very often subject to two evils. One is that, whatever outrage or shameful deed they might attempt, there is no one to hinder them or at least rebuke them, but even when they have acted wickedly and carried out the worst abominations, they are praised and extolled by their own people, and publicly commended as if they had offered a service to God. The other is that, although their conscience may gnaw at them inwardly, on the outside they admit no reproach, but reproach is dismissed with a sneer, lest correction should follow. But if anyone is caught who is reluctant to tolerate sinful conduct and does not applaud it triumphantly with joyful words and countenance, he is instantly held suspect, accused of ingratitude for a benefice he has received, and charged with the name

delatoris nomine et nota insimulatur, tanquam qui sedet in insidiis ut sagittet in occultis.

14. Et si forte in tantam insaniam proruperit quod dominum domus de quolibet excessu reprehenderit, vel etiam murmuraverit, e vestigio hostis publicus esse censetur, secluditur a consiliis, separatur a mensis, suspenditur a stipendiis, a clericis et capellanis habetur quasi ethnicus et publicanus, ab ostiariis et camberariis quasi fur et magus, a dapiferis dicitur "patibolismum," a pincernis "hydropisim," a cocis "febrem" aut "phrenesim." Non est in tota domo vel familia qui non inveniat in eo causam. Oculi omnium in eum spectant et aures eorum ad verba oris illius. Si locutus fuerit, dicetur blasphemasse; si tacuerit, dolos machinari. Universis est quasi clavus in oculo et gibbus in dorso. Si ingenuus est, degenerat; si servilis conditionis, patrissat; si sapiens est, desipit; si insipiens, versipellis est et, quando vult, sapit; si abundat, ex rapina aut furto; si pauper est, divina est ultio quae iusta merita retribuit iniquo.

15. Quid multa? *A planta pedis usque ad verticem capitis non est in eo sanitas.* Quia solum offendit dominum, a gratia excidit universorum, ad ultimum dicitur in multis offendisse, saepius correptum, sed numquam correctum, non debere ulterius sustineri, sed exterminari, quia iam manifesta sunt delicta. Nuper enim dixit quia nodus erat in scirpo, et quod nec ad preces pontificis plueret in hoc anno super Gelboe montes; quod domina domus non habebat nisi decem mutatoria vestium; sed et mulam patrisfamilias mulum

and mark of an informer, just like one who waits in ambush to shoot arrows in secret.

14. And if perchance this man has gone so far in his great madness that he has reproached the lord of the house for any excess, or even merely grumbled, he is instantly judged to be a public enemy, removed from councils, banished from tables, suspended from stipends, regarded as a heathen and a publican by clerics and chaplains, like a thief and a sorcerer by porters and chamberlains; he is called "drunkenness" by waiters, "dropsy" by cupbearers, "fever" or "frenzy" by cooks. There is no one in the whole house or household who does not find cause to blame him. The eyes of all observe him, and their ears are tuned to the words of his mouth. If he speaks, he will be said to have blasphemed; if he remains silent, he will be said to be plotting deceptions. To all he is like a sty in the eye and a hump on the back. If he is free-born, he is degenerate; if he is of servile status, he takes after his father; if he is wise, he is foolish; if he is foolish, he is devious, and sensible when he wants to be; if he is rich, it is from plunder or theft; if he is poor, it is divine vengeance which is repaying just rewards to an unjust man.

15. Why say more? *From the sole of his foot to the top of his head, there is no soundness in him.* Since he has offended the lord alone, he has fallen from the grace of all; in the end, he is said to have offended in many ways and, often chided but never corrected, should be borne no longer, but be banished, because now his faults are manifest. For he said recently that there was a knot in a bulrush and that it would not rain this year upon the mountains of Gelboe in response to the bishop's prayers, that the mistress of the house has no more than ten changes of clothes. But also he called the

nominavit; et multa in hunc modum quae si voluerit infitiari, ecce pro foribus qui eum convincant.

16. Quid ergo? Dignus iudicatur suspendio vel praecipitio; sed misericordius agetur cum eo, non quia huiusmodi et maiora horum non meruerit sed quia dominus eius misericors est, et honori proprio censuit deferendum. Recedat sine spe revertendi, vel quicquid percipiendi de servitio quinquenni vel septenni quo suis sumptibus militavit. Gravis siquidem vindicta et ultra quantitatem delicti longe extensa. Vae nobis, si singula delicta nostra simili talione punienda appendantur in statera! Cogitur miser ad deditionem vel exilium, quia *non est inventum in ore eius mendacium.* Satius quidem siluisset et dissimulasset, quo ad aestimationem eorum qui veritatem detinentes in mendaciis officioso discursu adulationibus deservire contendunt, *glutientes camelum et colantes culices.* In quorum ore invenitur semper, "est" et "non," ut quocumque res cadat victricis partis in sorte numerentur, ut quicquid contingat, in iniquitatibus suis se praevaluisse gaudeant et mercedem condignam reportent.

17. Duo igitur mala ista sunt quae praecipue divites comitantur, quibus non possunt de facili quia nolunt absolvi, si haec ut correptionem non admittant, et corripientes odio habeant. His non solum addicti sunt principes terrae aut episcopi, sed etiam fere omnes praelati et subiecti, ita ut invicem cotidie collidantur, nec possit alter alterum sustinere.

master of the house's she-mule a mule, and many things in this manner which, if he wanted to deny, behold there are those at the gates to convict him.

16. What follows then? He is judged worthy of hanging or a headlong fall. But he will be treated more mercifully, not because he has not deserved punishments of this kind, and still greater than these, but because his lord is merciful, and thinks that deference must be paid to his own honor. Let him depart without hope of returning, or of receiving anything from his servitude of five or seven years, during which he served at his own expense. Indeed, the punishment is severe and far exceeds the gravity of the fault. Woe to us if our individual faults are weighed in the balance to be punished with similar retribution! The wretched man is forced into forfeiture or exile, because *falsehood is not found in his mouth.* It would have been better to have kept silent and dissembled with respect to the estimation of those men who, suppressing the truth with lies, strive to devote themselves to flattery with officious activity, *swallowing a camel and straining out gnats.* On their lips is always found "yes" and "no," so that however a matter turns out, they are numbered in the ranks of the victorious side; so that whatever happens, they rejoice that they have prevailed in their iniquities, and they carry off the reward they have earned.

17. Therefore, these are two evils that especially attend rich men, from which they cannot easily be released because they are unwilling to be, if they do not admit these criticisms as correction, and they hate those correcting them. Not only are princes of the land and bishops given over to these evils, but nearly all prelates and their subjects even, so that they clash with each other daily, and cannot support

Praevaluitque ita clades ista iam circumquaque in domo domini, quod delicta non possunt corrigi, quia delinquentes non sustinent corripi.

18. Unde contingit nonnumquam quod sanum est corrumpi, quod rectum est praevaricari, quod utile est praetermitti, quod bonum est differri, quod honestum est non admitti. Ex quo provenit quod solutis compagibus vix aliquis ordo, vix aliqua professio, sibi cohaereat, sed sunt in eis contentiones et schismata, quia diversa sunt penitus eorum voluntates et studia, et quia in via Dei alius sic, alius sic, non dico currit, sed corruit, contingit cotidie mala innumera pullulare. Quibus dum non est qui falcem dum adhuc tenera sunt immittat, crescunt et confortantur, ita ut quae fuit herba minima fiat arbor immensa, et *velut agmine facto ruunt* ad perniciem, immo in perditionem, dum non est qui redimat neque qui salvum faciat.

19. Tu autem, dilectissime, non sic, sed *apprehende disciplinam, ne quando irascatur Dominus et pereas de via iusta.* Pone oculos tuos super semitas tuas, dirige in conspectu tuo viam tuam, ut possis dicere cum psalmista: *Lucerna pedibus meis verbum tuum, et lumen semitis meis.* Vide quae et quanta tibi commissa sunt, et cui vel quibus redditurus es rationem. Grave quidem est iugum quod forte spontaneus subisti, sed nec leve est onus quod portare consensisti.

20. Liberalium artium studiis satis olim indulsisti, sed nunc demum ad artem liberalissimam, ad artem artium, ad

each other. And this calamity has become so prevalent now on every side in the lord's house that faults cannot be corrected, because the transgressors cannot bear to be corrected.

18. Thus it happens that sometimes it is sensible to be corrupted, right to transgress, useful to be overlooked, good to be passed over, honorable not to be received. As a result, it comes to pass that scarcely any order, scarcely any profession holds together, because their bonds are dissolved. There are disputes and schisms in them, since their intentions and ambitions are completely different, and since on God's path one I do not say runs, but falls this way, another that way, it happens that countless evils spring forth daily. While there is no one who takes his scythe to them while they are still tender, they increase and grow strong, so that what was a very small plant becomes an immense tree. And *they rush like a massed column* to destruction, nay rather, to perdition when there is no one to provide rescue or safety.

19. You, however, most beloved, be not so, but *embrace instruction, so that when the Lord is angry, you do not also perish from the just way.* Set your eyes upon your path, make straight your way in your contemplation, so that with the psalmist you can say: *Your word is a lamp for my feet and a light for my paths.* Observe what things have been entrusted to you and how great they are, and to what person or for what you will render an account. Indeed, heavy is the yoke to which you have submitted, perhaps voluntarily, nor is the burden light that you have consented to carry.

20. Formerly you gave yourself over wholeheartedly to studies of the liberal arts, but now at length you have passed on to the most liberal art, to the art of arts, namely to the

regimen scilicet animarum, pertransisti. Vide igitur, quis, quid, quantum, qualiter, et a quo acceperis, et qualiter accepta oporteat te erogare, non ignorans quod scriptum est: *Cui plus committitur, plus ab eo exigetur.* Et cum augentur dona, rationes crescunt donorum. Bonum quidem esset villicare, nisi contingeret reddere de villicatione rationem. Nihil dulcius delicto, si delinquentes non punirentur; sed ex amaritudine quae a tergo subsequitur minus habet dulcedinis quicquid in facie voluptuose blanditur. Periculose enim nonnumquam digeritur quod interdum cum suavitate gustatur.

21. Forte a consideratione tui quae tibi plus esset necessaria, curis variis terentibus et distrahentibus longius recessisti. Sed redi ad cor tuum, consule conscientiam tuam, non enim est qui fidelius aut familiarius de singulis te possit erudire, quia non est amicus qui consulat tibi utilius, actor qui alleget contra te subtilius, iudex qui causam tuam iudicet aequius. Vocetur ergo ad diem legitimum conscientia tribus edictis, vel peremptorio uno, et si necesse est praestentur ei indutiae legitimae. Ipsa cum venerit, pro tribunali sedeat, ipsa si quid habet loco adversariorum proponat, ipsa testes suos, scilicet seipsum, producat, ipsa iudicium proferat, ipsa sententiam excipiat, et quae novit universa ipsa discutiat singula. Si invenerit unde gloriandum sit, apud se glorietur,

direction of souls. Therefore, look at who, what, how much, in what way, and from whom you have received this, and in what way you ought to disburse what has been received, in full knowledge of what is written: *To whom more is entrusted, more will be demanded from him.* And when gifts are increased, the accounting increases for those gifts. To be a steward of a farm would be a good thing, if it did not require accounting for that stewardship. Nothing would be sweeter than sin, if the transgressors were not punished; but on account of the bitterness which follows behind one's back, whatever flatters with delight in one's presence has less sweetness. For what is sometimes tasted with sweetness is often hazardous to digest.

21. Perhaps because of various cares wearing you down and drawing you away, you have withdrawn too far from that consideration of yourself, which would be more necessary for you. But return to your heart, consult your conscience, for there is no one who can more faithfully or familiarly instruct you about every matter, since there is no friend who could counsel you more usefully, no advocate who could plead against you more insightfully, no judge who could judge your case more justly. And so, let your conscience be summoned on the day appointed by law after three decrees have been proclaimed, or a final single one, and if necessary, let a legal delay be offered it. When your conscience arrives, let it sit in judgment, let it bring forth a response to its adversaries' arguments if it has any, let it produce its own witnesses, namely itself, let it pronounce judgment, let it receive the sentence, and, since it knows everything, let it investigate every detail. If it finds anything to take pride in, let it take pride inwardly, and so much the more agreeably as

et tanto iocundius quanto secretius. Si vero penes se repererit maculosum quid aut immundum, deducant oculi eius lacrimas per diem et noctem, et non taceant donec digne defleverit quod ignoranter aut ex industria deliquit.

22. Quis autem erit, sive de congregatione claustralium, sive de collegio clericorum, sive eorum qui utrisque ordine et honore praeferuntur, scilicet episcoporum, quem non in aliquo accuset conscientia sua? Si qui forte tales sunt, aestimo quia perpauci. Quis enim, teste scriptura, gloriabitur se habere mundum cor? Appareat de tot modo milibus unus, et dicat, "Ecce ego," nec deerit qui dicat, "*Vae soli, quia si ceciderit, non habet sublevantem!*"

23. Libet igitur intueri qualiter ecclesia detur in direptionem et qui sunt et qualiter ingrediantur in eam. Constat enim omnibus quod beneficia ecclesiastica, quamlibet modica, quamlibet extrema, nulli hodie conferuntur gratis aut vitae merito, sed omnia facta sunt venalia et turpi redacta sub pretio, sub quodam tamen obumbrationis velamine et iniquitatis dissimulatione. Palliant enim opera sua apud homines, et *facies suas exterminant,* et in conspectu eius qui corda intuetur et causas enormia quaeque committere non reformidant. Patientia eius et dissimulatione abutentes, adicientes praevaricationem praevaricationi et peccatum peccato, ac si patientia Dei peccatorum pariat oblivionem et dissimulatio impunitatem.

24. Dum enim patrimonium Crucifixi pretio distrahunt, et in usus pravos et detestabiles transferunt, quasi de impotentia Dei praesumunt, uti non retribuat unicuique pro

secretly. But if it discovers in itself anything defiled or unclean, let its eyes shed tears day and night, and let them not be at rest until your conscience has properly wept for what it has done wrong, whether unknowingly or intentionally.

22. Moreover, who will there be, whether from the congregation of cloistered monks or the community of clerics, or of those who are exalted in rank and honor above either group, namely bishops, whom his own conscience does not accuse for something? If by chance there are any such, I reckon that they are very few. For with scripture as witness, who will boast that he has a pure heart? From so many thousands, let just one appear and say, "Behold, I," and he will not be wanting who says, "*Woe to him who is alone, because if he falls, he has no one to lift him up!*"

23. Therefore, I should like to consider how the Church is given over to plundering, and who they are who assail it, and how. For it is known to all that ecclesiastical benefices, however small or large, are conferred on no one today for free, or for a deserving life, but all are put up for sale and received for a shameful price, though under a certain veil of darkness and a disguising of the injustice. Indeed, they conceal their works before men, and *they disfigure their own faces,* but, in sight of him who looks into hearts and motives, they do not fear to commit every outrageous act. By their dissimulation, they even abuse his patience, adding transgression to transgression and sin to sin, as if God's patience would produce forgetfulness of their sins and their dissimulation would beget impunity.

24. For while they divide up for sale the inheritance of the crucified Lord, they even convert it to perverse and abominable uses, as if they trust in the powerlessness of God, that

meritis, tradatque oblivioni in posterum quicquid in praesenti relinquit impunitum. De quo valde formidandum est quod tanto veniat districtior exactor quanto patientior exstitit creditor, eo quod percutiat et puniat durius quo peccantes et non repaenitentes sustinuit diutius. Timore igitur divino posthabito, qui est sapientiae initium, omnia quae libent licite prosequuntur, vendentes et ementes quae non possunt sub pretio redigi nec etiam ab hominibus aestimari.

25. Varia autem sunt genera huius commercii, omnes vero species eius pessimae et perversae. Alii igitur accipiunt ecclesias et ecclesiastica beneficia, nec prece nec praemio, sed nec pacto aliquo praeeunte, sed operante in eis valdissima virtutum gratia scilicet carne et sanguine. Nemo enim, teste Domino, *carnem suam odio habuit;* unde nonnumquam contingit ut pueris parvulis et adhuc paene in cunis vagientibus conferantur archidiaconatus ecclesiae, et ut *ex ore infantium et lactentium perficiant sibi laudem,* et digni a dignis laudentur, et nocentes esse innocentium testimonio comprobentur.

26. Erigitur itaque infantium aetas in laudem, cui committitur cura animarum, et grex Domini erudiendus, antequam amoveantur nutrix vel paedagogus. Adhuc pendet parvulus ad ubera, et iam personatum gerit in ecclesia! Ante accipit potestatem ligandi et solvendi quam possibilitatem loquendi, ante claves ecclesiae quam quicquam discretionis et intelligentiae. Incipit ante fructus maturos possidere

he will not repay each one according to his merits, and will forget in the future whatever he has left unpunished at present. Concerning this, one should fear that the more patient the creditor is, the more exacting will be the debt collector, because he will smite and punish more harshly the longer he has endured their transgressions and failure to repent. Therefore, setting aside divine fear, which is the beginning of wisdom, they boldly pursue whatever pleases them, selling and buying what cannot be reduced to a price nor even estimated by mortal men.

25. Now there are various categories of this traffic, but all of its kinds are most wicked and wrong. And so others receive churches and ecclesiastical benefices, not for a price or as a reward, nor indeed through any prearranged pact, but with the most powerful recommendation of virtues exerting influence in their case, namely flesh and blood. For no one, as the Lord is our witness, *ever hated his own flesh.* Thus, it often happens that archdeaconries in the Church are conferred on little boys and those practically still wailing in their cradles, so that *from the mouths of babes and sucklings they achieve praise for themselves,* the worthy are praised by the worthy, and they are shown to be guilty through the testimony of innocents.

26. And so, the age of infancy is held up to praise; to it is entrusted the care of souls, and the Lord's flock must be instructed by it before the nurse or the tutor is dispensed with. The little boy still hangs at the breast, and he already has an honored position in the Church! He has received the power of binding and loosing before the ability to speak, the keys of the Church before any discernment and understanding. He begins to take possession of mature fruits before he

quam possit prae immaturitate evelli ab ubere; ut tollatur nomen lactentis, cibatur solidis ante tempus ablactationis, priusquam metas attigerit pueritiae, virilis aetatis censetur ex nomine. Quam bene dispensabit res ecclesiasticas qui pro pomo uno citius solvetur in risum vel lacrimas quam si ei tres vel quattuor auferas aut conferas ecclesias!

27. In huiusmodi non desideratur ut proficiant sapientia, ut augeantur doctrina, muliplicentur gratia, sed tantum ut vivant et citius crescant, et ut virum mentiantur corpore, quem nondum possunt mentiri aetate. Temperatur a scholis, indulgetur otiis, subtrahitur virga, adhibentur balnea et cetera quibus *novellae plantationes* rigari solent in iuventute sua. Mittuntur interim Parisius, litterarum studiis erudiendi; qui postquam studio modicum vacaverint, ne laboris et studii vehementia absumantur et arescant, admittuntur tali et alea, et cetera quae sequuntur, ut respiret natura; et ne putentur non esse ingenui si huiusmodi ludorum fuerint ignari.

28. Sed et qui praesunt operibus, metientes circa eos parentum affectionem potius quam aetatis infirmitatem, illud Daviticum videntur sibi indesinenter audire: *Servate mihi puerum Absalon.* Unde concedunt eis quod petunt, permittunt quod volunt, dissimulant quod perperam faciunt. Salutata autem a primo limite grammatica sive logica, domum revertentes, quod superest temporis consumunt in aucupio et venatica, et utinam his occupationibus contenti essent, et cetera de quibus non est dicendum per singula non

can be prized from the breast because of his immaturity. To remove the name of nursling, he is fed on solid foods before the time of weaning; before he reaches the end of boyhood, he is considered, in name only, of manly age. How well he will manage the affairs of the Church, who dissolves into laughter or tears over an apple more quickly than if you take away or confer three or four churches on him!

27. There is no desire for boys of this kind to increase in wisdom, to be enriched by instruction, to be augmented by grace, but only to live and grow quickly, and in body to pretend to be the man whom they cannot yet pretend to be in age. He is held back from school, given over to leisure; the rod is spared, but baths are provided, and the other things by which *new plantings* are accustomed to be watered in their youth. In the meantime they are sent to Paris to be instructed in the study of letters. After they have applied themselves to study for a short time, lest they be worn out and wither away from the intensity of toil and study, knucklebones and dice are permitted, and all that follows, to allow respite for nature, and lest they be thought not to be noblemen if they are ignorant of games of this kind.

28. But also, weighing the affection of their parents for them rather than the infirmity of their age, those who superintend their activities seem to hear incessantly that saying of David: *Save for me the boy Absalom.* Thus they grant them what they ask, they allow them what they want, and they conceal what they do wrongly. Moreover, bidding farewell to grammar or logic after the first hour and returning home, they consume what is left of their time in fowling and hunting. And would that they were content with these occupations and would not undertake others about which it would

committerent. Quicquid enim deberent moribus inserendis et virtutibus acquirendis impendere, totum impendunt vanitati et luxuriae. Et quod in adolescente pessimum signum est, ita fiunt inverecundi et infruniti, ut illud prophetae eis specialiter dixeris attributum: *Frons meretricis facta est tibi; noluisti erubescere.*

29. Talibus potest episcopus secure et sine scrupulo conscientiae vices suas committere, et plebem a Domino sibi creditam ut erogent eis *in tempore tritici mensuram* commendare qui carnis voluptatibus quasi vermibus scaturiunt, qui aliena sine dilectu fortunae aut conditionis diripiunt, qui mane comedunt, et diem ac noctem insomnem potibus impendunt, qui decimas et oblationes fidelium in renes meretricum transfundunt, qui denique tot flagitia committunt, quod populus non solum erubescit ea referre, sed etiam abhorret audire. Et tamen adhuc sperant *quod influat Iordanis in os eorum,* exspectantes cotidie ut audiant vocem dicentem sibi, "*Amice, ascende superius.*"

30. Sic igitur istos in via sua properari aspicientes illi, quibus non est datum desuper ut caro et sanguis interpellet pro eis, dicentes secum, "*Nihil proficimus, ecce mundus totus post istos abit,*" Montem Pessulanum adeunt, artem et experimenta physicae diligenter addiscunt, post modicum vero temporis *venientes veniunt cum exsultatione portantes* pyxides suas, *super aegros manus imponentes* et curantes ubique. Applicant ergo se divitibus, aut certe ab eis evocantur, qui his

be wrong to speak in detail. For all the time they ought to devote to implanting morals and acquiring virtues, they devote entirely to vanity and luxury. And, which is the worst feature in a young man, they become so shameless and immoderate that you would say that the saying of the prophet was specially applicable to them: *Your face has become a harlot's; you would not blush.*

29. To such as these a bishop can entrust his own duties securely and without scruple of conscience, and to such he can commend the people consigned to him by the Lord, so that they might disburse to them *their measure of wheat in season.* But they are ones who are aswarm with the pleasures of the flesh as though with worms, who plunder another's possessions without regard for fortune or status, who eat in the morning and devote the day and sleepless night to drinking, who divert the tithes and offerings of the faithful to the loins of harlots, who in short commit so many shameful acts that people not only blush to tell them, but even shudder to hear them. Yet they still hope *that the Jordan will flow into their mouth,* expecting daily to hear a voice saying to them, "*Friend, go up higher.*"

30. So, therefore, those to whom it is not granted from above that flesh and blood should intercede on their behalf, when they see these men rapidly progressing on their way, they go to Montpellier, saying to themselves, "*We accomplish nothing; behold, the whole world follows them.*" They diligently learn the art and practices of medicine, but after a little time, *they come with rejoicing, carrying* their boxes of treatments, *laying their hands upon the sick* and curing them in every location. In this way they attach themselves to the rich, or at least are summoned by those who have employment

opus habent. Spondentur sub certa taxatione redditus, et quia non vacat ad praesens ecclesia assignatur certa annuatim de scriniis domini percipienda pecunia, donec vacaverit ecclesia vel praebenda quae conferatur ei pro mercede sua. Quae cum vacaverit, nisi fortior supervenerit, confertur ei in obligationem obsequii et solutionem scrinii. Onerosum enim est domino sed nec tutum famulo mercedes percipere de scrinio. Habentes igitur unde aptius serviant et altius ascendant, ad ulteriora aspirant.

31. Ornantur ergo variis apparatibus, calciantur discoloribus, vestiuntur multiplicibus, nomen et famam sibi comparant et conciliant donis et sumptibus. Quos cum viderint trabeatos incedere et regibus adhaerere, hi qui liberalium artium hucusque exstiterunt amatores, ignominiosum aestimantes rusticorum pulsus palpare et vetularum urinas inspicere, valefacto Parisius Bononiam se transferunt, corpus iuris quocumque labore adquisitum totum incorporant, transactoque tempore congruo revertuntur cum tripudio. Loquuntur enim linguis novis et sesquipedalibus verbis, docent enim homines lites facere, factas sopire, sopitas iterum suscitare. His oportet dare in instanti ecclesias, alioquin tollunt eas vi.

32. Hi sunt sine quibus nec principes nec praelati esse possunt. Sunt enim *pes claudo et oculus caeco.* Hos enim habent oculos ad intuendum in lege Domini viam iustificationum eius sed non ad exquirendum eam. Hos habent et pedes, sed

for them. Payments are promised them at a fixed rate, and since no church is free at the moment, a specific amount of money is allotted to be collected annually from the coffers of the lord until a church or prebend is free to be conferred on that person for his wages. When the church becomes free, unless a stronger man surpasses him, it will be conferred on him to bind him to obedience and to free up the money box. For it is irksome for the lord and not safe for the servant to take his wages from the money box. And so, having the opportunity to serve suitably and to climb still higher, they aspire to greater things.

31. Therefore, they are adorned with diverse forms of finery, furnished with shoes of different colors, dressed in many layers. They gain a name and fame for themselves and ingratiate themselves by gifts and spending. When they see those men wearing robes of state make their way and attach themselves to kings, these who have thus far been lovers of the liberal arts, considering it disgraceful to take pulses of peasants and to inspect the urine of old women, bid farewell to Paris and transfer to Bologna; with all their efforts they master the entire body of the law and come to embody it, and after a suitable period of time, they return with jubilation. Indeed, they speak a new language, with words a foot and a half long; in fact, they teach men to bring lawsuits, to settle the ones already brought, and to take up again the ones laid to rest. It is necessary to bestow churches on them immediately; otherwise they take them by force.

32. These are men without whom neither princes nor prelates can exist. Indeed, they are *a foot to the lame and an eye to the blind.* For they have eyes to see in the law of the Lord the way of his ordinances, but not to seek that way. They

potius ad faciendum eos romipetas in causis prosequendis quam ad dirigendos eos in viam pacis. Hi sunt qui pericula viarum in exteris regionibus experti, sub sole ignoto et aestivi aeris inclementia saepius morti expositi, tradiderunt corpora sua propter dominum suum ad supplicia. Ideo cathedrantur, et accipiunt pro palma cum redierint *baculum pastoralem.*

33. Sed contingit nonnumquam quod, dum negotia ardua explicanda suscipiunt ut ex eorum recompensatione sitis suae ardorem abundantius exstinguant oppressi vehementia laboris dissolvuntur in regione dissimilitudinis, eodemque pariter loco et die semitas claudunt vitae et concupiscentiae. Quorum bona omnia, tanto labore adquisita, tanta sollicitudine congregata, tanto studio intacta conservata, mox ad primos de morte rumores aut in rationes fisci, aut in usus domini fundi, aut in proprietatem cedunt sibi substituti. Qui dum in accessu suo similiter aut forte peius corruet, verteturque domus eius ad extraneos et haereditas ad alienos, dicente psalmista, "*Deiecisti eos dum allevarentur,*" quis pro delictis eius hostias placationis et expiationis faciet offerri, cum non sit de tota domo eius qui vel semel intra saepta illius sustineatur admitti? Sic utique tramite quo veniunt universa recedunt et quae habuerunt longum in colligendo spatium vix habeant in dispersione momentum.

34. Quid autem dicemus de his qui scienter pro causa iniqua fovenda et defendenda animam exhalarunt, cum constet quod quaestus et ambitio fuerint in proposito? Licet autem

have feet, but more for making them pilgrims to Rome in the pursuit of lawsuits than for directing them on the way of peace. These are men who, having experienced the perils of journeys in strange lands, and having been exposed often to death under an unfamiliar sun and the severity of summer heat, have handed over their bodies to suffering for their lord. And so they are enthroned, and they receive *a crozier* in place of a palm when they have returned.

33. But it happens often that, when they undertake matters difficult to unravel in order to extinguish in full measure their burning thirst by payment for those actions, overwhelmed by the intensity of the toil, they are abandoned to total estrangement, and in that very place and on that very day, they close the paths of life and longing. All their goods, acquired through great toil, gathered through great solicitude, preserved intact through great zeal, soon, at the first rumors of death, go either into the accounts of the royal treasury, or for the use of the lord's estate, or into the possession of their replacement. When this man through his accession falls in like manner, or perhaps worse, and his house is turned over to outsiders and his inheritance to strangers—as the psalmist says, "*You have cast them down when they were lifted up*"—who will have sacrifices of reconciliation and expiation offered for his sins, when there is not one from his whole household who is allowed even once to be admitted within its walls? At any rate, all things go back by the way they come, and what took a long time gathering, takes scarcely a moment to disperse.

34. Yet, what shall we say about these who knowingly waste their breath to support and defend an unjust lawsuit, for it is well established that profit and advancement are what they planned for? But although others see this saying

alii in his viderint adimpletum quod dicitur, "*Ducunt in bonis dies suos et in puncto ad inferna descendunt,*" non tamen possunt a cupiditate cohibere spiritum suum, et quamvis non possint usquequaque satisfacere desiderio suo satagunt tamen ne cadant a proposito. Et quia nolunt esse medici, nec esse possunt causidici, ne nihil agatur, ad curiam se transferunt, fiuntque notarii, circumeuntes terram et obambulantes eam, exspectantes donec ros et pluvia sufficienter descenderit super montes Gelboe, id est, donec satiati fuerint redditibus, pro quibus interpellat caro et spiritus gemitibus inenarrabilibus.

35. Qui quoniam non possunt nisi morte interveniente satiari, ipsi annos aetatis eorum saepe dinumerant, complexionem iudicant, qualitatem ponderant, facies considerant, infirmitates si quae sunt latentes a secretioribus explorant, ponentes sibi spem in morte alterius exspectantes sicut:

Rusticus exspectat dum defluat amnis; at ille
labitur et labetur in omne volubilis aevum.

Unde versantur in curia, persaepe donec penitus expilentur, vel donec capilli capitis omnino cani congregentur in locum unum, et in fronte appareat arida, et dicat, "*Usquequo gravi corde, ut quid diligitis vanitatem, et quaeritis mendacium?* Ite domum, prope venit Hesperus, ite capilli!"

36. Moriuntur autem nonnulli eorum sub exspectatione frustratoria, peritque opera et impensa. Alii autem eorum, quia non possunt consilia principum non transire, per

fulfilled in them, "*They spend their days in prosperity, and in a moment they go down to hell,*" yet they cannot restrain their spirit from avarice, and although they are not able entirely to satisfy their desire, they are nevertheless anxious that they not fail in their plan. And since they do not want to be physicians, and they cannot be barristers, lest they achieve nothing, they transfer to the court and become secretaries, roaming all round the land, waiting until dew and rains have fallen sufficiently upon the mountains of Gelboe, that is, until they have been satisfied with revenues, for which their flesh and spirit appeal with unspeakable groans.

35. Since they cannot be satisfied unless a person's death intervenes, they often count the years of people's lives, they judge their complexion, they ponder their condition, they examine their appearance, they seek to discover if there are illnesses concealed in their inner organs, while placing their hope in the death of another, waiting like:

> *A peasant waits while the stream flows by, but it glides along and will continue to glide along in its endless rolling course.*

Hence they remain at court, very often until they are completely bald, or until the hairs on their head are utterly white and gathered in one place, and hair appears scant on their forehead, and it says, "*How long will you be dull of heart? Why do you love vanity and seek falsehood?* Go home, hair, go home! The Evening Star approaches!"

36. Furthermore, some of them die of frustrated expectations, and their exertion and expense are wasted. Others of them, however, since the counsels of princes cannot fail to

manus notariorum admittuntur in gratiam et referunt fructum, tum quia timentur ne ab obsequio se subtrahant, tum quia formidatur ne abscondita palam faciant. Sive autem sic, sive sic promoveantur, non est absque fuco conscientia promoti aut promoventis. Sunt autem et alii tam hebetes et tam inepti quod nec ad pascendum porcos essent idonei, non quia defecerint in eis vires corporis, sed virtus mentis. Hos necesse est tanto robustius alieno fulciri suffragio quanto minus confidere possunt de proprio. Quibus enim sua deficiunt, aliena aut rogant aut rapiunt.

37. Mittuntur igitur a parentibus talium magnatibus xenia, exhibentur hospitia, datur mutuo pecunia, non tamen ad usuram, sed ut gratia inveniat gratiam in tempore opportuno. Offeruntur ergo Lincolniensi episcopo ut eos benedicat, Wintoniensi ut eis manus imponat, Lundoniensi ut eos ad quoscumque ordines promoveat, ut quasi ex hoc teneantur eis in ecclesiaticis beneficiis providere, praeeuntibus tamen paternis obsequiis, sine quibus nec benedictio Lincolniensis sanctificat, nec impositio manus Wintoniensis iuvat, nec promotio ordinis Lundoniensis aliquid praestat, sed quia venerunt et non *per aliam viam revertuntur in regionem suam*. Accipiunt igitur pro talium promotione non solum hi qui habent quod conferant, sed etiam hi qui eis adhaerent, ut negotium promoveant.

pass away, are admitted into favor through the efforts of secretaries, and they carry off fruit, both because it is feared that they might withdraw themselves from service, and because it is feared that they might publicly reveal secrets. But whichever way they are promoted, the conscience of both the promoted and the promoter is not stain free. Furthermore, there are also others so stupid and so senseless that they would not be fit to feed pigs, not because they are lacking in physical strength, but in excellence of mind. The less these are able to rely on their own aid, the more vigorously they must be supported by another's. For those who lack their own resources either ask for another's or seize another's.

37. Therefore, gifts are sent to important persons by the parents of such men, hospitality is shown, money is mutually exchanged, yet not for interest, but that favor may find favor at an opportune time. And so, gifts are presented to the bishop of Lincoln for him to bless the givers, to the bishop of Winchester to lay his hands upon them, to the bishop of London to promote them to any order whatever, so that from this moment the bishops are bound, as it were, to provide for them in ecclesiastical benefices. However, paternal services must pave the way, without which no blessing of the bishop of Lincoln sanctifies, no imposition of hands by the bishop of Winchester brings benefit, and no promotion in orders from the bishop of London conveys status, because they have come and do not *return to their own country by another way.* And so, not only those who have something to bestow receive gifts for the promotion of these men, but even these who are their adherents to advance the business.

38. Unde vacante praebenda vel ecclesia obsequia quae praecesserunt in re et quae sequuntur in spe non cessant clamare una voce dicentes: "*Osanna filio David,*" "*Memor esto verbi tui servo tuo in quo ei spem dedisti.*" Si detur quod petitur bene est, et terminus solvendi debiti prorogatur, et sunt omnia pacifica; sin autem, non est pax. Repetuntur enim mutuo data in instanti solvenda, improperantur obsequia saepius collata, computantur damna ex dilatione solutionis provenientia, nulla erit de cetero de amico confidentia. Quid ergo? Convocatis servis suis profert paterfamilias illud evangelicum: *Auferte ab eo minam, et date ei qui habet decem minas.* Quo facto *fiunt amici Pilatus et Herodes!*

39. Sunt autem et alii qui ne nota simoniacae pravitatis possint respergi, duo iugera vel tria secus ecclesiam comparant LX. vel C. marcis, ut ecclesiam percipiant gratis volentes apud homines famam, et apud Deum illibatam servare conscientiam. Sed numquid tales non aestimant, quod qui habent oculos non videant, et qui habent aures non audiant, et qui habent ora non loquantur super tam impudenti facinore et detestabili enormitate, quo Deum et homines se aestimant posse decipere vel circumvenire? Certe nequaquam, quia et si erratur *Deus non irridetur,* peccata hominum propter paenitentiam dissimulans et omnipotentiam suam parcendo et miserando manifestans.

40. Sunt autem et alii qui ut fratres et cognati magnorum filias ducant aut neptes, paternae haereditati cedunt et

38. Hence, when there is a prebend vacant or a church, the services that have preceded in fact and that will follow in expectation in the future do not cease to cry out with one voice, saying, "*Hosanna to the son of David,*" and "*Be mindful of your word to your servant, in which you have given him hope.*" If what is asked is given, it is well, and the term for paying the debt is deferred, and all is peaceful; but if otherwise, there is no peace. For instant payment is demanded for gifts given reciprocally, services often conferred are denounced, losses arising from the delay in paying are assessed; there will be no trust for a friend in the future. What then? Calling his servants together, the master of the household quotes that saying of the gospel: *Take that pound from him and give it to the one who has ten pounds.* After this is done, *Pilate and Herod become friends!*

39. Moreover, there are also others who, so that they cannot be defiled by the disgrace of wicked simony, purchase two or three acres alongside a church for sixty or a hundred marks, so that they can take possession of the church for free, wishing to preserve their reputation intact before men and their conscience before God. But do such men really think that those who have eyes do not see, and those who have ears do not hear, and those who have mouths do not speak about so shameless a crime and so abominable an outrage, by which they imagine they can deceive and defraud God and men? By no means is this so, because even if there is an exception, *he is not mocked,* but passes over men's sins unnoticed in the interest of repentance and reveals his own omnipotence by sparing and showing pity.

40. There are also others who, in order that their brothers and kinsmen may marry great men's daughters or granddaughters, disavow their paternal inheritance and

portioni quae eos iure haereditario contingebat publice renuntiant, ita tamen ut, ante contractum matrimonium vel post, redditus ecclestiasticos recipiant, qui paternae haereditatis quantitatem sesqualtera portione excedant. Quibus illud bene convenit quod in quodam loco cavit ecclesia felici commercio, pro terrenis caelestia, pro perituris aeterna commutant. Nec immerito, quia uno eodemque ex facto sibi et suis prospiciunt, et maiorum gratiam plenius et propensius adquirunt, qua adiuti possunt adepta in pace possidere et adhuc ampliora pacifice possidenda perquirere. Disposuerunt enim in corde suo ascensiones huiusmodi ut eant nequaquam de virtute in virtutem, sed de vitio in vitium, donec veniant in profundum.

41. Adhuc autem sunt et alii qui cum filiabus divitum ecclesias accipiunt in matrimonium, et quod legibus et decretis penitus prohibitum est, geminas simul ducunt uxores, alteram carnalem, alteram spiritualem. Qui autem ecclesias ita possident, nonne iusto titulo possident? Sed numquid huiusmodi contractus posset dissolvi et scribi *libellus repudii?* Numquid inter huiusmodi sponsam et sponsum sinerent canones celebrari divortium? Numquid huiusmodi matrimonia adhuc hodie sustinet et dissimulat ecclesia? Si quis vero talibus obloquatur, statim aut suffocatur et confunditur muneribus, aut publicis clamoribus arguitur esse invidus et malitiosus.

42. Sunt et alii qui personas ecclesiarum aere alieno ultra quam sint solvendo oneratas solvunt a creditoribus. Et

renounce publicly the share which fell to them by hereditary right. Yet they do this in such a way that, either before or after the marriage has been entered into, they may receive revenues from the Church which exceed the amount of their paternal inheritance by one and a half times. It suits them very well that in a certain place the Church looks out for fruitful commerce, so they exchange heavenly goods for earthly ones, eternal rewards for those that will pass away. Not undeservedly, since by one and the same act they provide for themselves and for their own, and they fully and readily procure the favor of powerful men; aided by this, they are able to possess in peace what they have acquired and to search for still more peaceful possessions. For they have arranged in their heart these kinds of advancements, so that they do not proceed from virtue to virtue, but from vice to vice, until they come to the depths.

41. Moreover, there are still others who receive churches along with the daughters of rich men in marriage, and what is utterly prohibited by laws and decrees, they take two wives at one time, one carnal, one spiritual. Do those who possess churches in this way not possess them with a righteous claim? But could a contract of this kind really be dissolved and *a bill of divorce* be drawn up? Would canon law have allowed a divorce to be pronounced between a wife and husband of this kind? Does the Church today still support and turn a blind eye to marriages of this kind? But if anyone finds fault with such marriages, he is either immediately silenced and overwhelmed by bribery, or he is accused by public outcry of being envious and malicious.

42. There are also others who release from creditors important personages in various churches who are burdened beyond their means in paying their debt. They allow them

absolutos liberos abire permittunt, incumbentes pignori donec satisfiant creditori, quod sero solet contingere. Sufficienter enim cautum est quod summa crediti tanta exsistat quae debitorem per inopiam in perpetuum excludat.

43. Iterum autem sunt alii qui relictas sibi a parentibus facultatum copias in usus divitum indigentium largiter et liberaliter effundunt in hilaritate, ut cum tempus retributionis advenerit *mensuram bonam confertam et coagitatam* recipiant. Et cum beneficia aliqua ecclesiastica perceperint, iterum ea in usus consimiles impendunt, ut similis subsequatur effectus, sicque sorbent ut evomant, evomunt ut iterum absorbeant, oceano similes in quem aquae refluunt lege qua prius effluxerunt. Nonnumquam tamen tales, dum seminant in gaudio, contingit metere in maerore. Quia:

Fallitur augurio spes bona saepe suo.

44. Alii autem, corpore robusti, corde astuti, obsequiis maiorum se devovent et eis officiose ministrant, ut gratiam eorum, immo gradum altiorem adquirant. Quos si diutius contingat a desiderio suspendi, clamant ad dominum in fortitudine dicentes, "*Usquequo Domine, oblivisceris me in finem, usquequo avertis faciem tuam a me? Memento mei in beneplacito tuo, et ne confundas me ab exspectatione mea.* Honori tuo plurimum detrahit, quod *ecce tot annis servio tibi nec unquam dedisti mihi haedum, ut cum amicis meis epularer*. Turpe quidem et ignominiosum erit, si usque ad histrionum consortia vel

to be released and go free, and they take over the mortgage until they satisfy the creditor, which usually is slow to happen. In fact, good care is taken that the sum of the loan is so great that it thrusts the debtor into poverty forever.

43. Again there are others who cheerfully squander, profusely and liberally, the abundant wealth left to them by their parents for the benefit of the rich in need, so that when the time of repayment arrives, they may receive *a good measure pressed down and shaken together.* When they have received any ecclesiastical benefits, again they spend these for similar purposes so that similar outcomes might ensue. Thus they swallow so that they might spew out, and they spew out so that they might swallow down again, like the ocean into which waters flow back according to the law by which they flowed forth before. Yet often it happens that such men, while they sow in joy, reap in sorrow, because:

Hope for the best is often deceived by its own omen.

44. Furthermore, other men, strong of body, cunning of mind, devote themselves to the service of the great and obligingly minister to them to secure their favor, or rather a higher rank. If it happens that they are kept anxiously awaiting their wish for very long, they cry out to their lord in their boldness, saying, "*How long, Lord, will you forget me to the end? How long will you turn your face from me? Remember me in your good pleasure, and do not confound me in my expectation.* It detracts very much from your honor that, *behold, I have been serving you for so many years and you have never given me a kid that I might feast with my friends.* Indeed, it will be a base and shameful thing if I sink from so great a man all the way to

obsequia a tanto viro cogente inopia descendero." Sicque multotiens beneficia optata extorquent et accelerant huiusmodi verbis quae licet diutius dilata variis tamen a longinquo satis praeempta fuerint obsequiis.

45. Quid autem refert merces clericorum a mercede laicorum, nisi quod pistor et pincerna et alii ministri certo numero taxata annuatim accipiunt stipendia, illi autem continua? Isti de anno in annum, illi ab anno secundo aut tertio in aevum suum. Feliciter differtur quod dilatione crescit et augetur, ubi mora non trahit ad se periculum sed generat incrementum. Nonne episcopi et ecclesiarum praelati longe libentius ministris laicis ecclesiastica darent beneficia si liceret accipere quam de aerario suo singulis annis sustinerent tantam pecuniam numerare?

46. Sunt autem adhuc et alii qui nec sanguinis linea, nec artis efficacia, nec muneris vel obsequii seu collusionis alicuius gratia adiuti, sola tantum adulatione et maiestativa quadam imperatorii vultus assumptione, impetrant, quicquid petierint vel praeceperint, quia non est tutum eos quovis pacto offendere, nec in manus eorum incidere. Horum est in aure percepta *super tecta praedicare* et verba in terra cadentia excipere et in altum extollere, *magnificare fimbrias,* noctem in fabulis et diem detinere in nugis. Horum est regum et principum generationes computare, et dominum domus loco competenti interserere, ut probetur regali de stemmate processisse. Horum est cum domino domus idem

the society and service of stage players when need compels me." And so, with words of this kind they often extort and hasten the desired benefices which, although long delayed, have nevertheless been fully purchased in advance by various services over a long period of time.

45. Further, how does the pay of clerics differ from the pay of laymen, except that the baker and butler and other servants receive wages fixed annually at a definite amount, but clerics receive continuous payment? The laymen from year to year, the clerics from the second or third year for the duration of their lifetime. Pay is happily deferred, because by delaying it, it grows and is increased, when delay incurs no hazard, but generates growth. Would not bishops and prelates of churches very gladly bestow ecclesiastical benefices on lay servants if they were allowed to specify the amount that each year they would pay out from their treasury?

46. There are still others also who, aided neither by family lineage nor efficient skill, nor by favor won with a gift or service or collusion, but only by flattery and a certain majestic patronage from the imperial countenance, obtain whatever they have sought or enjoined, since it is not safe to displease them in any way at all, nor to fall into their hands. Their role is *to preach on the rooftops* what is heard in the ear, and to take up the words falling to the earth and raise them on high, *to enlarge the hems of garments,* to spend the night in fables and the day in frivolities. Their role is to count the generations of kings and princes, and to put the lord of the house in an appropriate place to show his descent from royal stock. Their role is to want the same thing as the lord of the

velle, idem nolle, idem negare, ut benedicant eum in omnibus operibus suis et in omni loco dominationis suae.

47. Longum igitur esset modos omnes male ingredientium aut possidentium ecclesias enumerare. Quidam enim eas obtinent ad petitionem summi pontificis, quidam ad instantiam regis, quidam in ore gladii, quidam ratione occulta, sed tamen multiplici, alii sic et alii sic, sed fere omnes quotquot sunt uno spiritu quo ad votum vegetantur. Tantus est enim ardor ambitionis quod non potest etiam toto influente oceano exstingui; habentes enim unam aut duas ecclesias quae ad rei familiaris sustentationem salva honestate sufficerent, non sunt contenti nisi in singulis provinciis singulas habeant, ut sicut voluntas excedit modestiam ita numerus supergrediatur mensuram.

48. Insatiabilis autem est aviditas quam sufficientia non potest satiare. Succenditur ergo tanquam olla a facie aquilonis ardor immoderatae ambitionis, tantaque est libido cupiditatis quod ad explendum desiderium aestuantis animae nihil est quod formident attemptare. Veritas enim postponitur, honestas obliviscitur, iustitia despicitur, misericordia sepelitur, Deus excluditur, et homo non admittitur. Solus ille aliis beatior aestimatur, qui alium poterit aut circumvenire subtilius, aut supplantare validius, quod et cotidie perfacile est videre.

49. Contigit temporibus Henrici iunioris in Anglia quod refero. In provincia Cantuariensis archiepiscopatus erat

house, to not want the same, and to reject the same, so that they might bless him in all his works and in every place in his dominion.

47. In sum, it would take a long time to enumerate all the methods of those who wrongly enter into possession of or occupy churches. For certain men obtain them at the request of the pope, certain ones at the insistence of the king, certain ones at the edge of a sword, certain ones for a hidden reason, some for one reason and some for another, but almost all, however many there are, sharing a single spirit to animate them toward their wish. Indeed, so great is their burning ambition that it cannot be extinguished even if flooded by the entire ocean. For they are not content with having one or two churches that would suffice for the maintenance of their household, with their integrity preserved, unless they have churches in every see, so that just as their desire goes beyond moderation, so their number surpasses measure.

48. But the avarice which sufficiency cannot satisfy is insatiable. And so the ardor of their uncontrolled ambition is inflamed like a cauldron facing the north wind, and so great is their passionate desire that there is nothing they would fear to attempt to appease the longing of their impassioned soul. For truth is neglected, integrity forgotten, justice despised, mercy buried, God is shut out and man is not allowed in. That one alone is judged more blessed than others, who can either more subtly cheat another or more vigorously overthrow him, as is daily very easy to observe.

49. What I shall now relate happened in England in the time of Henry the Younger. In the see of the archbishop of Canterbury there was in a certain town a church whose

ecclesia in castro quodam aestimationis XL aut L marcis, cuius personatum per XL annos, aut eo amplius, gesserat vir quidam nobilis et approbatae honestatis. Fecerat autem sibi nomen magnum et famam hilarem in omni provincia sua, eo quod in strata publica situs hospitalem se omnibus exhibebat, omnesque tam divites quam pauperes ad eum divertentes in tanta hilaritate et opulentia excipiebat, quod universi mirabantur quomodo tantis expensis res tantilla potuit sufficere, vel, si sufficeret, quomodo potuit omnibus tanta iocunditate animi et vultus exhiberi. Erat autem iam grandaevus et processerat in diebus multis. Exceperat autem in domum suam clericos regis praetereuntes in multis equitaturis multotiens, et splendide exhibuerat ut moris erat et reverentia regia exigebat. Erat autem unus eorum hospes ei frequentior, et ideo amicus familiarior. Servierat enim ei saepe et multum non solum in exhibendis hospitiis, sed etiam in donis variis.

50. Contigit autem regem Henricum transfretare in Normanniam clericumque eius praefatum ad locum solitum declinare. Exceptus est et exhibitus sicut semper consueverat. Cumque laborem itineris et prolixae noctis taedium variis sermonibus et potibus abbreviarent, coepit ille affectuose ab hospite suo sciscitari si quid esset in mundo quod sibi vel suis a rege vellet impetrari, dicens se id plurimum desiderare et tota virtute velle perficere. Quod ille audiens plurimum gavisus est, et gratias referens ait, "Ego iam senui et consumpti sunt paene dies mei, unum tamen est quod desidero et desideriis omnibus antepono, scilicet ut ecclesiam quam

valuation was forty or fifty marks. A certain noble man of approved integrity had been its parish priest for forty years or more. He had won a great name for himself and a reputation for cheerfulness in the whole diocese because, situated on a public road, he showed himself to be hospitable to all. He used to greet all who visited him, rich as well as poor, with such cheerfulness and bounty that all marveled at how so small a property could suffice for such great expenses, or, if it did suffice, how it could be made available to all with such great amiability of spirit and countenance. But now he was old and had lived a long life. Nevertheless, he often welcomed into his house the king's clerics who were passing by with a large mounted retinue, and gave them a fine greeting, as was his custom and as respect for the king demanded. One of those clerics was his guest quite frequently, and so a more familiar friend. In fact, the priest had provided for him often and generously, not only in showing him hospitality, but even with various gifts.

50. Now it happened that King Henry was crossing over into Normandy, and his aforementioned cleric visited that place as usual. He was welcomed and provided for as had always been the custom. And while they were relieving the fatigue of the journey and the boredom of the long night with various conversations and drinks, the cleric began to inquire kindly of his host if there was anything in the world that he wished to have granted for himself or his own by the king, saying that he desired this very much and wanted to bring it about with all his might. Hearing this, the priest was very glad, and thanking him, he said, "I am now old and my days are almost finished. Yet there is one thing that I desire and put before all other desires, namely, that in consideration of

de dono regio habeo rex cuidam sororis meae filio, iuveni in scientia litterarum bene erudito, pietatis intuitu conferret ut mihi succederet." Cui ille: "Ne dubites: exaudita est oratio tua, fiet tibi sicut petisti. Ecce ego ad regem proficiscor cito rediturus expediamque negotium, verbum autem istud non exeat in publicum nec communicetur alicui donec reversus fuero."

51. Festinavit igitur ad regem et ad reditum, veniensque in Angliam machinatoque consilio cum episcopo diocesiano praedictum virum ascivit, negotium consummatum esse asseruit. Ventum est coram episcopo, propositum est verbum, et iuvenis qui avunculo suo in ecclesia illa deberet succedere. Clericus vero regius pro utroque instantius episcopo supplicabat et persuadebat. Episcopus vero, et ipse doli conscius, faciem hilarem praetendens, videbatur pollicere negotium agi in veritate, quamquam aliter ageretur. Cumque multis precibus quasi nolens ad hoc a clerico regis cogeretur respondere, quod superstite persona non posset alteri de iure conferri ecclesia, sed si eam resignaret, quod suum erat libenter efficeret.

52. Accessit ille cum gaudio magno, ecclesiamque episcopo resignavit, tamquam securus quod nepoti suo ibidem conferretur. Clericus autem regis statim prosiliens, ait, "Domine episcope, constat quod vacat ecclesia ista, sed quia in fundo regio sita dinoscitur, nec potest nec debet alicui nisi ad eius praesentationem conferri." Et prolatis litteris regis

my loyalty the king would confer the church that I hold as the king's gift on a son of my sister, a young man who is well educated in the knowledge of letters, to succeed me." The cleric said to him: "Have no doubt: your prayer has been heard; it will happen as you have requested. See, I am going to the king and will return quickly, and I shall settle this matter; but do not let this conversation become public or share it with anyone until I return."

51. And so the cleric hurried to the king and hastened to return. Arriving in England, after contriving a plan with the bishop of the diocese, he received the aforementioned man and declared that the matter was settled. They came before the bishop, along with the young man who was to succeed his uncle in that church, and the matter was proposed. The king's cleric urgently implored and tried to persuade the bishop on behalf of both. But the bishop, aware of the deception and simulating a cheerful countenance, seemed to promise that the matter was being transacted in reality, although it was being transacted far otherwise. And when he was compelled by the king's cleric through many entreaties to respond to this proposal, as if unwilling, he said that the church could not lawfully be conferred on another while the beneficiary remained alive, but if he should resign it, the bishop would willingly grant what was his own.

52. With great joy, the priest assented and resigned the church to the bishop, confident that it would then and there be conferred on his nephew. However, springing up at once, the king's cleric said, "Lord bishop, it is certain that this church is vacant, but since it is known to be situated on the king's land, it cannot be conferred on anyone, nor should it be, except according to the king's right of presentation."

ad episcopum quibus praecipiebatur quod primo vacantem in fundo regio in episcopatu suo praesentium latori dilatione postposita conferret, ait, "Ecce ista est prima vacans, praeceptum prosequere." Factumque est ita. Instituitque episcopus illum personam in ecclesia illa, aliumque inanem et vacuum abire permisit. Reversus est autem tristis et eiulans, sed non in domum suam, satellites enim alterius praevenerant et occupaverant universa. Vixit autem in mendicitate et miseria toto quo superfuit tempore, nec aliquid aliquando a supplantore suo potuit extorquere. Iam forte uterque eorum in cineres suos solutus est, memoria vero facti non poterit de facili oblivione deleri.

53. Sed et alius quidam cum multo tempore affectasset ecclesiam quandam, nec eam aliqua circumventione vel machinatione posset adipisci, contigit personam ecclesiae illius gravi infirmitate correptum usque ad extrema deduci, quod audiens ambitiosus ille cucurrit quamcitius ad canonicos religiosos qui in vicino commanebant, postulavitque habitum ad succurrendum quasi ex parte ipsius, et eo impetrato reversus est ad aegrotum, eumque induit ignorantem quid circa eum ageretur, immissumque feretro in coenobium deportavit. Ubi cum aliquantis diebus elapsis sanitatem recepisset, videns se delusum voluit in domum suam reverti. At ille prohibebat eum, dicens, "Ne venias, quia si veneris non reverteris." Sicque habitum et ordinem quem nesciens

And after a letter of the king to the bishop was brought forth, in which orders were given to confer without delay on the bearer of the letter at hand the first vacant church on the king's land in his diocese, the cleric said, "See, this is the first vacant church; execute the order." And so it was done. The bishop appointed that cleric as beneficiary in that church, and he allowed the other to go away empty-handed and without a benefice. The priest returned sad and lamenting, but not to his own house, for the agents of the other man had gone ahead and taken possession of everything. Furthermore, he lived in poverty and misery for the rest of his life, and he could not ever wrest away anything from his supplanter. Both of them, as it happens, have now been reduced to ashes, but the memory of the deed cannot easily be expunged in oblivion.

53. In addition, a certain other cleric had aspired to a certain church for a long time, but could not acquire it by any deception or contrivance. Then it happened that the beneficiary of that church was seized by a serious sickness and brought even to the point of death. Hearing this, that ambitious cleric ran as quickly as possible to the regular canons who were dwelling in the neighborhood, and asked for a habit, as if to succor him with it. After he obtained it, he returned and put the habit on the sick man, who did not know what was being done to him. Then the cleric placed him on a litter and brought him to the monastery. After some days had passed, when the man had regained his health, seeing that he had been tricked, he wanted to return to his own house. But the cleric prevented him, saying, "Do not come home, because if you come, you will not return." And thus he was forced against his will to keep the habit and adhere

suscepit coactus est nolens observare, vix tamen obtento necessaria sibi de suo quoad viveret ministrari.

54. Longe autem aliter alteri contigit, rege Henrico in finibus Walliae cum exercitu agente. Rumor subito ad curiam perlatus est quod clericus quidam, dives valde, diem clausisset extremum. Habebat autem idem multas ecclesias pretiosas, unam tamen pretiosiorem inter alias. Quo audito clericus quidam qui inter alios gratiam in oculis regiis ampliorem invenisse gloriabatur, surrexit velociter, et petiit a rege litteras ad abbatem quendam pro ecclesia praedicta. Quibus impetratis, quia abbas ille ad quem spectabat donatio octo dierum itinere distabat a rege, festinavit, ne alius praecurreret et apprehenderet bravium et praeriperet benedictionem. Mutatis igitur non semel equitaturis, et quibusdam interfectis, ac sociis itineris impotentioribus obiter relictis, bis quattuor dietas fere duabus confecit, substitit enim citra locum ubi abbas morabatur decem miliaribus, non quia voluntas progrediendi deficeret sed virtus propria, comitum et equorum, regionis ignotae error suspectus, et nox pro parte iam exacta, ulterius progredi prohibebat.

55. Fatigatus autem ex itinere, et tristior effectus audito quod eo die ecclesia alteri esset collata, acrius coepit aegrotare. Versusque ad parietem nec cibum nec consolationem voluit accipere. Unde in crastino, utroque homine, altero

to the order which he unknowingly received, securing with difficulty the right to have the necessities of life supplied to him from his own property as long as he lived.

54. However, another cleric had a quite different experience while King Henry was campaigning with his army in the territory of Wales. A rumor was suddenly brought to court that a certain very rich cleric had died. The man held many valuable churches, yet one among them was particularly valuable. When the news was heard, a certain cleric, who used to boast that among the others he had found greater favor in the king's eyes, rose up quickly and sought a letter from the king to a certain abbot to lay claim to the aforementioned church. After this was obtained, he set off in haste lest another might preempt him, seize the prize, and snatch the benefice, for that abbot on whom the grant depended was eight days' journey distant from the king. And so, after his horses had been changed more than once, and some even killed, and after the weaker of his companions had been left behind along the way, he completed the eight days' journey in just two. He stopped ten miles short of the place where the abbot resided, not because his will to proceed failed, but because his own strength and that of his companions and horses, the suspicion that they were going astray in an unfamiliar region, and the fact that the night was already partly advanced, all prevented him from proceeding farther.

55. Worn out from the journey, and saddened when he learned that on that day the church had been conferred on another, he began to fall seriously ill. Turning toward the wall, he wanted neither food nor consolation. Hence, on the next day, failing both inwardly and outwardly because of

prae fatigatione, altero prae anxietate frustrati desiderii, deficiente, obdormivit in mortem, delatusque est ad abbatiam, et abbati ante mortuus nuntiatus et expositus quam ipse causam adventus sui exponeret. Adhuc litterae regis facientes pro vivo recenti claudebantur sigillo et iam mortuus claudebatur sepulcro. Priusque scitum est quare non recederet quam cur tam subito adveniret. Ante passus est ruinam quam petitio eius pateretur repulsam. Nondum abbas regiae petitioni abnuerat, et ipse de non petendo ulterius iam satis dabat. Si mortuus est pro ecclesia quam ita ambierat, non est causandus rex, qui pro clerico suo scripsit, neque abbas qui rei nescius nec concessit nec negavit, immo ipse, qui in deferenda abbati petitione regia et nimis moratus est et nimis festinavit. Sicque dum nimio hiatu anhelavit ad obtinendum non habita, prius habita perdidit quam obtineret quod optavit.

56. Multa possent ambitiosorum exempla proponi, priusque deficeret scribenti ea vita quam materia, unum tamen placet adhuc inserere. Fuit in provincia Eboracensi ecclesia quaedam duobus clericis ita assignata quod alter mediam partem, et alter mediam possideret, fructusque provenientes aequa lance dividerent, ita quod neuter alteri praeesset vel subesset. Sed quia *omnis potestas impatiens consortis erat* coepit alter eorum, quia vir potens erat, graviter ferre quod consortem debuit admittere vel admissum sustinere, sustinuit tamen ad tempus cogitans et excogitans quomodo posset socium suum supplantare. Saepe a cogitationibus suis frustratus destitit, rursumque ne desisteret ipse sibi suggessit, sedens autem semper in insidiis vias multas excogitavit

weariness and the anguish of disappointed desire, he died and was brought to the abbey. His death was reported and made known to the abbot before he himself could make known his reason for coming. The king's letter on behalf of the man so recently alive was still sealed, but the dead man was already enclosed in a tomb. And it was known why he was not returning before it was known why he had arrived so suddenly. He suffered death before his petition suffered denial. The abbot had not yet refused the king's request, and the cleric was already giving assurance of no further requests. If that man died for the church which he had so coveted, the king who wrote on behalf of his cleric should not be blamed, nor the abbot who in total ignorance neither assented nor refused, but rather the cleric himself, who, in carrying the royal request to the abbot, both was too slow and too hurried. And so, while he aspired to gain what he did not have, he lost what he had before he gained what he wanted.

56. Many examples of ambitious men could be set forth, and the writer's life would run out before his material. Yet I intend to insert one more example here. In the province of York, there was a certain church assigned to two clerics in such a way that one had half and the other had half, and they apportioned the proceeds with equal shares, so that neither man was superior or inferior to the other. But since *all power is intolerant of a partner,* one of them, because he was a man of position, began to be irked that he had to accept a partner or tolerate his acceptance. Yet he bore it for a time, weighing and pondering how he could dislodge his colleague. Often he gave up his planning in frustration, but again he urged himself not to give up. Always waiting in ambush, he

quibus socium supplantaret, et utrorumque portionem perciperet, visaque est ei pars sua aut nulla aut modica sola consortium gratia, tantoque suum magis parvipendere, quanto acrius alienum desideravit.

57. Viso ergo quod via nulla superesset quae si veritate niteretur ad votum pertingeret, convertit se ad dolos excogitandos quibus praevaleret. Accedensque ad causidicum quendam, qui et filius erat cuiusdam potentis de provincia, pepigit cum eo foedus, data pecuniae quantitate non modica, tali scilicet conditione, quod ille eum et socium eius super tota ecclesia sua impeteret, et ipse post litem contestatam aut iuri suo cederet aut quasi invitus rem sibi abiudicari sustineret, ut ex hoc socium suum ad idem faciendum facilius impingeret, et ille cum ita utrumque evicisset, et partem utrorumque possideret, ei in integrum partem utramque restitueret.

58. Facta igitur conventione ista inter eos, et sigillorum appositione firmata, missum est ad curiam Romanam propter litteras negotio necessarias, quibus impetratis causidicus ille in ius traxit utrumque. Post indutias igitur legitimas et altercationes varias, ambitiosus ille qui utrumque voluit possidere defecit in causa, et sicut praelocutum fuerat possessio ei abiudicata et adiudicata alteri, qui et in possessionem missus est statim. Alter vero qui adhuc possidebat, pro seipso viriliter agens, confugit ad appellationes, quas opera et impensa diligentius prosequens obtinuit in causa sua.

pondered many ways to dislodge his colleague and to take possession of both their shares. His own portion seemed to him either nothing at all or only small on account of the partition between them, and so much the less did he value his own as he more eagerly desired the other's.

57. Therefore, when he saw that no way was left to attain his desire if he relied on the truth, he turned to devising deceptions by which to prevail. Approaching a certain advocate, who was also the son of a certain powerful man in the diocese, he concluded a contract with him after a considerable amount of money was paid, on the following terms: the advocate would lay a claim against him and his colleague over their entire church. After the suit was contested, he would resign his entitlement, or, with a show of unwillingness, he would acquiesce to the legal forfeiture of the property, so that by this ploy he would more easily force his colleague to do the same, and when the advocate had won out over each of them and possessed the shares of both, he would restore both shares entirely to him.

58. And so, after this covenant was made between them and confirmed by the affixing of seals, they sent to the curia at Rome for the documents needed in the matter. When these had been secured, the advocate dragged both men into court. After legal delays and various disputes, that ambitious cleric who wanted to have both shares failed in his suit, and just as prearranged, possession was denied to him and adjudicated to the advocate, who also was immediately sent to take possession. But the other cleric who still had possession of his own share, acting vigorously on his own behalf, had recourse to appeals; pursuing these very diligently with exertion and expense, he prevailed in his suit.

59. Viso autem ambitiosus ille quod a spe sua penitus cecidisset, accessit ad causidicum volens possessionem suam recipere. Ille autem restitit ei in faciem, asserens se legitime possidere et canonicum habuisse ingressum. Adiecit etiam ut si vellet chirographum inter eos factum proferret in medium, in quo continebatur quod cum totam ecclesiam obtineret, totam ei restitueret. Nondum totam obtinuit, sed partem unam; cum vero totum possideret, iuxta quod convenerat inter eos, totum restitueret. Sicque ambitiosus partem amisit pro toto, immo partem et totum, et alter accepit partem pro toto, malens possidere partem quam totum.

60. Licet autem ambitiosi se et alios spe sua videant saepius defraudari, non tamen pedem referunt nec frena moderantur, sed quasi equus currens in praelium, sic feruntur in praecipitium. Quid quo flagitio perquirant non curant, dummodo sortiantur quod desiderant. Haec est febris cotidiana quae cunctos corripit, nullum fere immunem relinquit, quae ideo non potest curari, quia materia non potest digeri. Hoc est venenum aspidum quod est insanabile, quo qui tactus fuerit de die in diem amplius tabescet. Hoc est fermentum quod universam massam corrumpit, et *a planta pedis usque ad verticem capitis* gravi ulcere totum corpus perfundit.

61. Libidine enim dominandi sive praesidendi omnes inflammantur, ut iugum dominationis alienae et servitutis propriae a cervicibus suis excutiant, in eius comparatione

59. After that ambitious cleric saw that he had utterly failed in his expectation, he approached the advocate, wishing to recover his possession. However, the advocate opposed him to his face, asserting that he legally possessed and held the canonical right of entry to the property. He also added that if the cleric wished, he would produce in public the written agreement made between them in which it was specified that when he obtained the whole church, he would restore the whole to him. He had not yet obtained the whole, but one part; indeed, when he possessed the whole, he would restore the whole, according to what was agreed between them. And so, the ambitious cleric lost a part for the whole, or rather, a part and the whole. The other cleric, preferring to possess a part rather than the whole, received a part instead of the whole.

60. But although the ambitious clerics often see themselves and others cheated of their expectations, yet they do not turn back or hold back the reins, but like a steed running to battle, so are they borne onward toward a precipice. They do not care with what shame they acquire anything, as long as they obtain what they wish for. This is the daily fever that seizes all, that leaves almost no one immune, that cannot be cured, because the morbid matter cannot be dissipated. This is the vipers' venom that is without remedy; one who has been infected by it wastes away more and more from day to day. This is the leaven that spoils the whole lump, and *from the sole of the foot to the top of the head,* it spreads painful sores over the whole body.

61. Indeed, all are inflamed with a passion for ruling or presiding, to shake from their necks the yoke of another's rule and their own servitude; in procuring this end, a man

omnia quae habet homo dabit in commutatione illius. Hinc est quod tanta ambitione quaeruntur et comparantur redditus et ecclesiae, ut ex eorum fructibus percipiant unde sibi principes concilient, potestates alliciant, familiaritates maiorum adquirant, aliis praeemineant, et de gradu in gradum ascendant.

62. Non sufficiunt quindecim aut viginti ecclesiae, nisi in omni cathedrali ecclesia totius regni adquirant praebendam unam, cui necesse est ut brevi tempore adiciatur decanatus, aut tale aliquid. Sed non sic furor eorum quiescit, sed adhuc manus eorum extenta desuper, et videns se cum Herode placuisse Iudaeis, quia occidit Iacobum, apponit ut apprehendat et Petrum. Et ne quid desit in ulla gratia, commutatur aut comparatur archidiaconatus manu, lingua, vel obsequio. Quo nacto dicunt, "Feliciter addat mihi Deus et alterum." Multiplicatis igitur intercessoribus quaeritur episcopatus, et spes certa adipiscendi concipitur quoniam *de praeteritis trahit argumenta futuri.*

63. Frequentatur ergo curia regis solito frequentius, dona ministris pluunt uberius, vocantur curiales ad convivia propensius. Excipiuntur legationes pro regiis negotiis expediendis in longinquis regionibus propriis sumptibus, ut, domino rege interrogante, "Petre, *amas me?*" secure possit responderi, "*Tu scis, domine, quod amo te,* nam et *animam meam pono pro te.*" Probatio vero dilectionis est exhibitio operis. Nemo autem maiorem caritatem habet quam ut animam suam ponat pro amicis suis. Currunt ergo et discurrunt olfacientes sedes vacantes, diligentius inquirentes quae cui

will give in exchange for it all that he has. Hence it is that revenues and churches are sought and procured with such great ambition, so that from their proceeds they may have the means to win princes over to themselves, attract the powerful, acquire friendships with the great, surpass others, and ascend from rank to rank.

62. Fifteen or twenty churches do not suffice, unless in every cathedral church in the entire realm they acquire one prebend, to which in a short time it is necessary that a deanery be added, or some such thing. But their madness does not cease even so; rather, their hand is still stretched out, and seeing that it has pleased the Jews and Herod, because it killed James, it further acts to seize Peter also. And lest anything should be lacking in any regard, an archdeaconate is exchanged or procured by action, by speech, or by service. After this has been obtained, they say, "May God happily add yet another office for me." And so, once the number of intermediaries has been increased, a bishopric is sought, and a sure hope of attaining it is harbored, since *one draws evidence of the future from the past.*

63. Therefore, the king's court is frequented more frequently than usual, gifts to ministers rain down more copiously, courtiers are invited to banquets more readily. Commissions are received for settling the king's business in distant regions at their own expense, so that when the lord king asks, "Peter, *do you love me?*" it can be safely answered, "*You know, Lord, that I love you,* for *I even lay down my life for you.*" Indeed, the proof of love is the performance of works. Moreover, greater love no man has than to lay down his life for his friends. And so they hasten and scurry about, sniffing out vacant sees, diligently seeking which outweighs which,

praeponderet, quae et quot sint praedia, et quod pretium eorum et qualiter possint dilatari. Nulla fit mentio de loci benignitate, sed de divitiis. Ultima quaestio est de fructu animarum, prima de fertilitate agrorum et fecunditate nummorum. Quia ubi amor ibi oculus, ubi dolor ibi digitus.

64. Si vero sedes non vacaverint, anni praesidentium crebro calculantur; universa secretius explorantur: si caligant adhuc oculi, si dentes defecerunt, si facies pallore suffunditur, si manus tremula alterius officio sustentetur, si pes labans vicario baculi fruatur obsequio, si sensus integros et si se habet bene ad oblata. Et ne *segnius irritent animum demissa per aures quam quae sunt oculis subiecta fidelibus,* simulatur peregrinatio ad sanctum loci, ad exsolvenda vota olim in naufragatio facta, ubi videatur et alloquatur episcopus, et sciatur si spes de eo est vel desperatio.

65. Si adhuc vegetus est, dicitur serpentis edulio iuventus eius ut aquilae renovari; non decessurum nisi percussum malleo. Iam enim annos Nestoris adimplevit, et ideo iam delirat et ad ineptias committitur pueriles. Si vero aliqua laboraverit infirmitate, dicitur sine spe convalescendi aegrotare, unde periculosum est tales praesidere de quibus certum est quod de cetero non poterunt ministrare. Quomodo enim alium potest regere qui seipsum non potest sustentare? Quomodo sufficiet alteri qui non sufficit sibi? Satius et sanius consilium esset in claustrum aliquod secedere, ibique horam extremam praestolari, quam ita praesidere. Perit

what and how many estates there are, what their value is, and how they can be enlarged. There is no mention of the benignity of the place, but of its wealth. The last question is about the fruit of souls, the first about the fertility of fields and its fecundity in cash. Because where love is, there is the eye; where sorrow is, there is the finger.

64. But if sees are not vacant, the age of those presiding over them is calculated often; every detail is secretly investigated: if the eyes grow dim yet, if the teeth are missing, if the face is pale, if a trembling hand is supported by the kindness of another, if an unsteady foot avails itself of the supplementary service of a staff, if he has senses unimpaired and if he responds well to the Communion bread. And, lest *things absorbed through the ears stir the mind more slowly than those which are presented to trustworthy eyes,* a pilgrimage is feigned to the local saint to pay vows once made in a shipwreck, where the bishop may be seen and spoken to, and it can be ascertained if there is hope in his case, or not.

65. If the bishop is still vigorous, his youth is said to be renewed like the youth of an eagle by the food of the serpent; he will not die unless hit with a hammer. For he has already completed the years of Nestor, and therefore now is out of his mind and is given over to childlike folly. But if he suffers from some infirmity, he is said to be sick without hope of recovery; hence it is dangerous that such men preside over matters which it is certain that they cannot attend to anymore. For how can he guide another, who is unable to hold himself up? How will he deal appropriately with another, who does not do so with himself? It would be a better and more sensible plan to retire to some cloister and there to await the final hour than to be preeminent like this. The

clerus et populus, quia non est qui verbum salutis praedicet, qui errata corrigat, qui diripientibus bona ecclesiae resistat vel contradicat, qui se murum pro domo Domini opponat, qui ministerium sollemnitatibus praecipuis debitum persolvat. Rex et archiepiscopus, ad quos negotium in primis respicit, et quibus principaliter incumbit, dicuntur privata ex causa dissimulare, alioquin prospicerent ecclesiae et populo pereunti.

66. Haec et alia nonnulla garriunt ambitiosi in sugillationem praesidentium, cupiditate potius praesidendi inflammati quam amore iustitiae ducti. Oculis enim lippiens plus odit lucem quam tenebras, et naris sordida male discernit odores. Si autem viderint curialibus obsequiis et exercitationibus nihil suam praevalere industriam, sed a voto suo amplius elongari, altius ingemiscunt et ardore ambitionis interius acrius exuruntur, flamma exire prohibita interiora depascens fortius debacchatur, *quoque magis tegitur tectus magis aestuat ignis.*

67. Quaeritur ergo et invenitur callis compendiosior ad votum consequendum. Viae enim longioris discursus vagos et erroneos semita brevis potest redimere; et medicina austerior efficacius interdum solet subvenire. Revertentes igitur ad propria, ecclesias ingrediuntur cathedrales, et, quasi omnia mundana post tergum reliquerunt, studia exteriora commutant, opera priora abdicant, dies et annos perditos conqueruntur, et tempora multa inutiliter defluxisse. Nunc autem, quia dies mali sunt, volunt tempus redimere et in

clergy and the people are lost because there is no one to preach the word of salvation, to correct their faults, to resist or gainsay those who plunder the goods of the church, to place himself as a wall before the house of the Lord, to render the service due to special celebrations. The king and the archbishop, whom the matter especially concerns and to whom it chiefly falls, are said to turn a blind eye for personal reasons; otherwise they would look out for the church and its suffering people.

66. The ambitious clerics prattle these words and sundry others to denigrate those enjoying preeminence, incited rather by a passion for their own preeminence than guided by a love of justice. For a man with inflamed eyes hates the light more than the darkness, and a blocked-up nose discerns odors badly. But if they have seen that their diligence in courtly service and practices fails to prevail, but they are kept further away from their desire, they groan all the more deeply and are inwardly burned more severely by the ardor of ambition; the flame, prevented from going forth, consuming their inner parts, rages more intensely, and *the more the hidden fire is concealed, the more it rages.*

67. Thus, they seek and find a shorter way to attaining their wish. For a short path can substitute for the errant and meandering byways of a longer journey, and bitter medicine is sometimes wont to heal more effectively. So, returning to their own properties, they enter cathedral churches and, as if they have left behind all worldly things, they wholly alter their outward attachments. They renounce their former works, they bewail their wasted days and years, and lament that much time has slipped away to no end. Now, however, since the times are wicked, they want to make up for lost

brevi tempora multa explere. Sufficit circuisse terram, et obambulasse eam. Nihil est subtilius intuenti, quicquid mundus blanditur. Nulla est rebus transeuntibus neque hominibus fides adhibenda.

68. Abiectis ergo pompis et reiecta sindone, ornamentisque aliis quibus hucusque utebantur, mediocribus vestiuntur, scilicet superpelliceis lineis et pellibus agninis, ut lupus rapacitatis et vulpis astutiae sub pelle ovina delitescat, horas canonicas praeveniunt et subsequuntur orationes peculiares et genuflexiones angulares. Reficiuntur pauperes in plateis, ut videant transeuntes opera eius et glorificent Patrem qui in caelis est. Vestiuntur nudi, visitantur infirmi, sepeliuntur mortui, ceteraque opera misericordiae ita sollemniter exercentur exterius et caro ieiuniis et vigiliis ita attenuatur interius, ut omnes mirentur et dicant: "*Non est inventus similis illi qui conservaret legem Excelsi,* igitur deo iureiurando deberet crescere in populo Dei."

69. Si vero adhuc fraudentur a desiderio suo, nec gradibus istis *tollantur in altum ut lapsu graviore ruant,* descendunt inferius, et quasi aries gradu retrogrado feruntur ut fortius impingant. Nullo autem sciente vel suspicante, subito in coenobia descendunt, monachum induunt, servantes tamen fidem saeculo quem sic relinquunt. *Haec* autem *mutatio dexterae Excelsi* non ita fit nemine praescio, ut res subito facta se citius, fama mediante, diffundat, fiatque omnibus eo amplius nota quo minus praecognita. Et quoniam nonnullos propositi sui socios ibidem reperiunt quos similis

time and achieve much in a short period. Enough of traveling and roaming the earth. To the perceptive observer, all the blandishments of the world are nothing. No trust should be accorded to passing things or to perishing men.

68. Therefore, rejecting all finery and shunning fine linen, along with other adornments that they previously enjoyed, they now dress in ordinary clothes, namely, in linen surplices and lambs' skins, so that the wolf of greed and the fox of cunning can hide under sheep's skin. They arrive before the canonical hours, and they hold their own private prayers with genuflections in corners. The poor are fed in the streets, so that those passing by may see his works and glorify the Father who is in heaven. The naked are clothed, the sick are visited, the dead are buried, and other works of mercy are practiced outwardly so scrupulously, and the flesh is so weakened by fasts and vigils inwardly, that all marvel and say: "*There is not found his like to keep the law of the Most High,* and so by a binding oath he ought to become great among God's people."

69. But if they are still foiled in their desire and not *raised on high by those advancements, so that they collapse in a heavier fall,* they sink down lower and, like the ram, they back up in order to strike more forcefully. With no one knowing or suspecting, they suddenly betake themselves to monasteries. They put on the monk, though keeping faith with the world that they have abandoned in this way. However, *this change of the right hand of the Most High* does not happen with no one knowing beforehand, so that a thing done suddenly spreads quickly by the agency of rumor, and the less it was known beforehand, the more fully it becomes known by all. And since they find not a few partners to join them in their

succendit ambitio, quibusdam singularis vitae studiis insistunt, aliisque fratribus longo aliter vestiuntur et vivunt.

70. Hi sunt qui, iuxta Salomonem, *risum reputant errorem et gaudio dicunt, "Quid frustra deciperis?"* Hi sunt qui consuetudine loci non sunt contenti, nec conditione communi, et, ut omnibus praeferantur in omnibus operibus suis, quadam gaudent singularitate. Omnia quasi perperam facta diiudicant, vitam aliorum lacerant et suam eligunt, desolationem ecclesiae Dei conspectu publico iugiter lamentantur, verba mellita toxicatis interrumpunt suspiriis, capite obstipo et pede lento incedunt, palpebras oculorum quasi congelatas longo tractu demittunt, et cum Martino oculis et manibus in caelum semper intenti invictum ab oratione spiritum non relaxant.

71. Et quia non sunt sicut ceteri, hominum vitam arguunt singulorum, subiectos opprimunt, pares despiciunt, superioribus non obediunt, sed eis sicut et ceteris detrahunt. Insimulant enim reges et principes de tyrannide, episcopos de insolentia, clerum de incontinentia, populum de imperitia, nec est aliquis quem aliqua non aspergant nota. Unum autem est quod maxime venantur, scilicet ut omnia opera eorum praedicentur in plateis et ascendat clamor eorum aures regis, ut cum sedes aliqua vacaverit reminiscantur eorum et dicat, "*Amice ascende superius. Qui enim se humiliat exaltabitur. Te enim vidi iustum coram me ex omnibus gentibus.*"

undertaking there, whom similar ambition inflames, they adopt certain pursuits of the solitary life, but they dress and live far otherwise than the other brothers.

70. These are the ones who, according to Solomon, *think that laughter is a mistake, and with joy say, "Why are you deceived baselessly?"* These are the ones who are not satisfied with local practices or with the common state of being, and in order to be esteemed before all others in all their works, they rejoice in their certain singularity. They decide that everything is done incorrectly. They censure others' way of life and choose their own way. They continually lament in the sight of all the desolation of God's Church. They intermingle honeyed words with poisoned sighs. They walk with head bowed and slow step. They lower their eyebrows as if they had been frozen for a long period, and like Saint Martin, ever intent upon heaven with eyes and hands, they do not release their unconquered spirit from prayer.

71. And since they are not like the rest, they reprove all men's way of life, they oppress those subject to them, despise their equals, and do not obey their superiors, but disparage them just as they do all others. Indeed, they accuse kings and princes of tyranny, bishops of arrogance, the clergy of excess, and the people of ignorance, nor is there anyone whom they do not taint with some mark of reproach. Moreover, there is one thing which they especially seek, namely, that all their works be proclaimed in the streets and their cry might ascend to the ears of the king, so that when some see is vacant, he remembers and he says, *"Friend, go up higher. For he who humbles himself will be exalted. Indeed, I have seen that you are just of all the people before me."*

72. Hae sunt igitur viae quibus ascenditur hodie in domum domini, per quas gradiuntur fere universi. Hae sunt semitae per quas subintrant ambitiosi, quorum tanta est multitudo quod non potest comprehendi, licet delinquentium culpam non minuat, sed eo magis augeat, quo fortius efficit ut quod a multis peccatur relinquatur inultum. Quod quidem non ideo minus est peccatum quia inultum, sed eo forte gravius quo multitudinis viribus agitur ne corrigantur excessus. Qua vero via ad honores ecclesiasticos ascendendum esset, non solum canones et etiam leges insinuant saeculares.

73. Unde et imperator Iustinianus inter alia sic ait: "Maxima in omnibus sunt dona Dei a superna collata clementia, sacerdotium et imperium. Illud quidem divinis ministrans, hoc autem in humanis praesidens ac diligentiam exhibens, ex uno eodemque principio utraque procedentia humanam exornant vitam. Ideoque nihil sic erit studiosum imperatoribus sicut sacerdotum honestas, cum utique pro illis ipsi semper Deo supplicent. Nam si hoc quidem inculpabile sit, undique et apud Deum fiducia erit plenum; imperium autem recte et competenter exornet traditam sibi rem publicam, erit consonantia quaedam bona omne quicquid est utile humano conferens generi.

74. "Nos igitur maximam habemus sollicitudinem circa vera Dei dogmata et circa sacerdotum honestatem, quam illis obtinentibus credimus, quia per ea maxima nobis dona dabuntur a Deo, et ea, quae sunt, firma habebimus, et quae nondum venerunt adquiremus. Bene autem universa

72. And so, these are the ways by which people rise up to the house of the lord today; the ways by which almost all advance. These are the paths on which the ambitious enter. Their vast number is so great that it cannot be grasped, although it does not lessen the guilt of those wrongdoers, but increases it all the more as it vigorously acts to ensure that the sins of many are left unpunished. Indeed, it is no less a sin because it is unpunished, but perhaps more grievous, in that excesses are left uncorrected through the strength of numbers. But not only canon law, but secular laws also make clear by what way one must ascend to ecclesiastical honors.

73. Hence even the emperor Justinian says, among other things, the following: "The greatest of all gifts of God conferred by his celestial mercy are priesthood and empire. The former attends to divine matters, but the latter presides over human affairs and exercises diligence in them. Proceeding from one and the same source, both enhance human life. Thus, nothing will be of so immediate a concern for emperors as the honest reputation of priests, since they should surely always pray to God for them. For if the priesthood is indeed blameless, there will be complete assurance on every side and before God; moreover, should the imperial rule rightly and properly enhance the commonwealth entrusted to it, there will be a certain benign harmony conferring on humankind everything that is beneficial.

74. "Therefore, we have the greatest concern about the true teachings of God and about the honest reputation of priests, which we entrust to those preserving it, because through this the greatest gifts will be bestowed on us by God, and we will keep secure those gifts which we already have, and will obtain those which have not yet come to us.

geruntur et competenter, si rei principium fiat decens et amabile Deo. Hoc autem futurum esse credimus, si sacrarum regularum observatio custodiatur quam iusti, laudati, adorandi inspectores et ministri verbi Dei tradiderunt, apostoli et sancti patres custodierunt et explanaverunt.

75. "Sancimus igitur sacras per omnia sequentes regulas, dum quispiam sequenti omni tempore ad ordinationem episcopatus perducitur, considerari prius eius vitam secundum sacrum apostolum, si honesta, si inculpabilis et undique irreprehensibilis sit et in bonis testimonium habeat, et sacerdotem decens et neque ex officiali aut ex curiali fortuna veniat. Neque ex idiota mox clericus, deinde parvum aliquid praeteriens episcopus appareat, sed aut in virginitate degens a principio, aut uxorem siquidem habens ex virginitate ad eum venientem neque filios odibiles. Alioquin qui praeter haec aliquid agit, et ipse cadat sacerdotio, et qui eum ordinat extra episcopatum sectabitur hanc legem offendens. Sed neque ineruditus exsistens sacrorum dogmatum ad episcopatum accedat, prius autem aut monasticam vitam professus, aut in clero constitutus, non minus mensibus sex, uxori tamen non cohaerens. De cetero autem nulli permittimus a positione legis uxorem habenti talem imponi ordinationem.

76. "Sicut bonam gratiam vel gloriam in eo qui ordinandus est quaerimus, ita etiam in eo calumniam qui frustra accusavit punimus. Si autem aliquis dicat conscium se esse

Moreover, all things are governed well and properly if the foundation of the state is worthy and amiable to God. We believe that this will happen if the observance of holy rules is preserved, which just, esteemed, venerable students and ministers of God's word have transmitted, which the apostles and holy fathers preserved and explained.

75. "Therefore we decree, following the holy rules in every respect, that when anyone for all time to come is brought to ordination to the episcopate, first his manner of life should be closely considered according to the holy apostle to see if it is honorable, guiltless and completely blameless, if it has supporting testimony from good men, is befitting a priest, and does not derive from the ranks of officials or courtiers. Do not let someone from the common crowd come forth first as a cleric, then afterward a bishop who neglects to say something about his children; but he should be celibate from the first, or if he has a wife, she should come to him as a virgin, and have no unacceptable children. Otherwise, anyone who acts contrary to these precepts should be expelled from his priestly office, and the one who ordains him in contravention of this law will be severed from his bishopric. But also, do not let one who is ignorant of sacred teachings be admitted to the episcopate, but first let him be professed in a monastic life or be established in the clergy for not less than six months, and not be united to a wife. Furthermore, we permit such ordination to be bestowed in the future on no one who has a wife in contradiction of the law.

76. "Just as we require a good reputation or honor in a man who is to be ordained, so also do we punish a false charge by one who has accused without cause. Moreover, if

alicuius illicitorum ei, non prius mereatur episcopi ordinationem quam querelae examinatio fiat et undique innoxius appareat. Quod si post huiusmodi contradictionem non passus is qui ordinem facit legitimam examinationem imponi causae currat ad ordinationem, sciat quod ab eo fit pro nihilo esse, sed is qui contra legem fit, cadat sacerdotio, et qui sine probatione ordinationem imponit et ipse similiter sede cadat sacerdotali."

77. Item Leo: "Si quemquam ad episcopatus gradum provehi Deo auctore contigerit, puris hominum mentibus nuda electionis scientia sincero omnium iudicio proferatur. Nemo gradum sacerdotii pretii venalitate mercetur. Qualiter quisque mereatur, non quantum dare sufficiat, aestimetur. Profecto enim quis locus tutus et quae causa poterit esse excusata, si veneranda Dei templa pecuniis expugnentur? Quem murum integritati aut vallum fidei providebimus, si *auri sacra fames* in veneranda penetralia proserpit? Quid denique cautum poterit esse aut securum, si sanctitas incorrupta corrumpitur? Cesset altaribus imminere profanus ardor avaritiae et a sacris aditis repellatur piaculare flagitium.

78. "Itaque castus et humilis eligatur nostris temporibus episcopus, ut locorum quocumque pervenerit, omnia vitae propriae integritate purificet. Non pretio sed precibus ordinetur antistes. Tantum in ambitu debet esse sepositus ut

anyone should say that he knows of a person's unlawful acts, let that person not be entitled to ordination by a bishop before there is an examination of the complaint and he is shown to be innocent in all respects. But if, after an objection of this kind, the one who is performing the ordination does not allow a lawful examination of the case to be conducted, but rushes to ordination, let him know that his action is null and void, and let the one who becomes a priest contrary to the law be expelled from the priesthood, and let the one who ordains him without examination similarly be expelled from his priestly rank."

77. Likewise, Leo says: "If it happens that someone is promoted to the office of bishop by God's authority, let the knowledge of his election be openly proclaimed to the undefiled minds of men, and the judgment of all be uncorrupted. Let no one purchase the office of priesthood for a price through venality. Determine how much each one is deserving, not how much he can afford to give. For indeed, what place will be safe and what cause could be legitimate, if the venerable temples of God are obtained for money? What defense for integrity or what protection for faith shall we provide if *the accursed hunger for gold* creeps into venerable sanctuaries? Finally, what would be safe or secure, if uncorrupted holiness is corrupted? Let the impious ardor of avarice cease to threaten altars, and may sinful wickedness be driven from holy shrines.

78. "And so, in our times let a chaste and humble man be elected bishop, so that, wherever he goes, he will purify everything by the integrity of his own life. Let a bishop be ordained not for a price, but by prayers. So much ought he to be distanced from desire for advancement that when sought

quaeratur cogendus, rogatus recedat, invitatus effugiat. Sola illi suffragetur necessitas excusandi. Profecto enim indignus est sacerdotio nisi fuerit ordinatus invitus. Cum sane quisquis hanc sanctam et venerabilem antistitis sedem pecuniae interventu subisse, aut si quis, ut alterum ordinaret vel eligeret, aliquid accepisse detegitur, ad instar publici criminis et laesae maiestatis accusatione proposita a gradu sacerdotii retrahatur. Nec solum deinceps honore privari sed perpetuae quoque infamiae damnari decrevimus, ut eos quos facinus par coinquinat et aequat, utrosque similis poena comitetur."

79. Item Iustinianus *Constitutione novella:* "Prae omnibus illud observari sancimus, ut nullus per suffragium alicuius muneris episcopus ordinetur. Si quid autem tale committatur, ipsi dantes et accipientes, et eorum mediatores, damnationi subiciantur. Et propterea qui dat et qui accipit, et mediator sacerdotii aut cleri honore removeatur. Quod autem pro hac causa datum est ecclesiae illi vendicetur cuius voluit sacerdotium comparare. Si forte laicus mediator pro hac causa aliquid accipiat, in duplum id ecclesiae restituat." Item: "Sed neque quemlibet venerabilis domus gubernatorem aut aliam quamcumque sollicitudinem ecclesiasticam agentem, dare aliquid illi a quo constituitur aut ulli personae liceat pro commissa sibi gubernatione. Qui vero dat aut accipit aut mediator fit, clero nudabitur acceptis vendicandis

out he must be compelled; that called upon he draws back, and that summoned he flees. Let the impulse to excuse himself alone cast a vote in his favor. For indeed, he is unworthy of being a priest, unless he has shown reluctance to be ordained. However, when anyone is found to have received this holy and venerable office of bishop by means of money, or to have accepted something to ordain or elect another, let him be removed from the order of priesthood after an indictment has been set forth, just as for a public crime or treason. And we decree that they not only be deprived of their honored position, but also condemned to everlasting disgrace, so that a like punishment attends both of those whom the same outrage defiles and makes equal."

79. Also, in the *Novels,* Justinian says: "Above all, we decree that this be observed: that no one be ordained bishop through the influence of any gift. Furthermore, if any such action is carried out, let those giving and those receiving, and their go-betweens, be subject to condemnation. And on that account, let the one who gives and the one who receives, and the go-between, be removed from their honored position of priesthood or clergy. Moreover, let what was given for this reason be claimed for that church whose priesthood a person wished to purchase. If by chance a layman receives anything for this reason as a go-between, let double that be returned to the church." Also: "Let no rector of a venerable house or one exercising any other ecclesiastical responsibility be allowed to give anything to that man by whom he is appointed or to any person for the rectorship entrusted to him. Indeed, one who gives or receives or becomes a go-between will be stripped of his clerical office after reparations claimed have been received for the venerable

venerabili loco. Si autem secularis sit qui accipit aut mediator est, quod datum est duplum eidem venerabili loco ab ipso praebeatur."

80. Item: "Sancimus cum opus fuerit episcopum ordinare, clericos mox in tribus decreta facere personis propositis sacrosanctis Evangeliis, dicentes in ipsis decretis quia neque propter aliquam donationem aut promissionem aut amicitiam hos elegerunt. Sed et scientes eos rectae fidei et honestae vitae esse et litteras nosse, et quia neque uxorem neque concubinam neque filios habent, neque hos curiales aut officiales esse." Item: "Sed neque curialem aut officialem clericum fieri permittimus, unde ex hoc venerabili clero iniuria fiat, nisi forte monasticam vitam aliquis eorum non minus xxv annis impleverit. Tales enim ordinari praecipimus quarta propriae substantiae sibi retenta, reliquis partibus curiae et fisco vendicandis, si in clero constituti, monacho condecentem vitam impleverint." Item: "Ab episcopis Deo amabilibus secundum divinas regulas religiosos clericos cum multa fieri inquisitione et boni testimonii viros ordinari sancimus, litteras omnimodo scientes, eruditos, sed nullos magis in sacris ordinationibus diligimus quam cum castitate viventes aut cum uxoribus non cohabitantes."

81. Haec quidem principes saeculi. Sed super his doctores ecclesiae plura sunt prosecuti quae tamen omnia iam viluerunt et abierunt in desuetudinem. Illudque unum omnibus

position. Moreover, if he is a member of the secular clergy who receives something or is a go-between, let double what was given be rendered by him to that same venerable position."

80. Also: "We decree that when it becomes necessary to ordain a bishop, the clerics then make a decree before three persons, after the most holy gospels have been displayed, declaring in those decrees that they have not elected these men on account of any gift of money or promise of such, or friendship; that they know them to be men of proper faith and upright life, and to possess a liberal education; that they have neither wife nor concubine nor children, nor are they courtiers or officials." Also: "But neither do we allow a courtier or an official to become a cleric, since from this harm may come to the venerable clergy, unless by chance one of them has followed the monastic way of life for not less than twenty-five years. Indeed, we order such men to be ordained with a fourth of their property retained for themselves, the remaining portions to be claimed for the court and the treasury, if, when joining the clergy, they have followed a way of life befitting a monk." Also: "We decree that clerics in religious life should be appointed by bishops pleasing to God, according to the divinely inspired rules, after much inquiry, and that men of good repute should be ordained, men who are versed in letters in every way, and learned; but in holy ordination we love none more than those living chastely and not cohabiting with wives."

81. Princes of the world have said these things. But beyond these, doctors of the Church have developed more precepts, which nevertheless have all now become worthless or fallen into disuse. Only that one seems to outweigh

aliis praeponderare videtur, quo dicitur, "Quod principi placet legis habet vigorem." Unde cum principum et potestatum gratiam sibi quacunque ex causa conciliaverint, omnia de iure sibi licere aestimant, nec est quod de cetero abhorreant, post assensum principis quicumque obviaverint reus est maiestatis. Instarque sacrilegii est illum aestimare indignum quem princeps elegerit, illique non oboedire quem ipse aliis praeposuerit.

82. Sed et ut auctoritatibus approbent quod penitus reprobum est, facta tyrannorum commemorant, consuetudines pravas licet rationi omnino contrarias quo tempore pravo inductae sunt, et sub dissimulatione correctionis induruerunt, palam recitant: qualiter scilicet princeps ille vel ille cognatum aut familiarem suum in ecclesiam illam violenter intruserit; qualiter illos ad eligendum minis et terroribus coegerit; qualiter ille episcopatum vel abbatiam publice vendiderit; quomodo alter appellationes ad sedem apostolicam in terra sua fieri prohibuerit; quam impune alius ecclesias et loca sacrata conflagraverit, altaria et capsas sanctorum auro et argento nudaverit; qualiter alius partem patrimonii Crucifixi in fiscum redegerit; quomodo alter primatem suum vel metropolitanum suum in exilium egerit eiusque omnia diripuerit; qualiter quidam maritali toro relicto scorto adhaeserint uxoresque legitimas reliquerint, vel carceri mancipaverint aut manibus propriis suffocaverint; quomodo alii venerabiles ecclesiarum praelatos a

all others which says, "What is pleasing to the prince has the force of law." Hence, when men have gained the favor of princes and powerful people for themselves for any reason, they reckon that all things are legally permitted to them, nor is there anything that they would shrink from thereafter. After they have gained the assent of the prince, whoever opposes them is guilty of treason. And it is a kind of sacrilege to judge anyone unworthy whom the prince has chosen, and not to obey one whom he has appointed over others.

82. But also, in order to demonstrate with precedents what is utterly reprehensible, they recount the deeds of tyrants; they openly recite perverse practices even though they were completely contrary to reason in the perverse times in which they were introduced, and in which they became firmly established in the guise of correction: namely, how one prince or another forcibly imposed his kinsman or follower upon the Church; how he forced the Church to choose them by threats and terror; how one openly sold a bishopric or an abbacy; in what manner another prohibited appeals to the apostolic see to be made in his kingdom; how another burned churches and consecrated places with impunity; how he stripped altars and reliquaries of the saints of their gold and silver; how another paid a portion of the patrimony of Christ crucified to the royal treasury; how another drove his primate or his metropolitan bishop into exile and plundered all his possessions; how, after they had abandoned the marriage bed, some took a mistress and left their lawful wives, or imprisoned them or strangled them with their own hands; how others kept it secret that venerable prelates of churches were killed by their henchmen; how

satellitibus occisos dissimulaverint, ecclesiamque Dei conculaverint, et in flagitiis et facinoribus variis nullo obloquente libito licitum coaequaverit. Quisquis igitur coram populo novit huiusmodi copiosius enarrare et ad evacuandam plebis fidem exempla prava proponere, ille maior est in regno eorum qui traditiones suas legibus divinis praeferunt, et timorem Domini postponunt.

83. Si quis vero iustitiae et veritatis zelator exsistat, qui pro veritatis assertione vel modicum quid proferat, statim hostis publicus dicitur, et laesae maiestatis reus iudicatur. Et si in proposito huiusmodi perseveravit, nec statim conversus egerit paenitentiam dicens se errasse in invio, et non in via, aut in carcerem retruditur aut exsilio damnatur. Si vero *viros sanguinum* sanctificaverit, si polluta quaelibet munda dixerit, si audito sanguine aure surda pertransierit, si ad omnes nutus principum voce et ore arriserit, et vitia eorum pessima palpaverit et palliaverit, ille *est amicus Caesaris,* et totius multitudinis pravae et perversae eum sequentis. Ille debet, quia dignus est, inter primos amicorum conscribi et ab universis venerari. Illi debentur salutationes in foro et *recubitus primi in convivio.* Illi ad primam vocem pandenda sunt ostia et inter primos vocandus est ad consilia secretiora, quoniam magnae fidei est et industriae, utpote *in quo sunt varii thesauri absconditi saptentiae et scientiae.*

84. Tales consiliatores habet hodie non solum curia regum, sed et domus pontificum. Tales sunt in saeculo. Tales et

they trampled upon God's Church, and in their various shameful acts and wicked deeds they equated what was permitted with what was pleasing, with no one to criticize them. And so, whoever knows how to recount more abundantly instances of this kind before the people, and to set forth perverse examples to undermine the faith of the common folk, is greater in the realm of those who prefer their own practices to divine laws, and who set aside fear of the Lord.

83. But if any zealous supporter of justice and truth should come forward, a man who should utter even a small statement in defense of the truth, he is instantly called a public enemy and judged guilty of treason. If he persists in an assertion of this kind, and does not immediately change and repent, saying that he has lost his way and is not on the right path, he is either cast into prison or condemned to exile. But if he has sanctified *men of blood,* if he has called any unclean things clean, if he has passed by with a deaf ear when bloodshed is reported, if he favors by utterance and expression all the commands of princes, if he flatters and palliates their worst vices, he *is a friend of Caesar's,* and of the whole perverse and depraved crowd following him. Since he is a worthy man, he ought to be enrolled among his foremost friends and revered by all. To him are owed greetings in the market and *first places at the feast.* To him doors should be opened at the first greeting, and he should be among the first summoned to privy councils, because he is a man of great trust and diligence, as one in whom *are hidden various treasures of wisdom and knowledge.*

84. Today, not only the court of kings, but also the houses of bishops have such counselors. Such men are in the world.

in claustro et tales rem publicam et ecclesiasticam administrant et leges condunt iniquas, non ut iuste iudicent inter filios hominum, sed ut subvertant iudicium et circumveniant filios pauperum, subsannantes potius quam suscipientes quod dictum est per prophetam: *Iudicate pupillo, defendite viduam et venite et arguite me, dicit Dominus.* Sed numquid apponet ut aliquando Deum arguat qui ita homini mortali adulatur, quod Deum obliviscitur, ita terrenis inhiat, quod de caelestibus nec semel cogitat? Sed quo amplius aspirant ad honores, salutis suae magis fiunt immemores, ut merito videatur eos increpare psalmista dicens, "*Homo cum in honore esset non intellexit, comparatus est iumentis insipientibus et similis factus est illis.*"

85. Quid enim bestialius quam quod creatura rationalis creatori suo non vult esse obnoxia, sed illud semper si detur optio eligat unde homini placeat et Deo displiceat? Quid bestialius quam seipsum ita *odio inexorabili* persequi quod nec aliquando sui ipsius velit misereri? Animalia bruta canes insequentes fugiunt, pedem referunt si praecipitia advertunt, loca tutiora libentius inhabitant, minus tuta devitant, aves caeli laqueos et pisces maris hamos etiam latentes declinant, et homo, cui soli inter ceteras creaturas data est discretio, ita desipit et per desideria illicita defluit, quod conditionem suam non attendit, sed pecora campi stoliditate antecedit, illud affectans ardentius quod subvertit efficacius, illud sine intermissione sitiens quod semel bibitum exstinguit in aeternum, illud reputans inhonestum quod

Such men are in the cloister, and such men govern the commonwealth and ecclesiastical affairs. They also establish unjust laws, not in order to judge justly among the sons of men, but to subvert justice and oppress the sons of the poor, deriding rather than accepting what is said by the prophet: *Judge for the orphan, defend the widow, and come and accuse me, says the Lord.* But will he not also add that the judge who fawns on a mortal man sometimes censures God, in that he forgets God and in so doing craves earthly goods, because he does not once think about heavenly ones? But the more they aspire to honors, the more they become forgetful of their own salvation, so that the psalmist seems to rebuke them rightly when he says, "*A man when he was in honor had no understanding; he was compared to senseless beasts of burden and became like them.*"

85. What is more bestial than the fact that a rational creature is unwilling to be subject to his creator, but if he has the chance, he always chooses how to please man and displease God? What is more bestial than for him to persecute himself with such *inexorable hatred* that he is never willing to show pity to himself? Irrational animals flee from hounds in pursuit. They draw back if they see precipices. They prefer to dwell in safe places; they avoid places that are unsafe. Birds of the sky shun snares, and fish of the sea avoid even hidden hooks. But man, to whom alone among all other creatures is given discernment, acts foolishly and degenerates through forbidden pleasures, inasmuch as he does not consider his own condition, but surpasses the herds of the field in stupidity, ardently aspiring to what is most likely to ruin him, thirsting without ceasing for what, once drunk, destroys him forever, considering disgraceful what in any

aliquatenus votis obviat nec famulari novit ad nutum, illud pestiferum quod voluptuosum suspendit desiderium, illud denique summum bonum quod libidinosum satiat appetitum, illud autem summum malum quod salutis est conservativum.

86. *Hae sunt occupationes pessimae* quas iuxta Salomonem dedit Deus filiis hominum; his implicantur non solum laici et clerici, sed etiam illi qui se profitentur—et utinam sint!—religiosi, scilicet monachi et nigri et albi et aliarum professionum viri magnifici seu Praemonstratae ecclesiae et Grandimontani, apud quos omnis ambitio non est hospes et advena, sed civis et domestica. Ut enim salva pace eorum loquar, multa praesumunt attemptare negotia quae ordini et honestati quam professi sunt non videntur convenientia, sed quae magis iter arduum quod ingressi sunt impediant quam expediant, et famam satagant decolorare quam vitae merito constat eos adquirere. Sicut enim contingit *ex modico fermento totam massam corrumpi,* ita nonnumquam ex paucorum delicto totius universitatis solet opinio denigrari.

87. Quid est quod sibi invicem adversantur et detrahunt, qui sub eodem duce eiusdem militiae titulo militant monachi scilicet et canonici albi et nigri, fratres Hospitales et Templi, Cartusienses et Grandimontani? Quorum omnium, sicut diversa est vita, ita diversa sunt studia. In omni enim congregatione sunt boni et mali et sicut quidam amplius aliis terrena despiciunt, ita alii aliis vehementius

way obstructs his wishes and has not learned to serve his pleasure, considering baleful what checks his desire for pleasure, and finally considering the greatest good what satisfies his lustful appetite, but considering that the greatest evil what is the preserver of his salvation.

86. According to Solomon, *these are the worst occupations* that God has given to the sons of men. In these are engaged not only laymen and clerics, but even those who profess themselves to be religious—and would that they were!—namely, monks, both black and white, and distinguished men of other orders, whether of the church at Prémontré or Grandmont, among whom all ambition is not a foreigner or a stranger, but a citizen and a maidservant. For (to speak while preserving peace with them) they dare to undertake many affairs which do not seem consistent with the order and integrity that they have professed, but which rather impede than expedite the arduous journey that they have entered on, and they strive to tarnish the reputation which it is certain that they seek to acquire by the merit of their way of life. For just as it happens that *the whole lump is spoiled by a little leaven,* so often from the fault of a few the reputation of the whole community is accustomed to be blackened.

87. Why is it that they oppose and disparage each other, men who serve under the same leader and under the banner of the same service, namely monks and canons, white and black, brothers of the Hospital and the Temple, Carthusians and Grandmontines? Just as the way of life is different for all of these, so are their pursuits. For in every community there are good men and bad. Just as certain ones despise earthly possessions more than others, so some men covet them more eagerly than others, and most attentively devote

concupiscunt, et tramitem quo altius ascendant officiosissime excolunt et ut velocius bravium apprehendant, potestates saeculi sollicitant. Magnorum gratiam sibi conciliant, obloquentes muneribus placant, principibus et praelatis suis sumptibus saepe ministrant.

88. Considera igitur, dilectissime, qualiter ascendant huiusmodi, quomodo et quales introeant in sancta sanctorum, et nacto tempore opportuno, et remoto tumultu aulico, quo ita vexaris quod nec dormiens potes esse immunis et interiorem conscientiae thalamum descende, et, clauso ostio, *argue, obsecra, increpa, insta opportune, importune,* eaque insinuante attende primo quis, quid susceperis et qualiter ingressus fueris. Non dico tu tantum, sed et omnes fere coepiscopi tui. "*Qui episcopatum desiderat, bonum opus desiderat*"; non dixit opes sed opus. Cum tamen de opibus adquirendis maior hodie quam de opere pontificali exercendo sollicitudo habeatur, vide si per ostium ascendisti in ovile ovium, alioquin fur es et latro, dicente Domino: *Qui non intrat per ostium in ovile ovium, sed ascendit aliunde, ille fur est et latro.* Fur non venit nisi ut mactet et perdat faciatque quod per prophetam dicitur: *Quod fractum erat non alligastis. Quod pingue erat devorastis. Quod debile et infirmum proiecistis.*

89. Quid autem faciet pater ille familias, pastor scilicet pastorum, cum visitaverit gregem suum et invenerit fures et latrones non per ostium sed per maceriam ascendisse in ovile ovium, videritque abominationes pessimas quas ipsi

themselves to the path by which to climb higher. And so as to seize the prize more swiftly, they solicit the powerful of the world. They procure for themselves the favor of important men; those who reprove them, they appease with gifts; they often serve princes and prelates at their own expense.

88. Consider, therefore, most beloved, how men of this sort climb upward, what kind of men enter the holy of holies and in what way. And when you find an opportune time, after you have set aside the bustle of the court, which so troubles you that not even while sleeping are you able to be free of it, then descend to the inner chamber of your conscience. With the door shut, *reprove, entreat, rebuke, be instant in season and out of season,* and at the prompting of conscience consider first who you are, what you have received, and how you have begun. I do not speak of you alone, but also nearly all your fellow bishops. "*One who desires a bishopric desires a good work*"; he did not say wealth, but work. But since greater care is taken today in acquiring wealth than in carrying out episcopal duties, see if you have climbed up into the sheepfold through the door. Otherwise you are a thief and a robber, as the Lord says: *He who does not enter the sheepfold through the door, but climbs up another way, that man is a thief and a robber.* A thief does not come except to slaughter and destroy and to do what is said by the prophet: *What was broken you have not bound up. What was fat you have devoured. What was weak and feeble you have cast out.*

89. Furthermore, what will that master of the house do, I mean the shepherd of shepherds, when he has visited his flock and found that thieves and robbers have not climbed up into the sheepfold through the door, but over the wall, and he has seen the worst abominations that they commit,

faciunt, gregemque dissipatum et a bestiis captum et dilaceratum? Numquid dicet alicui eorum, "*Amice, quomodo huc intrasti?*" Non utique quia nec nomine amici nuncupabit eos, sed mittet eos in carceris tenebras exteriores, *ubi fletus et stridor dentium et novissimus dolor peior priore.* Ne aduleris tibi in conscientia tua, similis factus eis *qui consuunt pulvinar sub omni cubito,* sed cum eo cui, teste Domino, *non erat similis in terra,* qui et ait, "*Verebar omnia opera mea,*" et iterum, "*Sidera non sunt munda in conspectu eius.*"

90. Operum tuorum diligens scrutator accede et vide si vitae merito dignus fueris sacerdotio, si morum sanctitas tanto sit digna officio, si virtutum operibus aliis possis esse exemplo, si in lege divina ita eruditus es ut habeas unde *proferas nova et vetera* a te ipso. Si hoc ante ingressum habuisti, secure potuisti ingredi; si tamen ingressus tuus fuit legitimus, forsitan respondes mihi et dicis, "Legitime ingressus sum, quia vocatus et coactus, non intrusus." Si ita est, bene est. Sed videamus utrum vocationem istam magis provocaverit et procuraverit amor personae, an meritum vitae, an favor aut formido potestatis regiae.

91. Pace omnium loquar, nonne cotidie tales eliguntur non solum episcopi sed et abbates in ecclesia Dei quorum non tantum vita et mores, sed et lingua et facies ignota est eligentibus? Numquid legitima aut libera est electio ubi dicitur: "Hic est quem prae aliis rex promoveri desiderat, hic

and has seen the flock scattered and caught by beasts and torn to pieces? Will he say to any of these, "*Friend, how have you entered here?*" Certainly not, since he will not call them by the name "friend," but will cast them into the outer darkness of prison, *where there is weeping and gnashing of teeth, and the last pain is worse than the first.* Do not flatter yourself in your conscience, like those *who sew a cushion under every elbow,* but join with him *whose like was not found in the earth,* as the Lord attests, and who says, "*I feared all my works,*" and again, "*The stars are not pure in his sight.*"

90. As an assiduous examiner of your own works, approach them and see if by the merit of your life you are worthy of the priesthood; if the holiness of your character is worthy of so great an office; if you are able to be an example to others by your acts of virtue; if you are so learned in divine law that you have a source from which *to bring forth* out of yourself *things new and old.* If you had this worthiness before your entry into the episcopate, you could have entered unhesitatingly. If your entry was truly lawful, perhaps you respond to me, "I have entered lawfully, since I was invited and constrained, not imposed." If it is so, well and good. But let us consider whether love of your person, or the merit of your way of life, or the favor or fear of royal power did most to call forth and prompt that invitation.

91. With peace toward all, let me speak. In God's Church today are not only such men elected as bishops, but also as abbots, whose way of life and character are not only unknown to those electing them, but also their speech and face? Is it really a lawful or free election when the following is said: "This is the one whom the king desires to be promoted before all others; this is the one for whom the king

est pro quo rex specialiter rogat, hic est de quo rex vult indubitanter ut fiat. Hunc habebitis et non alium; hunc eligite. Alioquin duriora audietis, fietque ab aliis, vobis inconsultis et irrequisitis et in subversionem libertatis et liberae electionis vestrae, quod fieri modo posset a vobis."

92. Mittuntur interim fratres Hospitalis et Templi, post eos Cluniacensis ordinis et Cistercii, postea vero Cartusienses et Grandimontani, omnes cum litteris ratihabitationis, omnes conscii regiae voluntatis, omnes viri vitae spectabilis, qui ita spiritu Dei ducuntur quod faciem hominis non accipiunt, qui *nec ad dexteram nec ad sinistram* pro capitis abscisione *declinarent.* Qui denique tanti ac tales sunt quod eorum verbis non credere, eorum consiliis non adquiescere, eorum mandatis non obtemperare, quasi scelus esset idolatriae.

93. Accelerantes igitur et cito euntes, adeo ut invicem cohortari se videantur et dicere, propter pusillanimes forte et pigritantes, "*Occupet extremum scabies,*" quo et ad quod admissi sunt veniunt, dicentes propter nimiam caritatem qua eos dilexerunt se advenisse zelo tractos iustitiae et pietatis. Mutantque vultus et verba secundum qualitatem negotii, ne quid omittant de contingentibus, praemittunt preces, proponunt exempla, praedicant bona, promittunt prospera, adducunt hinc rationes, hinc allegationes, hinc persuasiones, hinc pericula, hinc commoda; commendatur circumquaque persona!

specifically asks; this is the one for whom the king unhesitatingly wishes this to happen. Have him and no other. Elect him. Otherwise, you will be subject to harsher terms, and this role will be performed by others, while you will be unconsulted and unsought, bringing about the overthrow of your freedom and free election, as now can be exercised by you."

92. Meanwhile, brothers of the Hospital and the Temple are sent, and after them, brothers of the order of Cluny and Cistercians, and lastly Carthusians and Grandmontines, all with letters of ratification, all informed of the king's will, all men of admirable life, who are so guided by the spirit of God that they do not look upon a man's face, who *turn aside neither to the right or the left* on penalty of beheading. Finally, such is their greatness and quality that not to trust their words, not to assent to their counsels, not to obey their commands would be tantamount to the sin of idolatry.

93. Therefore, making haste and proceeding so quickly that it seems they are urging each other on and saying, with regard to the fainthearted and sluggish, "*Let the itch take the last one,*" they arrive at the place and for the purpose they have been sent. They declare that they have come because of the very great affection they felt for those men, drawn by a zeal for justice and duty. They adapt their expressions and words according to the nature of the transaction, so as not to omit any incidentals. They begin with prayers; they set forth examples; they predict good things; they promise prosperity; they adduce reasons, assertions, and persuasive points, cite risks and benefits; the person is commended in every way!

94. Si quaeratur de sanctitate vitae, Iohannes baptista est; si de sapientia, Cato est; si de eloquentia, Tullius est; si de mansuetudine, Moses est; si de zelo, Phinees; si de fide, Abraham; si de patientia, Iob; si de humilitate, Maria; si de sollicitudine, Martha; si de constantia, Laurentius; si de praedicatione, Paulus; si de conversatione, Benedictus. Quid multa? Quicquid volueris erit, dummodo eligatur, etsi non est in eo unde praesumatur de praeterito vel praesenti. *Quia potens est Dominus de lapidibus istis suscitare filios Abrahae,* et *honores mutant mores,* praesumendum est de futuris. Sed nec *ab eventu facta notanda putes, potens est enim Deus omnem gratiam abundare facere in eo, ut in omnibus semper omnem sufficientiam habeat.*

95. Si autem haec omnia ad persuadendum non suffecerint, alia via incedendum est. Si non profecerunt fomentationes et ungenta, adhibenda sunt cauteria, ut quibus non profuit otium, vexatio det intellectum. Fit ergo aeris mutatio subita, eclipsis apparet inopinata, *sol convertitur in tenebras et luna in sanguinem,* splendor in caliginem et dies in noctem, pluviae in fulgura et spiritus aurae lenis in tonitrua, densantur minae et descendunt, non *sicut imber super herbam, aut stillae super gramina* sed sicut nix et grando in tempestate valida et *sicut ficus mittit grossos suos.*

96. Adsunt pro foribus ministri regii ad alligandos contradicentes in compedibus et non consentientes in manicis ferreis, et nisi consenserint hac nocte, mane dispergentur sicut pulvis a turbine. Qui enim fuerunt hesterno amici et

94. If one asks about his holiness of life, he is John the Baptist; if about his wisdom, he is Cato; if about eloquence, he is Cicero; if about mildness, he is Moses; if about zeal, he is Phineas; if about faith, Abraham; if about patience, Job; if about humility, Mary; if about solicitude, Martha; if about his constancy, Lawrence; if about preaching, Paul; if about his way of life, Benedict. What more shall I say? He will be whatever you want, provided that he is elected, even though there is nothing in him that can be taken for granted about the past or present. *Since the Lord is able to raise up sons to Abraham from these stones,* and since *honors change character,* we can take for granted the future. But *you should not think that deeds should be stigmatized for their outcome, for God is able to make all grace abound in him so that in all works he may always have all sufficiency.*

95. However, if all these methods have not been enough to convince one, it is necessary to proceed by another way. If applications of poultices and ointments have not helped, cauteries must be applied, so that harassment may bestow understanding on those on whom the pacific approach has had no beneficial effect. So, there is a sudden change of atmosphere, an unexpected eclipse appears, *the sun is turned to darkness and the moon to blood,* brightness to gloom and day to night, rains to lightning and the breaths of mild air to thunder. Threats grow thick and fall, not *as a shower on the herb or drops upon the grass,* but as snow and hail in a powerful storm, and *as the fig tree lets fall its unripe fruits.*

96. Royal agents appear before the gates to bind in chains those who object, and those who do not agree in manacles of iron. Unless they will agree this very night, they will be scattered in the morning like dust by a whirlwind. For those

proximi et quasi fratres confoederati lege indissolubilis matrimonii scripserunt iam *libellum repudii,* et pro quibus parati erant exponere cervices, pronuntiantur regis et regni hostes capitales, digni *ut suspendatur mola asinaria in collo eorum et demergantur in profundum.* Et ut omnia ordine iudiciario compleantur, nec aliquid extraordinarie praesumatur, mittitur ad diocesianum episcopum ut vinculo anathematis innodentur, ne sit eis refugium pro qua dimicant domus domini, sed secure mittant in eos manus suas satellites immundi et canes impudici.

97. Si autem adhuc steterint nec si consenserint ut *cornua tribuant peccatori,* aliud excogitatur consilium, modus invenitur aptior, medicina efficacior, via compendiosior: differtur confiscatio possessionum, dissimulatur dissipatio personarum, cohibentur manus satellitum, ne forte tumultus fiat in populo qui possit dispendium generare negotio. Alio modo intrudendus est, quia iste modus nimis esset notorius et manifestus. Dividitur ergo in partes universitas, *separantur quasi oves ab haedis:* iuvenes a senioribus, minores a maioribus. Conveniuntur seorsum et singillatim; proponuntur hinc minae, inde blanditiae, hinc poena, inde gloria. Videas quasi iterum martyres assistentes coram tyrannis excogitatis suppliciis, compelli ut sacrificent idolis vel comedant de idolaticis. Promittitur minoribus maiorum degradatio et

who were friends and neighbors yesterday and, as it were, brothers united by the law of indissoluble marriage, have now written *a bill of divorce.* Those for whom they were ready to risk their necks are proclaimed mortal enemies of the king and kingdom, worthy *to have a millstone hung about their neck and to be drowned in the depths of the sea.* And so that all may be fulfilled in accordance with judicial procedure, and nothing assumed that is out of the ordinary, the matter is sent to the diocesan bishop so that they may be bound by a bond of excommunication, so that the house of the lord for which they struggle may not be a refuge for them, but those vile accomplices and shameless dogs may lay their hands on them with impunity.

97. Moreover, if they still stand fast and will not consent to *yield horns to the sinner,* another plan is devised, a more suitable method is found, a more efficacious medicine, a quicker way. Confiscation of possessions is put off, the dispersal of persons is concealed, and the hands of accomplices are held in check, lest perchance there be an uproar among the people that could cause a delay in the matter. The bishop must be imposed upon them by another method, because this method would be too widely known and exposed. Therefore, the whole community is divided into parts, *just as sheep are separated from goats:* youths from elders, lesser from greater. They are assembled separately and singly. Threats are made here, flatteries expressed there; punishment is set before them here, glory there. You could imagine martyrs, as it were, standing before tyrants with their punishments already devised, being forced to sacrifice to idols or to eat from idolatrous sacrifices. To lesser ones is

illorum substitutio, promittitur maioribus gradus altior, potestas amplior, dignitas eminentior, licentia diffusior.

98. Si qui vero sunt qui a spe huiusmodi percipiendi necessario ceciderunt, quos aut infirmitas suspendit corporis aut penitus succidit impotentia senectutis, ne ex inaffectione fiant difficiles, promittuntur nepotibus et cognatis eorum redditus et praebendae etiam primo vacantes. Sed et cum aliis a quibus consummatio negotii plenius pendet certius et secretius convenitur firmanturque nonnumquam pactiones, interposita fide, qua nihil est foedius vel infidelius. Sed et quidam sunt qui (prudentiori, ne dicam impudentiori, utentes consilio, iuxta quod scriptum est, "*Dum dolet, accipe*") antequam res eo usque processerit quod non possit retrocedere, oblata recipiunt, et eodem relicto ad alium qui simili febre desiccatur statim convertuntur, quia plus promisit et pepigit tantoque citius promissa, immo pacta, persolvet quanto amplius timet ne alter tollat quod ipse affectat.

99. Oritur autem lis magna nonnumquam inter competitores, inimicitiae inexorabiles. Est igitur videre quasi puellam nobilem et formosam procis expositam, qui omnes parati sunt propter eam obtinendam et in carcerem et in mortem ire. Iactitant ergo se invicem, alius de potestate et nobilitate generis, quia est *atavis editus regibus,* alius quod somniavit in Parnasso et saepius de fonte bibit caballino, alius quod totum Corpus Iuris subiecit pedibus suis, alius

promised the degradation of the greater and their substitution; to greater ones is promised a higher rank, greater power, loftier dignity, wider license.

98. If there are any who have unavoidably lost hope of obtaining something of this kind, men whom either infirmity of body incapacitates or weakness of old age entirely disables, revenues and also the first vacant prebends are promised to their nephews and kinsmen, lest through disaffection they become troublesome. But agreement is also surely and secretly reached with others on whom consummation of the matter fully depends, and often covenants are confirmed, with pledges given; nothing is more foul or faithless than this. There are also some who (exercising more prudent, not to say more shameless policy, according to the written precept "*While he is in pain, take*") receive offerings before the matter has gone so far that it cannot go back. After that one candidate has been abandoned, they immediately turn to another who is being burned up by a similar fever, because he has promised and agreed to give more, and the more he fears that another will take what he aspires after, the more quickly he will fulfill his promises, or rather agreements.

99. Furthermore, great strife often arises between rivals, and inexorable enmities. It is like seeing a noble, beautiful girl, the object of suitors who are all prepared to risk prison and even death for the sake of winning her. Thus, one after the other they brag about themselves: one about his power and nobility of birth, since he is *sprung from royal stock;* another that he dreamed on Mount Parnassus and often drank from the horse's spring; another that he has the entire *Corpus iuris* subject at his feet; another that if he were not held

quod nisi prohiberetur sacerdotio, Hector aut Achilles esset in militari officio, alius quia scientiam habet rerum gerendarum et negotiorum regni administrandorum, alius quod regnum in manu eius est et potestas et imperium. Iste blanditur patri et matri. Ille fratribus eius et amicis adulatur. Alter accedit ad dominum fundi ut hos et illos reprimat et eam sibi accipiat.

100. Sic agitur hodie cum ecclesiis vacantibus. Quae est enim hodie ecclesia quae non cogatur aut circumveniatur ad eligendum? Si quis autem de libertate electionis et de non eligendo per potentiam vel oppressionem regiam quicquam proposuerit, statim dicitur, "Non sunt modo miraculorum tempora." Quasi dicant:

Saturnus periit, perierunt et sua iura.
Sub Iove nunc mundus, iura Iovis sequere.

Numquid exspectabit ecclesia, iam tot annis desolata, donec vocetur quis sicut Nicolaus ad Mirrensem et Elphegus ad Wintoniensem? Absit! *Mundus in maligno positus est,* illud potius observandum est quod dicitur, "*Si poteris, recte; si non, quocumque modo rem.*"

101. Si quid vero in eo est, quare secundum canones non sit admittendus ad sacerdotium, quamvis ita notum sit et publicum quod *lippis et tonsoribus pateat,* tamen non est amovendus quia potest et expedit circa eum dispensari. Quemcumque titulum opposueris, confestim delebitur aut ratione

back by his priesthood, he would be a Hector or Achilles in military service; another that he possesses the knowledge for managing affairs and administering matters of the realm; another that the kingdom is in his hands, both its power and its authority. One flatters her father and mother. Another fawns on her brothers and friends. Yet another goes to the lord of the estate to quash each and every one and win her for himself.

100. So it is done today with vacant churches. For what church is there today which is not subject to compulsion or deception in making its choice? Moreover, if anyone asserts anything about freedom of election and about making a choice free from royal authority or oppression, the immediate reply is, "These are not now times of miracles." As if to say:

> *Saturn has perished, and his laws have perished; now the world is subject to Jove; follow Jove's laws.*

Will a church, now abandoned for so many years, wait until someone is summoned like Nicholas to Myra and Alphege to Winchester? God forbid! *The world is situated in wickedness;* rather, that saying must be observed which says, "Enrich yourself *in the right way, if you can; if not, however you can.*"

101. But if there is any objection to a man whereby he should not be admitted to the priesthood according to the canons, even if it is such common knowledge that it is *evident to the bleary-eyed and to barbers,* yet he must not be disqualified, because it is possible and expedient for him to be granted a dispensation. Whatever objection you have raised, it will be nullified without delay, either by reason of a

exempli aut conductitio clamore vulgi. Si igitur dixeris, "Adhuc puer est, et longe citra aetatem quae convenit sacerdoti," statim dicetur tibi, "Et Daniel dum adhuc puer esset, salvavit Susannam quam presbyteri seniores voluerunt damnare, et senes a puero condemnati sunt." Et illud: "*Caesaribus virtus contigit ante diem.*"

102. Ignobilis est genere vel servilis conditionis: haeres non quaeritur Caesaris sed successor piscatori. Pusillae staturae est; sed nec Ieremias magnus erat, nec ipse Iohannes praecursor, *quo maior inter natos mulierum non surrexit.* Rudis est et illiteratus; Petrus et Andreas non fuerunt philosophi quando facti sunt apostoli. Linguam gentis ignorat; Augustinus linguam Anglorum nescivit et praedicatione sua eos ad fidem convertit. Uxoratus est; tales praecipit apostolus promoveri, sed et apostoli dicuntur circumduxisse uxores. Reliquit uxorem suam; cui matrem suam Christus in cruce commendavit, prius eum vocavit a nuptiis. Publice scortatus est; sed hoc Bonifatium martyrem nequaquam a regno caelorum exclusit. Fisco regio deputatus est et functionibus publicis alligatus; beatus Thomas martyr, de cancellaria regis ad Cantuariensem transivit ecclesiam. Stultus est; *quae stulta mundi sunt elegit Deus, ut confundat sapientes,* quia *sapientia huius mundi stultitia est apud Deum.* Timidus est; et *Ioseph, qui iustus erat, cum audisset quod Archelaus regnaret pro Herode in Iudaea,* timuit illo ire, et Ionas ad Ninivitas. Vinolentus et gulosus

precedent or by the hired outcry of the common crowd. Therefore, if you say, "He is still a boy and far short of the age that is fitting for a priest," you will be told immediately, "Daniel also, while he was still a boy, saved Susanna, whom elder priests wanted to condemn, and the old men were convicted by a boy." And: "*Virtue came to the Caesars before its time.*"

102. If he is lowborn or of servile status: an heir of Caesar is not being sought, but a successor to a fisherman. If of small stature: but neither was Jeremiah tall, nor John the Baptist, the forerunner of Christ, and *no one greater than he arose among those born of women.* He is ignorant and illiterate: Peter and Andrew were not philosophers when they were made apostles. He is unacquainted with the language of the people: Augustine did not know the language of the English, yet he converted them to the faith by his preaching. He is a married man: the Apostle ordered such men to be promoted, and further the apostles are said to have been married. He left his wife: Christ on the cross commended his own mother to one whom he first called from a wedding. He has associated with harlots: but this in no way excluded Boniface the martyr from the kingdom of heaven. He was assigned to the royal treasury and involved in public taxation: blessed Thomas the martyr transferred from the king's chancery to the church of Canterbury. He is a fool: *God chose the foolish things of the world to confound the wise,* because *the wisdom of this world is foolishness before God.* He is fearful: *Joseph also, who was a just man, when he had heard that Archelaus was ruling in Judea in place of Herod,* feared to go there, and Jonah feared to go to Nineveh. He is a drunkard and a glutton:

est; Christus ipse dictus est potator vini et carnium devorator. Somnolentus est; Petro, cui data est potestas ligandi et solvendi, dictum est a Domino in passione, "*Una hora non potuisti vigilare mecum?*"

103. Impetuosus est et percussor; numquid non percussit Petrus Malcum, servum principis sacerdotum? Iracundus est; et Barnabas et Paulus ab invicem recesserunt. Senioribus suis contradicit; et Paulus Petro in faciem restitit. Contentiosus est; et inter discipulos Iesu facta est contentio. Vir linguosus est; nonne Paulus appellatus est seminiverbius? Militiam armatam exercuit; legio Agavum militum cum beato Mauritio sub Caesare militaverunt. Vir sanguinum esse dicitur; Moyses, cum quo locutus est Deus, *Egyptium clanculo interfectum in sabulo abscondit.* Manifestum perpetravit homicidium; Samuel coram omni populo interfecit Agag, regem pinguissimum. Debilitatus est toto corpore; tanto robustior in spiritu. Caecus est; Paulus ab Anania ante in apostolum consecratus est et baptizatus quam lumen reciperet. Mutus est; Zacharias in ordine vicis suae mutus ministravit. Surdus est; audientibus nihilominus potest praedicare. Valetudinarius est; Gregorius in infirmitatibus praevalidis strenue rexit ecclesiam. Elephantia percussus est; et verus ille sacerdos noster apparuit non habens speciem nec decorem, ita ut iuxta prophetam aestimatus tanquam percussus a Deo.

104. Auctoritate summi pontificis culpis exigentibus depositus; multi prius depositi postea sunt restituti, qui postmodum viriliter pro ecclesia Dei se opposuerunt. Vanus et superbus est; beatus Bricius licet vanus fuerit, Martino ta-

Christ himself was called a wine drinker and a meat eater. He is given to slumber: during his passion the Lord said to Peter, who received the power of binding and loosing, "*Could you not watch one hour with me?*"

103. He is impetuous and violent: did Peter not strike Malchus the servant of the high priest? He is subject to anger: both Barnabas and Paul separated from each other. He speaks against his superiors: Paul also opposed Peter to his face. He is contentious: there was contention among Jesus's disciples. He is talkative: was Paul not called a babbler? He has engaged in armed military service: a legion of Theban soldiers at Agaune served under the emperor with Saint Maurice. He is said to be a man of blood: Moses, with whom God spoke, *hid in sand the Egyptian he had secretly slain.* He has committed flagrant murder: Samuel killed Agag, the very fat king, in the presence of all the people. He is feeble in his entire body: so much more robust is he in spirit. He is blind: Paul was consecrated as an apostle and baptized by Ananias before he got back his sight. He is mute: Zacharias, in the course of his office, ministered though mute. He is deaf: nonetheless he is able to preach to those who hear. He is infirm: Gregory guided the Church vigorously despite very severe infirmities. He was stricken by leprosy: also that true priest of ours, Christ, appeared without beauty or comeliness so that according to the prophet he was thought to have been stricken by God.

104. He was deposed from office by authority of the supreme pontiff because his faults demanded it: many previously deposed have been restored later, men who afterward courageously took a stand in defense of the Church of God. He is vain and proud: although Saint Brice was vain, yet he

men successit. Deformis est; sed nec Martinus pulcher, sed deformis, fuisse describitur. Haereticus quando fuit; Augustinus, doctor ecclesiae, nonne Manichaeus aliquando exstitit? Idola coluit; Marcellinus, papa et martyr, coram fano compulsus turificavit. Ignoratur si sit baptizatus; Ambrosius est electus dum adhuc esset catechumenus. Persecutus est ecclesiam Dei; doctor gentium litteras accepit in Damascum, qui prostratus est saevissimus persecutor et erectus est fidelissimus praedicator. Non est qui eligat; Anglis non petentibus missi sunt Augustinus, Mellitus, Paulinus et alii quamplures. Non vacat ecclesia ubi intrudatur; qui praesidet, quia indignus est, deponatur, ut ei succedat. Constat quia avarus est; non est episcopi congregata spargere, sed dispersa congregare. Odiosus est omnibus; *qui hominibus placent confusi sunt, quoniam Deus sprevit eos.* Et, ut breviter dicatur, in omnibus ineptus est; *potens est Deus omnem gratiam abundare facere in eo.*

105. Nullus ergo titulus potest apponi quin eligatur (ne dicam intrudatur) pastor, immo lupus, in ovile ovium. Consentiunt igitur electioni quidam precibus, quidam terrore compulsi; quidam muneribus praeempti, quidam promissionibus decepti, quidam violenter coacti, quidam aliorum exemplo seducti. Constituto igitur die solemni convocantur amici et vicini, celebratur electio illa choris Domini alternatim laudantibus, pulsantibus signis et cantantibus organis; quibusdam vero gementibus et suspirantibus in cordibus

succeeded Martin. He is ugly: but neither is Martin described as being handsome, but ugly. He was a heretic at one time: was not Augustine, a doctor of the Church, for a time a Manichaean? He has worshipped idols: Marcellinus, a pope and martyr, was forced to offer incense before a temple. It is unknown if he has been baptized: Ambrose was elected bishop while he was still a catechumen. He has persecuted God's Church: the teacher of the Gentiles received letters for Damascus, and the most savage persecutor was thrown to the ground, but raised up the most faithful preacher. There is no one who would choose him: Augustine, Mellitus, Paulinus, and very many others were sent to the English, though they did not ask for them. There is no vacant church to push him into: let the one who now presides be deposed from office, since he is unworthy, so that he may succeed him. It is well known that he is greedy: it is not the role of a bishop to disperse what has been collected, but to collect what has been dispersed. He is hateful to all: *those who please men have been confounded, because God has scorned them*. In short, he is unsuitable in every way: *God has the power to make every grace abound in him*.

105. No pretext can be brought forward to prevent him being elected (not to say imposed) as shepherd, or rather as a wolf, into the sheepfold. So some consent to his election compelled by entreaties, some by fear, some men are bought off by bribes, some are beguiled by promises, some are violently forced, some are induced by the example of others. Therefore, on the day established for the ceremony, friends and neighbors are assembled, the election is celebrated with choirs alternately praising the Lord, with bells ringing and organs playing, but with some groaning and sighing in their

suis, et dicentibus, non palam tamen, sed in abscondito, "Merito haec patimur, quia peccavimus; *propter peccata enim populi permittit Deus regnare hypocritam* super terram."

106. Electio igitur taliter facta—immo taliter fieri coacta—numquid approbatur a Domino, quamvis probetur a clero et populo? Tu videris, viderint et ipsi qui tam exquisitis machinationibus procurant ut intrudantur quocumque modo. Suspirant tamen cum eliguntur et prae gaudio magno lacrimis uberrimis irrigantur dicentes, "*Discedite a me, quia homo peccator sum* ego et, peccatis meis exigentibus, contigit mihi ista tribulatio. Recedite a me, obsecro, et domui Dei idoneum pastorem providete, quia ego indignus sum et penitus insufficiens curae pastorali, utpote qui saecularibus negotiis usque hodie implicatus, nondum *degustavi quam suavis est Dominus.* Hei mihi quam subito praeoccupavit calamitas ista, cum praefixerim et certo certius statuerim in animo meo, quod in hoc anno *pedem meum in compedem* artioris religionis inicerem, et ecce furtim sublatus sum et ignoranter huic infortunio expositus. Scio enim, et vero scio, quod mors in ianuis est, quia iniurias ecclesiae Dei irrogatas non potero dissimulare etiam si oportuerit me mori pro ea. Sinite me, dilectissimi, sinite me liberum ad vitam solitariam quam praeelegi recedere et nolite me miserum tantis tormentis applicare. Nescitis quid facitis; sedes ista sanctorum est et sancti deberent introire in eam, non quales ego sum qui nec habeo apud me unde proferam *nova et vetera* nec aliquid sentio in me quo audeam talia praesumere.

hearts and saying (though not openly, but secretly), "We suffer this deservedly, since we have sinned, for *because of the people's sins God permits the hypocrite* to reign over the earth."

106. Is an election carried out in this way—or rather brought about by compulsion in this way—confirmed by the Lord, even though it is approved by clergy and people? Consider this, and let those also consider who bring about by such refined machinations that they are thrust into office by whatever means they can. Yet, they sigh when they are elected, and in the face of great joy they are drenched by copious tears, saying, "*Depart from me, for I am a sinful man;* because my sins demand it, this tribulation has befallen me. Leave me, I beseech you, and provide a suitable shepherd for the house of God, for I am unworthy and utterly insufficient for pastoral care, since up to this very day I have been involved in worldly affairs, and I have not yet *tasted how sweet the Lord is.* Ah, me! How suddenly this calamity has overtaken me, since I had determined and most assuredly made up my mind that this year I would put *my foot in the fetters* of stricter religious observance. Behold, I have been swept away by stealth and exposed to this misfortune unawares. For I know, and I know truly, that death is at the gates, since I will not be able to conceal the injuries inflicted on the church of God even if I must die for it. Allow me, most beloved, allow me to withdraw freely to the solitary life which I have previously chosen and do not subject me in my wretchedness to such great torments. You do not know what you are doing; this is a see of saints, and saints ought to enter into it, not such men as I am, who neither have at my disposal the means to bring forth *things new and old,* nor do I feel anything within me by which I could dare to anticipate

Quomodo possum alienae vitae speculator accedere qui propriam nescio nec sufficio diiudicare? Ut quid vota vestra in me contulistis, qui magis merui ruinam quam cathedram, severitatem iudicii quam dignitatem sacerdotii, *cum publicanis et peccatoribus* deputari quam super capita hominum imponi?"

107. Et haec dicens conturbato spiritu fremens et discerpens seipsum cadit retrorsum, volens ut in manibus suis portent eum, ne forte, dum a populo premitur *offendat ad lapidem pedem suum*. Tantis igitur argumentis contra se utitur quod eo ipso quodammodo dignus esse videtur. Capitur ergo, trahitur, et consecrandus metropolitano offertur. Evocantur a sedibus suis coepiscopi. Veniunt quidam, quidam litteras excusatorias transmittunt, quandoque pro, quandoque contra, sicut fecit sanctae recordationis Rogerius Wigorniensis. Cum enim quidam ad episcopatum, nescio si dignus, fuisset electus, et Cantuariae consecrandus a Ricardo archiepiscopo de more advenisset, praefatus Wigorniensis episcopus metropolitano et suffraganeis suis scripsit, dicens, "Ego huic electioni nec consentio nec consentiam, nec subscribo nec subscribam, nec praesentiam meam exhibeo nec in posterum exhibebo et vos scitis quare. Tu autem, Domine, miserere nostri." Ita vix ille, moribus, fide, et sanguine praeclarus, satis innotuit quare suam consecrationi subtraheret praesentiam, malens offensam apud homines incurrere quam *caput peccatoris* contra Deum et conscientiam suam *impinguare*.

such things. How can I come forth as an examiner of another's life, I who have neither the knowledge nor competence to judge my own? Why have you bestowed your choice on me, I who deserve ruin rather than a bishop's throne, severity of judgment rather than the dignity of priesthood, to be counted *with publicans and sinners* rather than to be set over the heads of men?"

107. Saying these words, while groaning, troubled in spirit, and reviling himself, he falls backward, wishing that his electors may bear him up in their hands lest, while he is propelled forward by the people, *he may happen to dash his foot against a stone.* And so, he employs such powerful arguments against himself that in a certain way he seems deserving of that very thing. So he is taken hold of, dragged off, and brought to the archbishop to be consecrated. His fellow bishops are summoned from their sees. Some come, some send letters of excuse, sometimes for, sometimes against the election, as Roger of Worcester (of blessed memory) did. For when a certain man had been elected to a bishopric (I do not know if he was worthy), and he had come in the customary way to Canterbury to be consecrated by Archbishop Richard, the aforementioned bishop of Worcester wrote to the archbishop and his suffragan bishops, saying, "I do not agree to this election, nor shall I agree; I do not endorse it, nor shall I endorse it; I do not present myself, nor shall I present myself in the future, and you know why. But you, Lord, have mercy on us." In this way that bishop, a man distinguished for his morals, faith, and ancestry, made very well known why he was withholding his presence from the consecration, preferring to incur disfavor among men than *to anoint the head of a sinner* in opposition to God and his own conscience.

108. Refert Iohannes Carnotensis episcopus in libro quodam egregium quiddam in talibus accidisse: "Regnante Rogero Siculo contigit vacare ecclesiam Avellanam. Campaniae, Apuliae, et Calabriae Robertus, iam dicti regis cancellarius, praesidebat, vir quidem in rebus gerendis strenuus et sine magna copia litterarum acutissimus, in primis provincialium facundissimus, eorum non impar eloquio, verendus omnibus privilegio potestatis et morum elegantia venerabilis, eoque mirabilior in partibus illis quod inter Longobardos, quos parcissimos, ne avaros dicam, esse constat, faciebat sumptus immensos et gentis suae magnificentiam exhibebat. Erat enim Anglicus natione.

109. "Ad eum utique viri tres accesserunt, abbas quidam, alter archidiaconus, tertius laicus quidam praepositus fratris sui clerici causam agens, singuli clam pro iamdicto episcopatu grandem pecuniam offerentes. Quid multa? Adhibitis familiaribus, seorsum cum unoquoque eorum convenit de pretio. Emptio ergo et venditio undique perfecta est, de solutione implenda sufficientissime cautum pignoribus et fideiussoribus datis, diesque praefixus est electioni sollemniter celebrandae. Cum itaque ad diem archiepiscopi, episcopi, et multae venerabiles personae convenissent, praefatus cancellarius competitorum causas et quid cum unoquoque eorum egisset exposuit, dicens se exinde ex

108. John, bishop of Chartres, reports in a certain book that a remarkable event happened in a case such as this: "During the reign of Roger of Sicily, it happened that a church at Avellino was vacant. Robert, the chancellor of the king just now named, was governing Campania, Apulia, and Calabria. He was a man of vigor in managing affairs and very intelligent, but without a great abundance of literary education. Among the leading men of the province he was the most fluent and not inferior to them in eloquence; a man to be feared by all because of his special claim to power and revered for the grace of his character. For this reason, he was all the more admired in those regions because among the Lombards, who are known to be very frugal, not to say avaricious, he used to incur vast expenses and to display the generosity of his race. For he was English by birth.

109. "At any rate, three men approached him: an abbot, an archdeacon, and the third, a layman who was a provost pleading the cause of his brother, a cleric. Each one was secretly offering a great deal of money for the aforementioned episcopate. What more shall I say? After their confidants had been consulted, Robert came to an agreement separately with each one of them concerning a price. Thus, the buying and selling was completed on all sides, conditions were sufficiently stipulated about making payment after pledges and sureties were given, and a day was set in advance for the election to be solemnly celebrated. When archbishops, bishops, and many venerable pastors had gathered on the appointed day, the aforementioned chancellor explained the positions of the competitors and the business he had contracted with each of them, saying that he would

episcoporum sententia processurum. Damnatis ergo competitoribus simoniacis, pauper monachus et totius rei ignarus canonice electus, approbatus, et introductus est. Illi tamen coacti sunt solvere id in quo se obligaverant usque ad *novissimum quadrantem.*" Haec Iohannes Carnotensis.

110. Sed et alibi idem refert quod: "Cum ambitiosus quidam monachus ad abbatiam quam praeemerat vocaretur, ille modestiam simulans, ut avidius peteretur, onus refugeret, recusaret honorem et se palam tantae rei fateretur indignum, 'Plane,' inquit princeps, 'indignus es, quia eam clam, data mihi tanta pecunia'—summamque expressit—'emisti; sed quandoquidem per me non stat quominus pactio impleatur, liberum me haberi iustum est, et tu domum redeas et qui dignus est destitutae praeficiatur ecclesiae.'" Utinam sic ageretur hodie cum excusatoribus huiusmodi, quibus tamen, cum seipsos accusant, melius credendum esset ipsis quam aliis et recederet a domo Domini omnis immunditia et versutia diabolicae fraudis, nec accederent consecrandi viri sanguinum et dolosi.

111. Sed quid? Examinantur ante consecrationem ut omnia rite facta videantur et omnis scrupulus conscientiae circumstantibus auferatur. Interrogatur enim si hoc et hoc vult facere, si talis et talis vult esse, si haec et illa pro posse

proceed next according to the judgment of the bishops. Therefore, after the simoniacal competitors had been condemned, a poor monk, who was unaware of the entire matter, was canonically elected, approved, and established in office. However, those men were forced to pay what they had bound themselves to pay, to *the very last farthing.*" John of Chartres relates these events.

110. The same author reports elsewhere: "When a certain ambitious monk was summoned to the abbacy which he had already purchased, he feigned modesty so that he might be sought more eagerly. He shrank from the burden, refused the honor, and openly proclaimed that he was unworthy of so great a thing. 'Clearly you are unworthy,' said the prince, 'because by giving so much money to me'—and he related the sum—'you secretly bought this abbey. But seeing that it is not my responsibility that the agreement is not being fulfilled, it is right that I be considered free of obligation, and that you return to your house and a worthy candidate be set over the vacant church.'" Would that such self-apologists were treated like this today! Yet when they accuse themselves, they should be trusted more than others. Then every uncleanliness and every cunning trick of diabolical deception would depart from the house of the Lord, and men of blood and deceivers would not come forward to be consecrated.

111. But what should be done? Prospective bishops are examined before consecration, so that everything may be seen to have been done properly, and every scruple of conscience removed from the bystanders. In fact, a candidate is asked if he is willing to undertake one or another action; if he is willing to play one role or another; if he is willing to perform

adimplere. Respondet autem ad universa et singula, cum singultibus et suspiriis, "volo"; sed si crastino vel deinceps casus emerserit in quo dictis facta compensent et fiat quod scriptum est, "*Sic loquimini et sic facite,*" statim convertuntur retrorsum, et universorum quae in consecratione spoponderunt non solum non reminiscuntur, sed etiam eis penitus contradicere et plane obviare non erubescunt. Qui, cum de voluntate requiruntur, melius et verius responderent, "Nolo corde, volo ore et, si volo corde et ore, volo tamen tantum, nec possum opere." Non enim verbis sed operibus hominum fides adhibenda est et vix etiam operibus.

112. Videamus igitur quae sunt quae ante consecrationem hoc verbum "volo" totiens iterando promisisti et quae in consecratione ipsa suscepisti, et si opera tua verbis sint consona, nec sibi invicem obvient et adversentur dicta et facta. Si *os quod mentitur occidit animam* et iuxta psalmistam, dicentem, "*Perdes omnes qui loquuntur mendacium,*" vitium istud turpe et reprehensibile est in laico, quanto turpius et reprehensibilius in episcopo? Nonne ante consecrationem tuam coram Deo et hominibus primo promisisti quod omnem prudentiam tuam, quantum tua capax esset natura, divinae scripturae accommodares? Quod qualiter impleveris, tu videris et tui similes, non de omnibus vobis dico, sed de te et multis aliis quos constat sensum suum magis terrenis negotiis applicare et implicare, quam scripturis divinis. Cum

this or that duty according to his ability. He responds with sobs and sighs to each and every question, "I am willing." But if tomorrow or thereafter a situation arises in which deeds should match his words, and what has been written should come to pass, "*As you speak, so do,*" they immediately turn right around. Not only do they not remember all the things that they solemnly promised at their consecration, but they do not even blush to deny them completely and to oppose them openly. When asked about their willingness, these men would better and more truly answer, "I am unwilling in my heart, willing in speech, and, even if I am willing in heart and in speech, yet I am only willing, but unable to carry through in action." Indeed, not in men's words, but in the works of men should trust be placed, and scarcely even in actions.

112. Therefore, let us see what you promised before your consecration by repeating this word "willing" so many times, and what you undertook at the consecration, and if your works are in harmony with your words, and if your words and deeds are not in contradiction and opposed to one another. If *the mouth that lies kills the soul* and, according to the saying of the psalmist "*You will destroy all who speak falsehood,*" that vice is scandalous and reprehensible in a layman, how much more scandalous and more reprehensible in a bishop? Before your consecration, did you not promise first before God and men that you would devote all your intelligence, as much as your nature is capable of, to divine scripture? You and your like should look to how you have fulfilled that promise. I am not speaking about all of you, but about you and many others who, it is well known, apply and engage their mind more in earthly affairs than in divine scripture.

igitur coram Patrefamilias conservi tui venerint et dixerint, "*Domine, quinque talenta tradidisti mihi, ecce alia quinque superlucratus sum,*" tu, qui in sudario talentum tibi creditum repositum abscondisti, quid dices? Numquid causari poteris inscientiam tuam vel impotentiam? Si dixeris cum evangelico illo, "*Timui te, eo quod homo austerus es,*" timeo ne tibi sicut et illi respondeat, et dicat, "*Serve nequam,*" et cetera quae sequuntur.

113. Secundo, promisisti quod ea quae ex divinis scripturis intelligeres plebem tuam verbo et exemplo doceres. Attende quid dictum est, immo quid ipse dixeris: "verbo et exemplo." Quomodo potest episcopus plebem suam docere verbo quam non contingit videre semel in anno? Quomodo exemplo, quem centesima pars plebis suae nec alloquetur nec videbit aliquo tempore? Et si forte viderint et audierint, nisi verbis opera fidem fecerint, illud dicent de patre suo quod Isaac de filio suo: *Vox quidem, vox Iacob est, manus autem, manus sunt Esau.* Quid est quod episcopus praedicat non furandum et ipse cotidie insatiabiliter rapinis inhiat pauperum? Quid est quod peccantibus fratribus dicit dimittendum, qui delinquentibus in se non vult misereri in perpetuum? Hinc est quod verba obviant exemplis et exempla verbis, unde ut populus, ita sacerdos, quia a sanctuario Domini, unde prodire debuit aequitas, prodit iniquitas, unde humanitas inde crudelitas, unde exempla virtutum inde germina vitiorum.

114. Tertio, promisisti quod mores tuos ab omni malo temperares et ad omne bonum commutares. Vulgo dicitur

Thus, when your fellow servants come before the Master and say, "*Lord, you handed over to me five talents; behold, I have gained another five over and above,*" what will you say, who have hidden away in a handkerchief the talent entrusted to you? Will you be able to plead your ignorance or inability? If you say in the words of the gospel, "*I feared you, because you are a stern man,*" I fear that he will respond to you as to that man, and say, "*Wicked servant,*" and the rest that follows.

113. Second, you promised that you would teach your people by word and example what you were learning from the divine scriptures. Consider what was said, or rather what you yourself said: "by word and example." How can a bishop teach his people by word when he does not happen to see them once in a year? How by example, whom hundreds of his people will neither speak to nor see at any time? And if by chance they see or hear him, unless his works inspire confidence in his words, they will say about their father what Isaac said about his son: *Indeed, the voice is the voice of Jacob, but the hands are the hands of Esau.* How is it that a bishop preaches that one must not steal, and he himself craves insatiably every day the plunder of the poor? How is it that he says that brothers who sin should be forgiven, but is perpetually unwilling to have mercy on those who offend him? Hence it is that his words are at odds with his examples and his examples with his words. Accordingly, as the people act, so does the priest, since from the sanctuary of the Lord, from which justice ought to proceed, injustice proceeds; from which kindness ought, cruelty; from which examples of virtue ought, appear the seeds of vices.

114. Third, you promised that you would restrain your behavior from every evil and transform it to every good. It is

honores mutant mores, sed utinam in melius, non in deterius! Multi enim ex quo desiderium suum adepti fuerint et super alios potestatem acceperint, universos aspernantur et conditionis humanae immemores in socios naturae exercent tyrannidem, ut vel irae satisfaciant vel potestatem ostendant, non reminiscentes quod scriptum est: *Ducem te constituerunt, noli extolli, sed esto quasi unus ex illis.* Quod utique perrarum est hodie. Quis enim non magis extollitur quam humiliatur de accepta potestate? Quis est hic et laudabimus eum? Taliter vero per antiphrasim multorum mores vidimus commutatos, ut qui ante promotionem fuerunt mansueti et modesti, adepta cathedra, ita fiant elati et importuni quod vix possint sustineri. Impleturque in eis quod Anglico proverbio dicitur: "Cum licet homini quod libet, tunc demum qualis fuerit prodet."

115. Quarto, castitatem et sobrietatem custodire et docere promisisti. Nec immerito dicuntur castitas et sobrietas custodiri. Quid enim aliud est castitatem et sobrietatem custodire quam custos esse castitatis et sobrietatis, quas custodire et docere teneris: custodire quantum ad te, docere quantum ad alios? Castitas autem non solum observanda est in illis membris quae quasi specialia instrumenta videntur esse libidinis, sed etiam in aliis quae diversa exercent officia corporis et quodam gaudent privilegio dignitatis. Castitas enim est non solum a concubitu carnali abstinere, sed etiam omnes sensus corporis a noxiis excessibus retinere. Et digne quidem castitati sobrietas iungitur, quia altera de altera

commonly said that *honors change habits,* but would that it were for the better, not for the worse! For many men despise everyone from the time that they have obtained their wish and received power over them. Forgetful of their human condition, they exercise tyranny over the sharers of their nature, so that they either satisfy their anger or display their power, not recalling that it is written: *They have selected you as a leader; do not be exalted, but be as one of them.* This is surely very rare today. For who is not rather exalted than humbled after he has received power? Who is he, and we shall praise him? But we see that through antiphrasis the habits of many men have been so transformed that those who were mild and modest before their promotion, after they have obtained an episcopal throne, become so exalted and oppressive that they can scarcely be endured. In them is fulfilled the English proverb: "When a man is allowed to do what he pleases, then at last will he make known what kind of man he is."

115. Fourth, you promised to defend and to teach chastity and sobriety. Not undeservedly are chastity and sobriety meant to be defended. For what is to defend chastity and sobriety other than to be a defender of chastity and sobriety, which you are bound to defend and to teach: to defend with respect to yourself, to teach with respect to others? Furthermore, chastity must be preserved not only in those members that seem to be special instruments of lust, as it were, but also in others that carry out the different duties of the body and that rejoice in a certain special claim to dignity. Chastity means not only to abstain from carnal copulation, but also to keep all the senses of the body away from harmful excess. And indeed, sobriety is rightly joined to chastity

nascitur, et quadam familiari et amica cognatione ita foederantur in unum, ut numquam inter se dissideant, nec adversa sibi invicem sentiant. Si autem castus est homo tuus interior, debet et exterior ei conformari, et ipsius ad exemplum disponi. Absonum enim est, si lugeat animus et lasciviat oculus, si se comprimat mens interius et dilatent se membra exterius. Gravem quidem, sicut dicitur, sortita est castitas inimicum, quae raro vincit et crebro vincitur. Haec est virtus cui difficilius creditur et cui facilius nota suspicionis impingitur, quae quanto laboriosius adquiritur, tanto fructuosius possidetur. Haec ita custodienda est in seipso et docenda proximo ut sibi reservetur ad praemium honestatis, et proximo suo ostendatur ad exemplum virtutis.

116. Quinto, promisisti quod te semper et divinis negotiis mancipares et a terrenis negotiis et lucris turpibus alienares. Numquid divinum est negotium sedere ad regis scaccarium et ibi audire computationes et confabulationes a prima luce in vesperum? Numquid hoc spectat ad plenitudinem pontificalis officii, et sine his non posset cena duci? Ibi agitur de solutione nummorum, non de salute animarum, de pecuniis aerario inferendis, non de peccatorum animabus a diabolo eruendis. Ecclesiae cui ordinatus es episcopus vix per unum aut duos dies in anno, et tunc forte magis coactus quam spontaneus, solvis debitum pensum et ad scaccarium non

because one proceeds from the other, and by a certain intimate and friendly relationship they are allied together so that they are never at variance nor feel opposed to each other. Moreover, if your inner person is chaste, your outer person ought also to conform to chastity, and to be disposed to its example. For it is a discordant thing if the soul mourns and the eye is wanton, if the mind constrains itself inwardly, but outwardly the members venture widely. Indeed, as it is said, chastity, which rarely conquers and is repeatedly conquered, has been cursed with a troublesome foe. This is a virtue which is credited only with difficulty, and on which the mark of distrust easily fastens; one which the more laboriously it is acquired, the more profitably it is possessed. It should be so defended in himself and taught to his neighbor in such a way that it is kept for himself for the reward of a good name, and displayed to his neighbor as an example of virtue.

116. Fifth, you promised that you would always give yourself over to divine affairs and that you would remove yourself from earthly affairs and from filthy lucre. Is it really a divine affair to sit at the king's exchequer, and to listen there to computations and conversations from early morning until evening? Does this pertain to the fullness of the pontifical office, and without these activities could you not enjoy a meal? The business there is about the payment of coins, not about the salvation of souls; about bringing money into the treasury, not about rescuing the souls of sinners from the devil. Scarcely one or two days in a year do you perform the duty owed to the church for which you were ordained bishop, and then perhaps rather forced than of your own free will. It does not weary you to spend half the year at the

taedet, immo dulce est, dimidiare annum! Si quaeratur ubi possit inveniri episcopus a rustico, quamlibet simplici et longe posito, statim respondetur, aut "Sedet ad scaccarium," aut "In negotiis regis profectus est." Ordine igitur converso, immo perverso, mihi videris adimplere quod promisisti, scilicet divinis negotiis mancipari et a terrenis separari, cum potius sis terrenis mancipatus et a divinis alienatus.

117. Salva pace omnium dixerim quod in Normannia a quodam audivi, videlicet quod episcopi nostri temporis, et maxime regni Anglorum, curiam regis et scaccarium eius adeo officiose et incessanter excolunt, quod magis videntur ordinati esse ad ministerium fisci quam ad mysteria ecclesiae Dei. Miror siquidem et vehementer admiror, quod licet divini amoris vel timoris instinctu non compuncti, saltem populari subsannatione confusi, non revertuntur ad cor, considerantes quam absurdum sit et professioni eorum contrarium, talibus studiis occupari quae sibi sunt ad ordinis et honoris dispendium et subditis temeritatis ad exemplum. Numquid ista est lex Domini, in qua tenentur *meditari die ac nocte* episcopi: audire computationes fisci, habere custodiam sigilli, portare claves aerarii? Petro suisque sequacibus dictum est a Domino, "*Tibi dabo claves regni caelorum*"; numquid "claves thesaurorum"? Quid est quod cum ad ecclesiam venitur vix una missa, et ipsa succincte et cum acceleratione dicta, non sine taedio auditur, et, cum ad computationes

exchequer—in fact, you find it pleasant! If a peasant, however simple and far off, is asked where the bishop can be found, he immediately answers either "He is sitting at the exchequer" or "He has set out on the king's business." And so, you seem to me to fulfill what you promised in a reverse—indeed, perverse—manner, namely the promise to give yourself over to divine affairs and to be parted from earthly ones, since you are rather given over to earthly affairs and removed from divine ones.

117. With due respect to all, I will tell what I heard in Normandy from a certain person, namely, that the bishops of our time, especially in the kingdom of the English, busy themselves with the king's court and his exchequer so dutifully and so incessantly that they seem to have been ordained more for the ministry of the treasury than for the mysteries of God's Church. Indeed, I marvel and I am exceedingly astonished that although they feel no remorse at the prompting of divine love or fear, but are at least embarrassed by people's mockery, they do not return to their senses, considering how absurd it is and how contrary to their profession to be engaged in pursuits such as these, which are to them a loss of status and honor, and to those subject to them an example of indiscretion. Is this really the law of the Lord, according to which bishops are bound *to reflect day and night:* to listen to fiscal calculations, to have custody of a seal, to carry the keys of the treasury? The Lord said to Peter and to his successors, "*I shall give to you the keys of the kingdom of heaven.*" Did he say, "keys of treasuries"? Why is it that when the bishop comes to a church, scarcely a single Mass is said, and that summarily and speedily, and it is listened to with boredom. Yet when he sits for computa-

scaccarii sedetur, tota dies et nox pro parte sine taedio transiguntur? Vide igitur quam digne ministerium sibi creditum compleant, quibus est pro ecclesia aula regia, pro mensa Domini mensa nummularii, pro lectione Veteris et Novi Testamenti revolutio computi anni praesentis et praeteriti!

118. Sexto loco, promisisti quod humilitatem et patientiam custodires in teipso, et alios similiter doceres. Bene alios haec duo docebis si prius ipsa in teipso habueris, quia maiorem in huiusmodi efficaciam habent exempla quam verba; res superest omni tempore, verba fluunt. Duo igitur ista, humilitas et patientia, pernecessaria sunt non solum subiectis sed etiam praelatis; humilitas, quia qui sine humilitate virtutes congregat, quasi qui pulverem in ventum portat; patientia, quia, dicente Domino, *in patientia vestra possidebitis animas vestras.*

119. Sed numquid humilis est qui in aestimatione sui ceteros nihil esse reputat, quos dum parvipendit quasi singularis ferus incedit? Quomodo se humiliat qui ad hoc nititur ut se super omnes alios extollat? Forte dicet mihi aliquis, "Multi humilitatem servant in corde, licet elati esse videantur in opere, faciuntque nonnulla quae videntur redolere superbiam magis ut alios humilient quam seipsos exaltent." Quod tamen si verum est nescio; Deus scit. Difficillimum autem esse arbitror ut ad exteriora quandoque non transeant ea quae diutius in corde coaluerunt. Unde raro contigit quod bene conveniant et in una sede morentur humilitas cordis et

tions at the exchequer, the whole day and night are spent without boredom on his part? See, therefore, how worthily they fulfill the ministry entrusted to them, these men for whom the royal court substitutes for the church, the table of money changers for the Lord's table, and unrolling the accounts for this year and the past year for reading the Old and New Testament!

118. Sixth, you promised that you would maintain humility and patience in yourself and would teach others the same. You will teach these two qualities well to others if first you have them in yourself, since in matters of this kind examples have greater efficacy than words. A deed remains for all time; words vanish. And so, these two qualities, humility and patience, are very necessary, not only for subjects, but also for prelates: humility, because a man who accumulates virtues without humility is like one who carries dust into the wind; patience, because, as the Lord says, *in your patience you will possess your souls.*

119. But is he really humble, who, in his own estimation, thinks that the rest of men are nothing; who attacks them like a strange wild beast, considering them of little consequence? How does he humble himself, who strives to elevate himself above all others? Perhaps someone will say to me, "Many men preserve humility in their heart even though they seem to be haughty in their actions, and they do some things that seem redolent of pride, more to humble others than to exalt themselves." I do not know if this is true; God knows. However, I think it is very difficult for these qualities which have taken root for a long time in their heart not to make their way outward at some time. Hence it rarely happens that humility of heart and pride of action, abase-

superbia operis, deiectio spiritus et gestus elatus, cor contritum et humiliatum et vana extollentia sermonum et operum. Sicut igitur omnium virtutum humilitas est custodia, ita et earundem clipeus est patientia contra vitia. Haec utinam praelatis tam familiaris esset quam necessaria, idque agerent ut saepius eam oblivioni traderent quam saepe de ea cogitarent.

120. Sed quid est quod miles multis lacessitus iniuriis silet et sustinet, et quandoque percussus non percutit, et episcopus statim ad primos motus gladium suum exserit et percutit? Non dico quod patientia ita sectetur ut ubi percutiendum est non percutiat; sed ne dissimulet ubi non est dissimulandum et feriat ubi non est feriendum. Sed ita gladium acceptum moderetur patientia, ne vulneretur conscientia, sive praepropere fuerit exsertus sive nimis remoretur exserendus. Quid autem est quod velocior et vehementior est ad vindictam quamlibet expetendam episcopus in sacra scriptura eruditus quam rusticus laicus et illitteratus cum dicat Dominus, "*Mihi vindictam et ego retribuam*"? Estne ista patientia quam promittunt in semetipsis custodire et alios docere? Si verba sacerdotis aut vera aut sacrilega, quare volunt promittere quod nolunt adimplere, cum dicat psalmista, "*Vovete et reddite*"?

121. Septimo, promisisti traditiones orthodoxorum patrum ac decretales sanctae et apostolicae sedis constitutiones veneranter suscipere, docere atque servare. Si traditiones orthodoxorum patrum ea qua deceret reverentia

ment of spirit and a haughty bearing, a contrite and humble heart, and vain exaltation of words and actions go well together and are present in one place. Therefore, just as humility is the guardian of all virtues, so also is patience their shield against vices. Would that to prelates this virtue were as habitual as it is necessary, and that they would pursue it in such a way that they might more often forget about it than think about it often.

120. But why is it that a knight assailed by many insults keeps silent and bears it, and at times does not strike when struck, but at the first disturbance a bishop immediately draws his sword and strikes? I do not say that patience should be pursued in such a way that one does not strike where one should strike, but that one should not overlook it when something should not be overlooked and should not strike when something should not be struck. Let patience rule the sword at one's disposal in such a way that conscience is not wounded if the sword has been drawn overhastily or held back too much when it should be drawn. Moreover, why is it that a bishop instructed in sacred scripture is quicker and more eager to seek any vengeance than a simple and unlettered layman, since the Lord says, "*Vengeance is mine and I shall repay*"? Is this the patience that they promise to defend in themselves and to teach others? If the words of a priest are either true or sacrilegious, why are they willing to promise what they are unwilling to fulfill, since the psalmist says, "*Vow and pay*"?

121. Seventh, you promised reverently to accept, to teach and to preserve the traditions of the orthodox fathers, as well as the decretals and decrees of the holy and apostolic see. If the traditions of orthodox fathers were being

observarentur, non esset hodie tanta confusio in clero et populo, neque a terrena potestate ita concuteretur et conculcaretur ecclesia; non esset tanta praelatorum insolentia, sed nec subditorum inoboedientia. Sed quia caput debile est et infirmum, membra inferiora vacillant nec debitum prosequuntur officium. Mandata siquidem apostolica veneranter suscipiuntur, suscepta reverenter docentur, sed qualiter observentur planum est aspicere. Si scribat dominus papa, etiam sine omni coniunctione et adverbio plane et aperte ita ut nihil sit ambiguum, nihil contrarium, mandatum tamen eius nihilominus eluditur, et pro nihilo habetur. Et ne debito mancipetur effectui, hinc per appellationes suspenditur, hinc per aliud mandatum inhibetur. Dicuntur litterae hinc surreptitiae, hinc falsa suggestione et tacita veritate impetratae. Postremo, si mandato apostolico aliqua exhibetur reverentia, ille est in causa qui primus in orbe deos fecit: timor, non amor iustitiae aut reverentia personae. Si pauper quilibet oppressus appellaverit, non tenet appellatio; si dives ad appellationem convolaverit, defertur appellationi, cum non esset deferendum, sicque pauperibus cedit in dispendium iuris, quod repertum fuit ad remedium oppressionis. Paulo dictum est, "*Caesarem appellasti? Ad Caesarem ibis.*" Pauperibus vero hodie dicitur, "Vos appellabitis? Nos expilabimus!"

122. Si igitur mandata summi pontificis ita suscipis quod personarum acceptionem potius attendis quam veritatem et sinceritatem causae pauperis, nonne est apud te pondus et pondus, statera et statera, iudicium et iudicium, cum dicat

observed with the proper respect, there would not exist today such great confusion among the clergy and people. The Church would not be so agitated and abused by earthly power. There would not be such great insolence in prelates, nor such great disobedience in their subjects. But since the head is weak and infirm, the lesser members waver and do not perform their due office. Apostolic mandates are indeed received reverently; once received, they are taught respectfully. But it is plain to see how they are observed. If the lord pope writes plainly and openly in such a way that nothing is ambiguous, nothing inconsistent, even without any conjunction or adverb, yet his mandate is nonetheless evaded and disregarded. And so that it is not put into effect as it should be, it is protracted by appeals or prevented by another mandate. One letter is said to be illegitimate, another obtained by a false allegation and by suppressing the truth. Finally, if any respect is shown to an apostolic mandate, the reason is that which first made gods in the world: fear, not love of justice or respect for a person. If any downtrodden pauper makes an appeal, his appeal does not prevail; if a rich man has rapid recourse to an appeal, his appeal is deferred to, although it should not be deferred to. And so for the poor what was devised as a remedy for oppression leads to a forfeit of his rights. To Paul it was said, "*Have you appealed to Caesar? To Caesar you shall go.*" But to the poor today it is said, "Are you going to appeal? We shall pillage you!"

122. Therefore, if you accept the mandates of the highest pontiff in such a way that you pay attention to respecting persons rather than to the truth and soundness of a poor man's cause, do you have before you weight and weight, balance and balance, judgment and judgment, since the Lord

Dominus: "*Iuste iudicate, filii hominum*"? Miror qua fronte sciens et prudens praesumit iudicare iniuste, qui de omnibus iudiciis suis in illo tremendo et terribili iudicio iusto Iudici redditurus est rationem. Quid est quod dives, si pauperem impetit prima die vel secunda, aut certe tertia, reportat iudicium iuxta desiderium suum; iudicium vero pauperis, si contendat cum divite, differtur in septennium, vel certe usque in sempiternum? Si iusti in perpetuum vivent, qui huiusmodi amant et operantur iniustitias quo devenient? Quid autem de illis sentiendum est qui iustitiam prostituunt et in pretium publice redigunt, *vendentes et ementes eam etiam in templo,* sicut venduntur oves et boves in foro?

123. Octavo loco, professionem fecisti de oboedientia canonica exhibenda metropolitano et ecclesiae matrici, cui etiam manu propria sicut moris est subscripsisti. Si *melior est* testante scriptura *oboedientia quam victimae,* et plus est oboedire quam immolare, non est tutum ab oboedientia resilire, vel eam simulare ubi non est in veritate. Quod quidem multi faciunt hodie, pauci enim sunt qui oboediant eo modo quo oporteret oboedire. Si enim placet quod praecipitur, paretur, sin autem, statim excusatio impossibilitatis praetenditur, vel, ut iugum oboedientiae penitus excutiatur a collo, ad sedem apostolicam appellatur. Quaeruntur ergo variis laboribus et sumptibus immunitates et exemptiones ne oboediant abbates episcopo suo, vel episcopi archiepiscopo.

124. Quid autem est huiusmodi privilegia quaerere de non oboediendo, quam sedem suam ad aquilonem ponere, ut

says, "*Judge justly, you sons of men*"? I am amazed at the boldness with which a knowledgeable and intelligent man dares to judge unjustly, a man who is going to render an account of all his judgments to the just Judge at that fearful and terrible final judgment. Why is it that if he accuses a pauper, a rich man obtains a judgment according to his wishes on the first day or the second, or certainly the third; but judgment for a poor man, if he contends with a rich one, is put off for seven years, or no doubt even forever? If the just will live forever, where will men who love and work injustices of this kind end up? What should we think about those who prostitute justice and publicly reduce it to a price, *selling and buying it even in the temple,* just as sheep and oxen are sold in the marketplace?

123. Eighth, you professed that you would show canonical obedience to your archbishop and your mother Church, and you even signed the profession with your own hand as is customary. If, as scripture testifies, *obedience is better than sacrifice,* and to obey is worth more than offerings, it is perilous to shun obedience or to pretend obedience when it is not present in reality. Indeed, many do this today, for there are few who obey in the manner in which one ought. For if what is commanded is pleasing, they comply, but if otherwise, they immediately put forth an excuse of impossibility, or, in order to shake off completely the yoke of obedience from their neck, they appeal to the apostolic see. And so, through various efforts and expenses, they seek immunities and exemptions so that abbots may disobey their bishop, or bishops their archbishop.

124. What else is to seek privileges of this kind about disobedience, other than to set one's own see toward the north,

dicant cum illo, "*Similis ero Altissimo.* Quis enim ille est ut ego oboediam ei? Forsitan praedecessor meus oboedivit ei, sed non ego; *grossior* enim *est digitus meus* dorso *patris mei.* Conferamus parentes nostros et parentum proavos, divitias nostras et litteras nostras et qui inventus fuerit inferior superiori oboediat." Haec et alia huiusmodi proponunt qui aliis oboedire contemnunt. Quae omnia potius pullulant de fomite superbiae quam de humilitatis radice.

125. Nono loco, promisisti quod pauperibus et peregrinis omnibusque indigentibus propter nomen Domini velles esse affabilis et misericors. Bona certe promissio, si bene impleatur. Pauperum et peregrinorum ultimo loco facta est mentio, ut tenacius memoriae commendaretur. Multi sunt qui, in suscipiendis peregrinis et pauperibus et erogandis eleemosynis, diffusi sunt ut videantur ab hominibus. Quotiens enim conventus fit magnatorum, tunc munera multipliciter stillant de manibus misericordiae in sinum pauperum, cum vero se in sua secreto receperint, venientibus pauperibus et clamantibus, "*Domine, domine, aperi nobis,*" non est qui respondeat, sed clausa est ianua. Quod si forte adhuc pertinacius institerint, canibus vel certe verberibus longius amoventur. Affabilem itaque et misericordem decet esse episcopum, sed nequaquam ut laudes obtineat hominum, sed mercedem apud Dominum. Exilis admodum et arida est quantumlibet lauta refectio pauperum cui conscientia pura non perhibet testimonium, et e contrario, ut ait Gregorius, numquam manus vacua est a munere, si arca cordis referta fuerit bona voluntate. Non enim quid sed ex quanto pensat Deus.

so that they say with the prophet, "*I shall be like the Most High,* for who is he that I should obey him? Perhaps my predecessor obeyed him, but not I, for *my finger is thicker than my father's* back. Let us compare our parents and our parents' ancestors, our wealth and our learning, and let the one who will be found inferior obey the superior." Those who disdain to obey others make assertions of this kind or their like. All of them issue from the kindling of pride rather than the root of humility.

125. Ninth, you promised that you would be kind and merciful to paupers and strangers and all those in need for the sake of the Lord's name. Surely a good promise, if it were properly fulfilled. Mention was made of paupers and strangers in the last place, so that it might be more firmly committed to memory. There are many men who, in receiving strangers and the poor and in disbursing alms, roam far and wide so that people may see them. For whenever there is a gathering of great men, then gifts flow in abundance from hands of mercy into the bosom of the poor. But when they receive them in private in their own homes, to those paupers coming and crying out "*Lord, lord, open for us,*" there is no one who responds, but the door is closed. If by chance they still stubbornly solicit, they are driven far off by dogs or at least by whips. And so, a bishop ought to be kind and merciful, but by no means in order to gain people's praise, but rather a reward with the Lord. Certainly, refreshment of paupers, however sumptuous it may be, if a pure conscience does not bear witness to it, is very meager and scant, and, on the other hand, as Gregory says, a hand is never without a gift if the heart's coffers are filled with goodwill. For God weighs not what is given, but from how large a store it is given.

126. Ista sunt quae ante consecrationem suam coram Deo et hominibus promittunt episcopi, quae utique ad memoriam, si mihi credideris, crebro revocabis, considerans teipsum si adimplesti promissa, si dictis respondeant opera, si aliter de te sentiat conscientia propria, aliter aliena. Non enim attendas quid de te alii, sed quid tu ipse sentias, sive bonum sive malum. Si bonus es et male de te opinentur homines, cum id merita tua non exegerint, patienter sustine, nec nimis super hoc solliciteris, cum scriptum sit: *Si de mundo fuissetis mundus quod suum erat diligeret, propterea autem odit vos mundus quia de mundo non estis.* Verumtamen orandum est pro huiusmodi ad Dominum exemplo eius qui ait, "*Pater, dimitte illis, quia nesciunt quid faciunt.*" Sane rumor falsus cito evanescit, et ubi deficiente materia ignis defuerit, fumi vapor citius deficiet et in nihilum declinabit. Si vero malus fueris et bene de te quocumque pacto senserint, homines non tam ipsos quam teipsum seducis. In primis enim corrodit te vermis conscientiae tanquam lignum putridum interius et exterius dealbatum. Haec est pestis perniciosissima, quae nec potest gaudiorum intermixtione oblivisci, nec locorum mutatione declinari. Si igitur ea agis quae agere decet episcopum, non residente scrupulo in conscientia, coepta prosequere, sin autem, vel sero incipe. Melius est enim sero quam numquam incepisse.

127. Illud autem in omni religioso, et maxime in episcopo, elaborandum est, ut conscientia servetur illaesa, ut quicquid ipse fecerit, vel fama de eo praedicaverit, cum apostolo

126. These are the promises that bishops make in the presence of God and men before their consecration. These you will certainly often recall to mind, if you trust me, examining yourself to see if you have fulfilled your promises, if your deeds accord with your words, if your own conscience judges one way about you, but another's judges otherwise. For you should not listen to what others think about you, but what you yourself think, whether good or bad. If you are good and people think badly of you, although your merits have not warranted this, bear it patiently and do not be overly troubled about it, since it is written: *If you had been of the world, the world would love what was its own; however, since you are not of the world, the world hates you.* Nevertheless, you should pray to the Lord for men of this kind, according to his example who says, "*Father, forgive them, for they know not what they do.*" Truly, false gossip vanishes quickly, and when a fire has failed for want of fuel, the smoke very quickly evaporates and diminishes to nothing. But if you are bad and people think well of you somehow, you are not misleading them as much as you are yourself. For in the first place, the worm of conscience gnaws at you just as at wood that is rotten inside and whitewashed outside. This is a most baneful curse that cannot be forgotten by intermittent joys nor avoided by changing location. So if you are doing the things which it befits a bishop to do, with no scruple lingering in your conscience, proceed with what you have begun; but if not, then begin, late though it be. For it is better to be late than never to begin at all.

127. Moreover, every religious man, and especially every bishop, should strive for this: that his conscience be kept inviolate, so that whatever he has done, or whatever public

semper secure dicere possit, "*Gloria nostra hoc est testimonium conscientiae nostrae.*" Conscientia siquidem custodienda est ut pupilla oculi, et erudienda ad instar parvuli, quae quanto potest leviori iaculo vulnerari tanto debet sollicitius contra iacula praemuniri. In conscientia duo sunt praecipue iugi meditatione versanda, misericordia scilicet et iudicium; ita tamen ut cum de iudicio agitur, timor poenae misericordiae dulcedine temperetur, ne animum in desperationem adducat. Et rursum cum sibi mens humana de misericordia blanditur, austeritas iudicii ne licentius dissolvatur, quam sit formidabilis pensetur, sicque invicem sibi confoederentur timor poenae et amor gloriae, ne alterutrius vicissitudo inveniatur vel nimis intensa vel nimis remissa.

128. Recordare igitur, antequam dies vitae tuae veniant ad occasum, si per ostium ascendisti in ovile ovium, et quo nomine ex merito verius habeas censeri, pastoris an mercenarii. Vide si episcopum exhibeas in opere, quam tam sollemniter professus es ore. Sin autem, magis ingemiscendum est tibi sub onere quam gloriandum de honore. Res quidem magna est super capita hominum imponi et praelationis maiestate gloriari, sed meticulosum valde est quod oportet unumquemque reddere rationem de villicatione sua et ei praecipue apud quem non est locus adulationi, qui nec potest decipi, nec a veritate qualibet occasione deflecti.

129. Dura siquidem est, si bene consideretur, praelatorum conditio, quia quanto gradus altior tanto casus gravior,

opinion says about him, he can always confidently declare with the Apostle, "*Our glory is this, the testimony of our conscience.*" Indeed, the conscience must be guarded like the pupil of the eye, and trained like a little child, for the lighter the dart it can be wounded by, the more carefully should it be protected against darts. In conscience, two things must particularly be considered with constant contemplation, namely, mercy and judgment, yet in such a way that when the subject is judgment, the fear of punishment is tempered by the sweetness of mercy, lest it lead the spirit to despair. And again, when the human mind flatters itself on the subject of mercy, let it be considered how formidable the severity of judgment is, so that it might not be too lightly passed over. Let fear of punishment and love of glory be united together in such a way that the reciprocal influence of each is not found to be either too strict or too slack.

128. And so, before the days of your life come to their setting, call to mind if you have entered into the sheepfold through the gate, and also by what name you truly should be called based on your merits: shepherd or hireling. See if you show yourself to be a bishop in actions, as you so solemnly professed with your mouth. But if not, you should rather groan under your burden than boast about your dignity. Truly, it is a great thing to be set over the heads of men and to glory in the greatness of a prelate, but it is a very frightful fact that every man must render an account of his stewardship, and in particular to him with whom there is no place for fawning, who cannot be deceived nor turned aside from the truth for any reason at all.

129. If we carefully consider, the condition of prelates is harsh, because the higher the station, the harder the fall,

viciniusque imminet praecipitium ad ruinam quam ascensus ad gloriam. Si in temporalibus gloriaris, gloria tua transibit cum tempore, et qui ad tempus fuisti gloriosus, forsitan sine fine eris ingloriosus. Sacerdotium igitur opus esse aestimes, non dignitatem. Sic adimpleas officii debitum, ut potius te censeas ministrum quam dominum, non attendens eminentiam dignitatis sed periculum curae pastoralis. Alioquin, nihil tibi et illi qui ait, "*Ego sum pastor bonus.*" Unde et ad experimentum boni pastoris subiungitur: *Bonus pastor animam suam ponit pro ovibus suis.* Numquid et tu paratus es, ad exemplum illius, animam pro ovibus ponere, a quibus tam longe positus es corpore, nescio si mente?

130. Sed cum teneantur praelati subditorum se moribus conformare, quid est quod tanta est hodie in ecclesia dissonantia inter praelatos et subditos non solum actu sed etiam habitu? Quae est inter te et gregem tuum conformitas, cum ipsi profiteantur monachum, tu vero clericum, ipsi induantur saccis, tu autem sericis? Multa quidem est dissimilitudo vestium; utinam una sit facies animorum. Verumtamen mihi videtur non aliud esse monachum clericis vel clericum monachis praeponi quam albo pallio nigrum caputium assui. Dissimilitudo autem habitus discordiam generat nonnumquam animorum, dumque ordo et habitus inter se discrepant, ad dissensionem mentes facilius invitant. Cum enim eiusdem professionis et ordinis crebro inter se dissideant, mirandum non est si penitus diversi non conveniant, sed

and the headlong descent into ruin menaces more closely than the ascent to glory. If you glory in temporal affairs, your glory will pass away with time, and you who were glorious for a time will perhaps be inglorious without end. Therefore, you should reckon that the priesthood is a task, not an honor. You should carry out the duty of your office in such a way that you would consider yourself rather a servant than a lord, not paying attention to the eminence of your worth, but to the peril of pastoral care. Otherwise, you have nothing in common with him who says, "*I am the good shepherd.*" Hence also, this is added as characterization of a good shepherd: *The good shepherd lays down his life for his sheep.* Are you really ready, according to his example, to lay down your life for your sheep, from whom you are so far removed in body (I do not know if in mind)?

130. But since prelates are bound to adapt themselves to the ways of their subjects, why is it that there is such great disharmony in the Church today among prelates and subjects, not only in actions, but also in attire? What conformity is there between you and your flock when they profess the monk, but you the cleric; when they are clothed in sacks, but you in silks? There is certainly a great difference in garments; would that there might be a single appearance in minds. However, it seems to me that preferring a monk to clerics or a cleric to monks is no different than sewing a black cowl onto a white cloak. Moreover, difference in attire often produces discord in minds, and when order and attire differ among themselves, they easily incite minds to dissension. For when men of the same profession and order repeatedly disagree among themselves, it is no wonder if those who are completely different do not agree, but feel more

magis invicem contraria sentiant, licet in diversitate vestium non sit consummatio virtutum. Multi enim in habitu abiectiori spiritum elationis induunt, et e converso nonnulli *in vestitu deaurato* magis humiliantur quam superbiunt.

131. Familiare tamen est similia gaudere similibus, et unumquemque conditionis suae, professionis et ordinis socios singulari quadam caritate amplexari. Legimus autem Iohannem baptistam de vestis asperitate fuisse laudatum, Iohannem vero evangelistam sindone super nudum indutum, utrumque tamen a Domino electum et non mediocriter dilectum, et ad caelestis convivii mensam omni acceptione vestium deducta admissum. Potius enim honestas quam habitus, virtus quam vestis, appetenda est. Iocunda autem societas est, cum sibi invicem confoederantur vestis et vita religionis, ita ut quod gratiosum erat ex per se gratiosius fiat ex alterius coniunctione. Absonum autem valde est quod episcopus, qui in clero debet fieri forma gregis clericalis, vestis honestate non est contentus, sed ex eodem panno pallium et tunicam partiantur miles et episcopus, sacerdos ad sancta sanctorum ingrediens et miles castra expugnaturus aggrediens, ille qui potestatem habet ligandi et solvendi et ille qui gladio materiali super femur suum habet accingi.

132. Si forte conveniant proceres et episcopi, dummodo caput discoopertum non videas, vix habes in quo alterum ab altero discernas. Iurat laicus, iurat et peierat episcopus, venaticam exercet laicus, venatum pergit et episcopus,

opposition to each other, although the consummation of virtues does not lie in the diversity of vesture. Indeed, many men in the more abject attire put on a spirit of elation, and, conversely, some *in gilded garments* are humble rather than haughty.

131. It is well known that like delights in like, and that everyone embraces those who share his own status, profession or order with a certain special affection. However, we read that John the Baptist was praised for the roughness of his garment, but John the Evangelist covered his naked body with fine linen, yet each was chosen by the Lord and greatly loved and admitted to the table of the heavenly banquet with no regard for clothing. Indeed, we should strive after integrity before attire, virtue before vesture. Fellowship is pleasing when religious vesture and the religious way of life are united to each other, so that what was agreeable of itself may be more agreeable on account of being joined to the other. It is very incongruous that a bishop, who ought to be a model for the clerical flock among the clergy, is not satisfied with the high status of his vesture, but from the same cloth a knight and a bishop divide a pallium and a tabard, the priest approaching the holy of holies and the knight advancing on camps to attack them. The one has the power of binding and loosing, and the other has to be girt with the material power of a sword on his thigh.

132. If by chance noblemen and bishops assemble together, provided that you do not see their heads uncovered, you have scarcely any way in which to distinguish one from the other. The layman swears an oath, the bishop swears an oath and perjures himself; the layman engages in hunting, the bishop proceeds to the chase too; the layman glories in

aucupio gloriatur laicus, aucupio delectatur episcopus, pares voto et viribus proficiscuntur ad proelium miles et episcopus, a pari saecularibus causis et iudiciis intendunt saecularis potestas et pontificalis auctoritas, pariter fisco deputantur, pariter publicis functionibus occupantur et quia paria sunt studia, paria fiunt officia, vix discrepant solo ordine qui unum et idem sunt et sentiunt voluntate et opere.

133. Quid multa? Si subtilius perpendatur, illud propheticum nostris temporibus videtur adimpletum: *Et erit sicut populus sic et sacerdos.* Quid enim est hodie in saecularibus negotiis vel in lucris turpibus tam enorme quod sacerdotes abhorreant, aut gratia quaestus sive conciliandae gratiae magnatorum non exerceant? Horrendi facinoris detestanda crudelitas quae in Coventrensi ecclesia nuper facta est nonne pervenit ab occidente usque orientem? Ubinam terrarum commissum est tam enorme flagitium? Mitius egissent pagani cum Christianis, si in manus eorum incidissent, quam egit episcopus cum monachis. Testis mihi est Deus quod dolens et tristis admodum refero quod in ecclesia Coventrensi oculis propriis aspexi. In claustro et capitulo, quae loca contemplationi et confessioni specialiter deputata fuerant, vidi ego et alii nonnulli, eiectis monachis, meretrices publicas introduci et tota nocte cum lenonibus decubare, sicut in lupanari.

134. O mira patientia Dei, quae non statim percutit, sed adhuc impios in impietate sua prosperari permittit! Qua poena punietur flagitiosus et nefandus ille, qui tanti sceleris

hawking, the bishop delights in hawking. Equals in vows and in vigor, the knight and the bishop march to battle; secular power and pontifical authority equally direct their attention to secular issues and judgments. They are equally appointed to the treasury; they are equally occupied with public payment of taxes, and since their activities are equal, their official duties become equal too. Scarcely are they distinguished just by their order whose existence and experience are one and the same in will and in action.

133. What more shall I say? If we closely consider the matter, that prophecy seems fulfilled in our times: *And it will be as with the people, so also the priest.* For what is so outrageous today in secular affairs or involving filthy lucre that priests shudder at it, or that they do not engage in it for the sake of profit, or for gaining the favor of great men? Has not the abominable cruelty of that terrible outrage that was committed recently in the church at Coventry reached from the west to the east? Where in the world has so outrageous an infamy ever been perpetrated? Pagans would have dealt more gently with Christians, if they had fallen into their hands, than the bishop dealt with the monks. God is my witness that with grief and great sorrow I report what I saw in the church at Coventry with my own eyes. In the cloister and chapter, places specifically designated for contemplation and confession, I and some others saw that monks were driven out and common prostitutes brought in and lay there the whole night with their pimps, just as in a brothel.

134. Oh wondrous patience of God, which did not strike them immediately, but still permits the impious to prosper in their impiety! With what punishment will that disgraceful and wicked one be punished, who was the culprit of so

actor exstitit, aut ipse quicumque sit qui ei consensit? Si faciens et consentiens pari poena puniendi sunt, quid de eis censendum est qui tam nefando operi non solum subscripserunt, sed tamquam dignum annalibus auctoritate sua confirmaverunt? Ego neminem accuso, neminem damno. Sunt autem opera quae testimonium perhibent veritati. Tu videris si te in aliquo super his conscientia reprehendat, procul dubio enim in huius operis factores et fautores, sive principes sive praesules, ipse ulciscetur *qui aufert spiritum principum* et terribilis est super filios hominum; et cui illata est iniuria ipse cogitabit de vindicta. Sed et iam creditur, et a multis circumquaque praeconatur, quod Deus, ultionum Dominus, propter miserias inopum et gemitum pauperum gladium suum pro parte exseruit ut ulciscatur sanguinem servorum suorum.

135. Haec sunt igitur opera episcoporum nostri temporis. Haec sunt quae faciunt aut impune fieri permittunt. Haec sunt virtutum exempla quae posteris relinquunt, ut sit memoria eorum in maledictione. Haec sunt gesta praeclara futuris saeculis digno relatu memoranda. Cum appositus fueris ad patres tuos et pro carnis conditione corpus tuum resolutum in cineres, supererit tamen qui referat posteritati haec vel illa tuis temporibus accidisse, talia attemptata fuisse te praesidente et forsitan auctoritatem praestante; quodque modo dicitur occulte tunc super tecta praedicabitur publice, detrahentque pulveribus tuis et cineri ad quos

great a sin, or whoever he is who consented to it? If the one doing it and the one consenting to it should be punished with equal penalty, what must we think about those who not only have endorsed so wicked a deed, but who have by their own authority validated it as if worthy to be recorded in the annals? I accuse no one, I condemn no one. However, there are actions that bear witness to the truth. You must see if your conscience reproaches you in any way in regard to these matters, for without doubt the one *who carries off the spirit of princes* and who is terrible over the children of men will have his vengeance upon the perpetrators and promoters of this action, whether princes or prelates; and he on whom injury has been inflicted, will take thought for vengeance. But even now we believe, and many proclaim on every side, that God, the Lord of vengeance, because of the wretchedness of the needy and the lamentation of the poor, has for his part drawn his sword to avenge the blood of his servants.

135. These, then, are the actions of the bishops of our time. These are the things that they do or allow to happen with impunity. These are the examples of virtues that they leave to posterity, so that their memory is a curse. These are the renowned deeds to be told of in worthy recital by ages to come. When you have been laid to rest near your fathers and your body has been dissolved into ashes according to the nature of flesh, yet one will survive to report to posterity that such and such things happened in your time, and such things were attempted on your watch and perhaps on your authority. What is now said in secret then will be proclaimed publicly on the rooftops. Those to whom you have scarcely come down in name only will disparage your dust and ashes,

vix solo nomine pervenisti, et qui modo forsitan excusat superstitem tunc accusare non desinet innocentem.

136. Quod si remedium huic morbo adhibere volueris, necesse est ut id sedulo opereris quo famam facias detracto nubilo serenari, et magnificentia operum laudabilium *obstruat os iniqua loquentium.* Non dico quod simulationibus sicut quidam solent insistas, ut exinde famam quae ad utrumlibet facilis et difficilis esse solet adquiras; nec hominibus aduleris ut eis placeas, quia *qui hominibus placent confusi sunt, quoniam Deus sprevit eos,* sed ut huiusmodi operibus semper insistas quibus et Deo ex testimonio conscientiae placeas, et proximis praebens bene operandi exemplum omnem detractionis materiam subtrahas et aemulis tuis omnem suspicionis et sinistrae interpretationis aditum praecludas, ut probata virtus insipientes corripiat et malitia iniquitatis excogitatae virtutum argumentis redarguta erubescat. Sic enim *congeres carbones super caput eorum* qui oderunt te et *adorabunt vestigia pedum tuorum qui detrahebant tibi.* Nihil enim adeo volitantis famae flammas exstinguit et malitiam mendacium redarguit sicut manifestatio operis in contrarium cui verit-as et iustitia non possunt non perhibere testimonium.

137. Gloriosius autem est illud meditari et agere quo ab aemulo et inimico tuo invito laudem extorqueas, quam quo favorem ab amicis ampliorem adquiras. Amicus enim omni tempore diligit, nec in tempore temptationis recedit, semper in eodem statu mentis permanens, et varias fortunae

and one who perhaps now excuses a man during his lifetime will not cease to reproach even an innocent man then.

136. But if you wish to apply a remedy to this disease, you need to work diligently to remove the clouds and brighten your reputation, and to strive that the splendor of your praiseworthy works *silences the mouths of those who speak ill of you.* I do not say that you should devote yourself to pretense, as some are accustomed to do, so that thereafter you may secure a reputation which is wont to be both easy and difficult contingently. You should not fawn on men to please them, because those *who please men are confounded, since God has despised them.* But you should always devote yourself to works of a kind both to please God according to the testimony of your conscience, and to offer your neighbors an example of right action, depriving them of every opportunity for detraction and blocking your critics from every avenue of suspicion and pejorative interpretation, so that your proven virtue may reprove the foolish, and the wickedness of contrived malice blush with shame, refuted by the evidence of your virtues. For in this way *will you heap coals upon the heads of those* who hate you, and *those who used to disparage you will worship the tread of your feet.* Indeed, nothing so effectively snuffs out the flames of airy rumor and refutes the wickedness of falsehoods as the manifestation of contradictory actions, to which truth and justice cannot but offer testimony.

137. Moreover, it is more glorious to think and act so as to wrest praise from your rival and your enemy, unwilling though he be, than to win greater favor from your friends. For a friend loves you at all times and does not withdraw in a time of trial, remaining always in the same state of mind,

vices eadem constantia mentis excipiens, ita ut in tempore adversitatis pro amico surdus sit ad famam, caecus ad gratiam, insensibilis ad fortunam. Ideoque sollicitius procurandum est ut hostibus detrahendi materia subtrahatur potius quam amicis laudis occasio tribuatur.

138. Quia igitur *mundus iste in maligno positus est,* et chaos antiquum nobis videtur minari regressum, quia *omnis fere caro corrupit viam suam* et *veritas non est in terra,* quia falsitas exterminavit eam a filiis hominum, vix potest hodie hostis ab amico discerni. Officiosior enim est qui alium circumvenire intendit quam qui in veritate diligit. Quod est enim hodie claustrum, aut quae est congregatio, ubi veritati non praevaleat adulatio, ubi non sit *pondus et pondus, mensura et mensura?* Et quia tanta est multitudo ficte et fallaciter incedentium, fides et veritas nullatenus possunt prodire in publicum. Ille enim qui alteri amplius insidiatur ut eum subvertat, ipse est qui se artius diligere simulat et quem *odio inexorabili* in corde persequitur, ei in facie ulterius blanditur et venenum quo totus tabescit in mente, iocunda quadam faciei gratia vestit et venustat vultus hilaritate; coram benedicit, clam vero subsannat et detrahit. Obsequitur ei in publico quem vellet occidisse in occulto. Suffulcit umero quam vellet praemisso vertice in sterquilinium praecipitasse a collo.

139. Haec nisi fallor, tu ipse aliquando expertus es. Dum enim tibi (quae frequentius fallit) fortuna arrideret, et penes

and accepting the various turns of fortune with the same constancy of mind, so that in a time of adversity, on behalf of a friend he is deaf to public opinion, blind to favor, insensible to fortune. And so, we should more conscientiously see to it that the material for disparagement is taken from our foes than that the occasion for praise is imparted to our friends.

138. Therefore, since *this world is seated in wickedness,* and the chaos of old seems to threaten us with a return, since *almost all flesh has corrupted its way* and *there is no truth in the land,* since falsehood has exiled it from the children of men, today an enemy can scarcely be distinguished from a friend. Indeed, he is more diligent who aims to deceive another than who truly loves him. For what cloister is there today, or what community, where flattery does not prevail over truth, where there are not *differing weights and measures?* And since the number of those who walk in falsehood and deceit is so great, trust and truth can by no means make a public appearance. In fact, the one who lays most traps for another to destroy him is the very one who pretends to love him most deeply, and he flatters all the more to his face the man whom he pursues with *relentless hatred* in his heart. The venom by which his mind is totally consumed he clothes with a charming agreeableness of face, and makes his countenance pleasing by its cheerfulness; publicly he praises him, but privately he mocks and disparages him. He courts him in public whom he secretly wants to kill. He supports on his shoulders the very one whom he wants to hurl headfirst by his neck into a dung pile.

139. Unless I am mistaken, you have experienced these things yourself at times. For while fortune (which frequently

te resideret potestas regni et sacerdotii, multos et magnos habuisti adulatores. Innumerabilis fuit turba famulantium, sed rara admodum in veritate diligentium, quod et exitus ipse probavit. Quocumque locorum divertebas, excipiebaris ut angelus, colebaris quodammodo ut deus, in tantum ut non minimum sibi successisse confiteretur quisquis in conspectu tuo tibi beneplacitum quicquam posset eloqui aut operari. Tuis stipendiis militabat favor cleri et devotio populi, tibi ascribebatur quicquid laude dignum agerent universi et singuli. Confluebant ad te non solum consanguinei et contermini tui, verum etiam a finibus terrae venerunt, ut cancellarium viderent et audirent, immo auferrent aliquid ab eo.

140. Quidam carmina, quidam cantilenas et alia huiusmodi, quae non multo constabant, magnifice offerebant, ut ubertate frugum alterius seminum suorum inopiam sublevarent. Ipse vero omni petenti se dabat tantaque hilaritate ut nonnumquam vota petentium praeveniret. Sed et tanta fuit in dante liberalitas, ut in dando moram aestimaret repulsam, et personarum acceptionem pauperis et degeneris animi argumentum reputaret. Omnia succedebant ad votum, universa ita famulabantur ad nutum, quod cum fortuna foedus de non solvendo foedere crederetur pepigisse.

141. Erat enim rex et sacerdos utroque accinctus gladio, utriusque fungens officio, quod et ex multitudine diversorum ordinum et professionum quae praeibant et quae

deceives us) was smiling on you, and the authority of the realm and the priesthood remained in your possession, you had many mighty flatterers. Your throng of servants was countless, but the number of those who truly loved you was very few, as the actual outcome proved. Wherever you used to visit, you were received as an angel; you were venerated in some way as a god, to such a degree that whoever could say or do anything pleasing to you in your sight claimed that he had achieved no small success. The goodwill of the clergy and the fealty of the people marched at your behest; the praiseworthy deeds of all and sundry were attributed to you. Not only did your kinsmen and neighbors flock to you, but people came even from the farthest reaches of the land to see and to hear the chancellor, or more precisely, to obtain something from him.

140. Some men generously offered poems, some songs and other things of this kind that did not cost much, to compensate for the insufficiency of their own sowings by the abundance of another's produce. To be sure, the chancellor made himself available to all petitioners, and with such great affability that often he would anticipate the wishes of those petitioning him. The generosity of the giver was so great that he would consider a delay in giving to be a refusal, and distinction between persons evidence of a poor and ignoble spirit. All things conformed to his wishes; everything so complied with his will that he was believed to have made a pact with fortune that would not be broken.

141. For he was a king and a priest, girt with each sword and discharging the duty of each. This was easy to observe because of the multitude of different orders and professions that would lead the way before him and would follow after

sequebantur facile fuit intueri. Condixerant enim in eum hinc iudiciaria potestas regni, inde quod non minimum est in regno officium cancellarii, hinc ordo et auctoritas episcopi, inde honor et excellentia legati Romani. Multiplicis ergo tituli gratia multiplex eum comitabatur caterva. Stipabant enim milites ducem praevium, notarii cancellarium, clerici episcopum, varias causas habentes legatum, unusquisque suum et non illius attendens commodum. Tanta igitur fuit divitiarum abundantia, dignitatum gloria, amicorum et obsequentium copia, quod non crederes vel hominem amplius posse affectare vel fortunam affectanti plus posse conferre. Unde si hominis et fortunae statum instabilem aequa lance pensares, non immerito diceres hunc desideriis suis ampliora consecutum, hanc vero circa eum votum non potuisse adimplere, sed defecisse citra desiderium. Tot enim emerserant subito in quibus gloriaretur animus et iocundaretur corpus, ut satietas fastidium gigneret, ut identitas nauseam provocaret. Quorum importunitati ut interdum consuleretur, accessit crebra locorum mutatio, ita ut interdum praeferetur tugurium palatio, labor otio, civitati solitudo.

142. Cum igitur omnia supremum summae felicitatis gradum crederentur adepta et in eo statu stare a quo nec deici et ultra quem non posset promoveri, subito *fortuna faciem contraxit* et radios eius caligo inopinata obumbravit. Ventus ab aquilone veniens vix modicum mare turbaverat, cum nec

him. For there came together in him on the one hand, the judicial power of the realm, and on the other, the office of chancellor, not the least in the realm; on the one hand, the rank and authority of a bishop, and on the other, the honor and eminence of a Roman legate. Therefore, a multifarious crowd used to attend him on account of his multiple titles. Knights crowded round him as their leader and commander, secretaries accompanied him as chancellor, clerics as bishop, those with various cases to bring as legate, each one striving after his own advantage, not his. He had so great an abundance of riches, so great glory in his offices, so great a number of friends and followers that you would not believe that a man could aspire to more power, or that fortune could confer more on human aspiration. Hence, if you were weighing impartially the unstable status of human fortune, you would not unjustly say that this man had obtained more than his desires, and that fortune could not fulfill a wish for him, but only fall short of his desire. In fact, so many blessings of fortune, in which the spirit took pride and the body delight, had emerged in such a short time, that satiety caused loathing, repetition produced nausea. Now and then, in order to mitigate the oppressiveness they produced, he had recourse to frequent changes of location, so that sometimes a hut was preferable to a palace, toil to leisure, solitude to a city.

142. Therefore, when everything was thought to have achieved the pinnacle of supreme happiness, and that he had reached that status from which he could not be cast down and beyond which he could not be promoted, suddenly *fortune frowned* and unexpected gloom obscured her beams. A wind from the north had barely stirred up the sea a

adhuc armamenta navis dissoluta deficerent, nec violentia tempestatis solis radium aut spem subduxisset redeundi ad portum, cum ecce fere omnes quotquot fuerunt amici prosperitatis *conversi sunt in arcum pravum,* vertentes ei dorsum et non faciem.

143. Defluentibus igitur amicis quasi sub prima hieme arborum foliis, et in locum suum recedentibus aquis apparuit arida et frons prius capillata repente decalvata, fueruntque nonnulli qui cum Petro iurarent se non nosse hominem, quos tamen loquela manifestos faciebat qui fuerant cum eo. Sed et ipsi de quorum consilio specialius pendere et quibus firmius et fidelius videbatur inniti, mox ad primos titubantis fortunae sibilos, longius ab eo recesserunt, persequentes tamen eum et percutientes plaga pessima vehementer; tantaque exorta est in brevi calamitas, quod respectu illius nihil esse diceres quicquid prosperitatis praecesserat. Omnes enim amici eius spreverunt eum inter angustias, nec fuit qui consolaretur eum ex omnibus caris eius. Sed et eo usque processerunt quae sibi condixerant malitia et iniquitas, ut et opera eius bona detestarentur, et nomen eius quasi pestiferum quid abominarentur, seminantes cotidie mendacia excogitata, ut cor populi ab eo averterent et in odium eius excitarent. Successisse sibi plurimum aestimabat qui suos, si tamen aliqui reperirentur, confundere aut ei amplius posset derogare.

little, when the ship's tackle was not yet broken and giving way, and the fury of the storm had not extinguished the sun's rays or the hope of returning to port, when, behold, almost all who were his friends in times of prosperity *were transformed into a crooked bow,* turning their backs to him and not their faces.

143. And so, while his friends were falling away like the leaves of trees at the beginning of winter, and like waters receding to their separate locations, his brow that had hair before, now suddenly appeared bald and dry. There were some who swore with Peter that they did not know the man, yet their style of speech made plain that they were men who had been with him. Even those on whose counsel he seemed especially to depend and on whom he seemed more firmly and faithfully to rely, immediately at the first whispers of faltering fortune withdrew farther from him, though still pursuing him and smiting him strongly with the most telling blows. In a short time, such great misfortune arose that with regard to him, you would have said that whatever prosperity had preceded amounted to nothing. Indeed, all his friends spurned him in the midst of his distress, nor was there one out of all his dear friends who comforted him. The malice and wickedness that had conspired against him progressed to such a point that they even denounced his good deeds; they detested his name as a noxious thing, while daily disseminating contrived falsehoods to turn the hearts of the people away from him and incite them to hatred of him. Anyone who could confound his friends, if any could be found, or who could disparage him still further, thought that he had achieved a very great success.

144. Unum autem erat prae ceteris quod animo altius insedit et animas eorum *felle amaritudinis* inebriatas toxicati rancoris gladio perforavit, scilicet quod homo de gente non sua super eos acceperat potestatem et principis sui gratiam consecutus erat aliis ampliorem. In tantum autem furor eorum exarserat et odium iniquum mentes eorum medullitus occupaverat, quod etiam manus cruentas misissent in christum Domini, nisi malitiae temporis et persequentium consulens praesentiam suam subtrahendo declinasset. Sed numquid formidarent in episcopum alienigenam manum mittere, qui archiepiscopum et indigenam suum in ecclesia sua non abhorruerunt interficere, et nomen suum sempiterno opprobrio maculare?

145. Quisquis igitur fortunae statum instabilem cognoscere desiderat, ex tui casus consideratione plenius poterit erudiri, illudque poeticum in te praecipue dixerit adimpletum:

Et cum fortuna statque caditque fides.

Cum enim recordatus fueris malorum quae pro servanda quam domino tuo debuisti fidelitate perpessus es, non immerito poteris illud Daviticum decantare: *Amici mei et proximi mei adversum me appropinquaverunt et steterunt, et qui iuxta me erant de longo steterunt, et vim faciebant qui quaerebant animam meam.* Sed et cum tot essent tribulationes et angustiae tuae quot nec quidem sufficeres ea enarrare possentque vulnera tua prae multitudine telis supervenientibus dicere, "*Non habet in nobis iam nova plaga locum,*" ecce calamitas

144. Furthermore, there was one thing above all that remained deeply rooted in their minds and that pierced with a sword of poisonous rancor their souls saturated by *the gall of bitterness,* namely, that a man not of their own nation had received power over them and had gained, more than other men, the favor of their prince. Their rage was kindled so much, and unjust hatred filled their minds so thoroughly, that they would have even laid bloody hands upon the Lord's anointed if, mindful of the wickedness of the times and of those persecuting him, he had not avoided it by withdrawing his presence. But would men who had not recoiled from murdering an archbishop, their own countryman, in his own church, and defiling their own name with everlasting shame, have feared to lay hands on a foreign-born bishop?

145. Whoever wishes to understand the unstable state of fortune could be fully instructed by contemplation of your fall, and could say that in you that line of poetry had been particularly fulfilled:

Loyalty stands or falls with fortune.

For when you call to mind the evils that you have suffered for keeping the faith which you owed to your lord, you can justly sing aloud that saying of David: *My friends and my neighbors have drawn near and stood against me, and those who were near me stood far off, and those who sought my life used violence.* Although your tribulations and your hardships were so many that you could not even recount them all, and although your wounds, because of their numbers, could say, when new weapons were hurled against you, "*Now a new blow has no room among us,*" behold, a calamity quite omnibus aliis longe incomparabilis supervenit, rumor scilicet flebilis et in perpetuum omni Anglorum genti deflendus de captione regis Ricardi. Quem sicut natura in rebus bellicis strenue gerendis universo orbi admirandum edidit, ita fortuna deflendum exposuit, palam faciens universis quod tam apud divites quam pauperes in sola instabilitate sua sit stabilis. Cum enim universa crederetur enavigasse pericula et clementioris aurae facies iocundior arridens polliceri videretur circumquaque serenum, inopinatae tempestatis procelloso turbine suborto passus est, non in mari sed in terra, naufragium.

146. Accessit igitur dolorum tuorum ad cumulum lamentabile regis infortunium, et quasi non haberes unde gemeres de angustiis propriis, coactus es communicare tribulationibus alienis, in tantum ut novissimus dolor peior esset priore, possesque illud propheticum veraciter dicere: *Exspectavimus pacem, et non est bonum; tempus curationis, et ecce turbatio. Maestum factum in dolore cor nostrum, quia cecidit corona capitis nostri.* Crescentibus igitur quae postremo venerunt tribulationibus et angustiis quae etiam *super dolorem vulnerum tuorum non minimum addiderunt,* coactus es novis supervenientibus vetera proicere aut penitus aut necessario dissimulare.

147. Fluctuantibus igitur fortunae et labentis saeculi tempestatibus agitatus et ex rerum vicissitudine varia plurima tam ex propria quam ex aliena conditione expertus, utinam ipsa experientia eruditus, illud evangelicum diligentius

unequaled by all others has befallen us, namely, the doleful report, a cause of perpetual woe for the entire race of Englishmen, concerning the capture of King Richard. Just as nature brought him forth as a source of admiration for the whole world in his vigorous prosecution of wars, so fortune has set him forth as a cause of lamentation, making plain to all that among the rich just as among the poor, its stability lies only in its instability. For when he was believed to have sailed clear of all dangers, and the delightful prospect of a more gentle breeze smiled upon him, seeming to promise fair weather all around, he suffered shipwreck after the tempestuous gales of an unforeseen storm arose, not at sea, but on land.

146. And so, the king's misfortune added to the lamentable heap of your sorrows, and as though you did not have anything to bemoan from your own distress, you were forced to share the troubles of others to such an extent that the latest sorrow was worse than the first, and you could truly affirm that saying of the prophet: *We have looked for peace and there is nothing good; for a time of healing, and behold, trouble. Our heart is made mournful in sorrow because the crown has fallen from our head.* Therefore, with the increase of these latest troubles and hardships, which *added not a little to the sorrow of your wounds,* you were forced either to lay aside completely the old ones for the new that had come upon you, or necessarily to dissemble them.

147. So, impelled by the fluctuating storms of fortune and of this failing world, and much tested by the shifting vicissitudes of circumstance in your own person and others', would that, instructed by experience itself, you would diligently listen to and give heed to this passage in the gospel:

audias et attendas: *Martha, Martha, sollicita es et turbaris erga plurima; porro unum est necessarium.* Numquid non multa sunt necessaria, et maxime divitibus? Non enim circa tot et tanta sollicitarentur, nisi plurima essent necessaria. Qui enim in non necessariis sciens et prudens occupatur, cum non dubitet unum esse necessarium, aut stolidus est aut nimis obstinatus. Verumtamen ego credo quia unum necessarium est episcopo. Et quod est illud? Ita adimplere ministerium sibi creditum, ut in die illa magna, quando de villicatione sua redditurus est rationem, mereatur audire: *Euge, bone serve et fidelis, quia in pauca fuisti fidelis, super multa te constituam; intra in gaudium Domini tui.* Sed numquid ad officium spectat episcopi saecularia exercere negotia, occupationibus se ingerere saeculi, et his indesinenter delectari? Plebem Christi suscepit erudiendam, non praedia fisci custodienda. Nonne episcopi hodie, circumquaque relicto proprio officio, militum et rusticorum officium sibi usurpaverunt? Et ne ab eo destituantur, vel casu quolibet defraudentur, indulgentiam a summo pontifice et confirmationes quaerunt a rege. Quid igitur fiet in ecclesia Dei, si versa vice laici officium sibi usurpaverint episcopi et privilegiis se petierint communiri? Ex quo enim suum sibi violenter, ne dicam impudenter, praereptum vident officium, quid mirum si et ipsi diripiant et exerceant alienum?

148. Contigit temporibus felicis recordationis Theobaldi, Cantuariensis archiepiscopi, quod laicus quidam, curialis

Martha, Martha, you are concerned and troubled about many things; but one thing only is necessary. Is it really the case that not many things are necessary, especially for the rich? For they would not be concerned about so many and such great things if many things were not necessary. For the knowing and wise man who is occupied with unnecessary things, although he has no doubt that only one thing is necessary, is either stupid or exceedingly stubborn. Yet I do believe that one thing is necessary for a bishop. And what is that? To carry out the ministry entrusted to him in such a way that on that great day, when he will have to render an account of his stewardship, he deservedly hears: *Well done, good and faithful servant; because you have been faithful in a few things, I shall place you over many; enter into the joy of your Lord.* But does it really belong to the office of a bishop to administer worldly business, to apply himself to the affairs of the world, and to take unfailing delight in them? He has received Christ's people to be instructed, not the treasury's estates for his supervision. Have bishops today not assumed for themselves the role of peasants and knights, abandoning their own role in every respect? And, lest they be deprived of that role or cheated of it by any misfortune, they seek an indulgence from the supreme pontiff and ratification from the king. But then what will happen in God's Church if, conversely, laymen assume for themselves the office of bishop and they seek to be legitimated by charters? For when they see their own office taken away from them violently, not to say brazenly, what wonder if they too snatch away and occupy another's?

148. It happened in the time of Theobald, the archbishop of Canterbury of blessed memory, that a certain layman (but

tamen, et presbyter quidam ecclesiam cuiusdam clerici acciperent ad firmam. Cumque fructus obvenientes aequa lance partirentur, voluit laicus sacerdoti ad altare astare ut oblationes ad manum sacerdotis venientes pariter reciperet, quia de fidelitate ipsius minus confidebat. Sacerdos vero prohibebat eum, dicens hoc non licere, maxime cum ordinem nullum haberet, repulitque eum hac ratione multo tempore. Quod ille graviter ferens, et eo praecipue quia videbat cotidie quod parochiani rite et recte offerebant, sed sacerdos non recte dividebat oblata, cogitavit quid faceret quo eum sacerdos huius tituli obiectione a cornu altaris non repelleret, sed in oblationibus suscipiendis sicut et in aliis consortem admitteret.

149. Contigit autem praefatum Cantuariensem archiepiscopum saepius in anno ibidem hospitari, et quia locus ille ab urbium vicinia et commerciorum frequentia erat sepositus, quaelibet modica, dummodo necessitati temporis congruerent, ampliorem gratiam et favorem poterant promereri, quod ille considerans, archiepiscopo xenia crebro mittebat et clericis suis quotiens pertransiret, vel hospitandi gratia ad locum diverteret. Cum igitur notitiam domini Cantuariensis et suorum plenius esset adeptus, utpote qui omnibus ita officiosus tam crebro exstiterat quod omnes ei accepti beneficii ratione tenerentur, accessit ad clericos archiepiscopi, rogans et petens ut litteras domini sui pro eo ad

yet a courtier) and a certain priest both received the church of a certain cleric for its farm rent. When the profits falling to them were being divided equally, the layman wanted to stand near the priest at the altar to accept together with him the payments coming into the hand of the priest, because he did not have confidence in his trustworthiness. But the priest prevented him, saying that this was not permitted, especially since he held no holy order, and for this reason the priest rebuffed him for a long time. Chafing at this refusal, all the more since he saw every day that the parishioners were duly and rightly making offerings to the priest, but he was not dividing the offerings rightly, he considered what he should do so that the priest would not keep him from the horn of the altar by reason of this pretext, but would accept him as a partner in receiving offerings just as in other things.

149. It happened that the aforementioned archbishop of Canterbury often lodged as a guest in that place during the course of a year, and since that place was far removed from the vicinity of cities and the hustle and bustle of commerce, any little services, provided that they were suitable to the needs of the occasion, were able to earn greater gratitude and goodwill. Considering this carefully, that layman frequently used to send little presents to the archbishop and his clerics whenever he passed through there or turned aside to the place to take lodging. Thus, when he had fully gained the acquaintance of the lord of Canterbury and his men, since he had so frequently been so obliging to them all that they all were bound to him by reason of the favors they had received, he approached the archbishop's clerics, asking and entreating them to obtain a letter from their lord to his own

episcopum vicinum impetrarent. Quod audiens archiepiscopus, et gavisus se temporis opportunitatem accepisse quo posset acceptis beneficiis in aliquo respondere, libenter annuit scripsitque episcopo ut illum in petitione sua audiret, sicut se vellet ab ipso audiri, non exprimens tamen negotii qualitatem. Veniente igitur tempore quo clerici solent ad sacros ordines promoveri, accessit rusticus ille ad episcopum cum litteris archiepiscopi sui, petens ut eum presbyterum ordinaret. Episcopus vero videns personam corpore elegantem, aestimavit in aliis idoneam, uti eam quam commendabat tanti patris auctoritas, cuius petitio praeceptum quodammodo videbatur.

150. Cui ne maior videretur fieri iniuria si vel sustineret repulsam, vel ille quem misit de moribus aut scientia examinaretur in aliquo, iudicavit fieri petitionem eius, ordinavitque rusticum laicum ad presbyterii gradum. Ordinatus autem domum e vestigio reversus est, impatiensque desiderii sui statim ad excipiendas oblationes altari audacter se ingessit. Quem cum sacerdos durius increparet minareturque sententiam anathematis in eum promulgare nisi se ab huiusmodi praesumptione cohiberet, ille, sublato pileo et ostensa corona, obviavit ei dicens: "Sustine, Frater, sustine, ego presbyter sum sicut et tu; non poteris me de cetero amovere; diu est quod me defraudasti portione mea, amodo vero a pari partiemur." Quid multa? Res taliter gesta non potuit silentio sepeliri; rumor facti prodiit in publicum, tanto magis

local bishop on his behalf. The archbishop, hearing this, and rejoicing that he had gotten an opportunity to be able to reciprocate in some way for the favors he had received, willingly assented and wrote to the bishop to hear that man's request, as if he wanted himself to be heard by him, yet not passing judgment on the rights and wrongs of the case. And so, when the time came at which clerics are customarily promoted to holy orders, that villein approached the bishop with His archbishop's letter and asked that he ordain him a priest. Now the bishop, observing that the person was refined in body, judged him suitable in other ways too, for the authority of so great a father was recommending him, whose request seemed in some measure to be a command.

150. In order not to commit a great insult against Theobald if he either should be refused or if that man whom he sent should be examined in any degree about his character or his learning, the bishop decided that his request should be granted, and he ordained that coarse layman in the rank of priesthood. Once ordained, he returned home forthwith, and, impatient of gaining his wish, he immediately proceeded boldly to the altar to accept offerings. When the priest rebuked him harshly and threatened to promulgate a sentence of excommunication against him unless he restrained himself from presumption of this kind, he stood before the priest, removing his cap and revealing his tonsure, and said to him: "Hold on, Brother, hold on. I am a priest just as you are. You cannot remove me anymore. For a long time you have cheated me of my portion, but from now on we shall share equally." What more shall I say? Such a story could not be buried in silence. Rumor of the deed became public, regarded on every side with the greater

mirationi circumquaque habitus quanto prius inauditus, hominem scilicet laicum et uxoratum promotum ad sacerdotii gradum. Vocatus est igitur episcopus et accusatus qui eum ordinaverat, at ipse culpam in archiepiscopum refundebat. Suspensus est ergo rusticus a toro et presbyter ab officio altaris, quo etiam si uti liceret litterarum ignorantia penitus prohiberet.

151. Non igitur mirandum est si consimilia nostris temporibus contigerit attemptari, cum clericos cotidie videamus laicorum officium usurpare, propriumque ita habere neglectui quod vix velint se clericos profiteri. Sed et quod absurdius est, multi fatentur se esse quod non sunt, ut solo nominis titulo bona ecclesiastica possideant, cum penitus rudes sint et litterarum ignari. Si enim codicem eis ad legendum aperueris, quasi theatralibus ludis subito capti obstupescunt, nihil scientes nisi quod huiusmodi sunt instrumenta clericorum, sicut novit faber retia instrumenta esse piscatorum et piscator malleum et incudem instrumenta fabrorum, cum alter in arte alterius nihil sibi possit proprium vendicare, nisi quod scit instrumentorum nomina exprimere, cum usum aut artem eorum non habeat et tamen utilia inde provenientia plurimum concupiscat.

152. Sic igitur sunt hodie in ecclesia clerici sine scientia litterarum, sicut plerique milites sine usu et exercitio armorum, qui etiam nomen habentes ex re vocantur ab aliis Milites sanctae Mariae. Cum enim alii pergunt ad expugnanda castra, illi delitescunt pro bono pacis in ecclesia. Ita et

astonishment as it was unheard of before, namely, that a layman, a married man, had been promoted to the rank of priesthood. And so, the bishop who had ordained him was summoned and called to account, but he cast the blame back on the archbishop. Therefore, the villein was suspended from his marriage and the priest from the service of the altar, for, even if he were allowed to perform it, his illiteracy would utterly prevent him from doing so.

151. It is no surprise, then, if similar things happen to be attempted in our times, when daily we see clerics usurp the role of laymen and so neglect their own that they are hardly willing to declare themselves clerics. But what is even more absurd, many profess to be what they are not, in order to take possession of the goods of the Church on the sole pretext of that name, although they are utterly untaught and ignorant of reading and writing. For if you should open a book before them to read, they become stupefied, as if suddenly caught in a stage play. They know nothing except that things of this kind are the tools of clerics, just as a smith knows that nets are tools of fishermen and a fisherman knows that a hammer and anvil are tools of smiths, although each can claim for himself nothing of the skill of the other as his own. Each knows only how to name the tools, since he does not have experience or skill with them, and yet he very much covets the benefits that come from them.

152. So, there are in the Church today clerics without a knowledge of reading and writing, just as very many knights are without the experience and exercise of arms. These even have a name and are in fact called by others Knights of Saint Mary. Indeed, when others go off to capture castles, these men skulk behind in church in the interests of peace. And in

clerici nostri temporis, cum quidam Parisium et Bononiam, et loca cetera, diutius inhabitent, ut litterarum studiis familiarius et fructuosius invigilent, quorum vota plurimum commendanda sunt; alii litterarum studiis animum applicare contemnunt, sed occupationes alias quaerunt manusque mundas ob modicam stipem in profundum luti defigunt; adeoque inviluit hodie dignitas officii clericalis, tum prae ignavia tum prae multitudinis abundantia, quod facilius invenires bene eruditum in arte sua bubulcum quam presbyterum, citius opilionem industrium quam clericum litteratum.

153. Sed cuius crediderimus hoc esse delictum, vel cui specialiter imputandum? Nonne ei qui huiusmodi corrigere debuit et potuit sed forsitan dissimulavit? Pace tua, Willelme, et fratrum tuorum, quae dicenda sunt dixerim. Si in vinea *Domini Sabaoth* custos et cultor bonus, falce putationis focarias presbyterorum penitus amputasses, nequaquam tot *spuria vitulamina* in parochia tua pullularent. Si ad sacros ordines non nisi dignos et officio idoneos usque quaque promoveres, nequaquam tot fatuos et tamquam animalia bruta per campos errantia in diocesi tua reperires. Si viris bene litteratis et morigeratis, et non aliis, conferres ecclesias et ecclesiastica beneficia, non tanta illitteratorum scaturirent examina. Sed quia permittis germina mala radices facere, quae statim, ne germinarent, deberes eradicare, et promoves ad gradus altiores quos potius deberes degradare, et

our time, while certain clerics dwell for a long time in Paris, Bologna, and other places, in order to devote themselves intimately and beneficially to their scholarly studies (ambitions that are much to be commended), other clerics scorn applying their minds to scholarly studies and seek other occupations, and for the sake of a small donation they thrust their clean hands into deep mud. Today the dignity of the clerical office has become so cheapened, both because of laziness and because of the overflowing numbers, that you may more easily find a plowman well educated in his craft than a priest in his, more swiftly find a diligent shepherd than a learned cleric.

153. But whose fault do we believe this to be, or to whom specifically should it be imputed? Should it not be to him who should have and could have corrected abuses of this kind, but perhaps neglected them? With all due respect to you, William, and your brothers: let me say what must be said. If, as a good overseer and cultivator in the vineyard *of the Lord of Hosts,* you had completely lopped off the concubines of priests with a pruning hook, in no way would so many *bastard shoots* be sprouting forth in your parishes. If you promoted to holy orders everywhere none but worthy men and ones suitable for the office, in no way would you find in your diocese so many fools and dumb animals, as it were, roaming the fields. If you conferred churches and ecclesiastical benefices on well-educated men and virtuous ones, and on no others, so great a crowd of illiterate men would not be swarming forth. Since you allow bad seeds to take root, which you ought to have uprooted immediately so they do not germinate, you promote to higher offices those whom you ought rather to have demoted, and you

confers idiotis ecclesias quas eis auferre debueras, ut et personis et usibus melioribus eas delegares. Ideo surculi abortivi vineam et zizania segetem tuam suffocaverunt. Ordines sacri sine ordine sunt et honore, personae vero et clerici quasi pecora campi.

154. Quorum omnium ipse auctor est a capite qui, cum posset et ex officio teneretur huiusmodi corrigere, usus est dissimulatione. Ex cultoris enim negligentia, spinae et tribuli succrescunt in area. Quam quia ut oporteret et ipse scires et posses non excolis, merito spinas et tribulos germinabit tibi quae, cum volueris, non valebis evellere, quia iam proceram et condensam excreverunt in silvam, quae in primo germine brevi potuerunt conamine exstirpari. Vide ne dissimulatio correctionis audaciam delinquendi praestiterit subiectis et mansuetudo tua non solum tibi sed plebi tuae sit periculo, ne cum iam demum inceperis non posse, tunc primo incipias velle.

155. *Quia igitur iam hora est nos de somno surgere,* exsurge et *accingere gladio tuo super femur tuum, potentissime,* et considera quid deceat episcopum, et non tantum quid deceat sed quid expediat vicario Christi. Vide quam longe est ab officio et professione episcopi *circuire terram et obambulare eam,* et sine intermissione implicari negotiis saeculi. Ut quid occupas episcopatum cum episcopi non exerceas officium? Quando enim praedicas, quando baptizas, quando paenitentes reconcilias, quando haec vel illa quae episcopi sunt administras? Si praedia lata et possessiones magnas habere et eorum fructus cum iocunditate percipere, et gemmata manu

confer on half-wits churches that you ought to have taken from them to assign them to better persons and better uses. In this way barren suckers have choked the vine, and cockle has choked your crop. Holy orders are without order and honor, but priests and clerics are like herds in the field.

154. The source of all these abuses comes from the head, who practiced neglect when he was able and duty bound to correct things of this kind. Because of the cultivator's negligence, thorns and thistles spring up in the garden plot. Since you do not cultivate it as you should, and as you have the know-how and ability to do, it will naturally produce for you thorns and thistles, which you will not be able to pull out when you wish, because they have now grown into a tall, dense forest that could have been rooted out with little effort in its first sprouting. Take care that your negligence in correction does not produce in your subjects a boldness in wrongdoing, and that your clemency does not become a danger not only for you but for your people, lest you first begin to want to correct them when finally you no longer have that power.

155. *Since now is the hour for us to rise from sleep,* get up and *gird your sword on your thigh, oh most mighty.* Consider what befits a bishop, and not only what befits, but what is expedient for a vicar of Christ. See how far it departs from the office and profession of a bishop *to go about the land and roam through it,* and to be involved in affairs of the world without ceasing. Why do you hold a bishopric when you do not perform the duty of a bishop? For when do you preach, when do you baptize, when do you reconcile penitents, when do you perform this or that duty that belongs to a bishop? If to have vast manors and great estates, and to gather their fruits with

extendere benedictionem in latum et longum, est esse episcopum, quare hoc non exhibet laicus sicut et clericus? Negotia enim publica, et maxime fiscum contingentia, regni consuetudines, scaccarii computationes et alia huiusmodi, non multa egent litteratura, nec profunda Veteris aut Novi Testamenti scientia. Sed in confessionibus peccatorum recipiendis, in paenitentiis iniungendis, in verbo praedicationis, in exemplo aedificationis, in resistendo pro ecclesia Dei principibus, in misericordiae et aliarum virtutum operibus, necessaria est huiusmodi doctrina, et ut ait beatus Benedictus in *Regula* sua, cum de praelatis loqueretur: "*Oportet,*" inquit, "praelatum *doctum esse lege divina, ut* habeat *et sit unde proferat nova et vetera.*" Qualiter enim docebit quis quae non didicit?

156. Sed et ipse aliquando dicere consueveras, cum multa sint in clero de quibus erubescit ecclesia, illud inter alia ignominiosius est: quod sic ducitur episcopus ad librum sicut bos ad aquandum. Forsitan autem gloriaris apud te quia titulus iste tibi non potest opponi, aliosque in corde tuo despicis quos tibi in huius gratiae titulo comparari non posse cognoscis. Et quia *scientia inflat,* timendum est ne inde corruas per superbiam unde ascendere debuisti per gratiam non a te sed a Deo tibi collatam. Quid enim habes quod non accepisti? Cave igitur ne gradum acceperis in ruinam, qui datam tibi desuper doctrinae et scientiae gratiam populo tuo non communicas, sed abscondis ab eis pro quorum ignorantia redditurus es Domino in die iudicii rationem.

delight, and to extend a blessing far and wide with a jeweled hand is to be a bishop, why does a layman not do this just like a cleric? Indeed, public affairs, and especially those relating to the treasury, customary practices of the realm, exchequer accounts and other matters of this kind do not need much literacy nor a profound knowledge of the Old and New Testament. However, in hearing sinners' confessions, in imposing penances, in preaching, in providing edifying examples, in resisting princes for the Church of God, in works of mercy and of other virtues, learning of this kind is necessary. Just as Saint Benedict says in his *Rule* when he speaks about prelates: "*It is necessary,*" he says, "*for* a *prelate to be learned in divine law, so that he might* have *and be himself a source from which to bring forth things new and old.*" For how will anyone teach what he has not learned?

156. But also, you yourself were accustomed at times to say, since there are many things among the clergy for which the Church blushes with shame, that among others, this is the most disgraceful: that a bishop is led to a book just as an ox is to water. Perhaps, however, you take pride because this claim cannot be alleged against you, and in your heart you look down on those whom you know cannot be compared to you in claiming this gift of grace. And since *knowledge puffs us up,* you should fear, lest for this reason you fall through pride from where you should properly have ascended by a grace conferred on you not by yourself, but by God. For what do you have that you have not received? Therefore, beware that you have not received your rank to your ruin, you who do not impart to your people the grace of learning and knowledge granted to you from above, but conceal it from them, for whose ignorance you will render an account to the Lord on the day of judgment.

157. Numquid excusabit te sicut quosdam fratrum tuorum litterarum et legis divinae ignorantia aut provectioris aetatis impotentia, infirmitas corporis aut inopia rei familiaris? Haec omnia tibi sed contra te perhibent testimonium: legis scientia, aetas florida, corporis sanitas, rerum temporalium copiosa facultas. Quid ergo causae praetendere poteris ad excusandas excusationes in peccatis? Forsitan dices, "Quasi exul agor, nec licet mihi exercere officium meum, quoniam si liceret, libenter illud exercerem." Quod est illud officium tuum? Officium regale an officium sacerdotale? Forsitan vices regias exsequi non permitteris more solito, sed numquid ideo suspensus es ab episcopali officio? Si subtrahitur potestas regalis, numquid et auctoritas pontificalis? Si non licet de hiis quae ad fiscum pertinent disponere, numquid os tuum alligatum est ut non possis plebi tuae verbum Dei praedicare? Esto quod utrumque liceat tibi sicut licuit exercere, poterisne utrique sufficere? Cum alteri istorum necesse sit totum hominem impendere, quis est qui utrumque gladium sine alterutrius damno possit sufficienter portare? Si utrumque desideras, cum solus utrique non sufficias, aut erras in desideriis tuis, aut ex desiderio de viribus ultra vires praesumis.

158. Ex ipsa Salvatoris sententia accepimus quod *nemo potest duobus dominis servire.* Si vero uni difficile est ad votum ministrare, quanto difficilius duobus, et maxime cum crebro inter se dissideant et raro conveniant? Regnum et sacerdotium sic invicem confoederantur, ut saepenumero variis

157. Will ignorance of letters and of divine law excuse you, or the frailty of advanced age, the weakness of body or the want of personal possessions, like certain of your brothers? All these things bear witness in your case, but against you: knowledge of the law, the prime of life, health of body, a plentiful supply of temporal goods. Therefore, what reason will you be able to bring forward for pleading excuses for your sins? Perhaps you will say, "I am driven off as an exile, and I am not allowed to carry out my office, for if it were allowed, I would carry it out willingly." What is this office of yours? A regal office or a priestly office? Perhaps you are not permitted to carry out regal duties in the customary manner, but are you therefore suspended from your episcopal office? If regal power is withdrawn, is your pontifical authority also withdrawn? If you are not allowed to administer matters which pertain to the treasury, is your tongue constrained so that you cannot preach the word of God to your people? But suppose that you were allowed to exercise each office as you once were, could you satisfy both? Since it is necessary to devote the whole man to one of these offices, who is there who can adequately carry both swords without detriment to one or the other? If you desire both, when alone you might not satisfy both, either you err in your desires, or on account of your desire you trust your strengths beyond their strength.

158. From our Savior's own words we have learned that *no one can serve two masters.* If indeed it is difficult to serve one as we would wish, how much more difficult to serve two, and especially since they often are at odds with each other and rarely are in harmony? Kingship and priesthood are mutually united in such a way that often, for various reasons,

occasionibus inter se collidantur. Aliud enim semper vult dominari, aliud vero numquam subici. Aliud enim praedicat iudicium, aliud misericordiam, utrumque vult praeesse et neutrum subesse. Unde et graves inter ea oriuntur nonnumquam quaestiones quas raro contingit cum pace utriusque partis absolvi. Quod quam rarum sit ipsa rerum experientia potest edoceri.

159. Ex quaestione enim et conflictu consuetudinum regni et sacerdotii causa illa traxit originem, pro qua decertans pretiosus ille Cantuariensis archiepiscopus Thomas in ecclesia sua glorioso meruit coronari martyrio. Sed et ille aliquando regis fuerat cancellarius tantaeque potestatis ut post regem ipsum videretur totius regni dominus. Verumtamen, ex quo ordinatus est in episcopum, ulterius non est reversus ad cancellariae officium, sed nec etiam voluit ecclesiam quae eum vocaverat ingredi, aut consentire electioni, nisi omnino liber et absolutus ab omni potestate et exactione fisci, sciens quod utraque officia pariter non posset sine ordinis sui periculo expedire. Unde altero non transitorie neque ad tempus relicto, sed in perpetuum relegato, altero fideliter adhaesit et in eo usque in finem perseveravit; nec tamen id fecit coactus, sed spontaneus, cum adhuc eo tempore a regis gratia non excidisset, sed in ulteriorem ipsius amicitiam receptus, posset, si vellet, non solum cancellariam retinere, sed etiam quidquid a rege peteret impetrare.

160. Hunc utinam non quasi *per speculum et in aenigmate* intuearis, sed ita facie ad faciem ut opera eius imiteris,

they clash with one another. One always wants to rule, but the other never wants to submit. One pronounces judgment, the other proclaims mercy. Each wishes to preside, and neither wants to be subordinate. Hence, often serious disputes also arise between them; it rarely happens that these are resolved amicably on both sides. How rare this is can be taught from practical experience.

159. For from a dispute and conflict over the customs of the kingdom and the priesthood, that affair took its origin, for which the archbishop of Canterbury, that precious Thomas, fought and was found worthy to be crowned with a glorious martyrdom in his own church. He was also at one time the king's chancellor, and a man of such great authority that after the king himself he seemed to be lord of the whole kingdom. Nevertheless, from the time he was ordained bishop, he did not return any longer to the office of chancellor. He was even unwilling to enter the church that had summoned him, or to agree to his election, unless he were altogether free and released from all authority and from the raising of taxes, knowing that he could not carry out both offices equally without peril to his order. Therefore, with one office not abandoned provisionally or temporarily, but set aside forever, he clung faithfully to the other and persevered in it right to the end. He did not do this as one constrained, but of his own free will, since at that time he still had not fallen from the king's favor, but, admitted to his even greater friendship, he could have, if he wished, not only kept the chancellorship, but even obtained from the king whatever he asked.

160. Would that you might not look upon this man as *through a glass darkly,* but face to face, in such a way that you

attendens et diligenti memoriae commendans, quam devote dignitatem ordinis et officii episcopalis suscepit, susceptum quam strenue administravit et postremo quam gloriose ministerium suum consummavit. Ex his enim quae ei acciderunt in multis poteris erudiri, si tamen ea dignum duxeris intueri. Et ne de temporali ac transitoria alicuius gratia confidens praesumas et *ponas carnem brachium tuum,* ipse solus tibi satis sufficere debet ad exemplum. Non enim erat in toto regno Angliae qui in oculis regis ampliorem gratiam invenisset. Ad nutum eius gerebantur universa; ab ore illius pendebat consilium et facies regia; indignus erat auditu quem ipse aure non dignaretur; nullatenus potuit expediri quod aliquatenus vellet aut velle crederetur impedire; primus erat mane ad regem ingredientium et ultimus ab eo in vespera discedentium. Infectum, immo penitus frivolum erat quidquid eo inconsulto inciperet, vel cui ipse incepto statim non subscriberet. Ex omnibus verbis eius nihil cadebat in terram, et quod sero praecipiebat fieri dies crastina non facile vidit procrastinari. In expeditione militari, sicut manifestius apud Tolosam claruit, quam strenuus exstiterit et regis sui vices absentis quam magnifice suppleverit, pars adversa ex iactura et confusione propria laudes alienas tacere non potuit.

161. Quicquid ageret, non erat in aula regia qui ei vel in minimo obmurmuraret, sed, quod proprie est aulicorum,

might imitate his works, while considering and commending to your careful recollection how devoutly he accepted the dignity of his order and of the episcopal office, how vigorously he administered it once he had accepted it, and finally how gloriously he consummated his ministry. Indeed, you can be taught many lessons from the things that happened to him, if only you would consider them worthy of your regard. And so that you not be presumptuous, trusting in a person's temporal and transitory favor, and thus *make flesh your arm,* he alone ought to suffice as an example for you. For there was not a man in the entire kingdom of England who had found greater favor in the eyes of the king. All things were carried out at his command. The royal council and regal countenance used to hang on his words. Anyone whom he did not deem worthy of his ear was unworthy of a hearing. No measure at all could be taken which in some degree he wanted to block, or was believed to want to block. He was first to enter the king's presence in the morning and the last to part from him in the evening. Whatever was undertaken without consulting him, or which he did not immediately support once it was undertaken, never came to completion, or rather was entirely worthless. Of all his words, none fell to earth, and what he ordered to happen at a late hour, the following day did not see easily delayed. The praises of others for how vigorous he was in military service, as became palpably clear at Toulouse, and how gloriously he took the place of his absent king, the enemy itself could not pass over in silence because of their own losses and confusion.

161. Whatever he did, there was no one in the royal court who would murmur against him, even in the least. Rather, as

adulabantur ei in omnibus, summopere formidantes eum offendere quem rex ipse satagebat offensum placare et tristem blanditiis delinire. Ioseph in Aegypto apud Pharaonem minus posse crederes, nec tantum gratiae in oculis eius invenisse, quantum cancellarius in conspectu regis Angliae. Tantus enim erat mutuae dilectionis affectus alterius ad alterum, quod nullatenus crederes hunc aliqua ratione admittere incrementum, vel eum occasione aliqua posse dissolvi in perpetuum. Interim autem rebus inopinato casu commutatis, subito facti sunt ita ut ad invicem inimici, quod de pacis reconciliatione inter eos desperarent universi. Rex enim persequebatur eum odio adeo inexorabili, quod nec etiam ipso in exilium acto proscriptisque omnibus qui eum quocumque titulo contingebant aliquatenus potuit mitigari, sed in tantum furor regius exarserat, quod eum nominari in praesentia sua sustinere non poterat, sed nomen eius quasi mortiferum quid abhorrebat. Si quis vero adeo temerarius exsisteret, quod eum praesumeret vel archiepiscopum dicere vel proprio nomine exprimere, constabat quod regiam incurrisset offensam, itaque quod vix aut numquam ulterius cum eo rediret in gratiam.

162. Verbum autem istud non erat absconditum, sed *pervenit usque ad fines orbis terrarum.* Quotiens enim a summo pontifice cardinales ecclesiae Romanae ad pacis reformationem destinati fuerint, quot archiespiscopi et episcopi et alii magnae opinionis viri quaquaversum convenerint, quam sollicitudinem rex ipse et proceres Francorum impenderint difficile esset evolvere. Crevit autem ira regia de die in diem

is natural for courtiers, they used to fawn on him in every way, fearing exceedingly to offend a man whom the king himself took great care to assuage when he was displeased, and to soothe with flattery when he was out of temper. You would believe that Joseph had less power with Pharaoh in Egypt, nor had he found as much favor in his eyes, as the chancellor found in the sight of the king of England. So great was the affection of mutual love each had for the other that you would refuse to believe it would admit increase for any reason, or that it could ever be dissolved for any cause. But then circumstances changed through an unexpected turn of events, and suddenly they became such enemies that everyone despaired of a restoration of peace between them. Indeed, the king pursued him with such inexorable hatred that he could not be appeased at all, even after the archbishop had been driven into exile and all had been proscribed who were connected to him by any tie whatsoever. The king's rage was so inflamed that he could not bear to have him named in his presence but loathed his name as something deadly. Indeed, if anyone were to be so indiscreet that he ventured to speak of him as archbishop, or to utter his name, it is an established fact that in so doing he would have incurred the hostility of the king, and that he could only with difficulty, or never, return again to favor with him.

162. Moreover, this news was not hidden, but *reached to the ends of the world.* It would be difficult to enumerate how often cardinals of the Roman Church were sent by the supreme pontiff to restore peace, how many archbishops and bishops and other men of great esteem came together from all sides, and what care the French king himself and the leading men of France expended. However, the king's wrath

et, cum graviora quaeque peccata septenni soleant remitti paenitentia, indignatio eius non est ex tractu temporis remissa, sed magis accensa, sed nec aliquando quievit donec causae finem imposuit sors ultima quae archiepiscopum triumphali morte de medio tulit.

163. De praeteritis igitur trahere argumenta futuri, ex exemplo alterius plenius erudiri, ne ultra quam expedit de gratia praesumas humana. Non enim melior es patribus tuis, nec impossibile est quae eis contigerunt tibi posse contingere. Miror autem nisi aliquando ad teipsum reversus consideres quam vanum sit gratiam hominis mortalis tanto opere quaerere, quae quolibet modo adquisita, quantumcumque diu habita, non tamen est stabilis sed transitoria. Contingit autem nonnumquam quod multi, adepta quam praeoptabant gratia facilius ab ea excidant, et ipsi maxime qui magis de ipsa debebant praesumere et eam credebantur propensiori obsequio promeruisse. Obsequia enim interdum possunt gratiam non habitam adipisci, sed adepta ne defluat non possunt elargiri. Divina enim gratia sola est quae manet mutabilitatis ignara. Omnes vero aliae tales sunt, quicquid de eis praedicetur, quales subiecta promittunt.

164. Non facile crediderim quod maiorem aliquando inveneris gratiam apud regem Ricardum quam invenit beatus Thomas apud regem Henricum, nec tamen multo tempore gavisus est ea. Non dico quod regis gratiam parvipendas, vel eam dum salva conscientia retineri potest gratis deperdas,

increased from day to day. Although all the most grievous sins are customarily forgiven by a penance of seven years, his anger was not relaxed by the lapse of time, but more inflamed, nor did it ever subside until the fatal end, which took the archbishop from our midst by his triumphal death, put an end to its cause.

163. Therefore, you should derive lessons for the future from past events and be fully instructed by another's example, so that you do not count on human favor more than is expedient. You are not better than your fathers, nor is it impossible that what happened to them can happen to you. Moreover, I wonder if ever, when communing with yourself, you do not consider how vain it is to seek to such a degree a mortal man's favor, which, however it is gained and for however long it is kept, yet is not enduring, but transitory. Furthermore, it often happens that many men, after gaining the favor they wished, readily fall from grace, and especially those who should have the firmest claim on it and were believed to have earned it through unusually devoted service. Indeed, sometimes such services can gain favor that was not had before, but once gained they cannot guarantee that it will not depart. Divine favor alone is incapable of inconstancy, but all others are such as promise things subject to change, whatever is said about them.

164. I could not readily believe that you will ever find greater favor with King Richard than blessed Thomas found with King Henry, yet he did not rejoice in it for long. I am not saying that you should lightly esteem the king's favor, or that you should forfeit it cheaply, provided that you can retain it with a clear conscience, but that you not rely too

sed ne nimis de ea confidas, et sicut vulgo dicitur, "martinum relinquas ut salices apprehendas." Si sortis tuae mutationem subitam subtilius volueris intueri, quam vana et fallax sit mortalium gratia satis poteris demetiri. Quis enim te amplius familiaritatem et gratiam adeptus est apud quamplures et praecipuos Anglorum magnates? Sed ubi abundavit gratia superabundavit et malitia, non minus prona in detractiones dum adversa crebrescerent, quam prompta adulationibus militare cum prospera pullularent.

165. Sed numquid tibi soli et non alii hoc accidit? Immo certe innumerabilibus. Tu vero nec primus nec novissimus. Quidam enim te praecesserunt et quidam subsequentur, sicut et ipse quosdam praecessisti et quosdam subsecutus es. Et si aliquatenus novi mores hominum, et eorum maxime quorum *cum fortuna statque caditque fides,* successori tuo, ne supplantatori dixerim, posses secure illud dixisse, quod Porus Alexandro, cum ab eo caperetur, legitur intulisse:

Exemplum tibi sum qui, cum fortissimus essem,
fortius inveni. Ne dixeris esse beatum,
qui quo crescat habet, nisi quo decrescere possit
non habeat, multo gravius torquentur avari
amissi memores, quam delectentur habendo.

166. Gratia igitur humana laboriose adquiritur, et adquisita non sine labore servatur et inter servandum

much on it. As the proverb says, "You let a marten go to grasp willows." If you are ready to look closely at your sudden change of fortune, you can measure well enough how empty and deceptive is the favor of mortal men. For who gained friendship and favor more than you among very many distinguished magnates of England? But where favor has flowed freely, malice also has overflowed, no less prone to slander when adversities were increasing than ready to engage in flattery when prosperity was welling up.

165. But has this really happened to you alone and not to any other? No indeed! It has surely happened to countless people. Truly, you are not the first nor the last. For some have gone before you and others will follow, just as you have gone before some and followed others. And if I have some knowledge of the ways of men, and especially of those whose *loyalty stands and falls with fortune,* you could have confidently said to your successor (not to say supplanter) what we read that Porus replied to Alexander when he was captured by him:

> I am an example to you. Although I was powerful, I have discovered something more powerful. Do not say that he is blessed who has the means to grow greater, unless he does not have the means to grow smaller; greedy men are tormented much more grievously in remembering what has been lost than they are delighted in possessing what they have.

166. Therefore, human favor is gained with great effort, and once gained is not retained without great effort, and sometimes in the process of being retained, it slips away

nonnumquam elabitur, cui sedet in insidiis rerum vicissitudo, quae ei assidue novercatur. Gratia haec, si voluerimus verum dicere, non est gratia. Comparatur enim divitiis, conservatur obsequiis, possidetur coagulatione cognati sanguinis, raro autem alicui confertur vitae meritis, multis vero aufertur causa solius suspicionis. Et postremo, quod longe deterius est, multi propter gratiam humanam divinam postposuerunt, et postpositam penitus perdiderunt. Cum autem dicat apostolus, "*Si adhuc hominibus placerem, servus Christi non essem,*" difficillimum arbitror Deo simul et hominibus placere, dicente psalmista, "*Qui hominibus placent confusi sunt, quoniam Deus sprevit eos.*"

167. Quid autem est quod in adquirenda divina gratia ita sumus tepidi et torpentes quod vix aliquando expergiscimur? Immo occasiones et excusationes frustratorias proponimus, et salutem nostram de die in diem prorogamus, non ignorantes tamen quid nobis potius expediret? Et si forte, ut assolet, valitudo aliqua corporis supervenerit, cuius molestia mentis oculus ad intuendum interioris hominis statum retorqueatur, statim compungimur, contristamur, erubescimus, et tacti dolore cordis intrinsecus in lacrimas quandoque copiose defluimus, promittentes errata corrigere, si quid alicui abstulimus ad plenum restituere, de cetero nos a saecularibus curis seorsum facere, nihil illicitum aut ordini nostro contrarium attemptare, omnibus qui nos offenderunt vel laeserunt in aliquo ex animo pro Deo remittere, et si quos offendimus promissa satisfactione competenti veniam postulare.

from him for whom there waits in ambush a change of fortune, which constantly acts like a stepmother toward him. This favor, if we are willing to speak the truth, is no favor. For it is purchased by riches, preserved by services, possessed by shared family blood; it is rarely bestowed on anyone for the worthiness of his life, but is taken away from many merely on account of suspicion. Finally, what is far worse, for the sake of human favor many men have subordinated divine favor, and have utterly lost what they subordinated. Moreover, since the Apostle says, "*If I yet pleased men, I should not be the servant of Christ,*" I believe that it is very difficult to please God and men at the same time, for the psalmist declares, "*Those who please men have been confounded, because God has despised them.*"

167. Why is it that in gaining divine grace we are so tepid and torpid that we are sometimes scarcely awake? Indeed, we put forward pretexts and excuses for procrastination, and put off our salvation from day to day, though we are fully aware what profits us more. But if by chance some infirmity of body befalls us, as is wont to happen, and because of its affliction the mind's eye is turned toward contemplating the state of the inner man, we immediately feel remorse, we are saddened, we are ashamed. Touched inwardly by heartfelt sorrow, we sometimes pour forth abundant tears. We promise to correct our faults, to make full restitution of whatever we have stolen from anyone, to separate ourselves from worldly cares in the future, to undertake nothing unlawful or opposed to our order, to forgive wholeheartedly before God all who have offended us or injured us in any way, and to beg pardon if we have offended anyone, promising suitable satisfaction.

168. Si vero convaluerimus, ante omnia statuimus ut de cetero eorum non reminiscamur quae in tempore angustiae promisimus, et quasi iam securi, quod mortem non tantum distulerimus quantum evaserimus, rursum ad consuetudines pravas revertimur, et longe avidius quam antea negotiis saecularibus et carnis illecebris inhiamus. Unde plerumque solet contingere quod hi quos castigatio flagelli debuit erudire ad salutem, ipsa miseratio quam consecuti sunt induret ad mortem, et qui fuerunt ex timore sub flagello devoti, fiunt post flagella ex negligentia securi.

168. But if we should regain our health, above all else we decide that in the future we will not recall what we promised in our time of distress, and as if secure now because we have not so much deferred death as escaped it, we return to our perverse customs once again. We gape at worldly affairs and allurements of the flesh far more eagerly than before. Hence, it is very frequently accustomed to happen that those men whom the chastisement of the whip ought to have instructed toward salvation, the compassion which they have gained hardens toward death; those who became devout under the whip out of fear, become secure after the whipping out of neglectfulness.

APPENDIX

The Life of Saint Paul, the First Hermit

Iussit adorari Decius simulacra deorum.
Vir sitiens poenas et caedem catholicorum,
vir cedens vitiis, immo sedes vitiorum,
ad facinus praeceps, exlex, hostisque bonorum.
Qui nactus regnum, non protector populorum,
immo ferox studuit fieri populator eorum.
Par sibi nequitia, tot participando malorum,
Valerianus erat; mens ad scelus una duorum.
Coepit uterque deos summo studio venerari,
Christicolas gladiis et supplicio populari;
cladibus illorum neuter potuit satiari.
Nec tamen optanti licuit gladio iugulari,
hostis enim poenis poenas iubet accumulari,
morteque fit gravius mortem patiendo morari.
Sicque facit variis cruciatibus examinari,
quos mavult animae quam carnis morte necari.
Hac cupit ut pereant, et ad hoc ipsius anhelant
actus, iussa, doli, quod et haec exempla revelant.
Edicto statuit simulacra deum veneranda,
et membris Satanae dat membra Dei crucianda.
Aggreditur quendam culpantem sacra nefanda,
et tormenta parat, quae non credit superanda.
Quem Christi virtus dum servat glorificanda,
sic patitur poenas quasi sint lenimina blanda.

Decius commanded that images of the gods be worshiped. He was a man thirsting for the suffering and slaughter of catholic Christians, a man subject to vices, indeed, a seat of vices, inclined to outrage, lawless, and an enemy of good men. Once he acquired power, he was no protector of the people, but strove savagely to become their plunderer. By sharing in so many evils, Valerian was his equal in villainy; the two were of one mind in wickedness. With utmost zeal each began to revere the gods, to lay waste Christians with swords and torture; neither could be sated in massacring them. Yet to be killed by the sword was not permitted to one wishing it, for the foe ordered pain to be added to pain, and to delay death by suffering became more painful than death.

And so he caused those Christians to be tested by diverse torments whom he preferred to be slain by death of the soul rather than of the body. In this way he wished them to perish, and his actions, orders, and subterfuges aspired to this purpose, which the following examples also reveal. In an edict he decreed that images of the gods should be revered, and he gives the members of God to the members of Satan to be crucified. He assails a man who condemns the impious rites, and orders torments that he does not believe will be tolerable. While Christ's glorious power protects that man, he bears the pains as if they were soothing balms.

Hunc oleum fervens, hunc candens lamina laedit,
ipse tamen durat, nec in hoc discrimine cedit,
dumque Dei iussis, haec aspernatus, oboedit,
pro nihilo reputat poenas quas vincere credit.
Hinc igitur Decio dolor alto corde resedit;
hinc alias poenas excogitat, invenit, edit.
Melle iubet nudum sub sole calente perungi
corpus, ut a muscis nudum queat undique pungi,
ut queat ardori stimulorum laesio iungi,
sic cupiens tandem victoris nomine fungi.
Hinc alius Christi venit ad nova proelia miles,
cui fortes animos praebent anni iuveniles.
Non parat hic poenas, immo ludos pueriles,
ut vitiis animos queat enervare viriles.
Hos laqueos Nembroth, has fraudes insidiarum,
hos tendit casses, praedam cupiens animarum.
Hunc temptat poenis, hunc luxu deliciarum
temptat, ut enervet virtutes Christicolarum.
Nemo dolos novit quibus auctor nequitiarum
Christicolis fraudum parat impedimenta suarum.
Ducitur ecce locum iuvenis visurus amoenum,
quem varii flores reddunt dulcedine plenum.
Florida blanditur tellus caelumque serenum.
Cetera quid referam? Sunt omnia dulce venenum!
Dumque locum mirans puer huc illucque vagatur,
extruitur plumis torus ornateque paratur.
Ipse superpositus sertorum fune ligatur,
et mollis nexus tenet illum ne moveatur.
Omnibus egressis, meretrix speciosa vocatur,
ut blandis illum sermonibus aggrediatur.
Haec venit, accedit, nec eum temptare moratur.

Boiling oil and a white-hot metal plate give him pain, yet he endures and does not yield at this moment of trial. As he obeys God's commands, disdaining these torments, he pays no heed to the pains that he believes he will conquer. On account of this, therefore, sorrow settled in the depths of Decius's heart; on account of this, he devises, discovers, and brings forth new punishments. He orders the man's naked body to be smeared with honey under the hot sun, so that the naked man may be stung from every side by flies, and the hurt of those stings may be united to the burning, wishing in this way at last to secure the title of conqueror.

After this another soldier of Christ comes to these new battles, one to whom youthful years grant a steadfast spirit. For him, Decius does not order punishments, but rather boyish sport, to weaken through vice his manly spirit. Nimrod sets these traps, he spreads out these deceptive snares, he spreads these nets, wishing for the prey of souls. One man he tests with punishments, one with indulgence in delights, to weaken the resolve of Christians. No one knows the tricks with which the instigator of evil prepares his treacherous obstacles for Christians.

Behold, the young man is taken to see a pleasant place, which multicolored flowers fill with sweetness. The flowery earth and fair sky are alluring. Why should I report the rest? All are sweet venom! And while the boy roams here and there marveling at the place, a couch is strewn with soft down and elegantly made ready. Laid upon it, he is bound by a rope of garlands, and the soft coil holds him to prevent him moving. After all have departed, a beautiful harlot is summoned to approach him with seductive speech. She arrives, draws near, and wastes no time in tempting him.

Mox, licet invitus, complexibus illaqueatur,
utque satis gravius veneris stimulos patiatur,
oscula dat meretrix et blanda voce profatur.
Heu, qua fronte queunt temptamina cetera dici?
Ipsa pudenda capit, nec enim pudor est meretrici.
Quid super hiis faciat? Vinctus nequit hanc removere.
Si rogat, haec idcirco manus non vult cohibere.
Quod superest solum: nutu Domini miserantis,
mordet et in faciem linguam spuit oscula dantis.
Dumque voluptatis dolor efficitur medicina,
mens sua praecipiti non est absorpta ruina.
His aliisque modis Decius saevire paratus,
intulit innumeros servis Christi cruciatus.
Hinc quod quisque timens ne cederet his superatus,
linquebat patriam, poene terrore fugatus.
Tempore Paulus eo latuit, tormenta timescens.
Moribus egregius et mente sagax adolescens
hic erat, apprime fidei fervore calescens,
inque piis studiis et sancto dogmate crescens.
Desponsata viro soror huic erat huius in aede
mansit, ab infesta cupiens evadere caede.
Sed nec in hac potuit tutus requiescere sede,
quippe vir infandus cupit hunc exponere praedae.
Aurum dum mentis gliscit sitis anxia foede,
non prohibent propria scelus illud foedera caede.
Heu, quid nunc cupidis persuadet mentis egestas!
Omne docet facinus, res spernere cogit honestas.
Quod si forte datur actu saevire potestas,
non timet in sanctos dextras armare scelestas.
Ecce virum cupidum scelus hoc corrumpere novit,

Soon, though unwilling, he is ensnared by her embraces, and to make him suffer more strongly the spurs of passion, the harlot imparts kisses and speaks with an enticing voice. Ah! With what shame can the rest of her temptations be told? She grasps his private parts, for a harlot has no shame. What could he do about this? The fettered youth cannot drive her away. If he begs, she is unwilling on that account to restrain her hands. Only one thing is left: at the command of the merciful Lord, he bites off his tongue and spits it in her face as she kisses him. And while pain is made the remedy for pleasure, his soul is not swallowed up in a headlong fall.

Ready to vent his rage through these and other methods, Decius inflicts countless torments on the servants of Christ. Hence, since everyone feared that he might be overcome by these measures and yield, everyone tried to leave his fatherland, put to flight by fear of punishment. At this time Paul went into hiding, fearful of torture. He was a young man, distinguished in character and keen of mind, especially ardent in the heat of his faith, and advancing in pious studies and sacred doctrine. His sister was betrothed to a man in whose house he stayed, wishing to escape the savage slaughter. But he could not rest securely in this abode, for that unspeakable man wished to expose him for gain. Since his anxious soul shamefully thirsted for gold, his own marriage did not restrain the wicked scoundrel from murder.

Ah! What does poverty of soul now prompt greedy men to do! It teaches them every outrage, it compels them to spurn honorable deeds. But if they are granted the power for savage actions, that power does not fear to arm their wicked hands against saints. See, this wickedness was able to corrupt the greedy man, and through him it turned the

inque pium per eum fraudum molimina movit.
Declinans Decium Paulus cupiensque latere,
hunc adit, ut latebras queat eius in aede fovere.
Quem sibi dum cernit vultu verbisque favere,
nescit simplicitas pia subdola verba timere.
Fraus latet hostilis, simulato tecta favore,
plagaque subtilis ferit hunc ictu graviore.
Sed cautela piae comes extat simplicitati,
indagans odii vestigia dissimulati.
Sed quid ad haec faciat vel quod sibi speret asylum,
undique Fata suum cum certent rumpere filum?
Obstat laetitiae metus, obstat cura quieti,
sicque frequens letum fit ei dilatio leti.
Non os, non oculos delectant prandia, somni;
interimitque virum mors nulla, perit tamen omni.
Felix si sensum mors non sineret superesse!
Sed sinit, et semper superest ut possit obesse.
Sentit, ut a sensu numquam dolor amoveatur;
vivit ut haec vita mors esse sibi videatur.
Sic, dum sollicitus mortem timet, illa moratur,
et tamen hac timidus, necdum moriens, cruciatur.
Una salutis opem fuga spondet: ea parat uti;
fit fuga sicque suae vir consulit ille saluti.
Deserit ergo suos; profugus deserta peragrat;
terrea postponit, caeli dulcedine flagrat.
Aulas contemnit cedro vel marmore fultas,
et quae suppeditat locupletibus ampla facultas.
Spernere regales epulas potumque Lyaei,
importuna docet penuria pauperiei.
Haec instans inopem premit; hic tolerat patienter,

contrivances of deception against a holy man. While avoiding Decius and wishing to hide, Paul approaches this man to provide him with a hiding place in his home. While Paul detects from his face and words that the man is well-disposed to him, his pious innocence does not know how to beware deceitful speech. The hostile deception is concealed, hidden by pretended favor, and a subtle blow strikes him with a grievous stroke. But caution is a companion to Paul's pious innocence, tracking down the traces of disguised hatred.

But what was Paul to do in this situation, or what refuge might he hope for, when the Fates strive from all quarters to cut the thread of his life? Fear imperils his happiness, anxiety his repose, and thus the postponement of death becomes for him a repeated death. Meals do not entice his mouth, nor sleep his eyes; no death is killing him, and yet he dies in every way. Happy he, if only death were putting an end to feelings! But it does not, and feelings forever remain with power to stand in our way. His feelings are such that sorrow is never removed from his sensation; his life is such that this life seems to be death to him. Thus, full of anxiety, he fears death, but death tarries, and he is tormented, afraid of death while not yet dying. Flight alone promises a means of deliverance: he prepares to use it; he flees, and thus the man looks to his own deliverance.

And so, Paul leaves his family; a fugitive, he wanders through solitary places; he puts aside earthly goods; he is inflamed by the sweetness of heaven. He despises palaces built of cedar and marble, and things that great wealth supplies to the rich. Poverty's harsh scarcity teaches him to spurn regal banquets and the cups of Lyaeus. Poverty overwhelms the destitute man, pressing upon him; he bears it patiently, and

et fit onus gratum quo deprimitur violenter.
Iam sine deliciis se pauper vivere gaudet.
Iam nec eis uti, si copia suppetat, audet
ne sibi si requies haec momentanea detur,
segnius invigilet huic quae data semper habetur.
Hinc quod hic in requie cupiens gaudere futura,
mollia postponit; cupit, eligit omnia dura.
Antra domos, herbaeque cibos dant, pocula stillae
imbris; in hiis habitat, his vescitur, has bibit ille.
Gaudia conventus urbis, spectacula villae
pro nihilo reputat, nec comparat illa favillae.
Sic prius invitus qui mundi liquerat actus,
gaudet eos linqui; contemptor denique factus.
Sicque necem fugiens, eremum subire coactus,
iam cogi gaudet, virtutum culmina nactus.
Cogitur aeternae sibi quaerere gaudia vitae,
quodque necesse videt cupit, optat, agitque perite.
Sic quod vim patitur, nil officit hoc eremitae.
Vim patitur; potius sibi vim facit ut patiatur.
Taliter ambitur via qua caelum rapiatur.
Caelum furatur latitans ne comperiatur.
Ipsum mercatur qui se dat ut hoc capiatur.
Quattuor ergo modis quibus ad caelum properatur
nititur, insistens ut ad illum perveniatur.
A quo proposito ne mens sua praepediatur
ipse locum quaerit quo carni provideatur.
Est specus inventus, aditu praeclusus operto.

the burden by which he is sorely oppressed becomes pleasing. Now the pauper rejoices that he lives without luxuries. Now he does not dare to enjoy them, even if they should be in abundant supply, lest if this momentary repose should be granted to him, he would too inattentively keep watch for the one blessing which, once given, is granted forever. It is for this reason that, longing to rejoice in future repose, he sets aside what is soft here; he longs for and chooses all that is hard. Caves furnish his abodes, plants his meals, drops of rain his drink; he dwells in one, eats another, and drinks the third. The joys of company in the city, the sights a town offers, he counts for nothing, and does not count them equal to ashes.

Thus, the man who at first was reluctant to forsake the activities of the world rejoices that they are forsaken; in the end he has come to despise them. And so, fleeing death and forced to endure the wilderness, he now rejoices that he was forced, having reached the pinnacle of virtue. He is forced to seek for himself the joys of everlasting life, and what he sees is needful, he desires, wishes for, and expertly performs. Though he submits to force in this way, this does not hinder his hermit existence. He suffers force; or rather, he inflicts force on himself so as to suffer. In such a way he aspires to walk the path by which heaven is seized. While hiding to escape discovery, he takes heaven by stealth. In sacrificing himself he stakes his own person for this aim to be achieved. Thus, he relies on four ways which hasten the journey to heaven, pursuing them vigorously to reach that place. So that his mind not be hindered in its purpose, he seeks a place where he can provide for his flesh. He finds a cave blocked, with its entrance covered over. Opening it, he

Quem reserans gaudet, cum palma fonte reperto.
Intrat et hunc aptum caelo videt intus aperto,
in quo sit stabilis et psallat tempore certo.
Palma cibum, vestem; fons illi pocula praebet;
durum terra torum caro cum requiescere debet.
Cum torus iste Iacob, cum talia fulcra fuere,
nocte Deum vidit; datur ex re nomen habere.
Congreditur, vincit, benedicitur atque laborum
haec quod causa fuit, fit ei merces meritorum.
Cui quia par studuit Paulus fore culmine morum,
fit quod et ille fuit, supplantator vitiorum.
Huic patet in somnis erectio mystica scalae;
tendit hic ascendens ad donum spirituale.
Hic videt, hic scandit; vacat hic, subit iste laborem.
Huic bona pars cedit, tenet ille tamen meliorem.
Dum videt emeritam sic Martha vacare sororem,
non vacat, adquirens operando quietis honorem.
Virtutum numerare gradus vitiis prohiberis;
obluctans ipsis Iacob alter, Paule, videris.
Ecce Iacob luctans es, et Israel esse mereris.
Ergo quod optatur pete Martha; Maria frueris.
Arcem virtutum qui scandere nititur almam,
promittit requiem labor illi pugnaque palmam.
Scandit hic et vitiis obstans athleta probatur,
speque triumphandi labor athletae relevatur.
Spes ita solatur, rem spondens qua potiatur,
qua non frustratur quid danti participatur.
O res magna, gravi res quaeri digna labore!

rejoices when he finds a spring with a palm tree. He enters and sees it is suitable inside, even though under the open sky, a place in which to persevere and sing psalms at a fixed time of day. The palm supplies food and clothing; the spring supplies his drink; the earth furnishes a hard couch when the flesh needs rest.

When such was Jacob's couch, when such was his bed, he saw God at night; indeed, from this fact he is given his name. He contends, he conquers, he is blessed, and since this was the reason for his hardships, he received a reward for his merits. Because Paul strove to be his equal in excellence of character, he became what Jacob was, an overthrower of vices. To one, a mystical ladder reaching upward appears in his dreams; the other directs his ascent toward a spiritual gift. One sees the ladder, one climbs it; one is at ease, one undertakes toil. A good part falls to the one, yet the other has the better part. Thus, while Martha sees that her sister is deservedly at ease, she is not at ease herself, but secures the honor of repose by working. You are prevented by vices from ascending one at a time the steps of virtues; in struggling with these, Paul, you seem another Jacob. See, in wrestling you are a Jacob, and you also deserve the name of Israel. Therefore, as Martha, seek what you wish for; as Mary, you will have delight.

To the one who strives to climb to the welcoming citadel of the virtues, toil promises him repose, and the struggle a palm. He climbs up and, in his stand against vices, is proved an athlete, and the athletic toil is lightened by the hope of winning a triumph. Thus, hope comforts him, promising he will win a possession of which he will not be deprived, but receives a share with the giver. Oh great possession! Oh

Qua quisquis fruitur summo donatur honore;
res optanda, frui qua nemo potest meliore;
nemo pari. Fulgens quovis quantoque decore
spes igitur non est aliquo frustranda tenore,
namque fruetur amans mercede fruendo datore.
Hinc quod hic ascendens, firmo conamine gressus
figit ne recidat, terreno pondere pressus;
ne trahat error eum quem Christi gratia rexit;
ne vitium reprimat quem spes ad sidera vexit.
Haerens ergo Deo mens a terrestribus exit;
quo semel inspecto, non lumen ad ima reflexit.
Haec superis inhians, dum iuncta Deo requiescit;
usu victa bono caro iam requiescere nescit.
Flet caro, mens gaudet; teritur caro, mens hilarescit.
Haec gemit, haec plaudit. Haec horret et illa nitescit.
Sic quod mens optat discit caro subdita velle.
Sic iter Axa suae regit et moderatur asellae.
Axa regens asinam mens carnis habens dominatum
dicitur. Irriguum rogat illa daturque rogatum;
est hoc donatum cum delet flendo reatum;
quod cum dilatum regnum flet, hoc geminatum.
Hic igitur, cuius regitur caro sicut asella,
non queritur nec enim patitur fera foedaque bella.
Pax geritur caro dum teritur summaque quiete
mens fruitur; tantum queritur dispendia metae
quae petitur. Spes appetitur promissa monetae,
nec capitur pro quo graditur nisi fine diaetae;

possession rightly sought by heavy toil! Whoever delights in this possession is granted the highest honors; it is a desirable possession. No one can enjoy a better; no one can enjoy its equal. And so, shining in splendor of all sorts and amounts, the hope cannot be thwarted by any course of events, for the lover will delight in his reward as he delights in the giver.

This is the reason that in ascending, Paul plants his steps with firm tread, so that, crushed by an earthly burden, he does not fall back; so that error not draw him away, whom the grace of Christ has guided; so that vice not hold him back, whom hope has conveyed to the heavens. Thus, clinging to God, his mind takes leave of earthly things. Once God had been contemplated, he did not turn his gaze back to the depths below. Intent on things above, when joined to God, his mind finds rest; overcome by his virtuous behavior, his flesh now knows no rest. The flesh weeps, the mind rejoices. The flesh is worn down, the mind is merry. The one groans, the other applauds. The one is filthy, and the other shines. So, his subdued flesh learns to wish for what his mind desires. So does Axa guide and direct the way for a she-ass. The mind that has mastery over the flesh is said to be Axa controlling a she-ass. She asks for water and is granted what she asked for. This is given to him when Paul wipes out his guilt by weeping; the kingdom he weeps for when delayed is redoubled. And so the one whose flesh is guided like a she-ass does not complain, nor suffer fierce and filthy wars.

When the flesh is worn down, peace comes about and the mind enjoys the utmost repose; it only complains about the delays to the goal that is sought. The promised hope of a reward is eagerly desired, and what he lives for is not obtained

unde viae sibi quaque die mora longa videtur
usque oneris gravitas operis mercede levetur.
Hoc studiis spondendo piis spes certa levamen
deliciis dedit et vitiis certum moderamen.
Sed quod onus tulit ille bonus, quo sic relevari
promeruit, necdum valuit vel quis meditari.
Vix patuit, quod vir latuit, quae gratia forti
principio, quae religio, quae gloria morti.
Hinc medium vitae spatium de quo dubitamus
hoc humili reserare styli cursu paveamus.
Ergo quibus vel quam gravibus pugnis patiendo
restiterit, grave ne fuerit transisse silendo,
sed vetito ne quid licito plus aggrediamur
haec ab eo soloque Deo sciri patiamur.
De reliquis superest aliquis modus agnitionis,
quem patulo labor hic oculo monstret rationis.
Quis fuerit, qui reppererit Paulum latitantem,
cur ierit, cur quaesierit, docet hic dubitantem.
Egerat angelicam sub carnis tegmine vitam
Paulus, et ornarat iam canities eremitam.
Mens superis inhians hunc fecerat Israelitam
spondebatque sibi palmam virtute petitam.
Iam centum bis quinque tribus vir vixerat annis;
restabat pugili superatis palma tyrannis.
Iam caro marcescit, mens regnat, gloria crescit,
bellum rarescit, fugit hostis, et iste quiescit.
Iam cursus metas spondet sibi debilis aetas,
spondet completas vitaeque viaeque dietas.

except at the end of his journey. Thus the delay seems long on each day of his travels until the heaviness of his burden is lightened by the reward for his labors. By promising this solace for his pious zeal, assured hope put a confirmed check on pleasures and vices. But no one is yet able to conceive what hardship that good man bore, for which he deserved to be thus comforted. It has only become known with difficulty, since the man lived in obscurity, what grace there was in his brave undertaking, what holiness and glory in his death.

Moving on, let us fear to disclose with the humble flow of our pen the middle span of his life, about which we are uncertain. Thus, what struggles or how harsh the battles he withstood by his long suffering, lest it be a grievous matter to have passed over these things in silence, but seeing that we are forbidden to undertake more than is permitted, we leave to be known by him and by God alone. About the rest, some means to knowledge remain, which may the labor expended here show to the open eye of reason. This work teaches the doubter who it was who found Paul hiding, why he went, and why he sought him.

Paul had led an angelic life under the covering of the flesh, and now gray hair had graced the hermit. His mind, longing for things above, had made him an Israelite and promised him the palm sought by virtue. The man had now lived for two hundred and fifteen years; the palm of victory awaited him for his bouts in overcoming tyrants. Now his flesh wastes away, his mind gains ascendancy, his glory increases, warfare slackens off, the enemy flees, and he is at peace. Now his feeble age promises him the end of the course; it promises the completion of his journey on the

Dat Christi pietas imitari mente prophetas;
sic iuvat athletas dans dotes gratia laetas.
Cum superas ita delicias pater anticiparet,
iamque foret tempus quo lux eremi radiaret,
eius ne meritum vel fama diu latitaret,
haec est facta patens ut et illud notificaret.
Claruerat meritis Antonius inclitus ille
in cuius laudem calamizant organa mille,
quem vitae meritum sub religionis agone
fecerat emeritum dignumque decore coronae.
Hunc non illexit decus aut decor ambitione,
sed nec eum flexit metus aut favor a ratione.
Nil sibi cum vitiis, quia carnis ad infima pronae
obstans deliciis, hanc rexit religione.
Iam denos novies annos aetatis habebat;
florida canities meritumque caputque decebat.
Spiritui parens senio caro deficiebat,
atque vigore carens non ipsa labore carebat,
sed labor aetherei spondebat dona trophaei,
quodque daretur ei post proelia, pax requiei.
Sicque fuere spei sibi tempora canitiei
qui non iussa Dei dedit antea segnitiei.
Iam vitii pestis cunctis infesta modestis
nullis infestis studiis obstabat honestis.
Praeteritis maestis victisque quibusque molestis,
palmae caelestis servat sibi mens pia testis.
Omne videns igitur vitium virtute subactum,
nullum cui cedat eremi credit loca nactum.
Sed Deus huic Paulum, longo certamine fractum,
praeponi monstrat redditque virum stupefactum.

path of life. The kindness of Christ allows him to imitate the prophets in understanding; in this way grace aids his athletes, bestowing on them a happy dowry. When Father Paul anticipated such delights on high, and the time was now at hand for the light of the desert to shine forth, so that his merit and reputation should not be hidden for long, his reputation was made manifest to make known his merit too.

Antony, that illustrious saint, had become renowned for his merits. In his praise a thousand tongues make joyous song, for he was a man whom the merit of his ways in the struggle of the religious life had made deserving and worthy of the glory of a crown. Glory or grace did not entice him through ambition, but neither fear nor favor diverted him from true reason. He had nothing to do with vices, because while resisting delights of the flesh that tends to the depths, he ruled it by his religious way of life. He had lived for ninety years already; a rich crop of gray hair befitted his merits and his head. Still subject to the spirit, his flesh was failing through feebleness, and though lacking strength, it was not lacking toil, but the toil that promised gifts of celestial victory and the gift he would receive after his battles, the peace of repose. And thus the times of old age were a source of hope for him, since he had not previously turned God's commands over to idleness. Now baneful vice, hostile to all decent men, was no longer hindering his honorable pursuits with hostile ones. After all gloom had passed away and every difficulty had been overcome, his mind, a pious witness to the heavenly palm of glory for him, keeps watch.

Therefore, seeing all vice overcome by virtue, Antony believes that there is no one occupying the desert to whom he should take second place. But God points out that Paul, made feeble by long struggle, is ranked before him, causing

Orat hic ut Pauli mores cognoscat et actum,
spondeturque sibi spes, subsequitur rata pactum.
Nec mora, spe fretus, iter ignorans, parat ire;
spes, dubitare vetans, quaerendo docet reperire.
Non iter excusat labor; immo pericla subire
gaudet ut hunc adeat ad quem cupit ipse venire.
Nuntia lucis ei dederat vix signa sereni
caeli, cum strepitu reserat pater ostia leni.
Hinc deserta subit, qua vasta patent sibi parte,
et tremulos artus natura fulcit et arte.
Arte iuvante regit corpus natura senile,
et vir carpit iter quasi sit robur iuvenile,
quod pro colloquio iusti tolerare virile.
Cor reputat quasi det pro caro munere vile.
Sol a parte poli medius distabat utraque,
virque laborabat, fessus fervore viaque,
cum vir conspicitur speciei mixtus equinae,
incutiuntque metum formae spectacula binae,
ac simul armatur frons sacro stigmate; tutus
quaerit iter; lenis fit ei responsio nutus.
Barbara frendentis in verba ferae patuerunt
ora, tamen certi vestigia nulla dederunt.
Vox etenim stridens et barbara verba fuerunt,
unde nec agnosci nec discerni potuerunt.
Signa tamen dextrae nutusque viam docuerunt.
Hinc cursu celeres sed dissimiles abierunt.

Antony to be astonished. Antony prays that he may get to know Paul's character and deeds; hope is promised him and ratified following the pact. Without delay, relying on hope, though ignorant of the way, he prepares to go forth; forbidding him to doubt, hope teaches him to seek and find. Hardship does not excuse him from the journey; rather he is glad to endure dangers to draw near to him whom he longs to reach.

The messenger of light had scarcely shown him signs of a fair sky, when the father opened his doors with a gentle creak. From here he proceeds to the wilderness, where a desolate expanse stretches out before him, and he supports his trembling limbs by nature and by art. With the assistance of art, he controls his body which is aged in nature, and as if his strength were youthful, the man pursues his journey, which is a manly feat of endurance, in return for conversation with a just man. His heart considers that it is, as it were, a paltry gift he is giving in return for the rich one he will receive. Now the sun stood midway between each pole, and the man was hard pressed, made weary by the heat and the journey, when he spied a man conjoined with the shape of a horse. The spectacle of this hybrid form produced fear in him; at the same time he protected his brow with the holy sign. Now safe, he asks the way; his answer is a gentle nod. The beast gnashed his teeth, his mouth gave vent to strange words, yet they offered no indication of clear meaning. For the voice was shrill and the words foreign, and hence could not be recognized or distinguished. Yet the gestures of his right hand and nods showed the way. Thence, swift in course, but dissimilar, they parted from one another.

Currebat senior quem deficientia pridem
robora tardabant; aetas obstabat eidem;
sistere saepe gradum labor hunc aetasque coegit.
Unde sequens oculis, quod non pede nisibus egit,
dumque ferae cursum stupuit longeque sequente
haesit in aspectu, sibi evanuit illa repente.
Hanc tamen an speciem daemon simulaverit, an sit
talis alumna loci fera, res incerta remansit.
Sed non ista senis obstant spectacula voto,
nam memor huius iter carpit, terrore remoto,
promissumque Dei pertractans pectore toto,
it celer ut Paulo sumat nova gaudia noto.
Nec mora, monstrati carpens compendia callis
hac iter aggreditur, qua ducit saxea vallis.
O nova res! Celeri cursu dum transvolat arva,
eius in occursum festinat belua, larva.
Turpior huic hominis species staturaque parva.
Quodque dat humanae decor huic et gratia formae,
quaedam deformant decus excedentia normae.
Est facies hominis, sed cornibus aspera binis;
frons est apta minis, armis munita ferinis.
Nasus aduncus ei, frons torva, pedes caprearum:
quae tria deformem reddunt similemque ferarum.
Conveniunt in eo species rerum variarum,
nec sibi conveniunt nec enim decor ullus earum.
Absque sui specie, species simul esse videntur,
cum mixtae formae formosum nil operentur.
Ut pater advertit formae deformis homullum,
obriguit; flatum vix liquit ei stupor ullum.

The old man, whom failing strength was lately slowing, was running now, but his age was hindering him. Hardship and age forced him often to stay his step. And so he followed him with his eyes, since he had not the strength to pursue him on foot, and while he was amazed at the wild beast's pace and kept him in his sight, following him from afar, he suddenly vanished. Yet, whether a demon assumed this appearance, or a wild beast of this kind was native to the place, remained an uncertain matter. But this spectacle does not thwart the old man's vow, for, mindful of it, laying fear aside, he pursues his journey, and, reflecting on God's promise with his whole heart, he goes swiftly on, to receive fresh joys with the discovery of Paul.

Without delay, taking the short cut of a mountain path shown to him, Antony makes his way along a stony vale. Oh novel turn of events! While he crosses the plains in his swift course, a monster, a specter, rushes up to meet him. He has the appearance of a man, but very ugly and of small stature. Some aberrations from the norm of beauty deform whatever the elegance and grace of human form bestow on him. He has the face of a man, but shaggy, with two horns; his brow is suited to threats, fortified with bestial weapons. His nose is curved, his brow savage, his feet those of wild goats: these three features make him unsightly and similar to wild beasts. Appearances of different things come together in him, but they are not in harmony, nor is there any beauty in them. Without a species of their own, species seem to be joined together, although that mingling of shapes produces nothing beautiful.

As the father observed the ugly-shaped dwarf, he grew stiff with fear; in his astonishment he could scarcely catch

Quippe tot enormes artus cernens animalis,
mirator stupidus fit formae prodigialis.
Sed cruce munitus rediit mentemque recepit.
Unde nihil metuens citus huic occurrere coepit.
At fera multa feri vultus dans signa vel ire,
obvia festinat, velut accersita venire;
nec satis est placidos vultus ostendere; profert
palmarum fructus, quod pignora foederis offert.
Hiis velut obsidibus pacis dat homuncio signum,
quem probat humanum compassio, dona benignum.
Subsistit senior, figit vestigia terrae.
Indagat quis sit. Sic incipit ille referre:
"Qui pro velle ratis dat legibus esse creatis,
vique potestatis moderando praeest moderatis,
esse mihi gratis dedit et nutu bonitatis
providet; ipse satis dat; habundo rebus amatis.
Legibus ipse datis regor. Ortum debeo fatis,
namque inhiant vatis haec faucibus insatiatis.
Me vulgus stultum satirum vocat, et prece multum
sollicitat; vultum demittit; dat mihi cultum,
meque deum memorat. Metuit, reveretur, honorat,
indiget, exorat, dat dona, placere laborat.
Si fit ut implorat, mox terram sanguine rorat;
cui litat ignorat; nescit quem pronus adorat.
Fitque quod est pluris: quia credit ovilia ruris
esse mei iuris, fugit haec audacia furis.
Hinc mihi pastorum famulatur turba, suorum
curam dans pecorum, quasi sim spes omnis eorum.

his breath. Indeed, seeing so many freakish animal limbs, the astonished man marveled at the strange shape. But, fortified by the sign of the cross, he returned to himself and recovered his senses. Then, fearing nothing, he began to hasten to meet him. But the wild beast, showing on his wild face many signs to Antony to proceed, hastens to meet him, as if summoned to come; and it is not enough to display a gentle countenance; he offers him dates, an act which gives an assurance of amity. With these as if with sureties, the little man offers a token of peace; his sympathy proves him human, his gifts prove him kind.

The old man stands still; he plants his feet on the ground. He strives to learn who that person is. The creature proceeds to reply thus: "The one who gives being to creatures under fixed laws according to his will and rules those governed, regulating them by virtue of his power, freely gave being to me and provides for me by command of his goodness. He gives me enough; I abound in cherished possessions. I am governed by the laws I have been given. I owe my origin to the fates, for truly, seers gape at these things with insatiable jaws. Simple, common folk call me a satyr, and often entreat me with prayer. They bow their heads; they worship me and call me a god. They fear, revere, honor, need, implore me, give gifts and strive to please me. If they have a petition to make, immediately they bedew the earth with blood. They know not to whom they make offerings; they know not to whom they bow down to worship. And this happens, which is of more importance: the thief's daring takes flight, because he believes that sheepfolds in the country are under my power. Hence the band of shepherds serves me, giving me the care of their flocks, as if I am their entire hope.

Faunus amans nemorum dicor; vocor incubus; horum
sors mihi verborum provenit ab omine morum.
Me grex faunorum mittit, legatio quorum
est mihi multorum famulanti causa laborum,
Regi communi cui cuncti subdimur uni
commendans: 'Uni nos foedere paceque muni!'
Immo tua fretos prece reddat pace quietos
Christus; et hac laetos repleat foveatque repletos,
quem caelum, quem terra tremit, quem pace retenta
laudant, magnificant, dum lite carent, elementa.
Quis caelum, terram, quis fecit cetera? Christus.
Quis solo nutu tenet et regit omnia? Christus.
Quis bonitate sua nutrit viventia? Christus.
Ergo Deus rerum monstratur in ordine Christus.
Esse Deum verum scio, quem concordia rerum
quemque fatetur Erum mora noctis luxque dierum."
Dixerat, at senior de Christi nomine laetus
sic ait, ubertim fundens quasi flumina fletus:
"Heheu, quam caecos habet Alexandria cives,
in qua daemoniis servit cum paupere dives!
O gens infelix, quae gaudet in ordine tristi,
dum sibi laus Satanae placet et blasphemia Christi!
Tristibus applaudit et deflet laeta; cavenda
quaerit et haec refugit quae iure fuere petenda.
O locus infandus! O gens rudis! O fugiendus
ritus, quo fugitur blasphematurque colendus!
Idola caeca colunt. Cur? Nam caecantur et ipsi.

"I am called a faun, a lover of groves. I am called an incubus. These names are allotted to me based on the tokens of my behavior. The herd of fauns sends me on a mission—a delegation that is for me, in their service, a cause of many hardships—with a message to the universal King to whom alone we are all subject: 'Unite us in a truce and fortify us with peace!' Or rather, may Christ, for our trust in your prayers, grant us contentment in peace; may he fill us with this peace in our joy, and may he watch over us when we are filled, for before him heaven and earth tremble; him the elements, in the security of peace, praise and glorify as free from strife. Who made heaven, earth, and everything else? Christ. Who controls and rules everything by his will alone? Christ. Who sustains living things by his goodness? Christ. Thus, in the order of things Christ is shown to be God. I know him to be the true God, whom the harmony of the world and the length of night and light of day acknowledge as Lord."

He had spoken, but the old man, made joyous by the name of Christ, spoke as follows, while copiously pouring forth almost rivers of tears: "Ah! Alas! How blind are the citizens of Alexandria, where rich man and poor man alike serve evil spirits! Oh unfortunate race, that rejoices in a wretched way of life, taking pleasure in the praise of Satan and blasphemy of Christ! This people rejoices in misery and laments happiness; it seeks out things that should be avoided and shrinks from what should rightly be sought. Oh unspeakable place! Oh ignorant race! Oh religious practice truly to be shunned, by which he who should be worshipped is shunned and reviled! They worship blind idols. Why? Because they are blind themselves. They are obtuse. For what

Sunt hebetes. Quare? Quia mens caligat eclipsi.
Non radiat ratio. Cur? Lumen abest rationis.
Obstat namque sibi caligo superstitionis;
soli iustitiae nequeunt tenebrae sociari;
debet amans tenebras uri, non irradiari.
Quique volens patitur vel neglegit interiores,
ut per eas pereat, pertransit ad exteriores.
Has adeunt et in his pereunt qui, lumine spreto,
non obeunt, non intereunt, nisi duplice leto.
Prima brevis mors illa levis, sed posteriori
qui moritur, moriens oritur superestque dolori.
Deficiens, mortem sitiens, moriendo novatur;
sic ad idem redit ille quidem ne non moriatur.
Quam miser est qui sic superest, qui sic reparatur!
More rei mors finis ei, nec ut interimatur.
Mors miseri sine morte teri finis; cruciatur
fine carens, mortisque parens, in vita moratur.
Quos immortales colis, Alexandria, divos
mors aeterna tenet semperque terit redivivos
horum cultores; mors excipit ut crucientur.
Hisque tuos socias quo morti participentur.
Ecce ferae Christum Dominumque Deumque fatentur;
quemque tui cives contemnunt hae reverentur.
Et quid ad haec dices cum te damnare videntur
bruta, deique tui sine fine perire docentur?
Vae tibi! Vae meretrix, cui falli daemonis astu
cuique placet Dominum tanto contemnere fastu!"
Vix ea cum petulans aufugit bestia. Cursum
miratur senior; hinc arripitur via rursum.

reason? Because their mind is groping in gloom. Reason does not shine in them. Why? They lack the light of reason. For truly, the darkness of superstition shuts them off; darkness cannot be associated with the sun of justice. One who loves the darkness ought to be subject to burning, not illumination. And one who willingly endures or disregards inner darkness passes over to an outer darkness, to perish by it. Those draw nigh to this darkness and perish by it, who, having spurned the light, do not die, do not pass away, except by a double death. That first brief death is easy to bear, but one who dies the later death arises in that death and remains alive for affliction. While fainting, while thirsting for death, he is renewed by dying; in this way he returns to the same state so that he does not die. How wretched is the man who survives and is restored in this way! In the nature of things, death is an end for him, but not to destroy him. The wretched man's death, his end, is to be tortured without death; he is tormented without end and lingers in life as an author of death. Alexandria, death everlasting grips the gods whom you worship as undying, and it forever tortures their worshipers in their restored life. Death receives them to be tormented. You ally your people with these gods in their shared death. See, wild beasts acknowledge Christ as Lord and God; whom your citizens despise, they revere. And what will you say to this when dumb animals are seen to condemn you, and your gods are shown to perish forever? Woe to you! Woe, harlot, who take pleasure in being deceived by a demon's cunning and in despising our Lord with such great disdain!"

Antony had scarcely said these words when the unruly beast ran away. The old man marvels at his speed; then he

Post ea lux abiit, vir psallit nocte secuta,
mensque fit interius, fit ab hoste foris caro tuta.
Prospicit, et dubia iam luce subit lupa montem;
cogit anhela sitis vicinum quaerere fontem.
Haec abit; ille specum velox petit. Aspicit intus;
nil videt; ingreditur, sed ei specus est labyrinthus.
In tenebris latebras scrutatur spes senioris,
suspenditque gradus et flatum temperat oris.
Nec spes frustratur; lux cernitur; hic hilarescit,
et prae laetitia currens lassescere nescit.
Currit et offendit. Paulus strepitum pedis audit;
ne pateant aditus festinat et ostia claudit.
Quid, pater Antoni, tua mens cupit, optat, et ardet?
Numquid ad id properas ut cursus vota retardet?
Ecce quod optasti quaeris terrore remoto;
curris ut obtineas; nocet acceleratio voto.
Te fugit hoc quod amas; tu discis Tantalus esse!
Non vis differri, facis hoc properando necesse.
Qui petit hoc avidus quo paenitet abstinuisse,
abstinet invitus, cum contigerit tenuisse,
abstinet ecce tenens. O res gravis est caruisse,
et si sit praesens votum non obtinuisse!
En quem quaesierat iam laetatur reperiri.
Ipse tamen queritur voto non posse potiri.
Corruit ante fores, gemit, orat eas aperiri,
et sibi ni pateant, vult pro foribus sepeliri.
"Pacificis," inquit, "reseratur ianua quaevis;

takes up his journey again. After this, daylight disappears, the man sings psalms as the night comes on, and his mind is safe from within, his flesh from the foe without. He looks out, and now in the twilight a she-wolf approaches the mountain; a panting thirst forces her to seek a nearby spring. She vanishes; he goes swiftly to the cave and peers within. He sees nothing; he enters, but to him the cave is a maze. In the darkness, the old man in hope investigates its recesses. He stays his steps and holds his breath. And his hope is not disappointed. He sees light; he becomes cheerful, and running forward for joy, he does not grow weary. He runs and stumbles. Paul hears the sound of his feet; to close off the entrance, he hurries and shuts the doors.

Father Antony, what does your mind long for, wish for, burn for? Are you really hurrying to slow down the purpose of your journey? See, you are seeking what you wished for, with fear cast aside; you are running to obtain it, but your haste is harming your wishes. What you love is fleeing from you; you are learning to be Tantalus! You do not want to be delayed, but you inevitably cause this by hurrying. One who eagerly seeks what he regrets to be parted from is reluctantly parted when he happens to secure it. See, when he happens to have it, he holds back. Oh, it is a grievous thing to be deprived and not to have obtained a wish, if it is present!

Look! Antony rejoices that the one whom he had sought is now found. Yet he complains that he cannot obtain his wish. He falls down before the doors, he groans, he pleads that they be opened, and if they are not opened for him, he wants to be buried in front of the doors. "Let every door be opened to peacemakers," he says. "The door that is not

mitibus illa patet quae non est pervia saevis.
Si fera forte venit, subit ostia, clamat et audis;
si sit laesa, foves; homo venit et ostia claudis!
Unde, quis, et quare tua quaeram limina nosti.
Porta patere potest, quoniam non clauditur hosti.
Ante tuos postes moriar, nisi quod peto dones,
et solamen erit quod mortua membra repones."
Sic plangente viro iam fluxerat hora diei
sexta, nec ipse tamen tacet indulgens requiei.
Paulus ad haec: "Nemo sic orat ut ipse minetur;
nemo minans plorat, vel terret ut inde precetur.
O nova verba viri! Flet, et ingressum petiturus,
dicit ni reserem quod venerit huc moriturus."
Dixit et arridens pater introitum patefecit.
Hinc avidum Pauli praesentia grata refecit.
Miscent complexus, dant oscula, nomen uterque
alterius profert; satis est res mira superque.
Postquam complexus et amoris cetera signa
sunt data, laus Christo datur et fit gratia digna.
Hospite suscepto Paulus sedet, ora resolvit;
considet ille tacens auditaque mente revolvit.
Tunc pater: "Ecce virum cui vitam postposuisti,
hancque feris, eremo, fervoribus exposuisti.
Est homini macies, est incultum caput isti,
pro quo ferre viae discrimina non renuisti.
Cetera concludam, nec enim placet ista referre.
Hoc solum superest ut reddam terrea terrae.
Sed precor ut narres siquis colat idola vana,

accessible to violent men is open to the meek. If by chance a wild beast comes, approaches the doors, and cries out, you listen. If it is injured, you nurse it. A man comes, and you shut the doors! You know who I am, where I come from, and why I seek your threshold. Your gate can be open, since it is not an enemy it is closed to. I shall die before your doorposts, unless you grant what I ask, and it will be my consolation that you bury my dead limbs."

Now, while the man was lamenting so, the sixth hour of the day had already passed, and yet he is not silent, giving himself over to rest. To these words Paul replies: "No one prays thus in order to threaten; no one weeps while threatening, or frightens in order to entreat. Oh, what strange words the man speaks! He weeps and will seek entry; he says that unless I open the door, he has come here to die." The father said this and, smiling, he opened the entrance. After this, the welcome presence of Paul refreshed the eager visitor. They embrace, they bestow kisses, each says the other's name; it is a quite remarkable event, even beyond remarkable. After embraces and other tokens of love have been bestowed, praise and due thanks are given to Christ.

After he had received his guest, Paul sits down and begins to speak; Antony sits with him in silence and reflects on what he has heard. Then the father says: "Behold the man for whom you have scorned your own life and exposed it to wild beasts, wilderness, and raging heat. This man is wasting away, his head is unkempt, this man for whom you did not hesitate to endure the dangers of a journey. I shall pass over other facts, for it is not my wish to relate them. This alone remains, that I return earthly things to the earth. But I entreat you to tell if anyone now is worshiping vain

praevaleatne fides Christi doctrinaque sana;
quae genus humanum foveat protectio regis;
cuius ad imperium subeant moderamina legis;
si sua tecta novent, nova si sint oppida turbis;
si populo veteris placeat locus et situs urbis."
Dum fovet et stupidum reddit facundia talis,
corvus eis panem pernicibus advehit alis.
Tunc pater: "En nobis dat Christi gratia victum;
in se sperantem probat haec non esse relictum.
Anni ter deni bis praeteriere quod harum
et datur et reficit me copia deliciarum.
Fracti cotidie me panis portio pavit.
Integer est. Nobis Deus annonam duplicavit.
Providet ille suis, qui prandia nostra paravit.
Quam bonus et pius est! Haec praesens esca probavit!"
Dixerat; hinc ambo laudant dantemque datumque,
inque Dei laudem devotio mandat utrumque.
Fons erat admittens patulo spiramina divo;
pulchra loco facies, illimi gratia rivo.
Qui dat aquas recipit, qui fundit sorbet agellus,
et parit eructans quas ebibit arida tellus.
Palma secus fontem viret et loca reddit amoena.
Omnia delectant: fons, arbor, et aura serena.
Paulus eo veniens socio comitante resedit.
Orat uterque cibum frangi sed neuter oboedit.
Alterius meritis subiectio mutua cedit,
longaque lis oritur, nam lux cum lite recedit.
Ob foedus mite contendunt Israelitae
quod parit emeritae pax et concordia vitae.

idols, or if the faith of Christ and his sound teaching prevail. Tell what king's protection sustains the human race; to whose sway the government of law submits. Tell if dwellings are being built anew, if there are new towns for the multitudes, if the location and site of the old city are pleasing to people."

While such eloquence is comforting Antony and amazing him, a raven brings bread to them on swift wings. Then the father says: "Look! The grace of Christ is giving us food; this shows that one who hopes in him is not forsaken. For sixty years now, the fullness of these delights has been given to me and has refreshed me. A piece of broken bread has fed me every day. This loaf is whole. God has doubled the supply for us. He who has provided our meal takes care of his own. How good and gracious he is! This food before us has proved it!" He said these words; then both men praise the Giver and the gift, and their zeal prompts each to praise God.

There was a spring there sending its vapors into the expanse of heaven; the pleasing place with its pure stream had a lovely appearance. A little field which produces and pours forth the waters receives them again and reabsorbs them; the dry earth drinks up the waters which it disgorges forth. Beside the spring a green palm tree grows and makes the place pleasant. All are charming: the spring, the tree, and the fair breeze. Coming there with his companion, Paul sat down. Each one asks that the bread be broken, but neither obeys. The mutual submissiveness of each yields to the merits of the other, and a lengthy dispute arises, for the day departs as the dispute continues. The Israelites gently argue over an agreement that owes its origin to the peace and harmony of a well-lived life. The hermits are their own

Litis finitae testes sibi sunt eremitae.
Pax carnis domitae facit hac contendere lite.
Ne mora sit liti placet unus finis utrique:
distrahitur panis; remanet sua portio cuique.
Sumitur ergo cibus, satiantur eo comedentes,
procumbuntque solo proni de fonte bibentes.
Hinc laudes dantur Domino, grates iterantur,
psalmi cantantur; sic excubiae celebrantur.
Dum pugnant et in his speratur laurea castris,
instat et invigilat nox psalmis, spiritus astris.
Pernoctant vigiles solvuntque Deo vota,
suntque procul somni, procul otia quaeque remota.
Iam parat Oceani Phoebus dimittere portum;
nata prior natu patrium praenuntiat ortum.
Ipse fugans tenebras sequitur vestigia prolis;
haec praeit ut pereat venientis lumine solis.
Iam quod contulerat natae pater abstulit esse.
Coepit ei proles et utrique relatio deesse,
cum pater ista seni: "Mundus secernitur a me,
sicque mihi requiem dant grata silentia Famae.
Haec solet, ut fallat, fictis adiungere facta;
multis plura tamen reticet quandoque coacta.
His invita tacet quorum non est loca nacta;
unde quiete fruor, vitiorum matre subacta.
Sic fit ut a strepitu mundi sit mens mea tuta,
haec mihi dum tacuit, dum non est vana locuta;
quaeque tacere nequit, cui tot sunt ora soluta,
plus monacho didicit servare silentia muta!

witnesses to ending the dispute. The peace that comes from subduing the flesh causes them to contend in this dispute. Lest the dispute be protracted, a single outcome pleases both of them: the bread is pulled apart; each has his own portion. Thus, the food is consumed; they eat it and are satisfied, and they bend down to the ground, drinking from the spring. Then praises are given to the Lord, thanks are repeated, psalms are chanted. In this way their vigils are celebrated. While they fight and hope for victory in this camp, the night presses on and is devoted to psalms, their spirits to the stars. They pass the night awake and fulfill their vows to God; sleep is kept far removed, as is any rest.

Now Phoebus prepares to leave Ocean's haven; before his arrival, his firstborn daughter announces her father's rising. Putting darkness to flight, he follows his offspring's steps; she goes before, to vanish in the light of the approaching sun. Now the father took away the existence he had granted to his daughter. His offspring began to be parted from him, and for both the relationship was ended, when Father Paul said these words to the old man: "The world is cut off from me, and thus the welcome stilling of Rumor grants me repose. Rumor is wont to join facts to fictions in order to deceive; yet sometimes, under constraint, for many she keeps quiet about numerous things. However unwillingly, she is silent about those whose locations she has not penetrated to. Hence I enjoy a quiet life, having conquered the mother of vices. Thus it happens that my mind is safe from the world's uproar, while Rumor has kept silent about me, while she has uttered no empty words; though she cannot be silent, and has so many open mouths, she has learned to keep silence, more mute than a monk! By fleeing, I have kept her

Quam quoniam fugiens ne posset obesse removi.
Absens quae celat, quasi sint praesentia novi.
Te novi dudum, Domino mihi notificante;
ipse modo misit mihi quem promiserat ante.
Vita brevis superest, labor exiguus mihi restat;
spem mihi finitus labor et spes gaudia praestat.
Spe fiunt tuti, Christum patiendo secuti,
quorum cura cuti nocet invigilatque saluti;
quorum mens inhiat superis, et fomite nullo
est blandita suo carnis corruptio pullo;
quorum iumento faenum datur; haecque retento
omni momento residens caret impedimento.
Iam frenata diu non nostra repellit asella.
Spem parit emerito parens caro victaque bella;
emerito finis superest finique corona.
Imminet hic, datur haec; teneo caelestia dona.
Detur imago Deo, caro terrae, mens requiei
pugnanti finis, vincenti palma trophaei,
succedatque spei res: optatae specie
visio grata Dei, requies anni iubilaei.
Ut mundo cessi, pia semina pectore pressi;
nunc satio messi, lucror ex his quae bene gessi.
Mundo subductus tolero ieiunia, luctus;
uber aquae ductus rigat hos quos colligo fructus.
Terga premens asinae nec lora sinens fore laxa,
accipit irriguum quod suspirans petit Axa.
Dat geminum pater irriguum post arida culta,
terraque cultori respondens dat sata multa.

away, so she cannot obstruct me. Though absent, I know things that she hides as if they were present. I have long known about you, for the Lord has made you known to me. Now he has sent to me the one he had previously promised.

"A short life is left to me, little hardship remains; the end of hardship offers me hope, and hope offers joys. Those whose concern is to mortify the flesh and to devote themselves to salvation, in their hope find safety, following Christ in their suffering; their mind longs for things above, and the corruption of the flesh does not coax their young with any incitement, but their draft animals are given hay. At rest, with all motion held in check, their mind is without hindrance. Now long bridled, the little ass does not spurn our commands. Obedient flesh and successfully waged wars beget hope for the veteran soldier. For this veteran, the end is still to come, and, at that end, a crown. The end is near, the crown is given; I grasp the gifts of heaven. Let my image be given to God, my flesh to the earth, my mind to rest; let there be an end to the fight, a palm of triumph to the victor, and may the reality conform to my hope: the welcome sight of God, a much-longed-for vision, and the repose of the jubilee year.

"When I withdrew from the world, I planted pious seeds in my heart; now is the time to reap the harvest. I profit from all I have done well. Removed from the world, I endure fasts and afflictions; a copious stream of water irrigates these fruits that I gather. While sitting on her she-ass's back and not allowing the reins to be slack, Axa receives the watered land for which, sighing, she asks. Her father gives her two well-watered lands in place of dry fields, and the earth, in response to its cultivator, yields many crops.

Haec igitur purgans probet, opto, mystica vannus
cum mansura quies iubilaeus venerit annus.
Quid moror et longum decanto celeuma viator,
cum prope sit meta, data porrigat ipse Vocator?
Finis adest vitae, vetor ergo plura referre.
Scito quid incumbit tibi: terram reddere terrae.
Missus es ut dones supremo corpus honore;
qui te misit, erit merces hoc digna labore."
Haec pater. Hospes ad haec flet, plangit, eumque precatur
ut suus in tali comes esse via mereatur.
Ille: "Quid haec quaeris quae sunt tua, quod prohiberis?
Cum profectus eris, conservis compatieris?
Carne quidem posita Christo cupis associari;
sed decet hoc alios ut te possint imitari.
Doneris ergo bonum tibi nunc in carne morari,
ut possis meritis multorum participari.
Sed ne distuleris concedere quod peto munus,
supremoque meum dones hoc munere funus
quod dedit antistes Athanasius. Hoc mihi dones
palliolum; placet hoc; in eo mea membra repones.
Ergo monasterium pete, defer id, atque redito.
Mortuus ut fuero mox corpus in hoc sepelito."
Cur, pater Antoni, cur mitteris? An sibi pulchrum
quod prius horruerat tegmen petit atque sepulcrum?
Cum palmae foliis vir vivens indueretur,
cur sibi defuncto vestis rogat illa paretur?
Quod iam damnarant spatularum tegmina dura,
si corpus nudum putrefiat, quae sibi cura?
Nulla quidem! Labor ergo tuus cur quaeritur audi:
simplex ille novae quaerit molimina fraudi;

And thus, I pray, may the mystical winnowing-fan by the act of purging commend these crops, when the jubilee year comes with its everlasting repose. Why do I delay on my journey, and give voice to a long refrain, when the goal is near, when the Caller grants his gifts? The end of my life is at hand, and so I am forbidden to recount more. Know what role falls to you: to return earth to earth. You have been sent to confer the final honor on my body; the one who sent you will be your worthy reward for this task."

The father spoke these words, at which his guest weeps, wails, and begs him that he be thought worthy to be his companion on such a journey. He replies: "Why do you seek things that are your own, seeing you are denied? When you depart, will you have pity on your fellow servants? It is true you wish to lay aside your flesh and be united to Christ, but it is right for others to be able to imitate you. Thus, you receive as a blessing now to remain in the flesh, so that you can share in the merits of many. But do not delay in assenting to the service that I request, and bestow on my corpse this final gift which Bishop Athanasius has given you. Give me this cloak as a gift; this is my decision; shroud my limbs in it. Therefore, go to your monastery, bring it, and return. Bury my body in it, as soon as I am dead."

Why, Father Antony, why are you sent off? Does Paul seek for himself the fine covering that he had shunned before, and a handsome tomb? Since he, when alive, was clothed in palm leaves, why does he ask that this garment be procured for him when he is deceased? If the naked body putrefies, which now a rough covering of palm branches chafes, what does he care? Nothing, certainly! So, hear why your labor is requested. That guileless man requests your

falleris a Paulo, solatia nunc habuisti.
Mitteris ut pereat, id ab ipso promeruisti.
Si quis amore pio calet et tenet hoc quod amatur,
fit nimis immitis qui cogit ut amoveatur.
Vix tenet hic quod amat, et amatus abire precatur.
Hunc ita cogit amor ut non quod amat teneatur.
Num Pauli pietas subito mutata probatur,
qui prece cogit eum ne quod cupit hoc potiatur?
Absit id a Paulo ferus ut sit vel videatur,
cui pro perfecta pietate corona paratur.
Ergo fit huic pia fraus dum visio grata negatur,
nam moriente viro dolor absenti leviatur.
Quod suadet pietas fit, nam pius hospes oboedit.
Dum licet hic remanet; Paulus rogat ire; recedit.
Quippe stupens in eo veneratur cuncta videntem,
cum perpendit eum de praesule vera loquentem.
Oscula dans oculis manibusque, silet reverenter.
Exit, abit lacrimans; aestum tolerat patienter.
Cumque labore viae sit et aevi pondere fessus,
ipse tamen multo figit conamine gressus,
et ne deficiat, aetate gravante senili,
fulcitur baculo foris, intus mente virili.
Mens superat vires; quae nullo victa labore
in duris durat, renovata recente vigore.
Vir remeare volens currit quia flagrat amore.
Est absens corpus, mens cum Paulo seniore.
Viribus absumptis, sed adhuc redeunte labore;
cella patet, nec ei requies datur unius horae.

efforts for a strange deception. You are deceived by Paul; now you have received solace. You are sent away so that he may die; this you have deserved from him.

If someone is inflamed with pious love and clings to what is loved, anyone who compels his removal becomes exceedingly harsh. Antony has scarcely secured what he loves, and the beloved begs him to depart. So love compels him not to hold on to what he loves. Is Paul's pious love found to be suddenly changed, who compels Antony through entreaty not to possess what he desires? Far be it from Paul, for whom a crown is prepared for his perfect piety, to be or seem cruel. Thus, a pious deception is perpetrated on Antony in denying him the pleasing sight of Paul, for grief at a death is alleviated when one is absent. What piety persuades comes about, for the pious guest obeys. While it is allowed, Antony stays. Paul asks him to go; he departs. For, astonished at that injunction, Antony reveres Paul as all-seeing, since he thinks he is speaking the truth about the bishop.

Bestowing kisses on Paul's eyes and hands, he remains reverently silent. He leaves, he goes away weeping, he endures the heat with patience. And although he is worn out by the hardship of the journey and the burden of age, he directs his steps, though with much effort, and so as not to fail, as old age weighs him down, he is supported by a staff externally, by a manly soul within. His soul outdoes his physical strength; overcome by no toil, it endures in hardships, restored with fresh vitality. Wishing to return, Antony hurries on, because he burns with love. His body is absent, but his soul is with the aged Paul. His strength is spent, but his toil returns afresh; his cell stands open, but not a single

Illius adventum duo fratres opperiuntur;
occurrunt viso, tarde venire queruntur.
Hic gemit et gemitum suspiria crebra sequuntur.
Vir tacet haecque virum vidisse stupenda loquuntur.
Instant discipuli; silet hic et verba petuntur;
os aperit, verba singultibus impediuntur.
Vocis iter medium praecluditur, hocque negato
syncopat ipse sonum verbo vix dimidiato.
Nititur inde loqui sed oberrat lingua palato,
quaeque sonum tacuit profert repetens iterato.
Qui latet interius dolor occupat ora loquentis,
editus exterius sonus exprimit intima mentis.
Mens dolet uberius quo fit vox cassa dolentis;
lingua labat levius quo mens tegitur patientis.
Plus dolor occultus, tectus plus aestuat ignis;
Hoc patet, hoc certis probat experientia signis.
Hinc dum cura latens gravat, ipsa loquela negatur;
dum non erumpit per verba, magis cumulatur.
Vox praeclusa redit singultus ut ille recedit;
quod mentem laedit denudat et haec pater edit:
"Vae mihi, cui sine re monachi scio nomen adesse!
Cum desit meritum, nomen mihi constat abesse.
Me fateor monachum cultu, non moribus, esse;
quo careo, monacho magis expedit estque necesse.
Heu, quam dissimilis sum Paulo dogmate, vita!
Instruit exemplo vitae nos hic eremita.
Sero mihi notus, cito linquitur unicus ille,

hour's rest is granted to him. Two brothers are awaiting his arrival. When they see him, they run to him and complain that he is late arriving. He groans, and repeated sighs follow the groaning. The man is silent, but these sighs tell that the man has seen wonders.

His disciples press him with questions, but Antony is silent; yet they ask for words. He opens his mouth, but his words are stifled by sobs. His voice is cut off in midspeech, and when speech fails him, he cuts short the sound and with difficulty pronounces only half words. Then he strives to speak, but his tongue strays onto the roof of his mouth, and after producing no sound, it produces a sound repeatedly. The sorrow that is concealed within invades the speaker's voice; the sound he makes outwardly expresses the innermost sentiments of his soul. His soul grieves the more copiously, the more ineffective the grieving man's voice becomes. His tongue wavers, and so his mind is concealed. The more his grief is concealed, the more the hidden fire burns. This is evident; experience proves this by clear signs. Accordingly, while hidden care weighs heavy on him, speech itself fails; while it does not burst forth in words, care mounts up the more. The stopped voice returns as this sobbing recedes; the father lays bare what wounds his soul, and utters the following words:

"Ah me! I know that baselessly I have the title of a monk. Since merit is wanting, it is clear that the name does not belong to me. I confess that I am a monk in appearance, not in character; what I lack is especially useful and necessary for a monk. Oh, how unlike Paul I am in learning and in life! This hermit teaches us by the example of his life. That singular man became known to me too late and is taken away too

quem non laudo satis, si linguis effero mille.
Alter hic Elias heresque Iohannis; utrique
participat, consors vitae, morum, meritique.
Hunc paradisus habet, immo vir habet paradisum,
quo veniens sero vidi; liqui cito visum!"
Haec pater, atque manu tacitus sua pectora tundit.
Sunt animi testes gemitus quos pectore fundit.
Palliolum profert, exit, cellamque relinquit.
Instant discipuli; narrare rogant, pater inquit,
"Tempora temperiem verbis imponere debent;
ipsa quidem cautis dant verba; silentia praebent.
Ergo qui callet, sapit, et regitur ratione,
temporis haec variat motu, vice, conditione."
Dixerat. Aggreditur iter, illi digrediuntur.
Paulus ab hoc petitur, sed ab illis claustra petuntur.
It pater esuriens nec id optat quod comedatur,
huius enim patiens cupit id quo mens satiatur,
et cum ieiunans caro marceat et minuatur,
ipsa fames Pauli desiderio superatur.
Cogit id e cella ieiunus ut egrediatur;
sic fit ut ipsa fames, relevata fame, satiatur.
Alterius lux et radius micat ecce diei,
virque pius repetit citius metam requiei.
Iam poterat quod restiterat peragi tribus horis;
affuerat requies et erat mora parva laboris,
cum subitum pater intuitum defigit in astra.
Post obitum Paulum positum videt in nova castra;
emicuit clarusque fuit, radiante nitore.
Hoc meruit dum se studuit macerare labore.

quickly, whom I do not praise enough if I extol him with a thousand tongues. He is another Elijah and an heir of John; he is a partner of both, a sharer in their life, their character, and their merit. Paradise possesses him, or rather, the man possesses paradise. Coming to him late, I saw him; but after seeing him, I soon left him!"

The father says these words, and then in silence beats his breast with his fist. The sighs that he pours forth from his breast are witnesses of his soul. He brings forth the cloak, he departs, he leaves his cell. His disciples press him; they beg him to tell the story, but the father says, "The times must impose temperance on our words; they provide cautious men with words; they prompt silence. Therefore, one who is experienced, wise, and ruled by reason varies his words according to the impulse, situation, and nature of the times." He had spoken. He sets out on his journey, and they go their way. He goes to Paul, but they to their cells. The father proceeds, hungry and yet not wishing for anything to eat, for his suffering soul seeks that which satisfies the soul, and although his fasting flesh is weak and wasted, his hunger is overcome by his longing for Paul. That forces the fasting man to go forth from his cell; in this way it comes about that his hunger is satisfied, its pangs relieved.

Behold, the light and sunbeams of another day shine forth, and the pious man quickly seeks again his restful goal. Now in three hours what remained of the journey could be completed. Rest was at hand and there was a small pause in his struggles, when the father suddenly fixes his gaze on the stars. He sees Paul established after his death in the New City; he shone and was bright in radiant splendor. This he earned in striving to wear himself down with suffering. With

Cum superis abit innumeris ad regna polorum;
huius eris par si fueris consors meritorum.
Ut patris agnitus est sibi transitus atque trophaeum,
scit quia caelitus intrat hic inditus ad iubilaeum.
Mens tamen anxia flet sibi gaudia tanta negari
Fataque segnia fila tenacia nendo morari.
Fit gravis haec mora longaque tempora; nec valet horum
pellere taedia, nec sibi gratia grata sororum.
Dum vacat ultima fit sibi pessima; dum miseretur
parcere nescia; dum sibi fit pia saeva videtur.
Foedere fit fera, quae nisi foedera forte dedisset,
ad nova munera iam super aethera vir pius isset.
Iam patris istius ipse comes pius astra subisset,
quo nihil amplius aut sibi gratius ipse petisset!
Quod nunc Fata negant se sperat adhuc habiturum,
nam mora quod differt cum morte scit esse futurum.
Et quoniam senium cito spondet eum moriturum,
ipsum meta iuvat, nec credit iter breve durum.
Qui cupit esse comes heres succedit et unus;
linquitur huic uni morientis munera funus.
Esset ei potius comitari funera munus,
sed quia Fatorum rigor inconcussus habetur,
non prece, non pretio, quod proponunt inhibetur.
Hinc quod nec Paulus prece nec lacrimis retinetur,
nec valet iste sequi nec cum volet ipse sequetur.
Quod valet ergo patri supremum donat honorem,

countless numbers of those dwelling on high, he departs to the realms of the heavens. You will be his equal if you are the equal of his merits.

As Antony perceives the father's passing and his victory, he knows that by divine authority Paul enters there, summoned to the jubilee year. Yet his distressed soul laments that such great joys are denied to him, and that the stubborn Fates tarry in weaving their binding threads. This delay becomes burdensome and the time long; he cannot drive away its tedium, and he is not grateful for the sisters' period of grace. While the last of the Fates is idle, she becomes the worst for him; while she shows pity, she is incapable of sparing; while she is kind to him, she seems savage. By this pact she becomes cruel, for if she had not granted the pact, that holy man would have already gone to new rewards above the heavens. He would have already ascended to the stars as the pious companion of that father. He would have sought nothing better or more pleasing to him than this!

What the Fates now deny, Antony hopes that he will yet have, for what delay defers, he knows will come with his death. And since old age promises that he will die soon, that end point pleases him, and he does not believe the journey, short as it is, will be hard. The one who wishes to be his companion succeeds him as sole heir; to him alone are left the funeral rites, the duty owed to the dying. He would rather his role was to share in the funeral, but since the inflexibility of the Fates is preserved unshaken, what they dispose is swayed by neither prayer nor price. Thus it is that Paul is detained by neither prayer nor tears, and Antony cannot follow nor will he follow him when he wishes. And so, he gives to the father what he can: the final rites.

donat honore patrem, solvens in funere morem.
Cor gemitum dat et os planctus oculique fluorem;
nec satis est clausum sic expressisse dolorem;
currit ut hunc videat. Lenit dolor ipse laborem.
Currit ut credas avibus vel equis leviorem.
Iure, pater, curris visuque cupis satiari;
hoc etenim quaeris, scis cetera quaeque negari.
Iure videre cupis quem cum Domino dominari,
conregnare Deo scis, ipsi participari.
Iure sibi vivens moriensque cupis sociari,
quem vitae merito scis mortis fine beari;
cernere gaudet amans quod ab ipso constat amari.
Ecce dolet cernens sed spes facit exhilarari,
nam videt hunc genibus flexis ex more morari,
erecta cervice, Deum manibusque precari.
Ac primo sperans precibus lacrimisque vacantem
orat, id assimilans quod cernit eum simulantem.
Ut non audit eum solito suspiria dantem,
comperit exanimem gestu caelis inhiantem.
Hinc igitur pacem dans oscula sumit et offert
palliolumque patri dat ut ultima munera profert.
Obvolvit corpus, psalmos iterando revolvit;
taliter exsequiis ea quae sunt debita solvit.
Cum terrae durae desint fossoria iure,
iura sepulturae quae restant sunt sibi curae.
Non ligo conspicitur, non quo fodiat reperitur;
quod superest queritur. Clausus dolor his aperitur:
"Vae mihi! Vae misero! Quae iam solatia spero?

He gives the father honor, paying him the customary rites in burial. His heart offers sighs, his mouth lamentations, and his eyes flowing tears. Nor is it enough to have expressed his hidden sorrow in this way; he hurries to see him. Sorrow itself alleviates his hardship. He runs so fast that you would believe him swifter than birds and horses. Justly do you run, Father, and wish to be sated by the sight of him; truly you seek this, since you know that everything else is denied you. Justly do you wish to see him whom you know has dominion with the Lord, who rules with God, who shares his role. Justly do you wish to be united, in life and death, with him whom you know to be blessed because of the merit of his life in the final hour of death. The lover rejoices to see it confirmed that he is loved by his beloved.

Behold, in looking at him, Antony grieves, but hope cheers him, for he sees Paul still on bended knees as was his custom, with his neck upright and hands uplifted to God in prayer. Hoping, at first, that Paul was devoting himself to prayers and tears, he prays, imitating what he sees Paul apparently doing. When he does not hear him heaving sighs in his usual way, Antony discovers that he is dead, but still in the attitude of longingly gazing at heaven. And so, as he carries out the last offices, he gives and receives the kiss of peace, and bestows the cloak on the father. He wraps the body; he recites and repeats the psalms. With these rites he performs what is due. Since tools for digging the hard ground are of course lacking, the remaining rites of burial are a concern to him. He sees no hoe; he finds nothing with which to dig; he follows his only recourse: he laments. His hidden grief is revealed with the following words: "Ah, me! Ah, wretched man! For what solace do I now hope? If I seek

Non rediturus ero si cellae limina quaero;
nil faciam remanens et deficiam proficiscens.
Est mora nostra vacans. Pergam? Remanebo fatiscens?
Est ignava quies, labor intolerabilis; horum
sit mors nostra precor medium finisque duorum!"
Vix ea cum geminos videt ipse venire leones,
quos eremi vastae sibi transmittunt regiones.
Immo sui Deus athletae miseratus agones.
Est frons torva feris, iuba crispans, atque patentes
rictus ostendunt uncos ex ordine dentes.
Scintillant oculi quos obliquant venientes.
Exterrere queunt ungues et cauda videntes
motibus innatis; rugitibus immoderatis
panditur elatis minus innatum pietatis.
Haec et plura satis dant signa suae feritatis,
quae ponunt gratis nutu summae Deitatis.
Qui prius horruerat gelido sudore solutus,
haerens mente Deo videt hos accedere tutus;
accedunt Paulique petunt vestigia proni.
Rugit uterque iacens, quasi mens humana leoni;
haec de morte boni ceu nenia facta patroni;
plangit supponi necis illum conditioni.
Nec satis est illis hunc exsequiis dare planctum
sed foveam faciunt ubi vix queat abdere sanctum.
Post opus expletum Pauli successor aditur;
lingua dat obsequium quo pesque manusque potitur;
quod lingendo petunt benedictio dat senioris.
Annuit et redeunt sumpta mercede laboris.
Hinc humeros curvat, hinc temptat onus leve ferre.

out the entrance of my cell, I shall not return here. Remaining here, I shall do nothing, and departing, I shall be at a loss. My tarrying here is futile. Shall I go? Shall I remain, progressively enfeebled? Rest is unavailing, toil is intolerable. May my death, I pray, be the mediator and the end of both of these!"

Scarcely had he spoken these words when he sees two lions approaching, which the vast tracts of desert are directing to him, or rather, God in pity for the struggles of his athlete. The wild beasts have fierce faces and flowing manes, and their open jaws expose a row of curved teeth. Their eyes, which they turn aside as they approach, are flashing. Their claws and tails, with their natural movements, can terrify those who see them. In their unrestrained roaring, when raised aloud, is displayed an innate lack of mercy. These and more give signs enough of their ferocity, which they freely set aside at the command of the supreme Deity. Antony, who had previously shuddered, bathed in cold sweat, by clinging to God in his soul, confidently watches them approach; they approach and go directly to the feet of Paul, lying before him. Each one lies down and roars, as if a lion had a human mind, as if this was a dirge raised because of a good patron's death; each laments that Paul is subject to the terms of death. And it is not enough for them to offer this lament for his obsequies, but they make a pit where Antony can eventually bury the saint. After the lions' task is finished, they approach Paul's successor. Their tongue renders the service that foot and hand achieve; the old man's blessing grants what they seek by their licking. He nods approval, and they go back, having received the reward of their labor. Then Antony stoops his shoulders, he tries to take up the

Depositum tumulo condit; dat terrea terrae.
Ut Parcae Pauli vacuarunt stamine fusum,
res intestati cedunt heredis in usum.
Cumque relicta sibi videt ipse sui fore iuris,
eligit excipiens unumque, quod est sibi pluris,
vindicat, et manibus exponit cetera furis.
Vestis erat quam texuerat Pauli manus alma;
contulerat quae nutrierat sibi stamina palma.
Vindicat hanc heres quasi pignus habens pretiosum;
et merito decet illa virum tam deliciosum!
Ut redit ad cellam, patris illuc pignora defert;
tegmina purpureis sportam simulantia praefert.
Induitur tantum festis hac veste diebus
ut sit onus sanctum terrenis gloria rebus.
Narrat discipulis Pauli vitam meritumque.
Hic unum laudat; nos collaudemus utrumque.

light burden. He consigns to the grave what has been entrusted to him; he gives earthly remains to the earth.

As the Fates clear their spindle of Paul's thread, they hand over the intestate man's possessions to the use of his heir. When Antony sees that what Paul left to him will be his to dispose of, in receiving that bequest he chooses and claims one thing that is of more value to him, but leaves the rest exposed to the hands of a thief. There was a garment which the blessed hand of Paul had woven; he had gathered the strands that a palm tree had produced for him. His heir claims this, considering it a precious relic; and it justly becomes a man so luxury loving! As he returns to his cell, he brings there the father's relics; he prefers to purple garments these coverings made like a basket. Antony wears this garment only on feast days, so that glory in earthly things might be a holy burden. He tells his disciples about the life and worth of Paul. He praises him alone; let us praise both men together.

Abbreviations

AH = Clemens Blume and Guido M. Dreves, eds., *Analecta Hymnica,* 55 vols. (Leipzig, 1886–1922)

BHL = *Bibliotheca hagiographica latina antiquae et mediae aetatis,* 2 vols. (Brussels, 1898–1901)

CSEL = *Corpus scriptorum ecclesiasticorum latinorum,* 106 vols. (Vienna, 1864–)

DMLBS = R. K. Ashdowne, D. R. Howlett, and R. E. Latham, eds., *Dictionary of Medieval Latin from British Sources,* 3 vols. (Oxford, 2018)

OLD = P. G. W. Glare, ed., *Oxford Latin Dictionary,* 2nd ed., 2 vols. (Oxford, 2012)

PL = J.-P. Migne, ed., *Patrologiae cursus completus: Series latina,* 217 vols. (Paris, 1844–1855)

TLL = *Thesaurus linguae latinae* (Leipzig, 1900–)

TPMA = Samuel Singer, ed., *Thesaurus proverbiorum medii aevi: Lexikon der Sprichwörter des romanisch-germanischen Mittelalters,* 13 vols. (Berlin, 1995–2002)

Note on the Texts

Miracles of the Virgin

The edition follows the sole complete witness, London, British Library, MS Cotton Vespasian D. xix (late twelfth or early thirteenth century). It takes into account London, British Library, MS Arundel 23 (late fifteenth century), the only other manuscript to transmit even a single miracle. In addition, it refers to the *editio princeps* (Jan M. Ziolkowski, ed., *Miracles of the Virgin Mary, in Verse: Miracula sancte Dei genitricis virginis Marie, versifice,* Toronto Medieval Latin Texts 17 [Toronto, 1986]), two editions by others of single miracles, and two reviews of that edition which considered manuscript readings and offered textual criticism.

Cotton Vespasian D. xix presents a treasure trove of Nigel's poetry, with his epigrams, the *Miracles of the Virgin, The Passion of Saint Lawrence,* and *The Life of Saint Paul, the First Hermit.* Although closely associated with the poet's monastic house in Canterbury, it contains too many errors to be considered an autograph, contrary to the suggestion of John H. Mozley and Robert R. Raymo in their edition of *The Mirror of Fools:* Nigel de Longchamps, *Speculum stultorum* (Berkeley, 1960), 123. That said, it may have received polishing here and there from the author in both his *textura* and his cursive hands. (On hands in Vespasian D. xix, see Jan M. Ziolkowski, ed. and trans., *The Passion of St. Lawrence, Epigrams, and Marginal Poems* [Leiden, 1994], 43–49.) The rubric headings, which may not have been supplied by the author, have been retained. They were often marginal and have suffered damage from such vulnerable placement. When complete loss has occurred, headings have been supplied from the corresponding miracle in the standard edition of William of Malmesbury, but for the record these are not medieval but the creation of the editors: Rodney M. Thomson and Michael Winterbottom, eds. and trans., *The Miracles of the Blessed Virgin Mary* (Woodbridge, UK, 2015).

The contents of Arundel 23 hint at a connection with Christ Church: it contains a Nigel-heavy miscellany of Latin verse, with his *Speculum stultorum,* a *Vita Eustachii* that has been sometimes ascribed to him, his metrical list of the archbishops of Canterbury, and the text of Nigel's twelfth miracle. See John H. Mozley, "On the Text of the *Speculum stultorum,*" *Speculum* 4 (1929): 430–42, at 431, and David Carlson, review of *Miracles of the Virgin Mary, in Verse: Miracula sancte Dei genitrices virginis Marie, versifice,* by Nigel of Canterbury, ed. Jan M. Ziolkowski, *Speculum* 64 (1989): 475–77, at 476.

Manuscripts

A = London, British Library, MS Arundel 23, fol. 67r

C = London, British Library, MS Cotton Vespasian D. xix, fols. 5r^{I}–24v^{I}

Editions

B = André Boutemy, ed., *Nigellus de Longchamp dit Wireker: Introduction; "Tractatus contra curiales et officiales clericos"* (Paris, 1959), 256–60 (edition of lines 1749–932)

G = Albert Gier, *Der Sünder als Beispiel: Zu Gestalt und Funktion hagiographischer Gebrauchstexte anhand der Theophiluslegende,* Bonner romanistische Arbeiten 1 (Frankfurt am Main, 1977), 348–54 (edition of lines 37–340)

Z = This edition

Z[1] = Jan M. Ziolkowski, ed., *Miracles of the Virgin Mary, in Verse: Miracula sancte Dei genitricis virginis Marie, versifice,* by Nigel of Canterbury, Toronto Medieval Latin Texts 17 (Toronto, 1986)

Reviews

H = J. B. Hall, "Notes on the 'Miracula sancte Dei genitricis virginis Marie, versifice' of Nigellus de Longo Campo," *Studi Medievali* series 3, vol. 29 (1988): 423–43

K = Thomas Klein, review of Ziolkowski, *Miracles, Mittellateinisches Jahrbuch* 26 (1991): 329–31

Tract on Abuses

The Latin text of Nigel of Canterbury's *Tract* printed here is adapted from the critical edition of André Boutemy, ed., *Nigellus de Longchamp dit Wireker: Introduction; "Tractatus contra curiales et officiales clericos"* (Paris, 1959). The editor based the text principally on Cambridge, Gonville and Caius College, MS 427 (late twelfth to early thirteenth century), occasionally supplemented by London, British Library, MS Cotton

Cleopatra B. iii (thirteenth century) and Cambridge, Corpus Christi College, MS 441 (thirteenth century). The Gonville and Caius manuscript exhibits abundant erasures, corrections, and marginal notations. Boutemy concluded that this manuscript was an autograph, a view endorsed by Jan M. Ziolkowski. The alterations made to this base edition are chiefly corrections of misprints, acceptance of variants warranted by sense and context, and a small number of conjectures; all are recorded in the Notes to the Texts.

Edition

B = André Boutemy, ed., *Nigellus de Longchamp dit Wireker: Introduction; "Tractatus contra curiales et officiales clericos"* (Paris, 1959)

The Life of Saint Paul, the First Hermit

The Latin text of Nigel of Canterbury's *Life of Saint Paul* printed here is adapted from the critical edition of Leo M. Kaiser, "A Critical Edition of Nigel Wireker's *Vita sancti Pauli primi eremitae*," *Classical Folia* 14 (1960): 63–81. Kaiser prepared the text "from photostats" of the sole manuscript in which it survives: British Library, MS Cotton Vespasian D. xix (late twelfth to early thirteenth century), folios 45v–51r. This manuscript contains several other works by Nigel, among them the *Miracles of the Virgin* included in this volume. Jan M. Ziolkowski has argued convincingly that Nigel of Canterbury supervised the production of this manuscript and made corrections to the text in his own hand. Kaiser also consulted the earlier edition of André Boutemy, "Une vie inédite de Paul de Thèbes par Nigellus de Longchamps," *Revue Belge de Philologie et d'Histoire* 10 (1931): 931–63, which he called "an unfortunately hasty piece of work, seriously marred by some three-score errors" (Kaiser, "A Critical Edition," 63). There are, sadly, misprints and errors in Kaiser's text too. These are corrected and reported in the Notes to the Texts, along with some departures from his base edition, made after careful consideration of meter, context, and sense.

Edition

K = Leo M. Kaiser, "A Critical Edition of Nigel Wireker's *Vita sancti Pauli primi eremitae*," *Classical Folia* 14 (1960): 63–81.

Notes to the Texts

Miracles of the Virgin

31 memorem Z^1: memoraem *(with* e *added suprascript) C*

102 leues *corrected from* leuis *C*

110 hec *Z*: hic *C*

116 gignit *G*, Z^1: gingnit *C*

118 nimis *added suprascript above expunged* sitis *C*

157 tenaces *G*, Z^1: tenenaces *C*

184–85 *G conjectures that a distich has been omitted here.*

185 tinea corrumpens *C, G*, Z^1: corrumpens tinea *H, but* tinea *likewise with long first syllable in Passio sancti Laurentii 1223*

188 solet *G*, Z^1: sole *C*

191 tempore *corrected from* tempori *C*

194 que *C*: quo *H*

195 venies *C*, Z^1: veniens *emended G*

197 teritur Z^1: territur *C*

199 Egrescunt *C*: Decrescunt *H*

207 Penitet *C*: percuitet *read G*

210 in lacrimas *H (compare 2376 and Speculum stultorum 1454)*: in lacrimis *C*

parans *C*, Z^1: patans *read G*

214 non *G*, Z^1: no *C*

216 in lacrimis *corrected to* in lacrimas *C*

218 subiungens *C*: *emend to* subiungit?

231 non digne *Z*: condigne *C*

263 Christus veniens *corrected from* veniens Christus *with transposition marks C*

invisere *C*, Z^1: invadere *G*

264 sibi *G*, Z^1: sib *C*

266 tenebras Z^1: tenebris *C*

304 nocte Z^1: noctei C

310 contulit *G*, Z^1: constulit *C*

327 flammis *G*, Z^1: flamis *C*

329 domini corpus *corrected from* corpus domini *with transposition marks C*

333 facie *G*, Z^1: faciie *(with strokes over both* i's*) C*

337 subeunt Z^1: subueunt *C*

345 *C suggests punctuation between* terra *and* favi

382 nova *corrected from* nove *C*

392 premat *corrected from* premet *C*

393 carnis consurgat *corrected from* consurgat carnis *with transposition marks* C

410 videretur *C*: *H suggests emending* metri causa *to* uideatur *despite the matching imperfect subjunctive* obesset *in 409*

414 neuma *Z*: pneuma *C*

423 redisset *H*: venisset *C*

434 personet Z^1: personat *C*

437 tanta Z^1: tantus *C*

442 te *added suprascript with insertion sign C*

443 cecinit *corrected from* cernit *with* i *added suprascript with insertion sign C*

464 certior *Z*: tucior *C*, trucior Z^1, tristior *or* tetrior *H*

483 His placare *corrected by H from* Hoc placare *C*, hoc prosternere *from* hiis prosternere *C*

500 alteruter *Z*: alterutro *C*

utroque modo *C*: uterque *H*

501 auxilium Z^1: axilium *C*

514 madet *(compare 515)* Z^1: manet *C*

515 resonant *C*: resonat *H*

521 soporiferae *H*: soperifero *C*

587 alla *corrected to* allata *C*

619* vetitum *H*: uentum *C*; *after the hexameter comes a signe-de-renvoi* Ø *to signal the pentameter in the left margin, which has been lost almost entirely to trimming*

625 absumptis *C, H*: assumptis Z^1

attenuatis Z^1: atenuatis *C*

636 putant Z^1: putat *C*

647 iniquos *C, H*: utrosque Z^1

660–61 *title omitted C*

669 dogmata Z^1: dogmate *C*

695 producta virgo *corrected from* virgo producta *with suprascript transposition marks C*

727 queramur Z^1: queramus *(perhaps corrected in right margin) C*

729 futile *H*: fictile *C*, Z^1

829 submergerer Z^1: submergeret *C*

841 aspectu Z^1: asspectu *C*

864 negas *Z*: negat *C*, Z^1

866 consona Z^1: cosona *C*

903 nunc *H, C*: nec Z^1

921 voce Z^1: *resembling* uite *or* uice *because of squeezed letters C*

957 fero *K*: fere *C*, Z^1

967 <figu>ris Z^1: ..oris *C*, sub oris *H*

996 quaeve vel: que uel *C*, quene uel *or* queue uel *H; compare 2092*

1006 alta *C, H*: astra Z^1

1007 ebrietatis Z^1: ebritatis *C*

1023 inviolatus *C*: iuiolatus *C*

1024 amore Z^1: amore *C*

1032 inhonestabat Z^1: inhonestatem *C*

1037 claustra *corrected from* castra *with suprascript* clau *C*

1043 animi vires *corrected from* vires animi *with suprascript transposition marks C*

1051 nequibat Z^1: nequiebat *C*

1063 stipite Z^1: stepite *C*

1068 licet Z^1: licet decet *C*

1071 invidet Z^1: iuidet *C*

1077 pedes *added suprascript C*

1102 fratres *H*: fratris *C*

1160 cunctis *Z*: cuntis *C*

1170 ingressa *Z*: ingressam *C*

1208 senum Z^1: saenum *corrected from* sanum *C*

1216 hanc *added suprascript C*

1226 demonis *(added in left margin)* invidia *(final* a *added suprascript)*: angelus inuidie *C*

1233 vetustam *H (but note 1159)*: venustam *C*

1279 probaro Z^I: probarum *C*

1288 predicat *corrected from* predicant *by expunging* n *C*

1312 feta *corrected from* fetu

1314 facta *corrected from* facti

1331 noui iam predampnata *corrected from* iam predampnata noui *with suprascript transposition marks C*

1339 auras *corrected from* aures (a *written over earlier* e) *C*

1344 errasse Z^I: erasse *C*

1365 materna *K*: materno *C*, Z^I

1373 fatenti *corrected from* catenti (c *changed to* f) *C*

1385 Aegy<ptiacae> *Z, normalized from* Egi<ptiace> *H*: Egi...... *C*

1404 brevis Z^I: breui *C*

1408 nocte *H*: nocteque *C*, Z^I

1414 pneumatis *with* u *added suprascript C*

1433 per te *C, H*: pro Z^I

1474–75 *(title)* communicante Z^I: comunicante *C*

1489 uerum *H*: ueri *C*, Z^I

1494 labem *C*, Z^I: saltem *H*

1501 tanti causa *corrected from* causa tanti *with suprascript transposition marks C*

1554 optatam *C*: ob tantam *A*
optat *C (compare 2520)*: orat *A*

1556 suo *C*: parens *A*

1559 papap *C*: papa *A*, pappa Z^I

1565–66 *omitted A*

1567 igitur puero *C*: puero pueri *A*

1572 inquirens *C*: iniquirens *A*

1575 Mente *A*, Z^I: Mente *corrected from* Menta *by* e *added at end C*
puerorum *A*, Z^I: puerorumq *(abbreviation for* -rum *misread as* q*) C*

1579 fidelem *omitted A*

1580 *A concludes with two additional hexameters*: Ecce puer signo panem dum porrigit isti / uox data de ligno promittit gaudia Christi

1610 ista vel illa *(compare 1608)* Z^1: illa uel illa *C*

1620 possit *H*: posset *C*, Z^1

1647 septeno *H*: septena *C*

1665 septeno *H, K*: septena *C*, Z^1

1670 tot flores etiam *(for the sake of meter) H*: tot etiam flores *C*, Z^1

1727 utque *C*: *emend to* quique?

1734 sibi *added suprascript C*

1735 urbem *corrected from* orbem *by expunction of* or *and addition of* ur *suprascript C*

1737 Ipse *C*: *emend to* Ipsa?

1739 celebri *C, H*: celebris Z^1

1773 quod *(compare 1137–38, note* illud *in 1774)* Z^1: quid *C*

1774 si *H*: sic *C*, Z^1

1824 ipse *Z*: ipsa *C*

1869 ope *added suprascript C*

1897 superbos *added marginally to replace expunged* triumphos *C, H*

1930 det *corrected from* dat *C*

1932 dedidicere *B*, Z^1: dedicere *C*

1977 Summa *C*, Z^1: Sancta *H*

1978 <Dei> *H, K*: *no indication of omission C*, <sacri> Z^1

1982 idem Z^1: item *C*

2125 iuuet Z^1: iuuat *C*

2127 necesse Z^1: neccesse *C*

2128 nec *H*: et *C*, Z^1

libet *H*: licet *C*, Z^1

2130 nunc precio, nunc prece, nuncque dolo *C, H*: nec precio, nec prece, necque dolo Z^1

2166 anim *with* os *added suprascript C*

2182 n<equit> *or* n<egat> *added marginally to replace expunged* studet *C, H (compare Speculum stultorum 3446* dissimulare nequit*)*

2195 nihil *C, H*: nil Z^1

2215 austerae: austere *with* s *added suprascript C*

2258 facit *corrected from* fecit *C*

2280 est visa tibi: tibi uisa tibi *C*, Z^1; modo uisa tibi *H*

2283 casto Z^1: casta *C*

2299 Christi *(as the monogram* xpi*) added suprascript C*

2310 placet *with* t *added suprascript C*

2341 mei *added marginally to replace expunged* stude *C, H*

2347 leviter *added marginally, with a signe-de-renvoi to indicate placement before* vel *C*

2371 omnes *C, H*: omnis Z^1

2387 utrique *H*: uterque *C*, Z^1

2414–15 *The title in the left margin has largely disappeared through trimming and handling.*

2460 hos *K*: his *C*

2463 libidinis Z^1: libininis *C*

2471 remissius *corrected from* remissior *C, H*

2498 rogat Z^1: rogant *C, H*

2507 formidat Z^1: formidet *C*

2530 videns *C, H*: vides Z^1

2536 memor . . . velis *corrected from* velis . . . memor *with transposition marks C, H*: velis . . . memor Z^1

2539 libidinis: libinis *with* di *added suprascript C*

2541 precibusque: precibus *with* que *added suprascript C*

2566 detur *conjectured H*: *erasure C*, possis *conjectured* Z^1

2580 compatiendo Z^1: conpatiento *C*

2585 nimium Z^1: nimiaum *C*

2613 loquantur *C, G*: loquuntur Z^1

2637 recessit *G (compare 299, 335, 8954)*: secessit *C*, Z^1

2641 compuncta Z^1: compucta *C*

2666 thronos *Z*: thoros *C*

Tract on Abuses

Pref.55 putes: putas *B*

14 ingenuus: ingemus *B*

21 longius: longuis *B*

aequius: acquius *B*

26 posthabito: potshabito *B*

34 circumeuntes: circueuntes *B*

36 aut: au *B*

57 quae: quam *B*

59 ecclesiam: eclesiam *B*

67 perditos: perdit s *B*
71 vitam: vitum *B*
77 hominum: omnium *B*
mereatur: mercatur *B*
piaculare: peculiare *B*
78 quisquis: *omitted before* hanc sanctam *B*
antistitis: antistes *B*
decrevimus: decrevisnus *B*
79 subiciantur: subiiciantur *B*
82 alter primatem: alterprimatem *B*
86 omnis: omnes *B*
98 disiccatur: dessicatur *B*
99 atavis: attavis *B*
100 tempora: termpora *B*
106 Discedite: Dicedite *B*
107 impinguare: impingere *B*
115 ad: ab *B*
117 computi: compoti *B*
121 hinc: hine *B*
124 nostras: nastras *B*
125 affabilis: affabili *B*
133 publicas: publicae *B*
141 nauseam: nausiam *B*
144 christum: Christum *B*
155 gemmata: geminata *B*
160 potuit: pouit *B*
aliquatenus: aliquattenus *B*

The Life of Saint Paul, the First Hermit

19 simulacra: simularcra *K*
39 hos: has *K*
45 visurus: visivus *K*
ecce: esse *K*
62 idcirco: iccirco *K*
99 delectant: dilectant *K*

122 mollia: molli *K*
135 ambitur: ampitur *K*
139 illum: illus *K*
169 quid: quit *K*
172 frui: fruit *K*
176 firmo: formo *K*
185 horret: orret *K*
287 evanuit: vanuit *K*
293 noto: voto *K*
295 aggreditur: agreditur *K*
315 multa: mulla *K*
394 arripitur: aripitur *K*
398 anhela: hanela *K*
404 lassescere: lasscescere *K*
429 fluxerat: fluexerat *K*
466 mandat: mactat *K*
482 remanet: remanent *K*
524 pugnanti: pugnati *K*
549 nunc: nuc *K*
626 quos: quas *K*
669 esset: esse *K*
679 currit: curritur *K*

Notes to the Translations

Miracles of the Virgin

incipit *Here begin the miracles . . . in verse*: In the manuscript, the incipit before 619 reads "Here begins the second book," and that before 1581, "Here begins the third book." These two headings make unequivocal by extension that the first book begins here, even though it is not flagged overtly as such within the text or in a caption.

1 *the Virgin and Mother*: The line-opening phrase *Virginis et matris* pervades the *Miracles,* recurring from 7 through 2086.

2 *by devout love*: Nigel caps the poem with this line-ending phrase in 2690.

4 *terseness of verse*: The poet returns to the wording *brevitas metri* in 34–36.

5 *is daunting, but love is ardent*: For puns on the verbs *terreo, -ere* (frighten, daunt) and *torreo, -ere* (burn, scorch) before Nigel, see the eleventh-century Norman Latin poem *Jezebel* 130, "*Torret* nos baratrum—*terrent* magis ora luporum" (The abyss burns us—but the maws of wolves are more daunting), and Lambert of Deutz, *Carmina* 12.2, *Versus fratris Lamberti in monasterio sancti Laurentii: In ventilabro, a sinistris* (Verses of Brother Lambert in the monastery of Saint Lawrence: On a fan), "Arceo quod *torret;* mea sordes orbita *terret*" (I keep away what makes us hot; my course frightens off contamination [by implication, flies]).

5–6 *overcomes my capacities*: This expression *(vires vincere)* reappears among words alliterating on *v* in 2322.

6 *overcomes . . . overcome*: Nigel plays often on words with the same stem, here a verb *(vincit)* and a past participle *(victus)*, in 12–13 an adjective *(magnificum)* and a past participle (*magnificata*, twice), in 60 a simple verb *(emit)* and a compound form of it *(exemptam)*, and so forth.

12 *glorified in countless ways*: The ending *magnificata modis* cycles back in 1742, likewise amid alliteration on *m*.

18 *what is there that*: *Quid quod* is here construed as if it read *quid est quod*.

19 *She who alone lacks a peer*: The opening *sola carens simili* repeats in 999. The words *carens simili* are placed in this same metrical position in 308 and 1411 (and compare 596, *careat simili*).

20 *she alone can*: The phrase *sola potes(t)* is rife in the *Miracles*, from 248 through 2526.

26 *Virgin and Mother of God*: The wording *virgo parensque Dei* appears a dozen times in the poem, even more often without *-que Dei*.

29 *kindly care*: In this line, 351, and 919, the manuscript reading *pie* can correspond to the adverbial or adjectival forms *pie* or *piae*, as represented in the standard spelling of Classical Latin.

31–32 The conceit that a long time would not suffice to do justice to a given topic relates to the so-called inexpressibility topos: see Ernst Robert Curtius, *European Literature and the Latin Middle Ages*, trans. Willard R. Trask, Bollingen Series 36 (Princeton, NJ, 2013), 159–62. For a relevant parallel, see Ovid, *Metamorphoses* 15.418–20, where a day would not pass muster.

36 *so that*: As often in Medieval Latin, *quatenus* fulfills the same function as *ut* did in Classical Latin when introducing a final clause expressing purpose: see *DMLBS* under *quatenus, -inus* 3b.

37–340 This tale of a pact with the devil, similar to the later legend of Faust, became a crowd-pleaser in the Middle Ages. The story of Theophilus emerged in the Byzantine world in the sixth century or so, though the Greek forms never achieved much popularity. In contrast, versions are attested widely in western Europe, in prose and verse, in Latin and vernaculars, from the late ninth century on. Scenes from it are represented in numerous stained glass windows and manuscript illuminations. For a recent study, see Jerry Root, *The Theophilus Legend in Medieval Text and Image* (Cambridge, 2017).

37 *gusting wind*: The concept of the flesh as wind derives from Psalms 77(78):39.

38 *the state of the flesh*: The operative word is *condicio* (state), which stands in for *lex* (law) in Romans 7:23.

39 *beneath the likeness of the true*: See 1 Corinthians 13:5 and Ovid, *Epistulae ex Ponto* 16.45. Compare 2385.

44 *how bitter the day*: The image owes to Amos 8:10.

46 *to have atoned*: Nigel, who relies heavily on such perfect infinitives, avails himself again of the syncopated *piasse* in 236.

52 *fame*: Fame, good and bad alike, personified and not, was central in medieval culture. See B. G. Koonce, *Chaucer and the Tradition of Fame: Symbolism in "The House of Fame"* (Princeton, NJ, 1966), and Piero Boitani, *Chaucer and the Imaginary World of Fame* (Woodbridge, Suffolk, 1984).

53 *deputy*: The Latin *vicedomnus,* like its French derivative *vidame,* can designate a secular "vice-lord" as well as an ecclesiastical "archdeacon."

54 *the Church's*: On the scansion of *ecclesia* with a short second syllable, see *TLL* vol. 5, part 2, col. 33, lines 4–9.

61 *for the time being*: Here and in 593, 687, 707, 959, and 2247 *ad horam* means "for an hour, for a time." The phrase appears in the Vulgate Bible in 2 Corinthians 7:8, Galatians 2:5, and Philemon 15. See *TLL* vol. 6, part 3, col. 2959, line 63 through col. 2960, line 35.

63–64 In Medieval Latin literature, Envy is commonly depicted as "gnawing." The fullest portrayal of *Invidia* in Roman literature is Ovid, *Metamorphoses* 2.760–832.

69 *Why should I recall . . . all men*: The first half-line derives from Horace, *Satires* 1.8.40. The second is based on 1 Corinthians 9:22. Compare line 2680.

70 *to each individual one*: *DMLBS* under 2 *solus* 5e, defines *omnes . . . et soli* as "all and no others."

71 *bishop's soul . . . flesh's prison*: The commonplace of the body as

prison of the soul, which goes back to Plato (*Phaedo* 62b), arrived in the medieval West through such conduits as Cicero, *Somnium Scipionis* 3.2 [14.14], and Macrobius, *Commentarii in Somnium Scipionis* 1.10.6 and 1.10.9.

the stars: The equation of heaven with stars pervades the Bible, from Genesis 22:17 on.

75–82 Theophilus's refusal recalls the convention, from late antiquity on, in which pious men allegedly resist offers to become bishop. Sometimes prospective appointees must decline election twice out of modesty before having their third turndown accepted. This stock response is sometimes designated by the Latin *nolo episcopari* (I don't want to be made a bishop).

77 *my mind and life bite back*: Nigel similarly describes a mind that causes remorse in 181–82, 186, and 2363–64. In 2481 he writes of the mind being acted upon by guilt or fear.

78 *sweet evil*: The poet has a soft spot for the combination *dulce malum,* found in *Passio sancti Laurentii* 568 and *Speculum stultorum* 2609 and 2998. The turn of phrase owes to Job 20:12.

87–88 *a new appointee . . . to be fickle*: A dangerously close relationship was perceived between newness or innovation on the one hand and inconstancy or levity on the other. Bernard of Clairvaux referred to newness as the daughter of inconstancy: see Letter 174, "Ad canonicos Lugdunenses." An additional element in these two lines is the medieval usage of *novitas* to refer to the initial period in office of a newly elected official: see *DMLBS* under *novitas* 5a–b.

93–122 On anger and grief, see Nigel's *Speculum stultorum* 1251–502. The close nexus between the two emotions in medieval culture is explored in Stephen D. White, "The Politics of Anger," in *Anger's Past: The Social Uses of an Emotion in the Middle Ages,* ed. Barbara H. Rosenwein (Ithaca, NY, 1998), 127–52.

107–10 *serious . . . more serious . . . most serious . . . burden . . . burdened*: Employing the rhetorical figure of polyptoton, Nigel plays on the root of the adjective *gravis, -e.*

115 *goads of envy*: The goad of envy is a Christian Latin image found

for example in Augustine, *De spiritu et littera* 2.3, "non mediocribus invidentiae stimulis" (by no small goads of envy).

anger gives rise to madness: On the relationship between *ira* and *furor,* see note to 2441.

126 *become all the deafer after having heard the prayer*: English has the related expressions "to turn a deaf ear to" and "deaf to prayers."

133 *magus*: The Latin *magus,* most notable in the description of the three Wise Men or Kings in Matthew 2:1–2, often refers to a soothsayer, seer, or astrologer, specifically from what was then called the Orient. Nigel assumes that such an eastern wise man will be *ipso facto* a Jew. In the Theophilus story this character is customarily Jewish.

138 *circuses*: On the *circus* as a haunt of astrologers, see *OLD,* under *circus* 3a. Compare William of Malmesbury, *Miracula sanctae Mariae Virginis* 1.1.4, ed. and trans. Rodney M. Thomson and Michael Winterbottom, *The Miracles of the Blessed Virgin Mary* (Woodbridge, UK, 2015), 16–17.

140 *the night and place*: The Latin *noxque locusque* is marked by a conjunction *-que* (and) after each of the two elements, a device known as polysyndeton.

141 *the prince of devils*: For the expression (applied especially to Beelzebub), see Matthew 9:34 and 12:24, Mark 3:22, and Luke 11:15.

142 *of spirits*: Spirits are often heavenly and good, but because the "prince of devils" has been mentioned, the malignity of the ones here does not need to be spelled out further.

147 *If he wishes to be mine, let him deny Christ*: Nigel's Latin resembles closely Hrotsvitha of Gandersheim, *Theophilus* 114, "*Si meus esse cupit* scriptis *Christum*que negabit" (If he wishes to be mine, and will deny Christ in writing).

157–79 For the tightest parallel to these lines, see Ovid, *Metamorphoses* 15.473–76:

> Retia cum pedicis laqueosque artesque dolosas
> tollite, nec volucrem viscata fallite virga,

nec formidatis cervos illudite pennis,
nec celate cibis uncos fallacibus hamos.

Dispense with nets, traps, snares, and crafty schemes, and do not deceive the bird with a birdlimed twig, nor spook the deer with alarming feathers, nor conceal barbed hooks with deceptive bait.

157 *who has been burned by the fire*: On *ustus ab igne timet,* see Hans Walther, *Proverbia sententiaeque Latinitatis medii aevi: Lateinische Sprichwörter und Sentenzen des Mittelalters in alphabetischer Anordnung,* 6 vols., Carmina medii aevi posterioris Latina 2 (Göttingen, 1963–1969), nos. 11384, 11385, 11387, 12292, 22919, and 32289, and *TPMA* vol. 2, pp. 93–94 (under *brennen* 3.5).

clinging snares and shackles: See Walther, *Proverbia,* no. 18626. Satan is often likened to a fowler in medieval literature, thanks to the predominant interpretation of Psalms 90(91):3. See B. G. Koonce, "Satan the Fowler," *Mediaeval Studies* 21 (1959): 176–84. Nigel cleverly turns around such images usually applied to the devil, by having the fiend use them in describing the conduct of the Virgin Mary toward him.

159 *birdlime frightens birds*: A "viscous" or sticky substance made from the berries of mistletoe, birdlime is spread on twigs to trap birds. For early usage, see Gunner Mikkelsen, "Augustine and His Sources: The 'Devil's Snares and Birdlime' in the Mouths of Manichaeans in East and West," in *In Search of Truth: Augustine, Manichaeism and other Gnosticism; Studies for Johannes van Oort at Sixty,* ed. Jacob Albert van den Berg, Annemaré Kotzé, Tobias Nicklas, and Madeleine Scopello (Leiden, 2011), 419–25.

the hook makes fish fearful: The discussion concludes with the implication that a fish that has once experienced the hook will dread it. See *TPMA* vol. 5, p. 352 (under *Haken* 2). Thanks to exegesis of Job 40:20, Jesus was viewed as a fisherman who made himself the bait and crucified himself on the hook to catch the devil, who was conceived as a whale or Leviathan. See Johannes Zellinger, "Der geköderte Leviathan im *Hortus deliciarum* der Herrad von Landsperg," *Historisches Jahrbuch* 45 (1925): 161–77, and Werner von Koppenfels, *Esca et Hamus: Beitrag zu einer historischen Liebesmetaphorik,* Sitzungsberichte der Bayerische Akademie der Wissenschaften, philosophisch-historische Klasse, volume for 1973, part 3 (Munich, 1973), 39–43. For an exposition of the theology, see Nicholas P. Constas, "The Last Temptation of Satan: Divine Deception in Greek Patristic Interpretations of the Passion Narrative," *The Harvard Theological Review* 97, no. 2 (2004): 139–63, at 143–49.

166 *by his own snares*: For the motif of the would-be deceiver caught in his own snare, see Psalms 9:16 (9:14–15) and Sirach 27:29. The proverb was beloved in the Middle Ages: see *TPMA* vol. 3, pp. 151–53 (under *Falle* 1, "Wer andern eine Falle stellt / einen Fallstrick legt, fällt selbst hinein"). Compare 654.

177–78 *the blind goddess*: On Fortuna, who is mentioned constantly in medieval literature, see H. R. Patch, *The Goddess Fortuna in Medieval Literature* (Cambridge, MA, 1927).

178 *before and behind*: Because *ante retroque* is usually applied in reference not to time but to space (see *DMLBS* under *ante* 1a–b), a more literal translation would be "backward and forward."

185–86 *a never-resting worm . . . gnaws it*: Compare Proverbs 25:20 (not in all manuscripts), "sicut tinea vestimento et vermis ligno, ita tristitia viri nocet cordi" (as a moth doth by a garment, and a worm by the wood, so the sadness of a man consumeth the heart), Sirach 7:19, Isaiah 66:24, and Mark 9:43 and 9:47.

185 *destructive moth*: For *tinea corrumpens,* see Luke 12:33. As in *Passio sancti Laurentii* 1223, the noun here has a long first syllable.

190 *nothing in the world can be cleaner*: The wordplay on the noun *mundus* (world) and the adjective *mundus, -a, -um* (clean) occurs again in 336, 387, and, most important, 1964, "*qua nihil in mundo* car*ius esse potest*" (than whom nothing in the world can be dearer).

192 *seeing*: The Latin is marked by the syntactical inconsistency known as anacoluthon. Alternatively, emend *videns* (seeing) to *videt* (he sees). Compare the endings, likewise with *superesse* (to remain) followed by a form of *video, -ere,* of 1118 and 1635.

193 *death . . . begins to be a cause of fear*: The thought relates to *timor mortis* (fear of death), found in Sirach 40:4 and Hebrews 2:15.

195 *You will come*: The future *venies* is the equivalent of an imperative. The subject is Death. Whereas the prevailing image today is "death's door," the Middle Ages had a personification of Death as a skeleton (like our Grim Reaper) that showed up at the entrances of homes and in workplaces to knock and collect those whose number was up.

198 *death and his crime*: The Latin *morsque scelusque suum* offers another instance of polysyndeton.

215 *With the sting of his pains goading him*: The image of *stimuli doloris* (stings of grief) can be traced to Cicero, *Tusculan Disputations* 2.66.

216 *the spirit and flesh*: The body and soul were frequently personified in medieval literature, especially in debates between the two: see Piero Boitani and Anna Torti, eds., *The Body and the Soul in Medieval Literature* (Suffolk, 1999).

217–18 *Nothing brings relief . . . following words*: Though the meaning is clear, the syntax is flaccid. In translating, one approach would be to fill the ellipsis with a missing verb of speech, another, to treat the participle as a finite verb.

224 *Eternal woe*: In Medieval Latin the interjection *vae* (woe) is occasionally used nominally, as here.

226–27 *against my crime . . . against my crime*: These lines repeat a second half-line at the beginning of the following one, a rhetorical figure similar to epanalepsis. Compare 1304–5.

228 *not a human being but a worm*: The metaphor here owes to Job 25:6, "How much less man that is rottenness and the son of man who is a worm?"

229 *dung*: The Bible sometimes equates human beings and their activities with dung. The most relevant verse may be 1 Maccabees 2:62, "And fear not the words of a sinful man, for his glory is dung, and worms."

231 *underworld*: Only here does Nigel use *Tartara,* a classical designation for the infernal regions.

232 *fully*: On the construction *ad plenum,* see *DMLBS* under *plenus* 9g.

233 *The heavens, earth, and sea*: Nigel employs *sidera, terra, mare* as a line opening also in 2029. In content, he offers a cameo of the inexpressibility topos: see Curtius, *European Literature and the Latin Middle Ages,* 159–62. In this rhetorical convention, writers from Homer on have emphasized their inability to handle a subject. Here the poet channels such a sense of inadequacy through Theophilus, who implies that the whole universe could not give an accounting of the punishment he deserves for his sins.

235 The poet cites four cases of penitence from Holy Writ, first one pair from the New Testament and then another from the Hebrew Bible, not identical with those in William of Malmesbury, *Miracula sanctae Mariae Virginis* 1.1.11, ed. and trans. Thomson and Winterbottom, *Miracles,* pp. 18–19 (which include Peter, David, and the Ninevites). The examples given by Nigel are among the ones in the Latin prose life of Theophilus that Paul the Deacon of Naples produced during the last quarter of the ninth century by translating a Byzantine Greek version of the story.

Peter: On Saint Peter's weeping after his three denials of Christ, see Matthew 26:75, Mark 14:72, and especially Luke 22:62.

Paul: The apostle's tears are mentioned at Philippians 3:18.

David: Many episodes in 2 Kings (2 Samuel) establish David as the most lachrymose character in the Pentateuch: see 1:17, 3:32, 13:36, 15:23, 15:30, and 18:33. Even more than through his representation in the historical books, the biblical king was associated with repentance owing to one of the so-called Penitential Psalms: Psalm 50(51), commonly known as the *Miserere* (Have mercy) after the first word of its first verse in Latin, is understood to describe David's repentance after being confronted by the prophet Nathan, as described in 2 Kings (2 Samuel) 12.

Ninevites: Nineveh was the capital of Assyria. The reference pertains to the book of Jonah, where the prophet is bidden to go and to cry out against the city for its wickedness. Luke 11:32 reports that the men of the city repented, an inference drawn from Jonah 3:5–8, where the Ninevites proclaim a fast and don the coarse fabric known as sackcloth.

252 *both because you alone . . . accustomed to do so*: In Medieval Latin *tum* . . . *tum* could mean "both . . . and," as *cum* . . . *tum* and (more rarely) *tum* . . . *tum* did in Classical: see *OLD* under *tum* 10b, and *DMLBS* under *tum* 5a and 6a. The same two verbs as appear here, *potes* and *soles*, respectively, are emphasized in 2524.

257 *Since compassion displayed to enemies is extraordinary*: In this observation, Nigel refers to a fundamental teaching of Christianity: see in particular Matthew 5:43–45.

264 *life*: The words echo John 14:6, "Jesus said to him, 'I am the way, and the truth, and the life.'"

265–66 Here Mary is accorded the quality of lightness attributed to Christ and God in John 1:5, 1 John 1:5, and elsewhere.

267 *a moon*: The earth's satellite has often been presented as a symbol of the Virgin. As the moon throws back the sun's light, so Mary reflects God's glory. See in particular Revelation 12:1.

268 *is God and man*: The four words *deus est et homo* were a staple of Medieval Latin poetry.

274 *sway me with your tears*: The archetypal scene of such suasion was Aurora's manipulation of Vulcan, as described by Venus, in Virgil, *Aeneid* 8.384, "Te potuit *lacrimis* Tithonia *flectere* coniunx" (Tithonius's wife was able to sway you with tears).

284 *violent death*: The Latin *vimque necemque* affords yet another example of polysyndeton.

289 *be too extreme . . . they seem harsh*: Since no logical antecedent can be found for the adjectives *dira* (extreme) and *dura* (harsh) as the subject of the verb *sit,* the feminine *vicis* (circumstance) in the subsequent line is taken as the postcedent.

293–94 *mouth . . . heart*: The emphasis on these two organs owes ultimately to Romans 10:9–10.

297 *from the grave*: This expression is attested from late antiquity on. For early evidence, see *TLL* vol. 8, col. 1507, lines 43–44. Compare *AH* vol. 41, p. 77 (referring to the episode of Lazarus in John 11), "Hunc de mortis funere / festinat praepropere / Martha suscitare" (Martha hurriedly rushes to rouse him from the grave).

307 *star of the sea*: The title *Stella maris* for the Virgin Mary goes back

to late antiquity and became entrenched in the Middle Ages: compare 1429. The phrase figures prominently in the second line of the old hymn *Alma redemptoris mater:* see Maurice A. Canney, "Stella maris," *Revue de l'histoire des religions* 115 (1937): 90–94.

319 *feast day*: Compare the feminine *festa dies* here with the masculine *dies festus* in 681, both with the same meaning.

326 *all-too-evident facts of the matter*: Nigel constantly utilizes *res manifesta* as a set phrase, most often in this metrical position (see also 574, 744, 1242, 1740, and 2374), but also as a hexameter opening in 1739 and ending in 1891. The wording is often difficult to translate, in spite (or because) of its seeming simplicity.

327 *The charter is consigned to the flames*: The burning of the written contract was a major motif in both texts and images of the miracle.

329–34 When Theophilus takes Communion for the first time after being freed from contracting his soul to the devil, he undergoes transfiguration and illumination that render him angelic.

333 *A new sun glitters . . . in his face*: For the underlying conception, compare Matthew 17:2, "And he was transfigured before them. And his face did shine as the sun."

334 *an angel in his countenance*: Acts 6:15 is often interpreted to mean that Saint Stephen's face was illuminated with a divine radiance, like the brightness of an angel's face. For the device of framing a pentameter within the words for angel and man, compare 410.

337–38 *Earth enters earth . . . earthly stronghold*: This couplet sums up beliefs about the fate of the body and soul after death. It owes to verses in the Bible, such as Ecclesiastes 12:7, "And the dust return into its earth, from whence it was, and the spirit return to God, who gave it."

341–456 Dunstan (909–988) contributed centrally to the intellectual revival of tenth-century England. First as abbot of Glastonbury, then as bishop of Worcester and London, and finally as archbishop of Canterbury, the saint toiled to restore monasticism and culture. He encouraged the copying of manuscripts and inculcation of such arts as metalworking and music making. For the sources, see Williams Stubbs, ed., *Memorials of Saint Dunstan,* Rolls Series (London, 1874). For biography, see Douglas J. Dales, *Dunstan: Saint and Statesman,* 2nd ed. (Cambridge, 2013).

341–48 This description of England as a land gifted in its fertile natural setting and pious inhabitants calls to mind Bede's *Historia ecclesiastica gentis Anglorum* 1.1.

345 *A honeyed land of honeycomb, a milky nation of milk*: The underlying notion of the promised land "flowing with milk and money" derives from Exodus 3:17.

349–52 On England's much-touted devotion to the Virgin (and vice versa) in the Middle Ages, see Edmund Waterton, *Pietas Mariana Britannica: A History of English Devotion to the Most Blessed Virgin Marye* [sic] *Mother of God* (London, 1879).

353 *of Canterbury*: The Latin adjective *Dorobernensis* designates Canterbury, the noun for which *(Dorobernia)* appears in 413. Dunstan's association with the city came from his having served as its archbishop.

357 *pious*: Nigel takes advantage of two meanings that the adjective *pius* can have, the other being "merciful."

364 *grows with love*: Compare Ovid, *Metamorphoses* 10.333, "pietas geminato *crescit amore*" (devotion grows with the doubled love).

365–72 On the boy with the maturity of an old man, see also 1055 and *Passio sancti Laurentii* 629–34. On the lineage of the topos, see Curtius, *European Literature and the Latin Middle Ages,* 98–101, and Teresa C. Carp, "*Puer senex* in Roman and Medieval Thought," *Latomus* 39 (1980): 736–39.

369 *Love conquered*: The opening *Vicit amor* is related most closely to Ovid, *Metamorphoses* 10.26, but owes an indirect debt to *Ciris* 437, "Omnia vicit amor" (Love conquered all) in the *Appendix Virgiliana.* The ultimate inspiration is Virgil, *Eclogues* 10.69, where the verb is in the present tense: "Omnia vincit amor."

372 *You would marvel*: The verb here in the active is far more commonly deponent.

377 *Hagar*: Abraham's concubine, by whom she had Ishmael, a child

of "the flesh." Sarah was Abraham's wife, by whom she bore Isaac, a child of "the spirit" or "the promise." In due course, Sarah cast Hagar and Ishmael out of Abraham's household. The episode in Genesis 16–19 is allegorized in Galatians 4:22–24.

379 *the cloister of Glastonbury*: The abbey, which fell into ruin after the dissolution of the monasteries in 1536, was founded in the seventh century in Somerset. By the late Middle Ages it became one of the wealthiest cloisters in England.

382 *a new soldier*: The image of the good soldier of Jesus Christ goes back to 2 Timothy 2:3–4. On such military metaphors in the early Church, see Adolf Harnack, *Militia Christi: The Christian Religion and the Military in the First Three Centuries,* trans. David McInnes Gracie (Philadelphia, 1982).

390 *way . . . to the homeland*: The second Latin noun could be translated more literally as "fatherland." In figurative Christian usage, the homeland is heaven: see *TLL* vol. 10, part 1, col. 771, lines 1–24.

395 *Reducing to ash*: Man's fragile body dies and is reduced to ashes, as stated often in the Bible: Genesis 18:27; Job 13:12, 30:19, and 34:15; and elsewhere.

398 *so that the flesh mortified would live in Christ*: The foundational verse in the Bible for this thought is Romans 8:13, "For if you live according to the flesh, you shall die: but if by the Spirit you mortify the deeds of the flesh, you shall live."

401–14 In 2 Corinthians 12:1–6, Saint Paul discusses visions and revelations in which a man, either in the body or out of it, is caught up to the third heaven. William of Malmesbury describes similar experiences undergone by Dunstan, with the distinctive feature that the future saint brings back heavenly melodies to his fellow monks: see Robert Easting, "Access to Heaven in Medieval Visions of the Otherworld," in *Envisaging Heaven in the Middle Ages,* ed. Carolyn Muessig and Ad Putter, Routledge Studies in Medieval Religion and Culture 6 (London, 2006), 89–104.

401 *through the intercession of*: *Mediante* can denote "by the mediation of, by the grace of": see Franz Blatt, *Novum glossarium mediae*

Latinitatis (Copenhagen, 1957–), under *medians* (itself listed under *medio*) I. D.

414 *music and melodies*: The manuscript spelling of the first word in the pairing of nouns suggests *pneuma* (breath, spirit), when what is meant is the distinct word *neuma* (musical sound or note, tone, tune; compare *neumata* in 411).

415–18 Dunstan's fame as a metalsmith gave rise to the legend that he once wielded a pair of blacksmith's pincers to grab the face, jaws, or nose of a demon who sought to tempt him. On this story, see Hilary Powell, "Demonic Daydreams: Mind-Wandering and Mental Imagery in the Medieval Hagiography of St Dunstan," *New Medieval Literatures* 18 (2018): 44–74.

420 *the demon's schemes*: The underlying thought, with the turn of phrase *insidias diaboli,* derives from Ephesians 6:11. Compare *daemonis invidia* (the ill will of the devil) in 1226.

423 *Oh how novel . . . people today*: This line crops up again verbatim in 645. The substantive *modernus,* to denote a contemporary, was a creation of Late and Medieval Latin. See Kent Kraft, "Modernism in the Twelfth Century," *Comparative Literature Studies* 18, no. 3 (1981): 287–95.

424 *oh how pleasing . . . reverence*: The accumulation of words alliterating on *v* is remarkable. Compare 658.

425–42 After becoming archbishop, Dunstan reportedly built a church to honor Mary. As a reward, he had a vision in which he witnessed Mary conduct a choir of virgins in singing a hymn there. On this miracle, see Kati Ihnat, *Mother of Mercy, Bane of the Jews: Devotion to the Virgin Mary in Anglo-Norman England* (Princeton, NJ, 2016), 113–14.

433–34 *Let us sing in honor . . . pious mouths*: In wording, these two verses owe ultimately to the first two lines of a famous fifth-century hymn: see Sedulius, *Hymni* 1.1–2, edited in *AH* vol. 50, pp. 53–56, at 53, and *CSEL* vol. 10, p. 155, "Cantemus, socii, Domino cantemus honorem, / dulcis amor Christi personet ore pio." The proximate source is William of Malmesbury, *Miracula sanctae Mariae Virginis* 1.7.3, ed. and trans. Thomson and Winterbottom, *Miracles,* p. 34 (with the second and third words

"Domino, sociae," as in Nigel). William uses the same modified phrasing in his *Vita Dunstani* 2.27, ed. and trans. Michael Winterbottom and Rodney M. Thomson, *Saints' Lives* (Oxford, 2002), 286. All these preceding texts strongly support emendation of *personat,* in manuscript *C,* to *personet.* In Exodus 15:1 and 15:21 *cantemus Domino* (let us sing to the Lord) opens the so-called canticle of Moses, a song of praise to the Lord sung by him and the Israelites after the crossing of the Red Sea.

439–42 As the legend unfolds, Dunstan, when exhorted to participate, sings an antiphon.

439 *Christ the King*: The title of king appears twice in the Gospel of John, first in an exchange between Pontius Pilate and Jesus (John 18:36–37) and then in the notice that the Roman leader had prepared and fastened to the cross (Jesus of Nazareth, the king of the Jews; John 19:19). *Rex* soon became ubiquitous in Christianity as a descriptor of Jesus. It refers to the kingdom of heaven, where Christ is seated to the right of God.

443–46 *He sang of many more . . . saw there*: In these two couplets, Nigel plays again upon the inexpressibility topos: see Curtius, *European Literature and the Latin Middle Ages,* 159–62. Here he explains that he must make a selection because the number of options would otherwise overwhelm readers and him.

455 *whose likeness he strove to become*: In other words, Dunstan attempted to be the image of Mary on earth.

457–560 Julian the Apostate (332–363), although given a pious education, professed paganism and persecuted Christians once he became Roman emperor. On the Marian miracle, see Klaus Rosen, *Julian: Kaiser, Gott und Christenhasser* (Stuttgart, 2006).

461 *poisons under honey*: See *TPMA* vol. 6, pp. 179–80 (under *Honig* 4.5.2.2).

462 *a wolf beneath a lambskin*: The image has become associated with Aesopic fable: see Babrius and Phaedrus, *Fables,* trans. Ben Edwin Perry, Loeb Classical Library 436 (Cambridge, MA, 1965), p. 513, no. 451. It is also proverbial: see *TPMA* vol. 10, pp. 2–5 (under *Schaf* 1).

463 *adulthood*: The Latin implies *ad annos discretionis,* the age of dis-

cretion or majority at which a person is considered old enough to assume responsibility for action. The late teens would be a reasonable guess for the age Nigel had in mind.

467 *garlands of victory*: Like crowns of triumph, these rewards honor distinction, especially through martyrdom: see James 1:12.

470 *Basil the Great*: In 370 Saint Basil was named bishop of Caesarea, and in 379 died there.

472 *Caesarea in Cappadocia*: The city mentioned here, now Kayseri in present-day Turkey, was the capital of the Roman province of Cappadocia.

485 *tawny metal*: This phrase is trite in Latin poetry as a designation for gold.

487 *Faith is nowhere safe*: The quotation is from Virgil, *Aeneid* 4.373.

496 *the crowd of poor*: Alongside the Classical Latin adjective *pauper, -eris* (poor), Medieval Latin had the biform *pauperus, -a, -um.*

500 *in one of these two ways*: The line ending was commonplace in dactylic poetry from Propertius, *Elegies* 3.17.12 on. This literary tradition argues in favor of *utroque modo* in *C* against *uterque* in *H.*

502 *they knock and find the doors open*: See Matthew 26:10–11 and Luke 13:25.

507–8 *near the walls . . . mountain*: The topography does not dovetail with the physical reality of the ancient site, which was located on the plain. In the unlikely event that the place of worship mentioned by Nigel ever existed, it could have lain outside the ancient walls toward Mount Argaeus.

515 *the sky resounds with cries*: The inspiration here issues from Ovid, *Ars amatoria* 3.375, "crimina dicuntur, *resonat clamoribus aether*" (accusations are spoken; the sky resounds with cries). All other Medieval Latin poems that quote the Ovidian language have *resonat . . . aether:* see *Liber Maiolichinus de gestis Pisanorum illustribus* 1707, Walter of Châtillon, *Alexandreis* 9.107, and *Carmen Friderici* 2438. In contrast, the manuscript here reads plainly *resonant . . . ethra,* with a plural verb to accompany what could be understood as a syncopated poetic form in the neuter plural of the more commonly masculine noun *aether:* see *TLL* vol. 1, col.

1149, lines 34–36, and *DMLBS* under *aether* 1b. For the neuter plural the latter cites the influential early medieval English poet Aldhelm, *De virginitate* 429 and 1989, ed. Rudolf Ehwald, *Aldhelmi opera,* Monumenta Germaniae Historica: Auctores antiquissimi 15 (Berlin, 1919), 371 and 435 (though in neither case with syncopation).

522 *relieving . . . with sleep*: The idiom *dare membra somno* (to give the limbs to sleep) is common, but here *somno* is ablative with *levare* rather than dative with *dare.*

526 *Mercurius*: In the Middle Ages, legend held that Julian the Apostate was killed by a so-called military or warrior saint named Mercurius, whom the Virgin dispatched from the grave. Saint Basil the Great learned of the planned assassination from a vision. On one day, he finds Mercurius's weapons missing from his burial place in Caesarea; on the next, he discovers them back but covered with blood. The miracle is all the more wondrous for the 113 years between Mercurius's martyrdom in 250 CE and Julian's assassination in 363 CE. See Philip Shaw, "A Dead Killer? Saint Mercurius, Killer of Julian the Apostate, in the Works of William of Malmesbury," *Leeds Studies in English,* n.s. 35 (2004): 1–22, and Christopher Walter, *The Warrior Saints in Byzantine Art and Tradition* (Aldershot, Hants, 2003), 101–9.

533 *Persia*: The backdrop to the action here is the Perso-Roman War, which took place between March and July of 363. Emperor Julian's invasion ended when he died from wounds sustained in a skirmish as he and his army retreated.

539 *there in the same city*: The only locale that has been named is Caesarea in Cappadocia, where Mercurius was supposedly martyred and buried in 250 CE, during the persecution of Christians under Emperor Decius.

546 *out of a desire . . . matters*: This pentameter is reiterated at 1440.

561–618 Saint Ildephonsus, known as a musician and a theologian, served as metropolitan bishop of Toledo from 657 until his death in 667. During that time the city in central Spain was the capital of the Visigothic kingdom.

570 *the deceitful Jews*: In relating the trial and death of Jesus, the

Gospel of John singles out the Jews as those who conspired to kill Christ. The liturgy of Good Friday, which gave considerable weight to John's version, emphasized the culpability of Jews. The two other miracles in Nigel's poem that portray Jews depict them unfavorably, with deceit prominent in the second.

the sacrilege of Helvidius: In a tractate written around 380, this fourth-century heretic held the brethren of Christ (mentioned in, for example, Matthew 12:46, Mark 3:31–32, and elsewhere) to be actual sons born to Mary and Joseph after the birth of Jesus. In 383 Jerome refuted Helvidius in the polemic conventionally entitled *Adversus Helvidium*. See David G. Hunter, "Helvidius, Jovinian, and the Virginity of Mary in Late Fourth-Century Rome," *Journal of Early Christian Studies* 1, no. 1 (1993): 47–71.

588 *the bishop's vestment*: In due course the garment is described as snow-white: compare 595–96, 602, and 606.

593–96 *Who could express . . . no like*: Once again, Nigel avails himself of the inexpressibility topos: see Curtius, *European Literature and the Latin Middle Ages*, 159–62.

596 *the art of the stylus*: This rodlike implement had at one end a point for scratching the wax and at the other a blunt edge for smoothing it. The modern English *style* derives from the noun for this writing device.

602 *snow-white*: In Christian symbolism, white signifies virginity, red, martyrdom.

609–10 *While alive . . . stars*: Nigel departs from the account in William of Malmesbury by describing the free pass that Ildephonsus is accorded, which allows him out-of-body transit to heaven.

611–18 The archbishop's successor, identified by William of Malmesbury as Siagrius, suffers sudden death for ignoring the injunction that no one else should use the vestment and throne.

619* *The bishop's sin in seizing a forbidden honor . . .* : After being initially omitted, the pentameter with which the first book concluded was apparently added in the margin. Because of later trimming, it is no longer legible.

620 *The duke of the Normans, Rollo*: In 911 this Viking led his followers

in a siege of the northern French town of Chartres. Afterward, he concluded the treaty of Saint-Clair-sur-Epte, in which Charles III the Simple and the Franks ceded to him and his Northmen (or Normans) the lower Seine basin. This area later became the duchy of Normandy. Only long after the fact was Rollo himself styled its first duke.

623–24 *Fortune . . . to be feared*: Lady Fortune has been giving Rollo and the Normans preferential treatment. Since she gives no sign of withdrawing her support, the prospects of the Chartrians look grim.

629 *the road to peace*: Compare Romans 3:17, which could be translated "they are strangers to the road to peace."

631 *Chartres was now a prison*: The alliteration in Latin between the first syllables of Chartres *(Carnotum)* and prison *(carcer)* drives home the message.

639–52 In legend, Gantelme of Chartres (bishop from 898 to 911) displayed the Virgin's tunic or chemise as a standard on the city ramparts. It blinded the besiegers and put them to flight. The textile (now held to be a veil) was supposedly what Mary wore when giving birth to Christ. Presented to Charlemagne by the Byzantine emperor Constantine Porphyrogenitus and his wife, Empress Irene, this holy relic was transferred to Chartres by Charles the Bald.

653 *The victor goes off*: The paradox of "the victor vanquished" is pervasive in Latin poetry. The opening *Victor abit* is attested first in Ovid, *Fasti* 5.649.

654 *falls into its own snares*: See note to line 166 above.

663 *The honor of the see, not the burden*: The similarity of *onus* and *honor* led to much wordplay in Latin, starting with Ovid, *Heroides* 9.31, "Non honor est, sed onus" (It is no honor, but a burden). See August Otto, *Die Sprichwörter und sprichwörtlichen Redensarten der Römer* (Leipzig, 1890), p. 167, no. 828, and (on medieval verses that begin "Non honor est, sed onus"), Walther, *Proverbia,* nos. 17875–77.

Fulbert: This bishop of Chartres (d. 1028) was renowned for his learning. On his life and works, see Frederick Behrends, ed.

and trans., *The Letters and Poems of Fulbert of Chartres* (Oxford, 1976), xiii–xc, and Michel Rouche, ed., *Fulbert de Chartres, précurseur de l'Europe médiévale?,* Cultures et civilisations médiévales 43 (Paris, 2008). As Nigel mentions in 677–82, Fulbert was regarded as a major figure in the development of devotion to the Virgin, the institution of the feast of her nativity, and the composition of liturgical song to honor her on this day. See Margot Fassler, "Mary's Nativity, Fulbert of Chartres, and the Stirps Jesse: Liturgical Innovation circa 1000 and its Afterlife," *Speculum* 75, no. 2 (2000): 389–434.

683 *the cast of his mind*: Literally, "the thinking of his mind."

690 *the true light*: In John 1:9 Jesus is identified as "the true light [*lux vera*] that enlightens every man" and in 1 John 2:8 as "the true light [*lumen verum*]."

695–706 William of Malmesbury refers to this episode in *Gesta regum Anglorum,* 3.285.1, ed. and trans. Roger B. Mynors, Rodney M. Thomson, and Michael Winterbottom (Oxford, 1998), 518–19. Among many later treatments of the miracle, two Anglo-Norman texts provide further evidence of a specifically English tradition. The first is in Adgar, the second in the so-called second Anglo-Norman collection. See Paule-V. Bétérous, "À propos d'une des légendes mariales les plus répandues 'Le lait de la Vierge,'" *Bulletin de l'Association Guillaume Budé* 4 (1975): 403–11, at 408–9.

701 *touched by the holy liquid*: Because the Virgin's body was understood to have been taken up into heaven in the Assumption, she left few bodily relics. Drops of milk that she shed during life or in subsequent apparitions allowed an immediacy otherwise lacking and were preserved as relics, from the Holy Land (especially in the Chapel of the Milk Grotto) west throughout Europe (in many churches). The *imitatio Christi* (imitation of Christ) of being suckled by the Virgin was particularly desired. In this miracle, Fulbert reportedly collected in a vase drops of milk left on his chin. They subsequently became the object of reverence.

707–30 The fatigue that Nigel expresses as author is similar to that voiced by scribes in colophons and subscriptions.

707 *Let rest restore what is tired*: The poet gives voice to the medieval counterpart of "All work and and no play makes Jack a dull boy": creativity requires relaxation, much as a bow will not retain its tensile strength if not sometimes unstrung. See Glending Olson, *Literature as Recreation in the Later Middle Ages* (Ithaca, NY, 1982), 90–127.

708 *The page should let the pen rest; the wax, the stylus*: Nigel refers to two main media and utensils for writing in the Middle Ages. A page was one side of a folio (or leaf) of parchment, on which a scribe wrote with a pen (from *penna,* the Latin for "feather," meaning its sharpened quill). The wax signifies a tablet covered with that substance, on which a writer plied a stylus.

709 *a desiccated hand*: By metonymy, the poet transfers to the hand of the unnamed scribe the change that ink undergoes as it dries out. He may also have meant *aridus, -a, -um* at least partly in the rare sense "exhausted": see *TLL* vol. 2, col. 567, lines 39–41. Further, his use of the adjective could be informed by the gospels: in Matthew 12:9–13, Mark 3:1–6, and Luke 6:6–11, Jesus performs a miracle on a Sabbath by healing a man with a withered or paralyzed right hand *(manus arida).*

715–19 *Without rest . . . without rest*: Throughout this five-line passage, Nigel riffs on the wording *absque quiete.*

718 *here is rest without rest: toil*: The alternative translation, which gains support from the break between the two halves of the pentameter, would be "here is rest: toil without rest." The manuscript offers no punctuation to decide between the two choices. In either case the implication appears to be, "If you desire rest, then let me tell you what true rest is. It is the total state of rest that you will achieve if you keep toiling without resting."

722 *let the Muse guide . . . with hand*: This line may be an unintended QED for why the poet needs a break, because it reverses and contradicts the careful associations that he drew in 707–10. At the outset Nigel distinguished between the cerebral effort of a poet's composing with a stylus on wax tablet and the manual labor of a scribe's transcribing with a pen on parchment. Consequently, we would expect here for the stylus to be associated

with the mind and the pen with the hand, but instead we encounter the opposite.

Muse: Nigel leaves unspecified which of the nine goddesses he has in mind. His interest in the Muses is typically medieval: see Ernst Robert Curtius, "Die Musen im Mittelalter," *Zeitschrift für romanische Philologie* 59, no. 1 (1939): 129–88, and 63 (1943): 256–68.

723–24 *I pray . . . route*: The couplet could be punctuated with a comma following *precor* and a full stop or semicolon after *periclo.*

730 *this vessel*: Thanks to 1 Thessalonians 4:4 and 2 Timothy 2:21, an empty vessel or vase represented the dead, mortal body from which the living, immortal soul has departed.

732 *name and reality*: The relationship between name and reality fascinated Nigel, whether the two were complementary or conflicting.

733 *changed his clothing*: The cleric doffed secular garb and donned monastic habit.

739 *the duplicitous man*: The Latin here prepares the way for *simplicitatis ovem* (guileless sheep) in 746: etymologically, *duplex* means "twofold," *simplex,* "onefold."

741 *excuses all his crime*: Under *discriminare* 3 the *DMLBS* suggests translating the verb here as "to quash (a charge)."

751–52 *If there was any inconstancy . . . pardoned him*: His untainted reputation excused his lapses into levity.

759 *for a wretched woman*: In Medieval Latin quantitative poetry, most poets scan oblique forms of the noun *mulier* regularly with a long *e:* compare *mulieris* (769, 1200, 2485), *muliere* (1047, 1052, 1285, 1445), and *mulierum* (1307, 1351, 2533).

760 *with the fires of unlawful lust*: Literally, "unlawful fires." In Latin *ignis* was routinely applied figuratively to mean "the fire of love": see *OLD* under *ignis* 9a.

761 *toward her*: *Eidem* could be construed as the masculine nominative singular, but on all other occasions when Nigel uses the form, always at the end of a hexameter, it is the dative singular: compare 681 and 2601.

pleading and payment: Nigel has frequent recourse to the punning metrical pattern *prec(e)* . . . *preti(o)*. See also 763, 764, and 2141. The phrase originated in Ovid, *Fasti* 2.805–6, "*preci*bus *pretio*que / nec *prece* nec *pretio*." Horace, *Epistles* 2.2.173, has "Nunc *prece*, nunc *pretio*." In Medieval Latin, plays on the nouns *pretium* and *prex* became common in proverbs and adages: see Walther, *Proverbia*, nos. 4766, 7797, 13756, 15142, 16237c, 18599, etc.

786 *Hail, Mary*: The angelic salutation in Luke 1:28, delivered by the archangel Gabriel, announces to Mary the impending birth of Jesus. In Latin, this announcement, known formally as the Annunciation, begins *Ave gratia plena*, from which derives the famous prayer to the Virgin known in English as the "Hail, Mary." Beyond playing a central role in this miracle, the text is mentioned prominently in the final one of the pregnant abbess: see 2518.

790 *of Gabriel greeting her*: Since his speech to Mary is called a *salutatio* (greeting) in Luke 1:29, it makes sense for Gabriel to be described with the participle *salutans*.

813 *broke the nighttime silence of the monastic order*: On the vow of silence, see *The Rule of Saint Benedict* 42.1, "Monks should diligently cultivate silence at all times, but especially at night."

814 *the shepherd and sheep*: That is, the abbot and brethren.

as well as with gestures: Monks may communicate nonverbally, particularly with their hands, when their rules forbid them to speak. On signing among Benedictines during Nigel's period, see Scott G. Bruce, *Silence and Sign Language in Medieval Monasticism: The Cluniac Tradition, c. 900–1200* (Cambridge, 2007).

824 *office of the dead*: Translated literally, "office of death." This phrase likely denotes the Office of the Dead in the liturgy of the hours. This prayer cycle is said for the repose of the soul of a deceased individual.

830–31 *dark crowd* . . . *snow-white brightness*: Devils were traditionally black; angels, white. See Michel Pastoureau, *Black: The History of a Color* (Princeton, NJ, 2009), especially 50–60.

835–36 *But in weighing them* . . . *small*: This scene presents a "soul-weighing," designated technically as *psychostasis*, in which the good and the bad deeds of a recently deceased person are weighed out on the pans of a scale to determine whether the spirit will be damned or redeemed. In medieval Marian miracles, the Mother of God often intervened through angels to save the immortal essences of her devotees, despite their sins.

837 *Few things . . . against me*: Compare "He that is not with me, is against me" in Matthew 12:30 and Luke 11:23.

849 *Hold up*: Before the late twelfth century, the imperative of *sisto, -ere* was employed in poetry solely as a transitive verb, but here it is intransitive.

868 *Belial*: The term occurs more than two dozen times in the Hebrew Bible. In 2 Corinthians 6:15 it personifies vileness and ungodliness, in opposition to Christ.

869–70 *his life . . . death, conduct, and life*: Here, in the rhetorical figure known as chiasmus, elements *(vita, via, mors)* are presented in the hexameter in the order A B C, in the pentameter C B A.

873–74 *It is properly permitted . . . on another's*: See Deuteronomy 23:25, "If thou go into thy friend's corn, thou mayst break the ears, and rub them in thy hand: but not reap them with a sickle." Compare Walther, *Proverbia,* nos. 33290 and 36840.

889 *Hail, Mary . . . from the wailing*: The internal rhyme *ave . . . a vae* is more visible without normalization of the manuscript spelling *ve* to *vae.*

892 *the man's . . . poisons*: For punning on *vir* and *virus,* see *Apocalypsis Goliae* 190 (stanza 48.2), "Non *vir* sed *virus* est, virosa sanie" (He is not a man but a poison, with his noisome pus).

910 *by interposing a barrier*: *Obex* derives from the verb *obicio, -ere,* with which it is here coupled. The noun was employed variously as a metaphor. Here it designates a literal or a figurative obstacle, serving to defend or protect. English makes similar use of words such as bulwark or rampart, which denote specific architectural features.

912–18 The contrast of the old and the new man originated with Saint Paul (particularly Ephesians 4:22–24 and Colossians 3:9–10).

914 *in old times by a new law*: The contrast between the old and the

new law is likewise ultimately Pauline, as in, for example, Romans 7:6 and Hebrews 8:13.

918 *becomes a new and altered man*: The concept of the new man is set forth in Ephesians 2:15 and 4:24 as well as in Colossians 3:10.

919 *cenobite*: The two main types of monks were cenobites, who lived in monasteries under rules, and anchorites or hermits.

922 *his life . . . his clothing*: For the reality that monastic life and clothing might clash, see the proverb "the habit does not make the monk": see *TPMA* vol. 8, p. 229 (under *Kleid* 4, "Das Kleid macht den Mönch nicht aus").

926 *worthy of enjoying the love . . . the Virgin and Mother*: The manuscript does not punctuate. If the comma at the end of 925 is removed and one is added at the natural pause in the middle of 926, the pentameter could be translated as "he, worthy of enjoying love, gives priority alone to love of the Virgin and Mother."

927–28 *Hope . . . who is distressed*: Compare Proverbs 13:12, "Hope deferred makes the heart sick, but a longing fulfilled is a tree of life."

929 *the Adversary*: The Latin *hostis* is synonymous with *adversarius* in 1 Peter 5:8. In Hebrew, Satan means "adversary."

933 *the Evil One*: As in 2163, the substantive use of *malignus* for the devil owes ultimately to 1 John 2:13–14, 3:12, and 5:18–19.

935 *The Enemy . . . besets with schemes, seeking someone to devour*: Compare 1 Peter 5:8, "adversarius vester diabolus . . . *circuit, quaerens quem devoret*" (your adversary the devil . . . goes about, seeking someone to devour).

946 *chastises the chalices*: Nigel's unusual and perhaps even unique conceit is that a heavy drinker punishes goblets by draining them often.

947 *shaggy haired*: The line-ending phrase *hirsuta capillis* was conventionally applied to winter: for example, see Alcuin, *Carmina* 58.7, and Sedulius Scottus, *Carmina* 2.5.13. Its application here is puzzling. In describing the nape of the toper's neck, Nigel may have in mind nothing more than the poor hygiene and

grooming of a heavy drinker. If a more specific cause is needed, he could be describing an adverse reaction to drinking similar to the condition known as alcohol flush reaction.

953 *of wine*: Wine from the Falernian district, in the north of Campania, acquired such renown among the ancient Romans that the relevant adjective could be used without even needing to specify the drink.

955–70 The grouping of bull, dog, and lion reflects the influence of Psalms 21:12–14(22:11–13), 21:17(22:16), and 21:21–22(22:20–21). On the devil as a lion, see 1 Peter 5:8.

956 *the author of sin*: That is, Satan. In Prudentius, *Peristephanon* 11.38, the words *erroris . . . auctor* take up the same metrical positions.

957 *with a savage horn*: The manuscript reading of *fere* (almost, nearly) makes less sense logically. For the pairing of the adjective *ferus, -a, -um* and the noun *cornu, -us,* see Statius, *Thebaid* 4.449, and Bernard of Cluny, *De contemptu mundi* 3.132.

984 *the evil pest*: The noun *pestis,* already applied to harmful divinities in Classical Latin, became a descriptor of demonic forces in Christian Latin in late antiquity: see *TLL* vol. 10, part 1, col. 1931, lines 9–18.

997–1000 *I am the Virgin . . . heavenly offspring*: Because two main clauses exist in 997 and 1000, a full stop needs to be placed among the appositional phrases. For want of manuscript punctuation, the decision is somewhat arbitrary.

1003 *the fountain sealed up*: The image derives from Song of Songs 4:12 and 4:15, where it has been interpreted often as referring to the Christian belief that God took human form by becoming Jesus. This incarnation coincided with the Annunciation, the moment when the son of God became the son of the Virgin.

1013 *the rod*: The Latin *vimen* denotes a flexible branch. Here it is a utensil for the self-imposed penitential and ascetic discipline of flagellation, instead of the more common word *virga.*

1017–20 *Cologne*: The original Latin designation for the Roman colony from which the German city eventually developed was Colonia Agrippina, named after Agrippina, Nero's mother. This passage commences by juxtaposing *culta* and *Colonia.* The collocation plays on the etymological association of the city's name with the idea of religious worship inherent in the verb *colo, colere, colui, cultus* ("till," "cultivate," "worship," or, as here, "adorn" or "endow"). From this verb derive both the past participle and the main element in the toponym Colonia.

1021–22 *under the name of holy Peter a renowned monastery*: The cloister in question is Saint Peter's Abbey, founded in 840.

1025–28 Playing upon the Greek elements in *coenobita* (living in common), Nigel points out that this monk professed the same life as the others but failed to uphold the same moral standards.

1034 *rendered unmonastic*: The deponent has the active meaning "to make unmonastic, to render unworthy of a monk." Under *demonachari* the *DMLBS* defines this word as "to live unmonkishly."

1037 *the camps of Venus*: The metaphor of "the camps of love" is a play on Roman militarism that goes back to ancient love poetry: for examples, see Ovid, *Amores* 1.9, and Propertius, *Elegies* 4.135–38. Nigel adds the contrast between *castra* (camps) and *claustra* (cloisters).

1038 *scoundrel . . . cell*: In the Latin pronunciation of Nigel's day, the pun in *sceleratus* and *cella* would have been readily apparent.

1043–44 *Lovemaking, leisure, and wine*: The triad is a monastic equivalent to "wine, women, and song," a formulation famous from its use as the title of a bestseller (subtitled *Mediaeval Latin Students' Songs*) by John Addington Symonds (1840–1893) that was first published in 1884. On Venus's love for leisure, see especially Ovid, *Remedia amoris* 143, "Venus otia amat."

1048 *pitiable evidence of his adultery*: Compare Ovid, *Fasti* 2.808, "Falsus *adulterii testis* adulter ero" (I, an adulterer, will offer false evidence of your adultery), where the key words are flip-flopped. The choice by the Roman poet to modify *testis* with *falsus* argues for construing *miserabilis* with *testis* rather than *adulterii* (a witness to the wretched adultery).

1049–50 *rumor . . . takes wing*: The classic portrayal of Rumor (or Fame) personified and flying is *Aeneid* 4.173–88. Virgil's defining phrase was *Fama volat,* which opens *Aeneid* 3.131, 7.392, and 8.554. Nigel brackets his couplet within these two words.

1052 *fathered*: More literally, *satus* could be translated as "sown." One medieval view of reproduction maintained the Hippocratic model in assuming that to generate a new person required seeds from both mother and father. Thus each of the two had semen in the etymological sense. Against the hypothesis that Nigel has in mind the woman's seed here, see 1271 and 1357–58.

1055 On a young boy as mature as an old man, see note to 365–72 above.

1061–68 The topos of birth ennobled by virtue is analyzed by Curtius, *European Literature and the Latin Middle Ages,* 179–80. An influential expression of it is offered by Ovid, *Tristia* 4.4.1–2, "O qui, nominibus cum sis generosus avorum, / exsuperas morum nobilitate genus . . ." (Oh you who, though you are ennobled by the names of your forefathers, surpass your line in the nobility of your morals).

1075 *Peter*: The monastery was dedicated to this saint. One of the twelve apostles, Peter is often depicted as heading those saints who stand to the right of God in heaven. This privileged placement accords with the unique position in the Church that Jesus promised his follower in Matthew 16:18. Thanks to this primacy, it is understandable that Peter should be portrayed as having special powers of intercession in heaven—but not so special as Mary's.

1081–84 *King, who will rest . . . stigma*: These lines paraphrase Psalms 14(15):1–2, "Lord, who shall dwell in thy tabernacle? or who shall rest in thy holy hill? He that walketh without blemish, and worketh justice." The biblical verses are highlighted in the prologue to *The Rule of Saint Benedict.* With the "sanctuary of the sacred citadel," Nigel slightly recasts the Latin of these verses in the so-called Gallican version of the Psalms, which Jerome is traditionally held to have translated from Greek that originated in the earliest extant translation into that language, known as the Septuagint *(iuxta Septuaginta).* Its text here reads "quis habitabit in tabernaculo tuo" (who will dwell in your tabernacle). Jerome's final Latin psalter, based directly on the Hebrew *(iuxta Hebraicum),* contains different wording. Beyond reversing the two elements of the tabernacle and the mountain, the medieval poet redefines the former. Compare the stock phrase *in aede sacra* (in the sacred sanctuary), which first capped a line in Lactantius, *De ave phoenice* 122.

1119 *born of Roman citizens*: This status need not imply that the wife was brought to life in Rome and even less that she and her husband lived there, but the later mention of the senate points to the city.

1143 *of them praying*: In poetry the genitive plural of present participles sometimes ends in *-tum.*

1145, 1147 *infertile . . . barren*: The form and placement of the adjective *sterili* produces in these two lines a perfect ambiguity about whether the husband or the wife is infertile.

1147 *John*: The Baptist, born to Elisabeth and Zacharias when they were old (Luke 1:5–58).

1167 *Conversation, touching, seeing*: This verse alludes to three of the five "degrees of love," steps leading from initial contact between two lovers to fulfillment of their desires: see Curtius, *European Literature and the Latin Middle Ages,* 512–13, and Lionel J. Friedman, "Gradus amoris," *Romance Philology* 19 (1965): 167–77.

1168 *torches*: The image works well here, since torches were associated commonly in the Latin poetic tradition with both marriage, by metonymy from their use in wedding processions, and the flames of love: see *OLD* under *fax* 2a and 7.

1170 *having done so*: Since *ingredior, -i* is a deponent, the past participle would normally be active in meaning (as it is above in line 86, in *Passio sancti Laurentii* 718, and in *Speculum stultorum* 2705), but the manuscript reading *ingressam* would necessitate translating it as passive: "devastates her *once she has been entered.*" A compelling argument for emending to *ingressa* (with allowable lengthening of the final vowel at the close of the first half-line) is presented by *Speculum stultorum* 3766, "Intrat et ingressus atria lata replet" (arrives and, having entered, again fills up the wide halls).

1171 *is born out of nothing*: The subject of the verb remains *passio mentis–amor* (a passion of the mind, love).

1181 *No witness is present*: Literally, "everyone aware is absent."

1182 *conceal . . . crime*: Nigel's pronunciation would have produced a pun *(scelus celat)*. See also note to 1796.

1191 *bitter crop*: The metaphor owes to Galatians 6:7, with its message of "as you sow, so shall you reap."

1196 *stepmother*: The wicked stepmother, well-established throughout European folklore, planted an indelible imprint in Latin literature: see David Noy, "Wicked Stepmothers in Roman Society and Imagination," *Journal of Family History* 16, no. 4 (1991): 345–61.

1207 *Alone of her sex*: The epithet *sola sui sexus,* which would accord well with the Virgin Mary herself, is shocking here by way of contrast.

mirror of virtue: The tag *speculum virtutis* is attested in Paulinus of Périgueux, *De vita Martini* 2.113 and 5.688.

1238 *There is nothing in the world that escapes the man*: The English assumes *lateo, -ere* to be transitive. Alternatively, translate "Nothing in the world of men lies hidden (from him)." Especially in poetry, the form *virum* can be the genitive plural rather than the accusative singular of the noun *vir, -i.*

1242 *in a moment*: Here and in 2579, *in instanti* means "in an instant, immediately": see *DMLBS* under *instare* 8a, and Albert Blaise, *Lexicon latinitatis medii aevi* (Turnhout, 1975), under *instans* 2.

1243 *Peter*: Despite denying Jesus three times shortly before the Crucifixion, Peter became *primus inter pares* among the apostles. His leadership, as the rock on which the Church was built, instituted orthodoxy and set up apostolic succession. The idea was natural to label as "another Peter" an ecclesiastic who defended or strengthened the faith.

1249–50 *an angel inwardly too—but an evil one*: The expression "evil angels" sometimes describes spiritual beings who revolted against God, belonged afterward to the devil (Jude 6, Matthew 25:41), and worked to deceive God's people through false teaching.

1255–74 On incest as both a social problem and a literary theme in the Middle Ages, see Elizabeth Archibald, *Incest and the Medieval Imagination* (Oxford, 2001). On the Virgin Mary's saving of incestuous sinners, see especially pp. 134, 138, 189, and 223.

1264 *this genus and this species*: The distinction between these terms is basic in medieval logic: compare 1769 and 1865.

1289 *requests that a pyre*: From ancient times incest has been in many cultures a capital offense, with execution by burning one especially drastic form of punishment. Nigel's Latin puns on the noun *rogus, -i* and the verb *rogo, -are.*

1307–14 The slurs against women here, alliterating on the letter *f* to resonate with the Latin noun *femina* (woman), typify the proverbs and poetry of medieval misogyny: see Thomas Klein, *Carmina misogynica: Frauenfeindliche Proverbien und Gedichte des lateinischen Mittelalters,* Beihefte zum *Mittellateinischen Jahrbuch* 17 (Stuttgart, 2015). Compare 1351–56 below.

1311–12 *of a foul stench*: In the manuscript the phrase *foedi foetoris* has punctuation surrounding it and can be construed either with the preceding (as translated here) or succeeding phrase.

1313 *false*: In the manuscript both 1312 and 1314 contain corrections, from a dittography of *fetu* to *feta* and from *facti* to *facta.* It may well be that *ficta* (false) here should be emended to *foeda* (foul) or *feta* (pregnant).

1314 *a woman become a wild beast*: The Latin was first written *femina facti fera,* but *facti* was corrected to *facta.* The mistaken wording was likely suggested by the famous tag "dux femina facti," of Dido as founder of Carthage in Virgil, *Aeneid* 1.364.

1317–18 *Lucian . . . in the city*: Though *urbs* (city) could signify Rome in particular, that localization may not be intended here. Its bishop was the pope, but no such Lucian is recorded. In contrast, three supreme pontiffs bore the name Lucius. Since the senate is mentioned in this miracle, Pope Lucius I (253–254 CE) is likelier than his namesakes in the twelfth century, Lucius II (1144–1145 CE) and III (1181–1185 CE).

1325 *Oh father, oh pastor of the country*: The sustained alliteration on *p* with the related repetition of *t* in the middles of words may well have called to mind the sounds of the Paternoster.

1331 *from the mouth of a new prophet*: In a Christian context, a new prophet is often the same as a false one.

1337–42 On false rumor.

1338 *malign*: *Rodere* can mean either "malign" or "gnaw": compare the note to 63–64 above on gnawing envy.

1340 *Plowing a barren shore*: The image of plowing sand, proverbial already in Classical Latin poetry (for example, Virgil, *Aeneid* 4.212, and Ovid, *Heroides* 5.116), remained so in medieval European literature: see *TPMA* vol. 9, p. 442 (under *Sand* 4, "In den Sand säen").

1351–56 These lines reprise 1307–14 above.

1353 *A defiled vessel*: The expression *vas pollutum,* applied to an impure woman, owes to Leviticus 15:26.

1366 *banished him to the darkness of death*: Compare 2412–13, "Sic *ab*it eductus de valle *necis tenebr*osa" (In this way the cleric departs, led forth to life from the dark valley of death). The fundamental inspiration is Psalms 22(23):4.

1374 *feeling compassion for the wretch*: Here the manuscript reading *misere* is understood as *miserae* and read as a dative dependent on the verb *compatior, -i.* At least theoretically possible would be to read *misere* instead as adverbial: "Suffering wretchedly with her."

1377 *Peter denied the Lord three times*: See Matthew 26:34 and 26:69–75, Mark 14:30 and 14:66–72, Luke 22:34 and 22:56–62, and John 13:38.

1378 *Mary was filled with seven demons*: On this episode involving the Magdalene, see Luke 8:2.

1380 *The one receives the keys*: On Peter's receipt of the keys to heaven, see Matthew 16:19. This motif was stock in the iconography of the saint, customarily depicted with one or more large keys on his person.

the other washes feet: Mary Magdalene was generally identified with the unnamed woman who anointed the feet of Jesus: see Luke 7:37–38.

1381 On the Ninevites, see note to 235 above.

1383 David contrived the death of Uriah so that he might marry the deceased's wife, Bathsheba: see 2 Kings (2 Samuel) 11:3–27.

1384–85 David's reaction to the illness and death of his first child by Bathsheba is recounted in 2 Kings (2 Samuel) 12:21–23: he wept while the child still lived, because he thought that God might show mercy. Although the episode could explain Nigel's reference to the tears of weeping that cleansed David's bed, this couplet likelier refers to Psalm 50(51), ascribed to David—and one of the eight Penitential Psalms.

1385–86 Mary of Egypt (ca. 344–ca. 421), patron saint of penitents, was a harlot of Alexandria who went on a pilgrimage. In Jerusalem she was converted through an experience with an icon of the Blessed Virgin. Eventually she crossed the Jordan and eked out a stringently ascetic existence for nearly a half century in the wilderness. The definitive account of Mary of Egypt's life has been ascribed to Patriarch Sophronius (ca. 560–638) of Jerusalem. Its Greek prose was translated into Latin prose in the late eighth century in a version ascribed to Paul the Deacon of Naples as well as in another by an anonymous. The *vita* was also versified in Latin more than once, most notably for our purposes by Hildebert of Lavardin. See Konrad Kunze, *Studien zur Legende der heiligen Maria Aegyptiaca im deutschen Sprachgebiet,* Philologische Studien und Quellen 49 (Berlin, 1969), 9–39; Erich Poppe and Bianca Ross, eds., *The Legend of Mary of Egypt in Medieval Insular Hagiography* (Dublin, 1996); and Hugh Feiss and Ronald Pepin, *Saint Mary of Egypt: Three Medieval Lives in Verse,* Cistercian Studies Series 209 (Kalamazoo, MI, 2005).

1387 *The door of forgiveness lies open*: The metaphor *porta veniae* is applied often to the Virgin in hymns: see *AH* vol. 9, p. 52, no. 62, stanza 6a; vol. 30, p. 210, no. 103, stanza 1.4; vol. 38, p. 230, no. 17, stanza 50.3; vol. 40, p. 109, no. 110, stanza 3b.3; vol. 46, p. 202, no. 152; vol. 49, p. 331, no. 656; and vol. 50, p. 469, no. 323.

1391 *Entrust all hope to Mary, the wellspring of forgiveness*: This translation assumes that *veniae* (of forgiveness) modifies *fonti* (wellspring), whereas it could modify *spem* (hope): "Entrust all hope of forgiveness to Mary, the wellspring." For the former, compare 1418; for the latter, 325 and 1386. On Mary as *fons veniae,* see Hildebert of Lavardin, *Carmina miscellanea* 1.52.

1411–34 The Litany of the Blessed Virgin Mary, also called the Litany of Loreto, contains many epithets or titles in use from antiquity on that appear in this passage. The Litany in its definitive form was postmedieval, approved by Pope Sixtus V in 1587. But it had many precedents. In the twelfth century similar litanies transitioned from monastic origins into private devotions.

1411 *Peerless Virgin*: For *Virgo carens simili* (already seen in 308), see *AH* vol. 24, p. 57, no. 18, "Die Martis," prosa 2, stanza 1.3; and vol. 54, p. 432, no. 285, "De beata Maria," stanza 9.1.

1413 *glory of the world*: Compare *Gloria terrarum* with *AH* vol. 38, p. 215, no. 16 ("Psalterium 'Theotoca'"), quinquagena 1, stanza 23.1, "terrae gloria"; and vol. 48, p. 128, no. 107 ("Rhythmus quintus"), stanza 1.4, "Orbis terrae gloria."

paradise of delights: For *paradisus deliciarum,* see *AH* vol. 17, p. 31 ("In Festo Rosarii BMV"), In 2. Nocturno: Responsoria, stanza 3.4; and vol. 32, p. 200, no. 152 ("Oratio ad beatam Mariam"), line 13.

1416 *glory of earth*: Medieval readers would have been prepared for *gloria* with *soli* as the dative of the adjective *solus, -a, -um* (alone). Nigel's pairing with the genitive of the noun *solum, -i* (soil) would have caused a jolt, since the two words differ in the quantities of their initial vowels.

1417 *honeycomb*: The formulation *favus mellis* earned special status through the Vulgate Bible: Judges 14:8, 1 Kings (1 Samuel) 14:27, Proverbs 16:24, and Luke 24:42. Applied metaphorically, it is widely diffused in the hymnic tradition: see *AH* vol. 1, pp. 53, 122; vol. 3, pp. 39, 64; vol. 9, p. 24; vol. 13, p. 74; vol. 15, p. 204; vol. 21, p. 71; vol. 25, p. 266; vol. 35, pp. 27, 173; vol. 41, p. 126; vol. 46, p. 331; vol. 48, p. 112.

1418 *wellspring and way of forgiveness*: For *fons veniae* in hymns, see *AH* vol. 6, p. 54; vol. 13, p. 51; vol. 15, p. 58; vol. 17, p. 58; vol. 21, p. 79; vol. 24, p. 128; vol. 29, pp. 65, 200; vol. 30, pp. 191, 268, 278; vol. 31, p. 15; vol. 32, pp. 56, 68; vol. 36, p. 147; vol. 42, p. 132; vol. 45, p. 29; vol. 46, p. 166; vol. 48, p. 384; and vol. 50, p. 595.

1419–20 *a pure and hallowed vessel . . . a vessel granted as an honor*: Compare Sirach 43:2, understood as a reference to Mary as "an admirable vessel, the work of the Most High."

1419 *a vessel pleasing to the Lord*: Compare *AH* vol. 13, p. 104, *"Vas Domini gratum"* (A pleasing vessel of the Lord).

a pure . . . vessel: For *vas mundum* in hymns, see *AH* vol. 4, p. 249; vol. 22, p. 116; vol. 33, p. 35; vol. 35, p. 50; and vol. 36, p. 39.

1420 *sealed on every side*: On *undique signatum,* see note to 1003. For *vas signatum* (the sealed vessel) in hymns, see *AH* vol. 13, p. 86; vol. 20, p. 159; and vol. 44, p. 211.

1421 *king's bridal chamber*: Mary is so called because in her womb the divine was wedded to the human, as a bridegroom to his bride. For an example, see Psalms 18:6(19:5). The fuller expression of *thalamus regis* (with the words sometimes reversed) shows up in hymns a few times: see *AH* vol. 24, p. 78; vol. 32, p. 159; and vol. 46, p. 182.

the law's fulfillment: With the nouns in the opposite order, this phrase is also found in hymns: *AH* vol. 8, p. 150; vol. 15, p. 62; vol. 29, p. 107; and vol. 48, p. 284.

1423 *light that illuminates the senses*: The turn of phrase *lumen sensificum* appears twice in the *AH* in neither case applied to the Virgin: vol. 13, pp. 28 and 54.

1424 *extolling Christ*: The Latin *magnificans Christum* and *Christum magnificans* is encountered occasionally in hymns: see *AH* vol. 26, pp. 29, 221, and vol. 48, p. 278, only in the last instance referring to the Virgin.

1429 *Shining star of the sea*: On the shorter phrase *star of the sea,* see the note to 307. For the longer form, see *AH* vol. 5, p. 49; vol. 15, p. 107; vol. 24, p. 49; vol. 46, pp. 168, 395; and vol. 54, p. 434.

1431 *Virgin, glory of morals*: The pairing *decus morum* appears dozens of times in hymns. For the three-word *Virgo, decus morum,* see *AH* vol. 30, pp. 129, 159, and vol. 32, p. 105.

1434 *the highest grace of God*: The phrase *gratia summa Dei* occurs seldom in the hymnic tradition, but see *AH* vol. 11, p. 81.

1454 *in Rome or the world*: The opening plays on *urbi et orbi* (to the city [of Rome] and the world), a set phrase in papal bulls and other official announcements.

1455 *The purest of women*: The expression *mulier mundissima* is attested in a litany for the Blessed Virgin: see *AH* vol. 31, p. 211, no. 208, stanza 5.3.

1457 *by angelic citizens*: The place of which they are citizens is of course heaven. *Civibus angelicis* was stock in dactylic poetry from Carolingian times as well as in hymns: see *AH* vol. 11, p. 236; vol. 28, p. 244; vol. 40, p. 92; and vol. 49, p. 284.

1468 *an unclean spirit*: The phrase *spiritus immundus* is biblical: see Zechariah 13:2, Matthew 10:1 and 12:43, Mark 1:23, etc.

1475–546 On the extremely popular tale of the Jewish boy who took Communion, see Eugen Wolter, *Der Judenknabe,* Bibliotheca Normannica 2 (Halle, 1879); Theodor Pelizaeus, "Beiträge zur Geschichte der Legende vom Judenknaben" (PhD diss., Vereinigte Friedrichs-Universität Halle-Wittenberg, 1914); and Miri Rubin, *Gentile Tales: The Narrative Assault on Late-Medieval Jews* (New Haven, CT, 1999), 7–28. The story had Greek origin, being written down by Evagrius Scholasticus of Antioch (b. ca. 536–d. after 594) in his *Ecclesiastical History.* In the West it achieved attention from its inclusion in Gregory of Tours (d. 595), *De gloria martyrum.* Eventually it reached England, where it was incorporated in the collections of Abbot Anselm the Younger of Bury Saint Edmunds and of William of Malmesbury. Nigel distills the narrative to its basic elements: a Jewish boy partakes of the Eucharist, his father flings him in an oven, his mother's screams attract a crowd, and the boy turns out to be unscathed thanks to the intervention of the Virgin. The episode concludes as a witness tale, in that many other Jews are converted when their personal experience of the miracle causes them to accept Christianity. Nigel accords prominence to the boy's Jewish mother, leaving implicit that Mary herself is (in a Christian context) the archetypal Jewish mother.

1479 *Each sex and every age*: The common Latin formula *omnis sexus et aetas* has long elicited remark because of its implication that there are as many sexes as ages: see Curtius, *European Literature and the Latin Middle Ages,* 160. Even in Classical Latin, the adjective *omnis, -e* (all, every) was often applied to things that ordinarily occur in pairs rather than in larger numbers: see *OLD* under *omnis* 5b. The construction *omnis sexus,* found also in Nigel's own *Epigrams* 5.27, became standard in Medieval Latin: see James Houston Baxter, "Omnis sexus," *Bulletin Du Cange: Ar-*

chivum Latinitatis medii aevi 9 (1934): 103. Contrast in 1482 the equally routine *sexus uterque.*

1480 *the angelic food*: The Eucharist has been described as angels' food (compare Wisdom 16:20, *angelorum esca*). See also 1486, where the angels' food becomes (less ambiguously) bread.

1486 *fed him with angelic bread*: In other words, the priest gave the boy the bread consecrated in the Eucharist.

1494 *catastrophe*: The second word of the line can be explained if the verb is construed with both an accusative and a dative: see *DMLBS* under *parcere* 4b. A more drastic option would be emendation of *labem* (catastrophe) to *saltem* (at least).

1496 *hand*: *Dextera,* literally "right hand," is commonly syncopated to *dextra* in Latin.

1497 *The boy's distraught mother*: The comparable pattern of *illa parens pueri* in 1529 and 1533, with a penthemimeral caesura afterward, argues for punctuating after *pueri* rather than *maesta parens:* "the distraught mother, taking pity on the boy's grievous pain."

1498 *face with violent fingernails*: The scratching of the face to express sorrow in mourning, desperation, or both was a gesture ascribed often to women in ancient Greece and Rome: see Carl Sittl, *Die Gebärden der Griechen und Römer* (Leipzig, 1890), 27.

1502 *What offense did the wretch commit?*: Nigel stands apart from other medieval poets in having *quid miser* lead into a third-person rather than a second-person verb. Consequently, *miser* is a substantive (the wretch) rather than a vocative (oh wretch) designating the subject. These circumstances suggest that his inspiration may well have been Ovid, *Ex Ponto* 4.4.48, also a pentameter: "et 'Heu' dicas '*quid miser* ille facit?'" (and you may say, "Alas! What is that wretch doing?").

1503 *Spare the boy, father*: Note Nigel's soundplay, with alliteration on *p* until the caesura and mainly nasal consonants afterward: "*Parce, pater p*atriae, *n*ec *nomin*is i*mmem*or huius." The initial letters in the first three words highlight *pater,* the Latin for father; those in the rest of the line, *mater,* for mother.

1513 *not even a hair*: Underlying this hexameter is the idiom of not touching or harming a hair on a person's head.

1537 *gusts that bring dew*: Literally, "gusts of dew." The main point of comparison is Daniel 3:50, "et *fecit* medium *fornacis quasi* ventum *roris fla*ntem" (and made the midst of the furnace like the blowing of a wind bringing dew). Some Greek and Latin manuscripts of the book of Daniel contain three sections not found in the Masoretic text. The first of these, often named "The Prayer of Azariah and the Song of the Three Holy Children," is intercalated between Daniel 3:23–24: the apocryphon runs through 3:90, so that the former 3:24 becomes 3:91. It tells of three Jewish boys named Shadrach (Hananiah in Hebrew), Meshach (Mishael), and Abednego (Azariah), who are Daniel's companions in captivity at the Babylonian court. For refusing to venerate a golden idol set up by Nebuchadnezzar, they are thrown into a fiery furnace. They sing a song of worship, the so-called "Canticle of the Three Children," and survive untouched, rescued by an angel. The episode of salvation involving the three boys was well known in the Middle Ages, and an excerpt from it was the fourth text of Lauds in the Marian Office: see Rachel Fulton Brown, *Mary and the Art of Prayer: The Hours of the Virgin in Medieval Christian Life and Thought* (New York, 2018), 203–5.

1545 *Pisa*: In pairing this miracle with the following one, William of Malmesbury makes explicit that both take place in Pisa: *Miracula sanctae Mariae Virginis* 2.34, ed. and trans. Thomson and Winterbottom, *Miracles,* 99. Nigel leaves implicit that the next miracle likewise occurs in Pisa. Elsewhere the location is Bourges, as in Dominic of Evesham, or Constantinople.

1546 *to pious service and the liturgical hours*: The last phrase translates a single word that could be put into English most literally as "offices." The divine office designates the liturgy of the hours that many in the Church were and are required to pray. For the rest of these words, compare 1746, "virginis *obsequiis* invigilare *piis*" (to keep vigil in dutiful service to the Virgin). The operative ones go back to Venantius Fortunatus, *Vita Martini* 1.397, "*obsequiis* intenta *piis*" (intent on pious service).

1547–80 On this miracle, see Karin Fuchs, "Les collections de miracles de la Vierge: Rassembler, copier, réécrire; L'exemple du récit du pain offert à l'image du Christ," in *Miracles, vies et réécritures dans l'Occident médiéval: Actes de l'atelier "La réécriture des miracles" (IHAP, juin 2004) et SHG X–XII; Dossiers des saints de Metz et Laon et de saint Saturnin de Toulouse,* ed. Monique Goullet and Martin Heinzelmann, Beihefte der Francia 65 (Ostfildern, 2006), 67–91.

1547–48 *a respectable mother, with her boy of tender age*: The boy and the parents in this miracle are not identical with those in the preceding one. William of Malmesbury makes a similarly abrupt transition when he conjoins the same two miracles: *Miracula sanctae Mariae Virginis* 2.33–34, ed. and trans. Thomson and Winterbottom, *Miracles,* 97–99.

1548 *into the Virgin's church*: The choice of the noun *templum* is a little curious.

1550 *the benevolent goddess*: Also striking is this designation of Mary as a female god. Generally, the Virgin was kept carefully distinct, as the Theotokos, or "God-bearer," rather than a divinity herself.

1552 *released from her vow*: Alternatively, translate "relieved through her vow."

1554 *requests the Virgin's hoped-for aid*: The strong alliteration of *optatam optat . . . opem* in both lines argues against the variant reading in manuscript *A* of *orat* (prays for) in place of *optat* (requests).

1555–56 *a mother's likeness*: In Nigel's time representations of Mary seated would have all shown her with Jesus as an infant on her lap. The image described here is such a Madonna and Child. The phrase *matris imago* is found also at line 1978. It is impossible to translate fully, since to the boy the carving embodies, or even is, a generic real woman and mother, whereas to more sophisticated viewers it stood in for the Mother par excellence, namely, the Virgin.

1559 *Eat*: The normal form of the imperative would be *pappa,* close to the reading *papa* in *A*. The unusual *papap* in the main manuscript, which averts the hiatus between the second vowel of *pappa* and the first of *ait,* could be an effort to convey baby talk for "Eat, eat!" Other versions of the story have "Puppa, inquiens, papa" and "Pupe papa, pupe papa": see Fuchs, "Les collections de miracles de la Vierge," 79.

1569–70 *you will share food with me*: Compare Luke 23:43, "And Jesus said to him: Amen I say to thee, this day thou shalt be with me in paradise."

1576 *three-day period*: The stretch of time, mentioned also in 1570 and 1579, calls to mind the triduum, which commences on the evening of Maundy Thursday and closes with evening prayer on Easter Sunday.

1583 *revered by all*: This translation takes *cunctis venerandus* as a self-contained unit, as it is in 1941 (in the same metrical position). The Latin could instead be construed "venerable in all his habits and his respectable life."

1585 *would chant the customary hours*: The eight canonical hours of prayer comprise one time of praise during the night (inspired by Psalms 118[119]:62) called Matins (about 2 a.m.), and seven during the day (Psalms 118[119]:164): Lauds (at dawn), Prime (about 6 a.m.), Terce (about 9 a.m.), Sext (about noon), Nones (about 3 p.m.), Vespers (about 6 p.m.), and Compline (about 7 p.m.).

1596 *fragrant with . . . aroma*: Christian culture, equating olfactory states with spiritual ones, associated sweet smell with moral purity, especially in the so-called odor of sanctity.

1624 *who just recently was first is last among the people*: The thought owes to the Gospel of Matthew. In 19:30 Jesus declares that in the world to come, "And many that are first shall be last: and the last shall be first"; in 20:16, "So shall the last be first, and the first last."

1645–74 The intricate number symbolism, explained cursorily by the angel, is not unique to Nigel but also appears in other versions. See "Miracles de la Vierge, par Everard de Gately, moine de Bury Saint-Edmond," in Paul Meyer, "Notice du ms. Rawlinson Poetry 241 (Oxford)," *Romania* 29 (1900): 27–47, especially 27–34. The numbers refer to two Psalms, 53 and 118, used in the

Marian Office, as well as to the sections and verses into which they are divided. For Latin texts with indications of the psalms employed in the Hours of the Blessed Virgin Mary, see Edward Samuel Dewick, ed., *Facsimiles of* Horae de beata Maria virgine *from English MSS. of the Eleventh Century,* Henry Bradshaw Society 21 (London, 1902). On the Hours themselves (also known as the Little Office of the Virgin Mary), see Fulton Brown, *Mary and the Art of Prayer,* throughout but especially 1–45 and 161–235.

1645 *twenty-three charming types of vegetation*: The twenty-three pleasant herbs that the flowering earth produces are the twenty-two divisions of Psalm 118(119) ("Beati immaculati," a psalm used throughout the Hours of the Virgin) and the entirety of Psalm 53(54) ("Deus in nomine tuo," the first psalm at Prime in the Hours of the Virgin). Twenty-three had deep meaning in medieval numerology, in part because the alphabet of the Latin language contains that number of letters. For the symbolism of twenty-three, twenty-two, seven, and eight, see the relevant entries in Heinz Meyer and Rudolf Suntrup, *Lexikon der mittelalterlichen Zahlenbedeutungen,* Münstersche Mittelalter-Schriften 56 (Munich, 1987).

1647 *replete with sevenfold flower*: Psalm 53(54) ("Deus in nomine tuo") is divided into seven verses, if the two verses composing the title are omitted from consideration.

1649 *eight flowers*: Each section of Psalm 118(119) ("Beati immaculati") contains eight verses.

1654 *outdoes balsam with . . . scent*: "Balsam," or "balm," referred both to a plant and to the aromatic resin derived from it that was used as a healing medicinal ointment. The word, which comes up again in 1704, appeared a half-dozen times in the Hebrew Bible.

1664–66 *sevenfold flower . . . seven*: Psalm 53(54) encompasses seven verses (see above, note to 1647). The seven gifts of the Holy Spirit (wisdom, understanding, counsel, fortitude, knowledge, piety, and fear of the Lord) find their origin in Isaiah 11:2–3.

1679 *everything is not only good but supremely good*: The last couple of words recall God's final assessment of the creation at the end of the sixth day, in Genesis 1:31, "Viditque Deus cuncta quae fecerat, et erant *valde bona*" (And God saw all the things that he had made, and they were very good). After having previously designated his work merely "good" four times in Genesis 1:10, 1:12, 1:18, and 1:25, God heightens his praise.

1680 *not even the tongue of an eyewitness can say*: Nigel resorts yet again to the inexpressibility topos: see Curtius, *European Literature and the Latin Middle Ages,* 159–62. The phrase *dicere lingua* is often found in the presentation of one or another type of play upon the commonplace. The first use of it is Lucretius, *De rerum natura* 1.831.

1683–84 *receives him in her arms*: The phrase *in ulnas* (into the arms) is positioned solely at the ends of hexameters, from Virgil, *Georgics* 3.355, on. Whereas it is often used with the perfect of a compound from *capio, -ere* such as *suscepit* and *accepit,* Nigel shows his indebtedness to Claudian, *Carmina minora* 30.217–18, "*in ulnas / excip*eres" by following it directly in the following line with a form of *excipio, -ere.*

1685 The image of the Virgin suckling the child Jesus was widespread in medieval art and literature alike. Such a nursing Madonna is designated technically by the Latin *Maria lactans* or *virgo lactans,* by the Greek *Galaktrophousa.*

1687 *my beloved son*: The phrases *filius dilectus* and *filius meus dilectus* appear in the gospels (Mattthew 3:17, 17:5, etc.), the apocryphal Gospel of Nicodemus, and Latin hymns.

1689 *the creator of the world*: The wording *conditor orbis* is understandably common from late antiquity in Christian Latin poetry, almost always in this final position in hexameters. The expression is found also in hymns and the liturgy.

1703 *with heavenly nectar*: The placement of *caelesti nectari* in this metrical position can be tracked back to Ovid, *Metamorphoses* 4.252. The expression appears often in Christian poetry, from late antiquity on, even though *nectar* is not found in the Vulgate. In Classical Latin the noun referred to a sweet drink, made of wine, honey, and spices or derived from other plants, that was consumed by the gods and that could confer immortality. It was also connected sometimes with milk.

1704 *aromatic gums*: The word *thymiama* is Late Latin, a Christian loan from the Greek for incense. These substances are invoked often in the Bible, especially in Exodus 25:6, 31:11, 35:15, 35:28, 37:29, and 39:37. The first of these mentions singles out the pleasant smell of the gums ("thymiamata boni odoris"), a quality that is emphasized repeatedly.

1707 *heaven-granted*: The lengthening of the final vowel in *indulta* is entirely normal in Medieval Latin, because of its position at the penthemimeral caesura, occurring after the fifth half-foot in the dactylic hexameter.

1741 *the mother sweet as honey*: In medieval symbolism the honeybee, seen to embody virginity and virtues, represented the Virgin. Doctors of the Church devoted to preaching about her, with Bernard of Clairvaux being the prime example, were characterized as flowing with honey—*mellifluus,* in Latin. Nigel maintains the alliteration on the letter *m* across ten words, for the entirety of this line and the next.

1749–932 The miracle of the priest who knew only one Mass was one of the oldest Marian miracles to originate in the West and was widely known: see Pierre Kunstmann, "La Légende de saint Thomas et du prêtre qui ne connaissait qu'une messe," *Romania* 92 (1971): 99–117.

1750 *a simple person*: This description of the man, reemphasized in 1756, 1761, and 1764, conforms to a commonplace known as "holy simplicity": see Jean LeClercq, "Sancta simplicitas," *Collectanea ordinis Cisterciensium reformatorum* 22 (1960): 138–48, and Walter F. Veit, "Sancta simplicitas," in *Sensus communis: Contemporary Trends in Comparative Literature; Panorama de la situation actuelle en littérature comparée; Festschrift für Henry Remak,* ed. János Riesz, Peter Boerner, and Bernhard F. Scholz (Tübingen, 1986), 369–83. The phrase *simplicitatis homo* recurs in 1756 and 1934.

1759 *unskilled*: More literally, "not much" or, alternatively, "not notable in the art of grammar." The adjective acquired this sense only in postclassical Latin: see Blatt, *Novum glossarium,* under *multus, -a, -um* I. C. 2, as well as *DMLBS* under *multus, -a, -um* 5.

1759–60 *the art of grammar*: *Ars grammatica* denoted the manuals through which Latin grammar was taught.

1765 *What grammar is*: Nigel's thumbnail sums up the coverage of grammar exactly as his contemporaries understood it. Herrad of Landsberg, abbess of Hohenbourg, has above her depiction of Lady Grammar the inscription "Per me quis discit *vox littera syllaba* quid sit" (Through me one learns what utterance, letter, and syllable are). See Herrad of Hohenbourg, *Hortus deliciarum,* ed. Rosalie Green, Michael Evans, Christine Bischoff, and Michael Churschmann, Studies of the Warburg Institute 36 (London, 1979), vol. 1, *Commentary,* p. 104, and vol. 2, *Reconstruction,* p. 57.

1769 *genus . . . species*: On the two concepts, see 1865 as well as note to 1264.

1772 *Quintilian*: The Spanish-born rhetorician, famous in Rome, lived from approximately 35 to around 100 CE. His only undisputed extant work is the twelve-volume guide to rhetoric entitled *Institutio oratoria (The Institutes of Oratory),* completed at the end of the first century.

1779–80 *Hail, holy Mother*: An apostrophe beginning "Salve, sancta parens" is addressed to the Virgin in the *Paschale carmen* by the fifth-century poet Sedulius, in an account of the birth of Christ. The words became the antiphon of the introit for common Masses of the Blessed Virgin Mary.

1785 *This is the office that suits*: Compare 1791, which likewise is built upon the wording "Hoc est officium quod . . . convenit. . . ." As in 824 and 1546, the noun *officium* in both lines denotes an office in formal worship, meaning a prayer service conducted by a priest.

1786 *this same one*: The Latin *illud idem* looks at first as if it might be intended to draw a distinction that established a separate category from the anaphora on *hoc;* but instead it is synonymous. Translating as "that same one" would be misleading.

1787 This line refers to the doctrine of the Trinity, that one God exists in three persons of one substance, namely the Father, Son, and Holy Spirit.

1789 *to perform last rites*: The expression *solvere defunctos* could also be translated as "to discharge (or release) the deceased."

1790 *to reconcile . . . with God*: The reconciliation refers to the sacrament of penance (or confession). Thus the reconciliation at issue can be achieved through general absolution, as part of the penitential rite of the Mass.

1795 *goes around the whole earth*: The line alludes to the devil, just before he began to persecute the title figure in Job 1:7 and 2:2, where the operative phrase is *circuivi terram.* Here and in 2453 the verb *circuit,* ordinarily spelled *circumit* in Classical Latin, also evokes Satan as described in 1 Peter 5:8, "adversarius vester diabolus tamquam leo rugiens *circuit*" (your adversary the devil, as a roaring lion, goeth about seeking whom he may devour).

1796 *to hasten crime . . . to hastening it*: There is a *jeu de mots* here involving *scelus* and the verbs. In Nigel's pronunciation, *scel-* and *-cel-* would have sounded identical. For the same play, see *Passio sancti Laurentii* 951, "In scelus accelerat" (He hurries into crime), and 1910, "scelus accelerare parati" (prepared to hasten crime).

1801 *the substance of his property*: Many clerics received support—a living—to compensate them for services that they rendered to the Church. Such a benefit was often called in Latin *beneficium.* Sometimes it came from an allotment of land.

1809–10 *blinds the eyes of his . . . mind*: The first line contains the Latin for "mind's eye," the mental faculty of visualizing either recollected or imagined images. The couplet assumes, in keeping with a common metaphor, that a vice such as lust impairs vision of this sort—that it blinds the soul. The most relevant biblical verses are John 12:40 and 2 Corinthians 4:4.

1811–14 The passage refers to nepotism, to which Nigel returns more explicitly in 2213–16. He touches often upon the topic in the *Tract on Abuses.*

1813 *Undiscriminating love*: The adjective could mean even "imprudent" or "foolish."

1821 *without instruction in the law and with no expertise in the liberal arts*: Parish priests were expected to be sufficiently literate to fulfill their pastoral responsibilities, which required being able to undertand and convey the meaning of the liturgy through preaching. Not all met these standards, which must have created situations similar to the one described in this miracle.

1836 *sufficient reason*: So the Latin *sufficiens causa* is conventionally translated, although the principle of sufficient reason has been juxtaposed to various phrases that incorporate cause, such as efficient cause, final cause, formal cause, and material cause.

1851 *he pretended that he was proceeding*: Compare Luke 24:28, "et ipse *se finxit longius ire*" (and he made as though he would go farther).

1859–60 *tears that Peter's or Mary's*: Peter's weeping, mentioned already in 235–36, is described in Matthew 26:75, Mark 14:72, and Luke 22:62. Mary's weeping is highlighted above all in John 20:11.

1862 *the judge's*: In the Hebrew Bible, God is called a judge in his capacity of supreme arbiter who passes sentence upon all on earth. In the New Testament, Jesus too is named a judge, instituting a new standard of judgment according to the new law.

1869 *the Deity's ear*: Holy Writ refers to the ears of the Lord in, for example, 1 Kings (1 Samuel) 8:21, Psalms 17:7(18:6), and James 5:4.

1877 *the highest king*: In the Bible Jesus is not called outright the highest king but rather, by a construction that conveys the same thinking, "king of kings": see 1 Timothy 6:15 as well as Revelation 17:14 and 19:16.

1893 *become a wolf instead of a shepherd*: On the proverbial image of the shepherd transformed into a wolf, see *TMPA* vol. 6, p. 114 (under *Hirt* 6).

1895 *conform well*: The only citation for the adjective *convenus, -a, -um* in *DMLBS* is this line in the *Miracles.*

the behavior of bishops: The substantive *gesta,* translated here as "behavior," ordinarily refers simply to deeds or actions. As a literary genre, it designates written accounts of such exploits.

1897 *to spare the simple and to crush the proud*: Nigel rings a change upon Virgil's famous words in *Aeneid* 6.853, "*parcere* subiectis *et debellare superbos.*"

1901 *just man*: The phrase appears in both the Hebrew Bible and the New Testament. The first person thus described is Noah in Genesis 6:9, the last the centurion Cornelius in Acts 10:22. John is so called in Mark 6:20.

1904 *before the thirtieth day*: The phrasing equates roughly to "within a month." The specific chronology evokes Daniel 6:7 and 6:12, where a royal decree stipulates that during the coming thirty days *(usque ad dies triginta)* anyone who prays other than to King Darius will be thrown into the lion's den. At the same time, it resonates with the span of three days known as the triduum: see note to 1576.

1908 *terrified to an unbelievable degree*: The past participle *contremefactus* may well be a Nigellian neologism, with the intensifying prefix *com-* (completely) attached to the ordinary *tremefactus.* The apparent hapax legomenon *contremefacere* is included solely in the *DMLBS,* with the only citation being this verse.

1910 *of flesh and blood*: The choice of words brings to mind Ephesians 6:12, "For our wrestling is not against flesh and blood [*adversus carnem et sanguinem*]; but against principalities and powers, against the rulers of the world of this darkness, against the spirits of wickedness in the high places."

1915 *The common custom . . . avoided*: This hexameter has hiatus between the final syllable of *praelatorum* and the following *et.* The next word *consuetudo* is to be scanned as four syllables: the first *u* is to be consonantalized and *-sue* treated as a single long syllable. Compare *Tract on Abuses* Pref. 73, "qui mores hominum, quae *consuetudo* locorum" (what are the manners of men, what the customs of places).

1930 *their homeland*: More literally, the fatherland, meaning heaven. See note to 390, as well as Hebrews 11:14–16.

1933–2118 On the miracle of the image collateralized in a loan, see Erik Boman, ed., "Deux miracles de Gautier de Coinci" (PhD diss., Göteborgs Universitet, 1935), vii–xv. Boman distills the findings of Mussafia, Kjellman, and others. Among many versions in eastern and western languages alike, the legend is attested in two accounts of Russian travelers to Constantinople, one from around 1200 and the other from the second quarter of the fifteenth century, both of whom claim to have seen in churches images of the Virgin that had been given as surety by the Christian Theodore and that protected him from wrongful foreclosure by the Jew Abraham. The narrative is attested earliest in a text by a monk from southern Italy who lived sometime between 950 and 1050. The story is the first miracle in the *Liber de miraculis* by this Johannes Monachus. Eventually, William of Malmesbury incorporated the tale into his collection of miracles of the Virgin.

1933 *Constantinople*: Present-day Istanbul in Turkey, capital of the Eastern Roman Empire that in modern times has been conventionally called Byzantium in the West. The city is mentioned again in this same miracle in 2035. Here and there Nigel treats the fourth syllable of the adjective *Constantinopolitana* as long. This solution to metrical necessity was well established in twelfth-century poetry.

1935 *Theodore*: Theodore is a common and even stereotypical Greek name that means "God-given." A figure known to Nigel because of local connections, Theodore of Tarsus (602–690) was a Greek who grew up in Tarsus but spent time first in Constantinople and later in Rome before being installed as archbishop of Canterbury.

1939 *created out of a rich one*: If the second half-line should be construed as the subject to this predicate (as in 87, where the phrase also appears), the translation would be "As a man made suddenly poor out of a rich one is accustomed [to do]." Compare the anonymous verse *Gesta regum Britanniae* 2.269, "quam qui mendicat *factus de divite pauper*" (than the one who begs, when a poor man is created out of a rich one).

1945 *doors*: Most probably providing access to religious foundations: see *DMLBS* under *ostium* 1b, "door (of church or monastery)."

1952 *payouts . . . prayers*: Nigel here puns on the plural forms of the same nouns that he manipulates in the singular in 761, 763, 764, and 2141.

1957 *Abraham (for so he was called)*: In the Bible, Abraham was the founding father whose covenant of the pieces formed the basis of the special relationship between the Hebrews and God. The name of this patriarch, initially Abram but subsequently expanded by the epenthesis of a syllable, was etymologized in Genesis 17:5 as "father of a multitude." After Isaac and Joseph, Abraham was the third most common personal name among Jews in Angevin England: see Joseph Jacobs, *The Jews of Angevin England* (London, 1893), 344–69.

1977 *Highest Wisdom*: This edifice, now known as Hagia Sophia, was erected by Emperor Justinian I (r. 527–565) and dedicated to Holy Wisdom (the second person of the Trinity, the Logos).

1977–80 *fittingly painted . . . on a panel*: Whatever painted icons of the Virgin and Child may once have been located in Hagia Sophia disappeared when Byzantine Constantinople fell, first to the Fourth Crusaders in 1204 and later to Sultan Mehmed II of the Ottoman Turks in 1453. In contrast, the famous mosaic icon of the Theotokos, representing Mary with Jesus in this manner, remains in the half dome of the apse. A short distance east of the former cathedral, the most famous icon of the Virgin holding the Child, believed to have been painted by Saint Luke himself, was displayed in the monastery of the Panagia Hodegetria (all-holy way pointer). The painting there, which enticed flocks of pilgrims, could be meant here.

1996 *he can hardly count*: This observation, regarding what we might call uncountability, is related to the inexpressibility topos.

2000 *before the date for interest payment*: This translation assumes that the genitive modifies *ante diem:* see *TLL* vol. 5, part 1, col. 1059, lines 32–36 for such expressions as *dies pecuniae* (the day of payment), *solvendae pecuniae* (of rendering payment), and *creditae pecuniae* (of payment of a loan). Another option would be to put into English as "all his debts of interest to the Jew before the appointed day (deadline)." In either case, the specificity of the term *faenus* seems to be at odds with the rest of the story, where the issue is repayment of the whole debt and not just interest.

2002 *the more we want anything, the slower it comes*: The thinking here resembles such proverbs as the modern English "a watched pot never boils."

2005 *the strait*: The noun *fretum* could denote most broadly "the sea," but here specifically the Bosporus Strait, which connects the Black Sea with the Sea of Marmara and separates Europe and Asia. The waterway has infamously strong and treacherous currents.

2014 *reading*: The English assumes that the participle functions here in a sense used of literary texts, to refer to their contents: see *DMLBS* under *habere* 14d. The alternative would be to translate "having this brief poem (inscribed)" with the inference that Nigel was motivated by Ovid, *Metamorphoses* 9.793, "addunt et titulum; titulus *breve carmen habe*bat" (they add also an inscription; the inscription had this brief poem), and 14.442, "condita marmoreo tumulo *breve carmen habe*bat" (buried in a marble tomb, she had a brief poem).

2020 *credit*: More literally, "faith."

2027–28 *earth . . . fire . . . air . . . sea wave*: Nigel lists the four elements as they had been designated by the Greek philosopher Empedocles in the fifth century BCE and as they remained for two millennia afterward.

2037 *it will redound*: Emendation to the present subjunctive *cedat* (it would redound) would be tempting, so as to relieve the inconsistency of this lone indicative preceded by five subjunctives in a row and followed by two. The change would also align the line more closely with wording at the end of Juvenal, *Satires* 1.110, "vincant divitiae, sacro ne cedat honori" (let riches prevail, that he not give way to sacred honor). A scribe copying *perveniant . . . cedat . . . pereant . . . neget* could have slipped by changing *cedat* to *cedet.* But the mixed condition with the future as it stands could be deliberate, to bring home the certainty that the Virgin will deliver on her pledge.

2069 *the talents that had been loaned*: Here and in 2073, 2087, and 2095 the plural noun *talenta* carries two meanings. Taken generally, the Latin indicates weights of money. At the same time, it would have reminded Nigel's readers inevitably of the parable of the talents in Matthew 25:14–30 and Luke 19:12–27. The phrase *commissa talenta* refers to the parable in such later poets as Paulinus of Nola, *Carmina* 21.438, and Venantius Fortunatus,

Carmina 5.2.52 and *Epistulae Austrasicae* 14.22. On exegesis of the story in the Middle Ages, see Stephen L. Wailes, *Medieval Allegories of Jesus' Parables* (Berkeley, CA, 1987), 184–94.

2088 *despite what you say*: This phrase translates *tamen*.

2113 *an event worthy of a renowned narration*: Elsewhere it would make sense to translate as "frequent reporting," but doing so here would obscure the litotes of *celebris . . . celebri . . . celebrem*.

2122 *lazy repose*: The distrust of idleness ran deep in medieval Christianity, especially in monasticism. By itself, repose was not blameworthy but commendable. In contrast, laziness was a different story. See Siegfried Wenzel, *The Sin of Sloth:* Acedia *in Medieval Thought and Literature* (Chapel Hill, NC, 1967).

2131 *the wise virgin*: A less loaded translation, such as "the circumspect maiden," would block the resonances of the parable of the wise and foolish virgins in Matthew 25:1–13: the Latin words there are *prudentes* and *virgines.* See Wailes, *Medieval Allegories of Jesus' Parables,* 177–84.

2140 *all too undeservedly*: The adverb *indigne* conveys either the cleric's view that he deserves better or the poet's that the cleric is wrong to regret a rejection that saved him from sin.

2146 *sorcery*: More literally, "magic arts."

2159 *holy Mary*: English tends toward Virgin Mary (or the Blessed Virgin Mary); French, *Notre Dame* (Our Lady). Spanish retains *Santa Maria* (Saint Mary).

2163 *the Evil One*: See the note to 933.

2165 *Prince of Night*: Although the expression *princeps noctis* is not biblical, untold verses in the New Testament evoke oppositions between, on the one hand, darkness, night, this world, and Satan, and on the other, light, day, heaven, and God. Ephesians 6:12 refers to the struggle "adversus principes et potestates, adversus mundi rectores tenebrarum harum" (against principalities and powers, against the rulers of the world of this darkness).

2175–84 Lovesickness garnered considerable attention, from educated readers who attended to literary treatments in Ovid and others, as well as from physicians. On the symptoms of sleeplessness, breathing, crying, color, and anorexia that are enumerated here, see Mary F. Wack, *Lovesickness in the Middle Ages: The* Viaticum *and Its Commentaries* (Philadelphia, 1990).

2213 *special dispensation for a nephew*: The term "nepotism" descends directly from the Latin *nepos* (nephew). Men who had taken vows of chastity, especially popes and bishops, could extend to these relatives the preference for advancement that they might otherwise have accorded to their own offspring. Nigel railed against this failing in his *Tract on Abuses* and in his prose letter on the *Speculum stultorum*.

2223 *The cleric . . . approves them*: The hexameter is symmetrically structured, bracketed between the cleric and the girl, with his lust occupying center stage; between these elements are the chiastic *ista probat* and *probat ista*.

2227 *vow of virginity*: More commonly, vow of chastity *(votum castitatis)*. The so-called three evangelical counsels, or counsels of perfection, are chastity, poverty, and obedience.

2228 *holy orders*: Within the Catholic Church, bishops, priests, and deacons receive in their ordination holy orders. One of seven sacraments (baptism, confirmation, the Eucharist, penance, anointing of the sick, holy orders, and matrimony), this one defines those ordained as ministering to the spiritual needs of others in continuation of Jesus Christ's priesthood.

2231 *the holy sacraments*: The wedding, itself conferring the sacrament of matrimony, includes the partaking of the Eucharist in holy Communion.

2234 *wines, and fine fare*: The Latin *dapes* can denote a feast or banquet as well as the foods involved.

2241 *the Hours of the Virgin . . . Nones*: On the canonical hours in general, see note to 1585. Nones was reckoned a particularly dangerous time. It was the ninth hour of the day from sunrise, originally in the midafternoon but eventually moved earlier to our noon, which is a derivative. The concept of the noonday demon (Psalms 90[91]:6) designates an evil spirit that predisposes its sufferers, especially monks and clerics, to be remiss in their duties, just as happens here.

2269–70 *chanting Nones*: In illustrated Hours of the Virgin, Nones could be illuminated with a depiction of the crucified Christ with Mary at his side. The ninth hour is when Jesus cried out to ask why God forsook him—the time of the Crucifixion, Redemption, and prayer with the mediation of Mary.

2321–26 The cleric has had sin in his heart, even if he has not acted upon the thought. See Matthew 5:28, "But I say to you, that whosoever shall look on a woman to lust after her, hath already committed adultery with her in his heart."

2328 *A little leaven*: Compare 1 Corinthians 5:6.

2341 *what my purpose is*: Or construe *quae . . . causa mei* as an instance of the figure of speech aposiopoesis, with *amoris* left momentarily unsaid because of the speaker's emotionalism.

2342 *allow you to know*: Having written about the product of his labor—the fruit of his work—Nigel now alludes cleverly to the knowledge of good and evil that could be gained by eating from the forbidden fruit from one of the two trees in the garden of Eden.

2364 *first and foremost*: It is difficult to be certain what *imprimis* modifies.

2397 *with rods, clothing, and food*: Nigel probably refers to the flagellation (here the administration of self-inflicted pain by rods rather than whips, as voluntary penance), hair shirt (a rough garment, also known as a cilice, worn close to the skin), and restricted diet of an ascetic.

2399 *tears . . . laughter*: Shedding tears was viewed as a virtue, engaging in laughter as a vice: see Piroska Nagy, "Religious Weeping as Ritual in the Medieval West," *Social Analysis* 48, no. 2 (2004): 117–37, and Irven M. Resnick, "*Risus monasticus:* Laughter and Medieval Monastic Culture," *Revue bénédictine* 97, nos. 1–2 (1987): 90–100.

2400 *Scant sleep and food*: See Sarah Macmillan, "'The Nyghtes Watchys': Sleep Deprivation in Medieval Devotional Culture," *Journal of Medieval Religious Cultures* 39, no. 1 (2013): 23–42, and Teresa M. Shaw, *The Burden of the Flesh* (Minneapolis, 1998).

2405 *the final hour of death*: *Extremi temporis horam* refers to both his own last moment and the Last Judgment awaiting all humankind. Compare Numbers 24:14 and Deuteronomy 31:29.

2407 *the mortal body*: The Latin means, literally, "the body of death." The source is Romans 7:24, "Unhappy man that I am, who shall deliver me from the body of this death?"

2409 *dove*: The bird issuing from his mouth symbolizes death and his soul rising to heaven, a scene represented commonly in Christian art.

2411–12 *the spirit . . . free*: For the words *liber* and *spiritus* with this placement, see first Paulinus of Nola, *Carmina* 15.192.

2411 *the prison of the flesh*: On the body as imprisoning the soul, see note to 71 above.

2413 *the dark valley of death*: Nigel fuses the different readings of the two main Latin translations of Psalms 22(23):4: the Gallican, "in the middle of the shadow of death" *(in medio umbrae mortis)*, and Jerome's translation from the Hebrew, "in the valley of death" *(in valle mortis)*.

2415–22 These lines, prefacing the miracle "On the Pregnant Abbess," discuss the battle that a person must wage to protect the flesh against the assaults of the devil.

2423–690 On the origin and diffusion of this tale, see Eric T. Metzler, "The *Miracle of the Pregnant Abbess:* Texts and Contexts of a Medieval Tale of Sexuality, Spirituality, and Authority" (Ph.D. diss., Indiana University, 2001), 23–73. The first written version appears in the *Miracles* by Dominic of Evesham; the second, in those by William of Malmesbury.

2427 *the reckoning to be rendered*: This remark alludes to the accounting for her actions that she will have to give at the Last Judgment.

2441 *Anger . . . madness*: Medieval doctrine distinguished carefully between *ira* and *furor.* For example, see Richard of Saint Victor, *De eruditione hominis interioris,* 1.7, ed. *PL* vol. 196, col. 1241D: "Furor est perturbatio mentis, totius expers rationis. Ira est mentis perturbatio magna, sed a ratione non penitus aliena." (Madness is a disturbance of the mind, devoid of all reason. Anger is a great disturbance of the mind, but one not wholly estranged from reason.)

2442 *germinates and nurtures the seeds of dissent*: In English we speak of sowing seeds of discord. Such metaphors go back to Proverbs 6:19, "him that soweth discord among brethren."

2444 *the limbs to be subject to their head*: An old fable in Livy's *Ab urbe condita* 2.32.5–12 told of the revolt that the limbs mounted against the belly. Nigel could have run into the narrative in John of Salisbury, *Policraticus* 6.24, where its author claimed to have heard it from Pope Hadrian IV. A stock medieval contrast was drawn between the body and the soul.

2453 *he who traverses the entire globe*: On the devil in this capacity, see Job 1:7 as well as 1795 above.

2454 *that evil spirit*: In the Vulgate Bible *spiritus Dei malus* is found five times in 1 Kings (1 Samuel) (16:15, 16:16, 16:23, 18:10, and 19:9), describing a condition that takes hold of Saul. In the Middle Ages the expression denotes a demon or the devil.

2483–85 *Dissembling for a long time . . . concealment*: The cover-up described in these lines is uncovered in 2642–43.

2485–94 *what can a woman's cunning in its subtlety not detect?*: Nigel relies on an empiricism that he credits to the nuns who surround the unnamed abbess. They notice that she is in love, looks unlike her usual self, alters her diet, suffers insomnia, walks with a heavier gait, has a different complexion, and so forth.

2508 *schemes of her flock*: A common medieval metaphor assumed a shepherd exercising pastoral care over a flock against the wiles of the diabolic wolf. Here, exceptionally, the congregation itself engages in plotting.

2510 *(not undeservedly) she has forfeited*: In the *Tract on Abuses* Pref. 146, the poet places the perfect infinitive at the same point in the line, preceding it likewise with a word to effect etymological play: "quam constat *meritis demeruisse* suis" (which it has clearly forfeited by its faults).

2540 *polluted like a sow by foul mud*: The insult "dirty pig" had proverbial status in the Middle Ages: see *TPMA* vol. 10, pp. 320–22 (under *Schwein* 2.1–6, especially 2.3–4).

2555–61 Like all nuns, the abbess took vows and celebrated her mystical betrothal to Jesus Christ in a ritual. She violated this consecration by surrendering her virginity to an earthly lover.

2571 *giving to a nearby hermit this as a command*: On *dare in mandatis,* see

DMBLS under *mandare* 7b. On the hermit in literature of Nigel's day, see Paul Bretel, *Les ermites et les moines dans la littérature française du Moyen Age (1150–1250)* (Paris, 1995).

2573 *seven years old*: This age is reemphasized in 2664 and 2671. In medieval culture, the transition from infancy was held to begin when a child attained this number of years: see Nicholas Orme, *Medieval Children* (New Haven, CT, 2003), 6–7, 29, 46, 56, 67, 68, etc.

2607–34 This scene presents, as if a perfectly ordinary ecclesiastic procedure, a gynecological and obstetric examination of a nun, first by one pair of male attendants, then by another, and finally by the presiding bishop. On such procedures, see Kathleen Coyne Kelly, *Performing Virginity and Testing Chastity in the Middle Ages,* Routledge Research in Medieval Studies 2 (New York, 2000).

2657 *wailing*: Scansion requires treating the *i* in *vagiens* as a consonant (a phenomenon known as synizesis) or keeping the participle three syllables but shortening the initial one. The first solution is likelier, in view of Ovid, *Fasti* 2.405, "Vagierunt ambo pariter: sensisse putares."

2664 *has been completed*: In Medieval Latin, forms of *eo, -ire* often took the place of *sum, esse.*

2669 *turns back*: This could be translated as "goes to." In classical usage, the related line ending *conversus ad urbem* does not imply returning so much as turning round the head to look back: see Statius, *Thebaid* 7.146, and Valerius Flaccus, *Argonautica* 3.343.

2678 *pious studies*: The phrase could be translated "pious pursuits."

2680 *he was all things to each individual person*: Compare 69–70: "Fuit omnibus omnia factus, / omnibus et solis omnia solus erat" (He became all things to all men, and alone was all things to each individual one). In both cases the underlying inspiration is 1 Corinthians 9:22.

2681–82 Nigel delighted in the antithesis of the lord who behaved as a servant: compare *Passio sancti Laurentii* 168 and 581 as well as *Marginal Poems* 6.8.

2690 *devout love*: To round off the poem, Nigel concludes with the same two words with which he capped its opening distich. He couples them nowhere else in the *Miracles.*

Tract on Abuses

Pref. 27–28 *empty-handed wayfarer . . . robber's face*: Compare Juvenal, *Satires* 10.22.

Pref. 63 *Ovid*: Publius Ovidius Naso was banished from Rome by Augustus in 8 CE and sent to Tomis on the Black Sea for offenses that included *carmen et error* (a poem and an indiscretion).

Pref. 64 *Getae*: The Getae, a Thracian tribe living on the Danube, became synonymous with wild frontiers and savage people in the poetry of Virgil, Horace, and Ovid.

Pref. 74 *the court*: *Curia* in this line, and throughout the introductory verses to the *Tract,* refers to the royal court where William Longchamp served as chancellor of England. Later, Nigel directs his *libellus* (little book) to Ely, where William was bishop.

Pref. 88 *fear Greeks and their gifts*: Compare Virgil, *Aeneid* 2.49.

Pref. 155 Saint Etheldreda, or Audrey, founded a monastery at Ely. After her death in 679, her shrine attracted many visitors, and she became one of the most popular Anglo-Saxon female saints; several ancient churches, besides Ely, were dedicated to her.

Pref. 171 *food . . . drink*: Lyaeus, meaning "liberator," is a name for Bacchus, the god of wine; Ceres is the goddess of grain and fruits.

Pref. 225 Nicholas and Peter are almost certainly real persons, monks of Ely, hailed here as friends, just as John of Salisbury commissioned his *Entheticus maior* (lines 1667 and 1675) to greet his friends Odo and Brito at Canterbury.

Pref. 228 *a fever*: Alexander Neckham in his *Suppletio defectuum* 2.405 records the popular notion that after their consumption, eels might bring on fever: "comesta / anguilla corpus febricitare solet."

Pref. 246 *the legate*: William Longchamp was named papal legate in England in June 1190.

3 *in each of your offices*: Nigel here refers to William's roles as man of the state and man of the Church with the phrase *in utroque homine.*

lest you . . . the commandments: Horace, *Epistles* 1.13.19.

If you want life, keep my commandment: See Matthew 19:17.

4 *endures . . . raging sea*: See Ovid, *Heroides* 7.142.

My days . . . my heart: Job 17:11.

5 *Martha . . . Mary*: Luke 10:38–42 records that when Jesus visited their home, Martha bustled about serving her guests, while Mary sat at the Lord's feet listening to his words. Thus, in monastic literature, Martha came to signify the active life, Mary the contemplative life. The next line offers a good example of Nigel's fondness for alliteration, which I have tried to retain as much as possible.

6 *runs . . . attain the prize*: An allusion to 1 Corinthians 9:24.

a very few paces depends: The alliteration of *p* in *perpaucis passibus pendeat* suggests the runner's panting. Note Nigel's emphatic assonance of *a* in the following sentences (for the same reason).

7 *that man of our desires*: The angel Gabriel, in the guise of a man, addressed Daniel as "a man of desires" in Daniel 9:23.

I set my mouth against heaven: See Psalms 72(73):9.

I touch the Lord's anointed: See Psalms 104(105):15.

8 *Better are the wounds . . . a fawning enemy*: See Proverbs 27:6.

dry and lifeless: See *Rhetorica ad Herennium* 4.11.16, which cautions against a style that is "aridum et exsangue."

9 *eloquent voice*: Horace, *Ars poetica* 323 used the phrase *ore rotundo.*

the blessings of peace: Literally, "things that pertain to peace."

10 *you may bring forth . . . new and old*: See Matthew 13:52.

to write to you . . . spacious sea: Nigel employs a common medieval topos here, namely, to offer something superfluous, as "coals to Newcastle." He is also alluding to Horace, who had mocked the folly of carrying wood to the forest in *Satires* 1.10.34–35.

11 *to the one who has all will it be given*: See Matthew 25:29.

12 *that you are meek and humble of heart*: Matthew 11:29.

the mildness of Moses: Numbers 12:3 refers to Moses as a man most meek beyond all men who dwelt on earth.

my scythe into another's harvest: See Deuteronomy 23:25.

to judge . . . his own lord: See Romans 14:4.

13 *the mouth of fools spouts foolishness*: Proverbs 15:2.

14 *a sty*: *Clavus* literally means "nail'; see Numbers 33:55 for the phrase "nails in your eyes."

15 *From the sole . . . no soundness in him*: See Isaiah 1:6.

there was a knot in a bulrush: See Plautus, *Menaechmi* 2.1.22, and Terence, *Andria* 5.4.38. Both comic poets used the proverb "to look for knots in a bulrush."

the mountains of Gelboe: 2 Kings (2 Samuel) 1:21 invokes the mountains of Gelboe.

changes of clothes: Compare Isaiah 3:22.

16 *falsehood is not found in his mouth*: See Revelation 14:5.

swallowing a camel and straining out gnats: See Matthew 23:24.

18 *they rush like a massed column*: See Virgil, *Aeneid* 1.82–83. Note Nigel's pun on *perniciem* (destruction) and *perditionem* (perdition) here.

19 *embrace instruction . . . the just way*: See Psalms 2:12.

Your word . . . my paths: Psalms 118(119):105.

20 *To whom more . . . from him*: See Luke 12:48.

22 *Woe to him . . . to lift him up*: See Ecclesiastes 4:10.

23 *they disfigure their own faces*: See Matthew 6:16, which teaches that we should not disfigure our faces like hypocrites so as to appear to others to be fasting.

transgression to . . . forgetfulness of their sins: Note Nigel's heavy reliance (again) on alliteration of *p* in this passage, as in *praevaricationem praevaricationi et peccatum peccato.*

24 *divine fear . . . of wisdom*: Compare Proverbs 1:7.

25 *ever hated his own flesh*: Ephesians 5:29.

from the mouths . . . praise for themselves: See Psalms 8:3(2).

26 *of binding and loosing . . . the keys*: Compare Matthew 16:19.

27 *new plantings*: Psalms 143(144):12.

28 *Save for me the boy Absalom*: 2 Kings (2 Samuel) 18:5.

Your face . . . would not blush: See Jeremiah 3:3.

29 *their measure of wheat in season*: Luke 12:42.

aswarm . . . with worms: 2 Maccabees 9:9 and Exodus 16:20 employ the image of worms swarming.

who eat in the morning: Ecclesiastes 10:16 laments a land whose king is a boy and whose princes eat in the morning.

that the Jordan will flow into their mouth: See Job 40:18.

Friend, go up higher: Luke 14:10.

30 *We accomplish . . . follows them*: See John 12:19, where the Phari-

sees complain about Jesus that "the whole world has gone after him."

they come . . . carrying: Psalms 125:7.

laying their hands upon the sick: See Mark 16:18, where Jesus proclaims that in his name his disciples would cast out devils, speak in tongues, and lay their hands upon the sick, who would recover.

prebend: A stipend paid to clergymen from the endowment of a church.

31 *with words a foot and a half long*: Horace, *Ars poetica* 97, coined the phrase *sesquipedalia verba.*

32 *a foot to the lame and an eye to the blind*: See Job 29:15. The suffering Job claims that he had been an eye to the blind, a foot to the lame.

way of his ordinances . . . that way: Compare Psalms 118(119):27.

the way of peace: Romans 3:17 declares that all men are sinners, and "the way of peace they have not known."

a crozier: *Baculus pastoralis* literally means "a pastoral staff."

33 *they close the paths of life*: Nigel's circumlocution for "they die" seems to allude to Psalms 17:46.

You have cast them down . . . lifted up: Psalms 72(73):18.

34 *They spend their days . . . down to hell*: Job 21:13.

dew and rains . . . mountains of Gelboe: Compare 2 Kings (2 Samuel) 1:21. See the note to 15 above.

unspeakable groans: This alludes to Romans 8:26.

35 *A peasant waits . . . rolling course*: Horace, *Epistles* 1.2.42–43.

How long . . . seek falsehood: Psalms 4:3(2).

Go home . . . Evening Star approaches: *Capilli* (hair) here puns on *capellae* (she-goats) in Virgil, *Eclogues* 10.77.

36 *the counsels of princes*: Psalms 32(33):10.

the efforts of secretaries: *Manus notariorum* literally means "hands of notaries."

to feed pigs . . . excellence of mind: Compare Luke 15:15.

37 *return to their own country by another way*: See Matthew 2:12.

38 *Hosanna to the son of David*: Matthew 21:9 and 21:15.

Be mindful . . . given him hope: Psalms 118(119):49.

Take that pound . . . ten pounds: Luke 19:24.

Pilate and Herod become friends: See Luke 23:12, which reports the friendship that developed between Pilate and Herod.

39 *those who have eyes . . . do not hear*: For the image of eyes that do not see and ears that do not hear, see Ezekiel 12:2 and Mark 8:18.

he is not mocked: Galatians 6:7.

41 *a bill of divorce*: See Matthew 5:31.

43 *a good measure pressed down and shaken together*: See Luke 6:38.

Hope for the best . . . its own omen: Ovid, *Heroides* 17.234.

44 *How long, Lord . . . with my friends*: In this passage Nigel blends verses from Psalms 12(13):1, 105(106):4, 118(119):116, and Luke 15:29.

46 *to preach on the rooftops*: See Matthew 10:27.

to enlarge the hems of their garments: See Matthew 23:5.

47 *at the edge of a sword*: A common biblical expression.

48 *cauldron facing the north wind*: Jeremiah 1:13.

49 *Henry the Younger*: Henry II (1154–1189).

its parish priest: *Persona* can mean "parson," a beneficed priest.

53 *the regular canons*: Members of a religious community bound by vows and living under common rules.

55 *Turning toward the wall*: Compare 4 Kings (2 Kings 20:2), "[Ezekias] turned his face to the wall."

was still sealed . . . was already enclosed in a tomb: Nigel puns here on *claudebantur sigillo* and *claudebatur sepulcro.* This entire passage is replete with alliteration and clever wordplay.

56 *Many examples . . . before his material*: Nigel here employs the common medieval topos that an author's lifetime will be insufficient to cover his vast subject.

all power is intolerant of a partner: Lucan, *De bello civili* 1.93.

60 *the vipers' venom that is without remedy*: Compare Deuteronomy 32:33.

the leaven that spoils the whole lump: Compare 1 Corinthians 5:6.

from the sole . . . of the head: See Job 2:7. Job was stricken with ulcers "from the sole of the foot even to the top of his head."

62 *it killed James . . . Peter also*: Herod's persecution of the apostles James and Peter is reported in Acts 12:1–2.

by action: *Manu* can mean "by action or deed" or "by force."

one draws . . . from the past: André Boutemy, ed., *Nigellus de Longchamp dit Wireker: Introduction; "Tractatus contra curiales et officiales clericos"* (Paris, 1959), 168, notes that this is taken from Bernardus Silvestris's *Mathematicus*. See *PL* 171:1370.

63 *more frequently . . . more copiously . . . more readily*: The emphatic repetition is Nigel's.

do you love me . . . that I love you: See John 21:16–17.

I even lay down my life for you: See John 13:37.

fruit of souls . . . fecundity: I have attempted here to retain Nigel's alliteration: *fructu, fertilitate, fecunditate.*

where love is, there is the eye: The proverb *ubi amor ibi oculus* was used by John of Salisbury in his *Letters* 97 and 145. It seems to express a view similar to Jesus's admonition in Matthew 6:21 and Luke 12:34 that "where your treasure is, there will be your heart also." Augustine wrote of love as a source of vision in *De moribus ecclesiae* 1.17.31, and Hugh of Saint Victor expresses an idea similar to our proverb in *De sacramentis Christianae fidei* 2.13.11, "Ubi enim charitas est, claritas est" (For where there is charity, there is clarity).

64 *things absorbed . . . trustworthy eyes*: See Horace, *Ars poetica* 180–81.

65 *hit with a hammer*: The image here might allude to the slaying of Sisera by Jael with a hammer and nail driven through his head. See Judges 4:21.

the years of Nestor: Nestor is the archetypal old man of Greek mythology.

66 *the more the hidden fire is concealed, the more it rages*: Ovid, *Metamorphoses* 4.64. The verse appears in the story of Pyramus and Thisbe, whose love burned all the more because they concealed it.

68 *There is not found . . . Most High*: The closing line echoes the high praise for the patriarch Abraham found in Sirach 44:20.

69 *raised on high . . . heavier fall*: See Claudian, *In Rufinum* 1.22–23.

like the ram . . . more forcefully: Compare John of Salisbury, *Policraticus* 7.18, ed. C. C. J. Webb, *Ioannis Saresberiensis episcopi Car-*

notensis Policratici sive De nugis curialium et vestigiis philosophorum libri VII (Oxford, 1909), vol. 2, p. 167.

this change of the right hand of the Most High: Psalms 76:11(77:10).

70 *think that . . . baselessly*: See Ecclesiastes 2:2.

with head bowed: Horace, *Sermones* 2.5.92, describes Davus, a stock figure of Roman comedy, with his head bowed, *capite obstipo,* the phrase that Nigel employs here.

71 *Friend, go up higher . . . before me*: Luke 14:10–11, Matthew 23:12, and Genesis 7:1 are all reflected in the closing line here.

73 In this passage the term used for "priesthood" is *sacerdotium,* and for "supreme secular rule," *imperium.*

74–80 Nigel's extensive quotations from Roman emperors in the following paragraphs are taken from John of Salisbury, *Policraticus* 7.20, ed. Webb, vol. 2, pp. 182–90.

75 *Therefore we decree . . . the law*: The virtues of a bishop are listed in 1 Timothy 3:2–4.

unacceptable children: *Filii odibiles* probably refers to illegitimate or unwanted children.

77 *the accursed hunger for gold*: Virgil, *Aeneid* 3.57, *auri sacra fames.*

79 *in the Novels*: That is, in the *Novellae constitutiones.*

80 *to possess a liberal education*: *Litteras nosse* literally means "to have learned letters."

81 *What is pleasing . . . force of law*: Compare John of Salisbury, *Policraticus* 7.20, ed. Webb, vol. 2, p. 186.

82 *they recount the deeds of tyrants*: Compare John of Salisbury, *Policraticus* 7.20, ed. Webb, vol. 2, p. 187.

mistress: *Scortum* means "prostitute" but can also refer to a mistress.

83 *he is either . . . condemned to exile*: Compare John of Salisbury, *Policraticus* 7.20, ed. Webb, vol., 2, p. 186.

men of blood: See Psalms 58:3(59:2).

if he has passed by . . . bloodshed is reported: An allusion to the parable of the Good Samaritan, Luke 10:32.

is a friend of Caesar's: See John 19:12, "If thou release this man, thou art not Caesar's friend."

first places at the feast: See Matthew 23:6, where Jesus warns his followers not to imitate the scribes and Pharisees "who love the first places at feasts."

are hidden . . . wisdom and knowledge: The same is said of Jesus by Saint Paul in Colossians 2:3.

84 *Judge for the orphan . . . says the Lord*: Isaiah 1:17–18.

A man when he was in honor . . . became like them: Psalms 48:13(49:12).

85 *inexorable hatred*: Ovid, *Metamorphoses* 5.244–45.

86 *these are the worst occupations*: See Ecclesiastes 1:13.

monks, both black and white: This refers to Benedictines and Cistercians, respectively.

distinguished men: The phrase is surely used ironically here.

arduous journey: This might allude to Jeremiah 4:29.

the whole lump is spoiled by a little leaven: See Galatians 5:9 and 1 Corinthians 5:6. Nigel borrowed Saint Paul's image of a whole lump spoiled by a little leaven earlier (see the note to 60 above).

87 *brothers of the Hospital . . . Grandmontines*: The Order of the Hospital of Saint John (Knights Hospitaler) and the Knights of the Temple of Solomon (Knights Templar) were religious orders founded on military structure during the Crusades. The Carthusians were founded in France in 1084 to lead eremitical lives of austerity and piety; the order later established charterhouses in England. The Order of Grandmont (Grandmontines) was founded in England around the year 1100 and became known for its strict observance of poverty and silence. All of these orders, and several more, were roundly satirized by Nigel in *Speculum stultorum.*

so as to seize the prize more swiftly: Compare 1 Corinthians 9:24. See the note to 6 above.

88 *reprove, entreat . . . out of season*: See 2 Timothy 4:2.

he did not say wealth, but work: In this line Nigel puns on *opes* (wealth) and *opus* (work).

One who desires a bishopric desires a good work: See 1 Timothy 3:1.

He who does not enter . . . a thief and a robber: John 10:1.

What was broken . . . you have cast out: See Ezekiel 34:3–4.

89 *the flock scattered . . . torn to pieces*: The image of the flock scattered and falling prey to beasts is found in Ezekiel 34:5.

Friend, how have you entered here: Matthew 22:12.

where there is weeping . . . worse than the first: See Matthew 8:12 and 27:64.

who sew a cushion under every elbow: See Ezekiel 13:18.

whose like was not found in the earth: See Job 2:3.

I feared all my works: Job 9:28.

The stars are not pure . . . in his sight: See Job 15:15 and 25:5.

90 *to bring forth . . . new and old*: See Matthew 13:52. See the note to paragraph 10 above.

92 *turn aside neither to the right or the left*: See Proverbs 4:27 and Deuteronomy 17:11.

93 *Let the itch take the last one*: Horace, *Ars poetica* 417. Compare John of Salisbury, *Policraticus* 7.19, ed. Webb, vol. 2, p. 170, where this quotation also occurs.

begin with prayers . . . the person: In this passage, I attempt to preserve the alliteration of *p* in Nigel's Latin.

94 *Since the Lord . . . from these stones*: Luke 3:8.

honors change character: See note to 114.

you should not think . . . for their outcome: Ovid, *Heroides* 2.86.

for God is able . . . always have all sufficiency: See 2 Corinthians 9:8.

95 *the sun is turned to darkness and the moon to blood*: See Acts 2:20.

as a shower on the herb or drops upon the grass: See Deuteronomy 32:2.

as the fig tree lets fall its unripe fruits: Revelation 6:13.

96 *like dust by a whirlwind*: Ashes scattered by a whirlwind is an image from Job 21:18.

a bill of divorce: Matthew 5:31. See the note to 41 above.

to have a millstone . . . depths of the sea: See Matthew 18:6 and compare Mark 9:41.

97 *yield horns to the sinner*: See 1 Maccabees 2:48.

just as sheep are separated from goats: See Matthew 25:32.

98 *While he is in pain, take*: See John of Salisbury, *Metalogicon* 1.4, where *dum dolet, accipe* is presented as an adage of corrupt and greedy physicians.

99 *sprung from royal stock*: See Horace, *Carmina* 1.1.1, where the epithet applies to Maecenas, the patron of Horace.

he dreamed on Mount Parnassus . . . horse's spring: Compare Persius, *Saturae,* Prologue 1–2. Mount Parnassus was sacred to Apollo and the Muses, and home to the spring of Hippocrene, formed where the winged horse Pegasus struck the ground with his hoof.

Corpus iuris: That is, the *Corpus iuris civilis,* the body of civil law comprising the *Digest, Institutes, Code,* and *Novels,* which was assembled and promulgated during the reign of Justinian.

her father and mother . . . her brothers and friends: "Her" refers to the beautiful girl *(puella nobilis et formosa)* mentioned above.

100 *Saturn has perished . . . Jove's laws*: The couplet concerning Saturn and the passing of the Golden Age is found in various manuscripts of Ovid's *Heroides* after 4.132, but it is likely spurious.

Nicholas . . . Winchester: Saint Nicholas was bishop of Myra in Lycia (mod. Turkey) in the fourth century, but widely venerated in England, where some four hundred churches were dedicated to him. Saint Alphege, or Elphege, became bishop of Winchester in 984, and then archbishop of Canterbury in 1005; his popular cult as a martyr was defended by Saint Anselm. An earlier Saint Alphege had also been bishop of Winchester from 934 to 951.

The world is situated in wickedness: See 1 John 5:19.

In the right way . . . however you can: Horace, *Epistulae* 1.1.66.

101–4 *But if there is any objection . . . abound in him*: Nigel's language in these sections can be usefully compared to John of Salisbury, *Policraticus* 7.19, ed. Webb, vol. 2, pp. 175–78.

101 *evident to bleary-eyed men and to barbers*: That is, to everyone. See Horace, *Sermones* 1.7.3.

Daniel also . . . by a boy: For the story, see Daniel 13:45–64.

Virtue came to the Caesars before its time: Ovid, *Ars amatoria* 1.184.

102 *no one greater . . . born of women*: See Matthew 11:11 and Luke 7:28.

the Apostle: Saint Paul. See 1 Timothy 3:2.

Christ on the cross . . . from a wedding: Christ commends his mother to John, the "beloved disciple," in John 19:25–27.

Boniface the martyr: Boniface of Tarsus (fourth century) abandoned an immoral life and suffered martyrdom.

God chose the foolish things . . . foolishness before God: 1 Corinthians 1:27 and 3:19.

Joseph also . . . place of Herod: See Matthew 1:19 and 2:22.

Jonah feared to go to Nineveh: As told in Jonah 1:2–3.

a drunkard . . . a wine drinker: *Vinolentus* means "immoderate in wine drinking." Jesus is called *potator vini* (a drinker of wine) in Matthew 11:19.

Could you not watch one hour with me: See Matthew 26:40.

103 *did Peter not . . . high priest*: As told in John 18:10.

there was contention among Jesus's disciples: Compare Luke 22:24.

was Paul not called a babbler?: In Acts 17:18, Paul is called *seminiverbius,* a term that means "word sower," but which may also be rendered negatively as "babbler."

hid in sand the Egyptian he had secretly slain: See Exodus 2:12.

Samuel killed Agag, the very fat king: Compare 1 Kings (1 Samuel) 15:32–33.

Paul was consecrated . . . got back his sight: As told in Acts 9:12–18.

Zacharias . . . though mute: As told in Luke 1:8.

Gregory guided . . . very severe infirmities: See Paul the Deacon, *Vita Gregorii* 13.

without beauty or comeliness: Compare Isaiah 53:2.

104 *but neither is Martin . . . but ugly*: See Sulpicius Severus, *De vita beati Martini* 9.

Ambrose was elected . . . a catechumen: See Paulinus, *Vita sancti Ambrosii* 7.

a Manichaean: Manichaeism was a dualistic philosophy of religion that flourished in the fifth century but was condemned as a heresy by the Church; it had attracted Saint Augustine in his youth.

the teacher of the Gentiles . . . faithful preacher: See Acts 9:2, and 1 Timothy 1:13 and 2:7. Nigel puns here on *persecutor* and *praedicator.*

those who please . . . God has scorned them: Psalms 52:6(53:5).

God has the power to make every grace abound in him: 2 Corinthians 9:8.

105 *because of the people's sins God permits the hypocrite*: See Job 34:30.

106 *Depart from me, for I am a sinful man*: See Luke 5:8 and 13:27.

tasted how sweet the Lord is: See Psalms 33:9(34:8).

my foot in the fetters: See Sirach 6:25, where the "fetters" are Wisdom's.

things new and old: Matthew 13:52. This is the third instance in which Nigel alludes to this gospel passage. See notes to paragraphs 10 and 90 above.

with publicans and sinners: Matthew 9:11. The Pharisees complained that Jesus ate with publicans and sinners.

107 *he may happen to dash his foot against a stone*: See Psalms 90(91):12 and Matthew 4:6.

Roger of Worcester: Roger fitz Count, bishop of Worcester, consecrated on August 23, 1164, died at Tours on August 9, 1179.

Archbishop Richard: Richard, archbishop of Canterbury, consecrated April 8, 1174, died February 16, 1184.

to anoint the head of a sinner: See Psalms 140(141):5.

108–9 *During the reign . . . the very last farthing*: John of Salisbury, *Policraticus* 7.19, ed. Webb, vol. 2, pp. 173–74.

109 *the very last farthing*: Matthew 5:26.

110 *When a certain ambitious monk . . . the vacant church*: John of Salisbury seems to refer to either Robert, duke of Normandy, or Henry I, king of England, the sons of William the Conqueror. See *Policraticus* 7.18 and Webb's note to the text in his edition (vol. 2, p. 168).

111 *As you speak, so do*: James 2:12.

112 *the mouth that lies kills the soul*: Wisdom 1:11.

You will destroy all who speak falsehood: Psalms 5:7.

Lord, you handed over . . . over and above: Matthew 25:20.

I feared you, because you are a stern man: Luke 19:21.

Wicked servant: Luke 19:22.

113 *Indeed, the voice . . . hands of Esau*: See Genesis 27:22.

plunder of the poor: An allusion to "The spoil of the poor is in your house" in Isaiah 3:14.

as the people act, so does the priest: See Isaiah 24:2.

114 *honors change habits*: Here Nigel quotes the first three words of the proverb *honores mutant mores, sed raro in meliores* (honors change habits, but rarely for the better), and paraphrases the rest. The origins of the proverb remain shrouded in the past, but its popularity is attested by wide use among English authors. Nigel identifies the second proverb in this passage as specifically English: *Anglico proverbio.*

They have selected . . . as one of them: See Sirach 32:1.

116 *filthy lucre*: See Titus 1:7, which cautions a bishop to be "without crime" and "not greedy of filthy lucre."

without these activities could you not enjoy a meal: Compare Horace, *Ars poetica* 376: *poterat duci quia cena sine istis* (because the meal could be enjoyed without them).

117 *to reflect day and night*: See Psalms 1:2. The just man is described as one who meditates on the law of the Lord day and night.

I shall give to you the keys of the kingdom of heaven: Matthew 16:19.

the table of money changers: Matthew 21:12 and John 2:15 report that Jesus turned over the tables of money changers in the temple.

118 *in your patience you will possess your souls*: Luke 21:19.

119 *a strange wild beast*: Nigel's *singularis ferus* here seems to pun on *senglarius* (a wild boar).

go well together and are present in one place: Here Nigel is paraphrasing Ovid, *Metamorphoses* 2.846, on the union of majesty *(maiestas)* and love *(amor)*.

is patience their shield against vices: Hebrews 10:36 affirms that in the priesthood of Christ, "patience is necessary."

120 *Vengeance is mine and I shall repay*: See Romans 12:19 and Hebrews 10:30.

Vow and pay: Psalms 75:12(76:11).

121 *the reason is . . . respect for a person*: Statius, *Thebaid* 3.661, records that fear first made gods in the world.

Have you appealed . . . you shall go: Acts 25:12.

Are you going to . . . pillage you: Nigel concludes his point with a clever pun on *appellabitis* (appeal) and *expilabimus* (pillage).

122 *weight and weight . . . judgment and judgment*: The injunction is taken from Leviticus 19:36; compare Proverbs 16:11 and 20:10.

Judge justly, you sons of men: See Psalms 57:2(58:1).

render an account . . . final judgment: This passage affords another example of Nigel's emphatic repetition and alliteration: *tremendo et terribili iudicio iusto Iudici,* etc.

selling and buying it even in the temple: See Matthew 21:12.

123 *obedience is better than sacrifice*: See 1 Kings (1 Samuel) 15:22 and Ecclesiastes 4:17.

124 *toward the north*: There is an allusion here to the wickedness of King Achaz, who removed an altar of brass from before the Lord and set it "toward the north," as told in 4 Kings (2 Kings) 16:14.

I shall be like the Most High: Isaiah 14:14.

my finger is thicker . . . father's: See 2 Chronicles 10:10, where Roboam, son of David, was advised by the young men to threaten his people with a heavy yoke and to tell them that "my little finger is thicker than the loins of my father."

125 *Lord, lord, open for us*: Matthew 25:11.

a reward with the Lord: Wisdom 5:16 promises that "the just shall live forevermore, and their reward is with the Lord."

For God weighs . . . it is given: Here Nigel alludes to the "widow's mite" in Luke 21:3–4.

126 *If you had been . . . the world hates you*: See John 15:19.

Father, forgive . . . what they do: See Luke 23:34.

127 *Our glory . . . our conscience*: See 2 Corinthians 1:12.

128 *render an account of his stewardship*: Compare Luke 16:2.

129 *I am the good shepherd*: John 10:11.

The good shepherd . . . for his sheep: John 10:11.

130 *in gilded garments*: Psalms 44:10(45:9).

131 *John the Baptist was praised . . . with fine linen*: Matthew 3:4 reports on the attire of John the Baptist, and John the Evangelist is taken to be the "certain young man having a linen cloth cast about him" in Mark 14:52.

the power of binding and loosing: Jesus bestowed the keys of the kingdom and the power of binding and loosing on Peter in Matthew 16:19.

132 *provided . . . heads uncovered*: If their heads were uncovered, the bishops' tonsures would be revealed.

public payment of taxes: See the *Codex Iustinianeus* 8.54.4 on *functiones* (payment of taxes).

133 *And it will be as with the people, so also the priest*: Isaiah 24:2 and Hosea 4:9.

134 *permits the impious . . . impiety*: Compare Jeremiah 12:1, "Why doth the way of the wicked prosper?"

who carries off the spirit of princes: Psalms 75:13(76:12).

135 *What is now said . . . upon the rooftops*: Compare Luke 12:3.

136 *silences . . . speak ill of you*: See Psalms 62:12(63:11).

who please men . . . despised them: Psalms 52:6(53:5).

will you heap . . . heads of those: See Romans 12:20.

those who used to disparage . . . your feet: See Isaiah 60:14.

138 *Therefore, since this world . . . no truth in the land*: The first sentence is a patchwork of scriptural allusions: see 1 John 5:19, Genesis 6:12, and Hosea 4:1.

differing weights and measures: Proverbs 20:10.

relentless hatred: See Ovid, *Metamorphoses* 5.244–45. Nigel borrowed the same expression earlier, in paragraph 85.

140 *ignoble spirit*: An allusion to Virgil, *Aeneid* 4.13.

142 *fortune frowned*: See Ovid, *Epistulae ex Ponto* 4.3.7.

were transformed into a crooked bow: Psalms 77(78):57.

143 *who swore with Peter . . . speech made plain*: A reference to the third denial of Peter, as recounted in Matthew 26:72–73.

144 *the gall of bitterness*: Acts 8:23.

even laid bloody hands upon the Lord's anointed: Compare 1 Kings 24:7 (1 Samuel 24:6).

145 *Loyalty . . . with fortune*: Ovid, *Epistulae ex Ponto* 2.3.10.

My friends . . . used violence: Psalms 37:12–13(38:11–12).

Now a new blow has no room among us: Ovid, *Epistulae ex Ponto* 4.16.52.

the capture of King Richard: Richard I was captured by Leopold II of Austria on his way home from the Third Crusade in December 1192 and held for ransom in the castle of Durnstein. He was released and returned to England in March 1194.

146 *the latest sorrow was worse than the first*: Compare Matthew 27:64.

We have looked for peace . . . fallen from our head: See Jeremiah 14:19 and Lamentations 5:16–17.

added not a little . . . your wounds: See Psalms 68:27(69:26).

147 *Martha, Martha . . . only is necessary*: Luke 10:41–42.

Well done, good and faithful . . . of your Lord: Matthew 25:21.

148 *the horn of the altar*: The phrase *cornu altaris* occurs several times in the Old Testament, for example, Psalms 117(118):27 and Judith 9:11.

149 *villein*: *Rusticus* is meant as a derogatory term here.

153 *If, as a good overseer . . . in your parishes*: Note how Nigel's diction sustains the imagery of pruning and vineyards.

of the Lord of the Hosts: See Romans 9:29.

bastard shoots: Wisdom 4:3.

cockle has choked your crop: Compare Matthew 13:25–30.

155 *Since now is . . . rise from sleep*: See Romans 13:11.

gird your sword . . . most mighty: Psalms 44:4(45:3).

to go about . . . roam through it: Similar words refer to Satan in Job 1:7 and 2:2.

It is necessary . . . new and old: *The Rule of Saint Benedict* 64.9.

156 *knowledge puffs us up*: 1 Corinthians 8:1.

157 *the prime of life*: Catullus used this identical expression, *aetas florida,* in his lyrics (68.16).

is your tongue constrained . . . word of God: Compare 2 Timothy 2:9, "But the word of God is not bound."

carry both swords . . . the other: Gelasius I, pope from 492 to 496, proclaimed the doctrine of "two swords" that govern the world: consecrated power residing in the pope, and royal power centered in the emperor.

158 *no one can serve two masters*: Matthew 6:24 and Luke 16:13.

159 *He was even unwilling to enter*: That is, to take possession of the church as archbishop.

160 *through a glass darkly*: 1 Corinthians 13:12.

consummated his ministry: *Consummavit* invokes the memory of Jesus on the cross in John 19:30.

make flesh your arm: See Jeremiah 17:5.

nothing fell to earth: This seems to allude to Job 29:24, "And the light of my countenance fell not on earth."

161 *unexpected turn of events*: Nigel might be alluding to Becket's leniency in the case of a "criminous clerk" in 1163, or his refusal to consent to the Constitutions of Clarendon in 1164; both actions infuriated the king.

162 *reached to the ends of the world*: See Psalms 18:5(19:4) and Romans 10:18.

the French king: Louis VII, who supported Becket in his famous quarrel with Henry II.

163 *Therefore, you should . . . than is expedient*: An impersonal verb such as *decet* or *oportet* seems to be omitted in this sentence.

164 *You let a marten go to grasp willows*: The sense of this proverb seems to be that you neglect something valuable in order to chase something worthless. See Walther, *Proverbia,* nos. 24572–73.

165 *loyalty stands . . . fortune*: Ovid, *Epistulae ex Ponto* 2.3.10. See above, the notes to paragraphs 142 and 145. This is Nigel's fourth reference in the *Tract on Abuses* to Ovid's *Epistulae ex Ponto,* a collection in which the Roman poet laments his exile from Rome. Of course, such a sentiment reflects William Longchamp's situation at the time when the *Tract* was composed. Also, Nigel mentions Ovid by name and as an exile in the verse preface (Pref. 64).

I am an example . . . what they have: These verses, altered and with omissions by Nigel, occur in Walter of Châtillon's *Alexandreis,* 9.4713–19.

166 *If I yet pleased . . . of Christ*: Galatians 1:10.

Those who please men . . . despised them: Psalms 52:6(53:5).

The Life of Saint Paul, the First Hermit

1 The brief reign of Decius, Roman emperor from 249 to 251 CE, is noted for its persecution of Christians.

8 Valerian, another persecutor of Christians, served as Roman emperor from 253 to 260 CE.

20 *and he gives the members . . . crucified*: The imagery of this line is indebted to Saint Paul's famous analogy of the mystical body in 1 Corinthians 6:15, "Know you not that your bodies are the members of Christ." See also the same epistle at verse 12:27.

25 *a white-hot metal plate*: Horace, *Epistles* 1.15.36, "candens lamina."

35 *soldier of Christ*: 2 Timothy 2–3 established the image of the *miles Christi.* The long tradition of Christians doing battle with vices and sin was popularized by the *Psychomachia* of Prudentius.

36 *youthful years*: Ovid, *Metamorphoses* 8.632, "anni iuveniles."
a steadfast spirit: Horace, *Sermones* 2.5.20, "fortes animos."

39 Nimrod (Nemrod) was a mighty hunter *(robustus venator)* in Genesis 10:9.

45 *a pleasant place*: The rhetorical conceit of *locus amoenus* is called "the principal motif of all nature description" and amply treated by Curtius, *European Literature and the Latin Middle Ages,* 195–200.

48 *sweet venom*: *Dulce venenum* became one of many stock phrases referring to the fatal charms of women in misogynistic literature of the Middle Ages. See Ronald E. Pepin, "The Dire Diction of Medieval Misogyny," *Latomus* 52 (1993): 659–63.

54 *with seductive speech*: Proverbs 29:5.

58 *enticing voice*: Virgil, *Aeneid* 1.670–71, "*blandis*que moratur / *vocibus.*"

79 *thirsted for gold*: *Aurum gliscit sitis* plays on Virgil's famous expression, *auri sacra fames* in *Aeneid* 3.57.

96 The Fates *(Parcae)* are depicted as three sisters who spin, measure, and cut the thread of life. They appear later in this poem at 654–56, 663, 670, 733.

108 *the man*: Nigel uses the word *vir* several times in the *Vita Pauli* to signify a man of God, or "saint." See lines 204, 220, 271, 395, 429, 596.

113 Lyaeus, meaning "liberator," is another name for the god of wine.

114 *Poverty's harsh scarcity*: See Horace, *Carmina* 3.16.37, "*importuna* tamen *pauperies.*"

130 *pinnacle of virtue*: Nigel associates sanctity with having attained the pinnacle of the virtues at several points in the *Life.*

138 *four ways*: The "four ways" are not defined by Nigel, but he has been discussing Paul's embrace of solitude, contempt for earthly goods, prayer, and poverty.

145 *persevere*: Literally, "be stable." For a discussion of the concept of stability in Benedictine monasticism and Egyptian cenobitism, see Timothy Fry, ed., *The Rule of St. Benedict in English* (Collegeville, MN, 1981), 463–65.

148–49 *When such was Jacob's couch . . . his name*: In this passage, Nigel alludes to the patriarch Jacob's dream of a ladder ascending to the sky (Genesis 28:12–16), his wrestling with an angel, and his name changing to Israel (Genesis 32:24–28).

156 *One . . . one . . . one . . . one*: Both *hic* and *iste* in this line seem to refer to Paul, and reflect his roles in the active life and the contemplative life. Thus the immediate comparison to Martha and Mary in the following lines. See Luke 10:38–42.

158 *Martha . . . her sister*: See Luke 10.38–42 for the story of Martha and Mary.

187 Axa, the daughter of Caleb in Judges 1:13–15, is described as *sedens asino* (sitting on an ass). See note at line 532.

192 *guided like a she-ass*: Nigel will later (lines 519–20) invoke this simile of the flesh directed like a she-ass that is being curbed and driven with a stick.

218 *Israelite*: One of God's chosen people.

227 *athletes*: The word *athleta* (athlete, or champion) is here used with the Christian connotation of *athleta Christi* (champion of Christ) or *athleta Domini* (saint).

233 *tongues*: *Organa,* literally, "organs." Prudentius used this term to mean "tongues" in *Peristephanon* 10.2.

248 *baneful vice, hostile*: See Cicero, *Orationes in Catilinam* 1.11, "*infestam* rei publicae *pestem.*"

259 *to seek and find*: *Quaerendo . . . reperire* alludes to Matthew 7:7.

262 *The messenger of light*: Aurora, goddess of the dawn.

265 *by art*: *Arte,* referring to the skill of making a staff or walking stick, also enables the pun on *artus* (limbs).

272 *a man conjoined with the shape of a horse*: A centaur.

274 *the holy sign*: An exorcism achieved by the sign of the cross occurs also in *Speculum stultorum* 3579–80.

303 *brow savage*: Virgil, *Aeneid* 3.636.

318 *dates*: *Palmarum fructus,* literally, "fruits of palms."

321 *he plants his feet*: Virgil, *Aeneid* 6.159.

328 *with insatiable jaws*: *Faucibus insatiatis* implies "with mouths wide open in amazement."

339 *faun . . . incubus*: Fauns are sylvan deities; Faunus, the protector-god of shepherds, is often identified with Pan. Ovid linked fauns and satyrs *(faunique satyrique)* in *Metamorphoses* 1.193. Isidore defined an *incubus* as a nightmare or demon in his *Origines* 8.11, but in *De civitate Dei,* Saint Augustine referred to *incubi* as forest deities who lusted after women.

347 *earth tremble*: See Psalms 75:9(76:8).

357 *Alexandria*: Antony traveled from his desert cell to this celebrated city of northern Egypt to encourage Christians during a persecution under Emperor Maximinus in 311 CE. He also took part in the Arian controversy there in 355.

366 *gloom*: Literally, "an eclipse."

369 *the sun of justice*: Malachi 4:2.

372 *an outer darkness*: Compare Matthew 8:12 and 25:30.

411 Tantalus suffers a punishment in the underworld whereby the food and drink he ardently desires will forever elude his grasp. See Ovid, *Metamorphoses* 4.458–59.

437 *they bestow kisses*: Greeting with a kiss was a sign of the profession of common faith among early Christians. Saint Paul instructed his followers thus in 1 Corinthians 16:20 and in Romans 16:16: "Salute one another with a holy kiss."

447 *other facts*: Other debilitating symptoms of old age.

456 *on swift wings*: Virgil, *Aeneid* 4.180.

467 *There was a spring*: Ovid, *Metamorphoses* 3.407.

474 *bread*: *Cibum,* literally, "food."

477 *Israelites*: See note to 218.

487 *victory in this camp*: See the note at line 35 on battle imagery and the Christian struggle against sin. See also *The Rule of Saint Benedict* 1.4–5.

490 *Phoebus . . . his firstborn daughter*: Phoebus is the sun, his daughter the dawn. Although classical poets sometimes indulged in elaborate descriptions of daybreak and sunrise, Nigel develops a particularly strained conceit to describe sunrise following dawn here. In his prose *Life of Paul,* Saint Jerome required six words to convey this, while Nigel's poetic version takes six lines.

498–99 *the welcome stilling of Rumor . . . deceive*: The negative portrait of Rumor is heightened by Nigel's alliteration: *famae, fallat, fictis, facta.* For the phrase "join facts to fictions," compare Ovid, *Metamorphoses* 9.138.

505 *so many open mouths*: Compare Virgil's depiction of Rumor in *Aeneid* 4.183, "tot linguae, *tot*idem *ora so*nant" (so many tongues and as many mouths sound).

517 *draft animals are given hay*: See Psalms 103(104):14.

526 *jubilee year*: In this line (as well as in lines 536 and 652), *iubilaeus annus* represents the repose of eternal life in heaven. In the Old Testament, the jubilee was a year of sanctification and rest observed every fiftieth year. See Leviticus 25:8–17.

527 *pious seeds in my heart*: Planting spiritual seeds is a metaphor that derives from 1 Corinthians 3:6–8. Note that Nigel sustains the imagery of planting, watering, and harvesting through line 534.

532 Axa was the daughter of Caleb, who gave her watered land. See Judges 1:13–15.

535 *mystical winnowing fan*: Virgil, *Georgics* 1.166. The winnowing-fan was carried about during the sacred mysteries of Iacchus (Bacchus).

537 *refrain*: *Celeuma,* literally, a boatswain's command shouted to rowers to help them keep time.

542 *worthy reward for this task*: *Merces digna labore* echoes Saint Paul's doctrine that each one will receive a reward according to his labor (1 Corinthians 3:8), and the laborer is worthy of his reward (1 Timothy 5:18).

552 *final gift*: See Virgil, *Aeneid* 11.25–26.

553 Athanasius (ca. 296–373 CE) was the bishop of Alexandria and an uncompromising foe of the Arian heresy. A doctor of the Church, he wrote the famous *Life of Antony of Egypt.*

596 *the man . . . the man*: *Vir* refers to Antony.

598 *his voice is cut off . . . fails him*: Compare Statius, *Thebaid* 7.360–61. *Vocis iter* (the midpassage of his speech) also occurs in Virgil, *Aeneid* 7.534.

613 *baselessly I have the title of a monk*: In *The Passion of St. Lawrence, Epigrams, and Marginal Poems,* Mittellateinische Studien und Texte 14 (Leiden, 1994), 207, Jan Ziolkowski has shown that the conflict between *res* (the thing) and *nomen* (its name) is a recurrent theme in Nigel's works.

621 Elijah and John the Baptist are both identified as desert dwellers in scripture. The Hebrew prophet dwelt by the torrent of Carith at the Lord's command, and he was fed daily by ravens, which brought him bread (3 Kings [1 Kings] 17:3–6); the Gospel of Mark (1:3–4) records that "John was in the desert baptizing" and referred to him as "the voice of one crying in the desert."

646 *in the New City*: *In nova castra,* literally, "in a new camp." This expression refers to heaven, the New Jerusalem.

652 *by divine authority*: *Caelitus,* literally, "from heaven."

654 *the stubborn Fates*: Ovid, *Epistulae ex Ponto* 1.2.61, called the Fates themselves tenacious *(tenacia).*

658 *incapable of sparing*: Note the pun in *parcere nescia* on the goddesses' collective name, *Parcae.*

674 *the final rites*: Virgil, *Aeneid* 11.61.

711 *fierce faces*: See note to 303.

719 *cold sweat*: Virgil, *Aeneid* 3.175.

741 *so luxury loving*: *Deliciosus* is used ironically here, of course.

Bibliography

Editions and Translations

Bandeen, Betty Isobelle. "A Translation of the *Speculum stultorum* and *Tractatus contra curiales et officiales clericos* of Nigel Longchamp." M.A. diss., Radcliffe College, 1958.

Boutemy, André. *Nigellus de Longchamp dit Wireker: Introduction; "Tractatus contra curiales et officiales clericos."* Paris, 1959. See especially 256–60. (*Miracles of the Virgin,* lines 1749–932.)

———. "Une vie inédite de Paul de Thèbes par Nigellus de Longchamps." *Revue Belge de Philologie et d'Histoire* 10 (1931): 931–63. *(The Life of Saint Paul, the First Hermit.)*

Gier, Albert. *Der Sünder als Beispiel: Zu Gestalt und Funktion hagiographischer Gebrauchstexte anhand der Theophiluslegende.* Bonner romanistische Arbeiten 1. Frankfurt am Main, 1977. See especially 348–54. (*Miracles of the Virgin,* lines 37–340.)

Kaiser, Leo M. "A Critical Edition of Nigel Wireker's *Vita sancti Pauli eremitae.*" *Classical Folia* 14 (1960): 63–81. *(The Life of Saint Paul, the First Hermit.)*

Wright, Thomas. *Anglo-Latin Satirical Poets and Epigrammatists.* 2 vols. London, 1872. See especially vol. 1, pp. 146–230. *(Tract on Abuses.)*

Ziolkowski, Jan M. *Miracles of the Virgin Mary, in Verse: Miracula sancte Dei genitricis virginis Marie, versifice.* Toronto Medieval Latin Texts 17. Toronto, 1986.

Further Reading

Bailey, D. R. Shackleton. *Homoeoteleuton in Latin Dactylic Verse.* Beiträge zur Altertumskunde 31. Stuttgart, 1994. See especially 203–6.

——. "Textual Notes on Some Poems of Nigel de Longchamp." *Medium Aevum* 53 (1984): 282–90.

Cotts, John D. "The Critique of the Secular Clergy in Peter of Blois and Nigellus de Longchamps." *Haskins Society Journal* 13 (1999): 137–50.

Hall, J. B. "Notes on the 'Miracula sancte Dei genitricis virginis Marie, versifice' of Nigellus de Longo Campo." *Studi Medievali* series 3, vol. 29 (1988): 423–43.

Ihnat, Kati. *Mother of Mercy, Bane of the Jews: Devotion to the Virgin Mary in Anglo-Norman England.* Princeton, NJ, 2016.

Klein, Thomas. Review of *Nigel of Canterbury: Miracles of the Virgin Mary, in Verse,* edited by Jan M. Ziolkowski. *Mittellateinisches Jahrbuch* 26 (1991): 329–31.

Koopmans, Rachel. *Wonderful to Relate: Miracle Stories and Miracle Collecting in High Medieval England.* Philadelphia, 2011.

Mann, Jill. "Does an Author Understand His Own Text? Nigel of Longchamp and the *Speculum stultorum.*" *The Journal of Medieval Latin* 17 (2007): 1–37.

Ziolkowski, Jan M., ed. and trans. *The Passion of St. Lawrence, Epigrams, and Marginal Poems.* Mittellateinische Studien und Texte 14. Leiden, 1994.

Index

M = *Miracles of the Virgin; Tr* = *Tract on Abuses; LP* = *The Life of Saint Paul*